Churchill versus Hitler: War of Words

by Peter John

BENNION KEARNY

Published by Bennion Kearny Limited
6 Victory House
64 Trafalgar Road
Birmingham
B13 8BU

www.BennionKearny.com

Cover image: © Lee Bullen (LeeBullen.com)

Table of Contents

Introduction

According to Sir Ian Kershaw, Hitler's best recent biographer, "the 'duel' between Hitler and his arch-enemy Winston Churchill ... would in many ways determine the ... course of the [Second World] war"[1]. Yet, though much has been written on virtually every other aspect of that conflict, there has been, as far as I am aware, no attempt to trace the feud between its two most important protagonists.

Few feuds between politicians in different countries in modern history have lasted as long as that between Winston Churchill and Adolf Hitler, and none has had more momentous consequences for the world, or led to more bloodshed. One does not have to be a believer in the "Great Man" theory of history to believe that, had neither man lived, the history of Europe in the mid-20th century and beyond could have been radically different. Even the premature death of one of the antagonists could have had important implications for their countries and the world. For instance, had Churchill been killed, rather than seriously injured, when he was run over by a car in New York in 1932, Britain's most likely Prime Minister in June 1940, Lord Halifax, might have ended the Second World War after the fall of France. Hitler might then have attacked and defeated Russia the next year, with consequences which are incalculable. Churchill did not make peace with Nazi Germany, because he believed it important to re-establish a balance of power in Europe with a peaceful Germany, something obviously impossible while Adolf Hitler was dictator.

The purpose of this book is to chronicle the history of the two men's mutual antagonism in detail as it manifested itself in their writings, speeches and private conversations throughout the tumultuous times through which they lived, in the manner of Andrew Roberts's scintillating *Napoleon and Wellington*.

Introduction

Hitler's views on Churchill were influential on the decisions he made in the course of the Second World War. He thought, completely wrongly, that the British might be tempted to accept his repeated offers of peace in July 1940, so he hesitated before unleashing the *Luftwaffe* on Britain. This gave Britain crucial weeks to strengthen its air and land defences and helped Britain keep off the German aerial attacks in August and September 1940. Hitler's wish to answer Churchill's night bombing of Berlin in September 1940 led directly to the decision to bomb London repeatedly, costing him the opportunity to finish off the battered, reeling Royal Air Force, and possibly end the war. His belief, expressed to his Propaganda Minister, Goebbels, on 11 March 1945, that Churchill had "set himself the single and insane goal of destroying Germany, even if it means the destruction of England as well" meant that Germany had "no choice but to look around for other opportunities"[2] to reduce the number of her enemies.

Hitler's opinion about Churchill is generally taken to be one of contempt. Albert Speer, Hitler's court favourite and Armaments Minister, later noted that "he considered Churchill, as he often stated during the situation conferences, an incompetent, alcoholic demagogue"[3]. There are numerous quotes from his public speeches and private conversation which support Speer's claim. Hitler referred to Churchill as an "unscrupulous politician who wrecks whole countries"[4], a "puppet of Jewry"[5], and an "undisciplined swine who is drunk eight hours out of every twenty-four … who spends extravagantly and smokes without moderation"[6]. Hitler never admired Churchill in the same way that he did the Russian Premier, Josef Stalin, whom he described as "one of the most extraordinary figures in world history"[7]. However, there seems to have been an undercurrent of fear in his contempt. Several days before the outbreak of war, Hitler had warned an Englishman visiting him in Berlin that Churchill's return to office would "seriously set back the possibility of maintaining peace"[8]. He also asked British visitors to Germany in the mid-1930's about Churchill's position in Britain and attacked him by name in public speeches. Had Hitler really thought that Churchill was the undisciplined, drunken failure that he proclaimed him to be, he would surely have ignored his British critic, as he did with other out-of-office opponents in foreign countries in the 1930s.

Churchill's views on Hitler are well-documented. They were formed in the early 1930's, and Churchill stuck to them with remarkable tenacity, and despite great short-term damage to his political career. He viewed Hitler from the outset as a grave threat to European peace and the balance of power, and persistently argued that Britain should stop him, by force if necessary. Even when Hitler was triumphant, and when Churchill had no clear idea how the war could be won, Churchill refused to make peace or surrender, much to Hitler's astonishment and annoyance. He referred to Hitler in private throughout the Second World War as "that man", "that bad man" or "that wicked man". He would mention him publicly with a varied catalogue of abuse, calling him, for instance, a "guttersnipe" and a "monster of wickedness" and referring to his "bloodlust and ... hateful appetites", his "perfidy" and his insatiable "lust for blood and plunder" – all those terms in just one speech[9]. During the 1930's, in an attempt to persuade Britain and other countries to oppose Nazi Germany, Churchill's speeches focused on Hitler's threat to the international states system. Once he had managed to bring into being an international coalition against Hitler, however, and once the extent of Nazi atrocities during the Second World War became clear, Churchill mentioned the internal crimes of Hitler's regimes far more.

Churchill's views about Hitler explain more than simply why, despite briefly admitting the possibility in late May 1940, he did not give in to those in his Cabinet who would have made peace with Hitler after the fall of France, when Britain stood alone, ending the Second World War before America and Russia were involved. They explain why Churchill swallowed his long-held and utterly sincere hatred of Communism and gave crucial assistance to Russia (and urged the Americans to do the same) when Hitler invaded. They also explain why Churchill swallowed President Franklin Roosevelt's demand for "unconditional surrender" and made no attempt to extricate Britain from what was clearly a destructive war, and one which was likely to strengthen the power of the United States and the Soviet Union while weakening the British Empire. Indeed, the demand for unconditional surrender also had an impact on his opponent's course of action. According to his *Luftwaffe* adjutant, Nicolaus von Below, Hitler "mentioned the [demand for unconditional surrender] repeatedly and stressed that any idea of 'coming round' would now be completely senseless"[10].

Sources

The work covering this period of European history is vast and constantly growing. Much of it is extremely good. There has, however, been no parallel biography of the two men comparable to Lord Bullock's *Hitler and Stalin: Parallel Lives*. This cannot be due to a lack of primary source material, since the lives of both Hitler and Churchill were constantly scrutinised and recorded from their 20s onwards. Though neither Hitler nor Churchill published a conventional autobiography, both wrote autobiographically about their early years, Churchill in his illuminating and amusing *My Early Life*, and Hitler in his turgid and

Introduction

mendacious *Mein Kampf.*

In fact, there is an important difference between the available documentation about the two men's lives. As Kershaw puts it, "The combination of Hitler's innate secretiveness, the emptiness of his personal relations, [and] his unbureaucratic style ... mean that, for all the surviving mountains of paper ... the sources for reconstructing the life of the German Dictator are in many respects extraordinarily limited – far more so than in the case, say, of ... Churchill"[11]. This is particularly true of Hitler's life before 1920, when he was only known to a close circle of family and acquaintances. There is, however, a wealth of secondary material. At least a thousand biographies or biographical studies of Hitler have been published, many (for instance those by Lord Bullock, Joachim Fest, Norman Stone and Sir Ian Kershaw) of outstanding quality. With Churchill's life, on the other hand, the problem is an almost overwhelming abundance of primary sources, rather than a dearth. Sir Martin Gilbert's eight volume biography of Churchill, with its sixteen companion volumes of documents (and more projected), must surely be the most thorough study of a single human life ever undertaken. To Gilbert's monumental work must be added shorter books by, for instance, Roy Jenkins, Sir John Keegan, David Irving and Clive Ponting. Churchill himself wrote and spoke millions of words about the Second World War, and his part in it, before, during and after the conflict itself. He was rewarded with the Nobel Prize for Literature for the quality of his outpourings. His multi-volume *The Second World War*, indeed, at 1.9 million words including Appendices, skilfully mingles autobiography and history. Previously, Arthur Balfour famously said about Churchill's history of the First World War that Churchill had written a book about himself and called it *The World Crisis*. Churchill repeated this feat a quarter of a century later with another struggle and called it *The Second World War*. Churchill's writings cannot be taken as gospel truth. As he himself said, "this is not history, this is my case". However, they are nevertheless vitally important in reconstructing the history of his turbulent life.

These biographical and autobiographical writings are, of course, only a part of the volume of work on British and German history in the 1930's and early 1940's. There are also numerous other primary sources, including journals kept at the time (often either furtively or illegally, or both) by famous diarists such as Sir John Colville, Field Marshal Sir Alan Brooke (later Lord Alanbrooke) and Sir Charles Wilson (later Lord Moran) on the British side, and Josef Goebbels and Generals Alfred Jodl and Franz Halder in Germany. Goebbels' diaries alone run to 75,000 *pages*, or around 200 times the length of this book. There are hundreds of tons of official government documents, increasingly available online. Much of the Third Reich's official government archive was captured intact by the US

Army just as it was about to be destroyed in 1945, and it has been heavily studied by historians over the last several decades. The British government has, in recent years, begun to publish Cabinet documents and related papers for these tumultuous years on the Internet. Each nation had a large press from which I have quoted freely. The British press in the 1930's and 1940's was highly diverse, though the German press under the Nazis was, of course, heavily censored and rigidly controlled*. It is plainly impossible for any one person to master all of the primary sources, let alone the secondary sources which are derived from them. However, perhaps hubristically, I do not anticipate that any of my major conclusions are likely to be contradicted. Where I have had to engage in speculation, I have marked it clearly as such.

Written sources only record a small part of any person's life, even Churchill's. As he wrote to the great historian Sir Lewis Namier:

> "One of the most misleading factors in history is the practice of historians to build a story exclusively out of the records which have come down to them. These records are in many cases a very small part of what took place, and to fill in the picture one has to visualise the daily life – the constant discussions between ministers, the friendly dinners, the many days when nothing happened worthy of record ..."[12]

Sir Lewis may have been right that friendly dinners and constant discussions are generally unrecorded, but this is perhaps less true for politicians in the mid-twentieth century, and especially for these two men, than for any previous statesman. As this is mainly a book about attitudes and thoughts, behaviour at dinner parties and stories about off-the-cuff remarks made during train journeys can be almost as revealing as official papers and monumental historical studies. Anecdotes carry their own dangers, however, and the historian must treat them carefully. People can misremember, on purpose or unintentionally, and without knowing the context and tone of remarks, reciting anecdotes can be misleading. Nevertheless, they are important and entertaining. The story of the feud between Hitler and Churchill would gain nothing from the exclusion of these revealing anecdotes of which both men's lives are so replete. Where such anecdotes are relevant, even tangentially, I have sought to include them.

---

* The British ambassador to Berlin, Sir Neville Henderson, was in the habit of reading five newspapers per day. He later recorded that the wife of a Nazi official once said to him, "What on earth do you do that for? If you read one, you have read the lot."

Introduction

Studying these sources, it is immediately noticeable that Churchill spoke and wrote much more about Hitler than vice versa. This is especially true during the 1930's when Churchill was an opposition politician attempting to warn his mostly unheeding countrymen about the danger to Britain from the dictator across the North Sea. Hitler, as a head of state, had many other matters to claim his attention, including destroying Germany's democratic system and its federal structure, rearming, invading numerous European countries and persecuting national minorities. It is therefore unsurprising that references to Churchill in his speeches and conversation in those years were relatively few. It is also noticeable that Hitler's writings and speeches on Churchill were utterly devoid of the wit and sparkle which were often present in Churchill's opinions on Hitler.

Once the Second World War began, and in particular once Churchill became Prime Minister, he spoke much less about Hitler. His public writings inevitably dried up almost entirely, though his speeches and radio broadcasts continued. The explanation for this apparent paradox is that, in London and on his travels, Churchill dealt with allies and colleagues who were already fully committed to the fight against Nazism. At one critical stage of the Second World War, when Britain was suffering significant setbacks in the Mediterranean and Hitler was poised to attack Russia, a friend of Churchill's remarked that one Cabinet colleague took more of Churchill's time than Hitler did[13]. Though the remark may have been flippant, it reflects an important truth. Dealing with colleagues, allies and neutrals takes much more of a leader's time than dealing directly with enemies. Hitler, too, had to deal with allies and colleagues who were already fighting Britain. However, Churchill inevitably figured more in his speeches and conversation during the war, when he was Prime Minister, than during the 1930's, when he had been in Opposition. After Hitler's suicide, and with the free time granted by his defeat in the 1945 general election, Churchill wrote *The Second World War*, which allowed him to reflect on every aspect of his opponent's career with the leisured wisdom of hindsight. Hitler, obviously, could not undertake a similar dissection of Churchill's life. Whether he would have done had Germany won the Second World War must be speculation, but it seems doubtful. Though interested in history, the Nazi dictator would not have had the discipline or motivation for the research that such work would require.

What these two leaders thought about each other is certainly not separable, and indeed I have not sought to separate it, from the political and military events of their times. Fully to describe these tumultuous events, however, would increase the length of this book by an order of magnitude or more. I have, therefore, offered the barest of outlines of the history of the time, where it has been necessary to make the story comprehensible. My treatment of Hitler's Russian campaign, or the invasion of Britain, or the Munich crisis of 1938, may therefore seem reprehensibly superficial, and my outlines of almost-forgotten issues such as the plight of German-speakers in the Alto-Adige/Südtirol region of Italy in the 1920s correspondingly disproportionate. I have assumed some knowledge of the major events of the history of these years on the part of the reader.

I have told the story of the verbal and written struggle between the two men to a large extent chronologically, rather than thematically, because it flows better that way. It also avoids much repetition, though it does not eliminate it entirely. Each chapter therefore covers a given time period, though I have sometimes needed to refer to events outside the years allocated to each chapter. However, as Hitler and Churchill and their respective countries were grappling with each other in many places and using many means simultaneously, I have had to break down the chronological chapters thematically in many places, to make them easier to follow.

This account is mainly concerned with the public speeches, private conversation and writings of Hitler and Churchill. It seems appropriate to comment here on the two men's respective styles of oratory and writing, both because such commentary is interesting in itself, and also because it is useful in setting the scene and describing the sources for what follows. Books have been devoted to both Hitler's and Churchill's writings and speeches. What follows is a short discussion of the quality and style of their speeches, public and private, and writings.

Oratory

Both men were remarkable orators by the time they were 35 years old. Both were well aware of the fact, and took care to practice and develop their skill in this art. However, Churchill's talent was more universal than Hitler's. According to the German dictator's favourite architect, Albert Speer, Hitler's persuasiveness did not work over the telephone. Hitler would, therefore, never conduct important arguments over that device[14]. He clearly preferred a large audience. He told his photographer, Heinrich Hoffmann, "I must have a crowd when I speak. In a small, intimate circle I never know what to say … As speaker either at a family gathering or a funeral, I'm no use at all"[15]. Even in small groups, in fact, his loquacity was considerable. There are numerous anecdotes of his boring his staff to sleep with ranting monologues during the Second World War. As with most bores, he regarded his conversation as fascinating, however, and he looked with disfavour on anyone who nodded off.

Introduction

Nevertheless, his main claim to fame is as a master of set-piece public occasions, in which he was able to give a prepared speech. He could influence, then feed off, the audience's reaction. Reading those speeches with their repetitions and inaccuracies, whether in English or in German, one cannot get a sense of how persuasive they clearly were to their audience. However, their content certainly leaves an impression. There is no trace of self-doubt or humility in anything he says. He returns to the same themes (the iniquities of the Versailles Treaty, Bolshevism and the Jews, his years of struggle, Germany's peaceful intentions in Europe, etc., etc.) over and over again. He portrayed himself as a Messiah and demanded unquestioning obedience, and, tragically, tens of millions of Germans followed him on those terms.

Watching Hitler speaking on television or film today, while knowing the care which he took to perfect his delivery, he appears something of a ham actor. He exaggerates and screams for effect, rather than as a reflection of any genuine emotion he may be feeling. However, his speeches were clearly effective to Germans who were part of a crowd of people mesmerised by his words. On trial for his life after the Second World War, Göring testified later that, on first hearing Hitler, he felt that Hitler had "spoken word for word as if from my own soul"[16]. Also at the Nuremberg trials, Julius Streicher, Hitler's manic newspaper editor, said that, after hearing Hitler speak for three hours, he was "drenched in perspiration, radiant. My neighbour said he thought he saw a halo around his head; and I, Gentlemen, experienced something which transcended the commonplace. When he finished his speech, an inner voice bade me get up"[17]. Hitler could also give an extemporaneous speech to a large crowd to great effect, as is demonstrated by his speech in the *Bürgerbräukeller* during the 1923 Beer Hall *Putsch*. One eyewitness to this occasion was a professor of modern history and political science, whom we might therefore assume to be a sophisticated and critical observer. He commented: "I cannot remember in my entire life such a change in the attitude of a crowd in a few minutes, almost a few seconds ... Hitler had turned them inside out, as one turns a glove inside out, with a few sentences. It had almost something of hocus-pocus, or magic about it"[18].

Hitler was never elected to any legislature, so we will never know how he might have performed in a parliamentary debate. (Though, as dictator, he gave speeches to the Reichstag, these were set-piece occasions in which no debate occurred). As Hitler was not a German citizen until 1932, he was unable to stand for election to the Reichstag until he was on the verge of becoming Chancellor. However, it is very difficult to imagine him succeeding in Parliamentary debate: he would not have been able to apply himself in a sufficiently disciplined fashion to make himself master of a brief, then present arguments in the most effective form to an informed audience. On the other hand, Churchill was a master of Parliamentary debate, speaking early in his political career on subjects as diverse as reconstruction in South Africa after the Boer War[19]; the London and North Western Railway[20]; the 1903-04 Army estimates[21]; the uniform day for the periodical retirement of members of the Port [of London] Authority[22] and the flogging of "Coolie no. 277" in a mine in South Africa[23] (Churchill was opposed).

Hitler would also not have been able to work on a committee, except perhaps as a highly dominant chairman, delegating all the routine work to a compliant staff. He was congenitally unable to conciliate, compromise with and flatter opponents and neutrals, as all members of any elected assembly must sometimes do. In the early 1920s, when the Nazi Party was desperately short of funds, some American magazines offered him $20,000 for his photo, a fabulous sum of money at the time. "On principle", he remarked revealingly to a photographer, Hoffmann, "I never accept offers; I make demands"[24]. He knew only the all-or-nothing gambit: he resigned from the Nazi Party in 1921 rather than accept the slightest dilution in his dictatorial control. It is a pity that Hitler did not therefore follow a more conventional route to the top in a Parliamentary system. If he had done so, his career would most likely have been short and undistinguished.

Hitler was also able to exert influence on most, but not all, individuals in private. He was helped by his apparently hypnotic, though slightly protruding, eyes. His boyhood friend, August Kubizek, remembered that in Hitler's countenance: "the eyes were so outstanding that one did not notice anything else. Never in my life have I seen any other person whose appearance ... was so completely dominated by the eyes ... It was uncanny how these eyes could change their expression, especially when Adolf was speaking. In fact, Adolf spoke with his eyes, and even when his lips were silent one knew what he wanted to say"[25]. Kubizek's account may be unreliable in some parts, but this description of Hitler's ocular prowess rings entirely true. Many others throughout Hitler's career reported themselves spellbound by those organs. Ribbentrop, Hitler's foreign minister, testified before the Allied Military Tribunal that "I noticed particularly his blue eyes in his generally dark appearance, and then, perhaps as outstanding, his detached, I should say reserved - not unapproachable, but reserved - nature, and the manner in which he expressed his thoughts"[26]. Hitler could also use his eyes to indicate his mood. The Italian foreign minister, Ciano, wrote in his diary in October 1939 that "Hitler's eyes flash in a sinister fashion whenever he talks about his ways and means of fighting"[27].

Most people who talked to Hitler informally remembered his impassioned monologues, or rants. Reading accounts of Hitler's monologues throughout his life, from Kubizek's accounts to the records of his *Table Talk*, or recollections of

Introduction

colleagues in the notorious Berlin bunker in the last years of the Third Reich, one is amazed that even his courtiers could stand the repeated, dogmatic, and often wrong, expressions of strong opinions on every conceivable subject. It made no difference to Hitler whether or not he had any knowledge of the subject concerned. He was clearly a know-all with strong opinions on everything. Ribbentrop said that Hitler's "thoughts and statements always had something final and definite about them, and they appeared to come from his innermost self. I had the impression that I was facing a man who knew what he wanted and who had an unshakable will and who was a very strong personality"[28]. It does not seem to have occurred to Ribbentrop that having an unshakable will did not make a man right. Evidently for those wanting something to believe in, or just without ideas of their own, Hitler's personal magnetism was extraordinary. It was clearly also limited, however, to certain forms of expression and to large groups of people in the German-speaking countries.

Despite describing public speaking as "one of the most difficult of the arts ... I see too many things at once and jumble them up together in a foolish fashion ... A test which I nearly always fail"[29], Churchill made successful speeches to large crowds throughout his long political career. After hearing him speak in Newcastle, Hull and Sheffield, one of his secretaries thought that "morale ... was certainly raised by a visit from him. He knew just what to say ... He always raised a laugh at Hitler's expense"[30]. Churchill could also talk triumphantly on the radio and in Parliament (though according to one witness in 1940, he "hate[d] the microphone and when we bullied him into speaking ... he just sulked"[31]). Even one member of Hitler's staff admired his oratory: Dr Paul Schmidt, Hitler's interpreter, later wrote, "It was always a literary delight to hear Churchill, even though I by no means always agreed with what he said"[32]. He did not even confine his memorable addresses to the English language: in 1949, he addressed the citizens of Strasbourg in French. It is impossible to imagine Hitler making a speech in any language besides German.

We can still watch Churchill's set-piece speeches on film or read them in books or newspapers, but, given the passage of time, we can no longer experience for ourselves his magnetism in informal groups. Nevertheless, Churchill seems to have been remarkably persuasive in private conversation. Evidence from his colleagues throughout his career is almost unanimous, however. One Civil Servant who accompanied him on tours of devastated areas during the Blitz recalled, almost forty years later, "the uniquely unpredictable magic that was Churchill". With a quick reply to a question, he could transform "the despondent misery of disaster into a grimly certain stepping stone to ultimate victory"[33]. As First Lord of the Admiralty between 1911 and 1915, Churchill had frequent dealings with the Second Sea Lord and later Commander-in-Chief of the Grand Fleet, Sir John (later Lord) Jellicoe, who wrote subsequently that he "admired very much [Churchill's] wonderful argumentative powers. He surpassed the ablest of lawyers, and would make a weak case appear exceedingly strong"[34]. Stanley Baldwin, twice Conservative Prime Minister, explained Churchill's exclusion from the Shadow Cabinet in 1930, "I make up my mind [on an issue] then along comes Winston with his hundred-horse-power brain and makes me change it"[35]. Baldwin may have been joking, or exaggerating, but his underlying fear of Churchill's powers of persuasion is unmistakable.

Sometimes, Churchill could overdo it. A common complaint from people who talked to him informally was that he would do ninety per cent of the speaking, leaving them unable to get a word in. Talking to the American diplomat Sumner Welles, who was sent on a peace mission to Europe in 1940, an apparently tipsy Churchill delivered "an address of one hour fifty minutes, in the course of which [Welles] was never given an opportunity to say a single word". Even Welles acknowledged that Churchill's monologue "constituted a cascade of oratory, brilliant and always effective, interlaced with considerable wit"[36]. In contrast, Welles' record of his meeting with Hitler a few days before makes it clear that Hitler had allowed him to do a good part of the talking[37].

Unlike Hitler, who was never elected to any Parliament, and therefore never had to debate with equals, Churchill spent decades in the House of Commons, one of the world's most demanding debating chambers. He clearly attached enormous importance to his speeches there, and would spend hours or even days preparing them. The effort was not wasted. Even when Churchill was out of office, in the 1930's, the news that he was to speak would bring MPs back from the bars and tea rooms of the Palace of Westminster to what had been an empty House of Commons. He also spoke well on the radio and, at the end of his career, on television. Few who listened to his war-time speeches ever forgot them[†]. While awarding him the Nobel Prize for Literature in 1953 the Nobel Committee praised "his brilliant oratory in defending exalted human values"[38]. Perhaps the most famous comment on Churchill's speeches was made by Edward Murrow, an American radio journalist in London during the Second World War: that he "mobilised the English language and sent it into battle"[39].

[†] The author well remembers the accounts which his grandmother would give forty years later of listening to those speeches over the radio during the dark days of the Second World War. She was clearly one of the millions who found Churchill's oratory unforgettable.

Writing styles

Churchill used his pen as well as his mouth to persuade and to contribute to the historical record, while Hitler used his mouth almost exclusively. Hitler produced only two books, and published just one, *Mein Kampf*. He planned a third, a memoir of his First World War service, but never delivered the manuscript[40]. Articles attributed to him, and on which he claimed handsome fees, were published in the Nazi Party press in the 1920s and early 1930s, but it is unclear how much of them he himself wrote. Nevertheless, he described himself as a writer on income tax forms until he became Chancellor in 1933, after which sales of *Mein Kampf* made him the wealthiest author in Germany and a millionaire[41].

Hitler seems to have begun work on *Mein Kampf* before his imprisonment, and he wrote the second volume in 1925, after he was released. In fact, rather than writing it himself, he dictated it. One sympathises with the people he dictated it to. One of his secretaries later claimed that his "Bavarian" (though Hitler was in fact Austrian) dialect was so strong that it had to be "translated into German" before it could be written down[42]. The manuscript which he eventually delivered to his disappointed publisher, Max Amann, showed many basic errors in German grammar and spelling[43]. The book fully deserves the awful reviews it has received from anyone who has struggled with it‡. Though Hitler clearly wrote it to gain publicity and supporters for the Nazi cause, it is hard to imagine it convincing anyone except the already converted§. The bad reviews have kept coming since Hitler's crony from the trenches, Max Amman, published the book. William Shirer, an American journalist in Nazi Germany later said that he had "heard many a stalwart Nazi complain that it was hard going and not a few admit … that they were never able to get through … its … turgid pages"[44]. A British cabinet paper is not a usual place to find literary criticism, but one, from 1936, refers to *Mein Kampf*'s "great length" and "turgid style"[45]. One historian, writing in an Introduction to an English-language addition, has said that it is "lengthy, dull, bombastic, repetitious and extremely badly written … Most of its statements of fact and the entire tenor of its argument in the autobiographical

---

‡ It is worth noting that this is the *edited* version, which was worked on by editors and Hitler's publisher, Max Amman. The original manuscript must have been awful beyond belief.

§ A rare exception to this is Josef Goebbels, Hitler's Propaganda Minister, who in his diary compared Hitler to Christ and John the Baptist after reading the first volume of *Mein Kampf*.

passages are demonstrably untrue"[46]. The translator of that edition, no doubt in a bad mood with Hitler after labouring intensively on 782 turgid pages of badly written German, added:

> "he makes the most extraordinary allegations without so much as an attempt to prove them. Often there is no visible connection between one paragraph and the next … [Hitler's style] is without colour and movement. Hitler … was an expert [in mixed metaphors] … Here and there, amid his ponderous reflections, Hitler is suddenly shaken with rage. He casts off his intellectual baggage and writes a speech, eloquent and vulgar"[47].

The prize for the most concise and accurate review goes, however, to the British historian Hugh Trevor-Roper, who wrote in his famous introduction to *Hitler's Table Talk*, that *Mein Kampf* was "unread and unreadable"[48]. Churchill read *Mein Kampf* when it appeared in English in abridged form in 1933, translated by Edgar Dugdale, and commented on its message (though not its style) in his essay on Hitler in his 1937 book *Great Contemporaries* (see Chapter 4). After the Second World War, Churchill became yet another critic to use the word "turgid" in taking about the book, when he described *Mein Kampf* as "the new Koran of faith and war: turgid, verbose, shapeless but pregnant with its message"[49].

Hitler himself later regretted having written *Mein Kampf*, because of the light it shed on his programme and also because of its poor style, and he insisted that passages should be removed from the 1933 English version. He described it as "fantasies behind bars", adding, "if I had suspected in 1924 that I would become Chancellor, I would not have written the book … as to the substance there is nothing I would change"[50]. In what must be a first for a politician talking about his memoirs, Hitler advised Albert Speer, his favourite architect and later Minister of Armaments, not to read them[51].

Hitler's second book (known quite literally as the *Second Book*), on foreign policy, is written in a slightly more intelligible style than *Mein Kampf*, but only slightly so. It is more focused, more tightly argued, and above all, much shorter**. It does not mix questionable autobiography, political manifesto and spurious historicism in the same way that *Mein Kampf* does. It retains many of the same flaws, however. There are still extraordinary statements without any attempt at

---

** *Mein Kampf* is around a quarter of a million words in English translation, while Hitler's Second Book is about a third as long.

Introduction

justification, tedious repetition and discussions of many matters of which Hitler is obviously ignorant. Hitler did not publish this book during his lifetime, apparently because his publisher feared that it would hit sales of *Mein Kampf*. Chapter 2 of this book discusses in more detail what it reveals about Hitler's views of England.

Churchill's writing style is as different from Hitler's as it is possible to be. It is extraordinarily good. One of the pleasures of writing this book has been reading so much of his huge output. From his first book, published in 1898, to his last, published more than six decades later, he wrote in crystal-clear prose, without pretension. Though some of the language appears dated today, Churchill was often modest and understated where Hitler would have been bombastic and pretentious. While Hitler's writing is entirely devoid of wit, Churchill's senses of humour and of the absurd are on display throughout his books and journalism, and in particular in more personal writing, such as *My Early Life*, but also in his histories.

Like Shakespeare or Oscar Wilde, however, Churchill's greatest skill was as a phrase-maker. Again and again he is able to express a particular concept memorably, so that it sticks in the mind, and indeed many of his phrases have become the standard English-language description of their subject: "[British pilots] the Few"; "[Russia] is a riddle wrapped in a mystery inside an enigma"; "[a rival politician] a modest man who has a good deal to be modest about"; "[British naval traditions] rum, sodomy and the lash"[tt], and many others. His literary output, in contrast to Hitler's, was enormous. He had not inherited money, but was wildly extravagant in his lifestyle, while Hitler, like Stalin, lived relatively simply, at least until he became Chancellor of Germany. Churchill wrote, or co-authored, 43 books, including several multi-volume histories. He evidently planned even more: "I shall never live long enough to write all the books I have in mind"[52], he would remark to his private secretary.

Churchill's literary talent was also much more diverse than Hitler's. It was as widespread as any writer's has ever been. While Hitler's two books are essentially political manifestos, Churchill's books include a novel, personal memoirs, history books, two biographies and a book of biographical essays, a book on painting as a pastime and various collections of speeches. They are not

---

[tt] This comment may have been apocryphal. Perhaps it is almost as significant that people who knew Churchill *thought* he said it, rather than that he actually did.

all classics, to be sure, and some contain factual inaccuracies‡‡. Churchill's only novel, which he wrote at the start of his career, is basically a failure. The distinguished historian Sir Jack Plumb wrote of Churchill's *History of the English-Speaking Peoples*, that "as history it fails, it hopelessly fails; as a monument of a great Englishman's sense of the past, it is a brilliant success" and wrote of *Marlborough* that it was "a splendid work of literary art"[53]. His histories of both world wars, however, which blend history and autobiography, may not be definitive, but they are certainly classics, and their influence is obvious in every subsequent history of the events which they portray, whether those accounts agree with Churchill or not. As well as their feud during their lifetimes, Churchill and Hitler have fought a posthumous battle for their reputations. That Churchill has won hands down is due in some part to his work as a writer and historian.

---

[1] *Hitler, 1936-1945, Nemesis*, Ian Kershaw, p.286

[2] *Goebbels diaries*, 11 March 1945

[3] *Inside the Third Reich*, Albert Speer, p.418

[4] *Berlin Diary*, William L Shirer, p.455

[5] *Hitler's Table Talk*, 18 October 1941, p.72

[6] *Hitler's Table Talk*, 18 October 1941, p.369

[7] *Hitler's Table Talk*, 11 July 1941, p.8

[8] *In Search of Churchill*, Martin Gilbert, p.78

[9] *Churchill War Papers, Vol. III, The Ever-Widening War*, Martin Gilbert, p.835-838

[10] *At Hitler's Side*, Nicolaus von Below, p.164

[11] *Hitler, 1889-1936, Hubris*, Ian Kershaw, p.xiv

[12] *In Search of Churchill*, Martin Gilbert, p.246

[13] *The Fringes of Power*, 5 June 1941, Sir John Colville

[14] *Inside the Third Reich*, Albert Speer, p.338

[15] *Hitler was my Friend*, Heinrich Hoffmann, p.46

[16] *Nuremberg Trial Proceedings*, Volume 9, p.236

[17] *Nuremberg Trial Proceedings*, Volume 11, p.308

[18] Dr Karl Alexander von Mueller, quoted in en.wikipedia.org/wiki/Beer_hall_*Putsch*

[19] *Hansard*, 18 February 1901

[20] *Hansard*, 6 May 1909

[21] *Hansard*, 12 March 1903

[22] *Hansard*, 9 December 1908

[23] *Hansard*, 11 July 1906

[24] *Hitler was my Friend*, Heinrich Hoffmann, p.48

---

‡‡ Out of many possible examples, here is one. He writes in *The World Crisis*, Vol. 1, p.51, that "For nearly a thousand years, no foreign army had landed on British soil", ignoring the invasions by Prince Louis (later King Louis VIII of France) in 1216 and the Dutch Stadholder William of Orange (later King William III of England) in 1688.

Introduction

[25] *The Young Hitler I Knew*, August Kubizek, p.120-131

[26] *Nuremberg Trial Proceedings*, Volume 10, p.226

[27] *Ciano's diary 1937-1943*, Ciano, p.284

[28] *Nuremberg Trial Proceedings*, Volume 10, p.226

[29] *The Truth About Myself*, Winston Churchill, *Strand* Magazine, January 1936

[30] *Mr Churchill's Secretary*, Elizabeth Nel, p.79

[31] *The Harold Nicolson Diaries*, 1907-1963, ed. Nigel Nicolson, p.223

[32] *Hitler's Interpreter*, Paul Schmidt, p.274

[33] The Churchill War Papers, Volume 2, Never Surrender, p.789

[34] Quoted in *Castles of Steel*, Robert Massie, p. 63

[35] I was Winston Churchill's Private Secretary, Phyllis Moir, p.123

[36] *Report* on Mission to Europe, Sumner Welles, London, 12 March 1940.

[37] *Report* on Mission to Europe, Sumner Welles, Berlin, 2 March 1940.

[38] http://nobelprize.org/nobel_prizes/literature/laureates/1953/

[39] Edward R Murrow, CBS, subsequently quoted by President Kennedy in conferring honorary US citizenship on Churchill

[40] *Hitler's Private Library*, Timothy Ryback, p.81

[41] *The Rise and Fall of the Third Reich*, William Shirer, p.109

[42] *Until the Final Hour, Hitler's Last Secretary*, Traudl Junge, p.41

[43] *Hitler's Private Library*, Timothy Ryback, p.72

[44] *The Rise and Fall of the Third Reich*, William Shirer, p.109

[45] Cabinet Paper CAB/24/259

[46] *Mein Kampf*, Introudction by DC Watt, p.xi

[47] *Mein Kampf*, Translator's Note, p.vii-viii

[48] *Hitler's Table Talk*, p.xvi

[49] *The Second World War*, Winston Churchill, Vol 1, p.50

[50] *Hitler*, Joachim C Fest, p.204

[51] *Inside the Third Reich*, Albert Speer, p.678

[52] *I was Winston Churchill's Private Secretary*, Phyllis Moir, p.170

[53] Quoted in *Churchill, Visionary, Statesman, Historian*, by John Lukacs, p.124

1

Early Years (1874-1925)

Winston Churchill was born in 1874, 15 years before Adolf Hitler, in Blenheim Palace. This 187-room stately home in the Oxfordshire countryside had been his eighteenth century ancestor's reward for routing the French armies of Louis XIV several times. His father, Randolph Churchill, was Chancellor of the Exchequer in a Conservative Government, and for a time looked likely to become Prime Minister. He never fulfilled this promise, however, resigning from the government and then spending a decade "dying by inches, in public", becoming insane before death finally claimed him in 1895.

Churchill spent his life at the peak of Britain's social and political establishment, at a time when it was much more exclusive than it is today. Indeed, from his father's death until the birth of the then Duke of Marlborough's son in 1897, Winston was heir to the dukedom and to one of Britain's largest fortunes*, in an age before death duties, and when income tax was much lower than today. In his later words, "In those days, the world was for the few, the very few"[1]. Accidents of birth deprived him of financial security, however, and his high birth did not make him wealthy. In aristocratic England, inheritances descended

---

* It is certainly entertaining to wonder what might have happened had the 9th Duke died during this brief period, and Churchill succeeded to the title and estate. Sir Martin Gilbert (*In Search of Churchill*, p.287) states that Churchill could not have been Prime Minister in the 20th Century if he had succeeded to the title, though Lord Home of the Hirsel became Prime Minister in 1963, after renouncing his peerage, and, according to Andrew Roberts (*Holy Fox*, p.201), Chamberlain in 1940 took confidential soundings amongst the country's law officers about whether peers (in this case Lord Halifax) could sit in the Commons under emergency situations.

to first-born male heirs – other relatives often got nothing. As the extravagant offspring of a younger son, Churchill was never independently wealthy, despite his aristocratic pedigree and a large, though variable, income from his pen and Parliamentary and government salaries. On the contrary, on at least one occasion in his life, his wife was fretting about their possible bankruptcy, and on two other occasions (in 1929 and 1937) he suffered sharp financial setbacks when the American stock market crashed[2].

Despite once commenting that "there were a great many inept plutocrats in England"[3], Hitler seems to have admired the English nobility, saying that "England couldn't live if its ruling classes were to disappear" and that the English masses "ought to be ruled, for they are racially inferior"[4]. The concept of the English gentleman, with its connotations of noble birth, effortless superiority, fair play and self-control, was surprisingly popular in Germany during Hitler's lifetime[5], and Hitler is recorded as using it on several occasions. Instructing his subordinates to work together in armaments production, Hitler told them to behave to each other like "gentlemen", using the English word[6]. When he had been at war with England for four years, he actually claimed to be a "gentleman" himself in ticking off a slippery Field Marshal, though he apologised for using an English word[7]. Hitler also thoroughly approved of the practice of primogeniture which denied Churchill a share in his family fortune. In October 1941, he argued that the practice kept the family's fortune intact, whilst the younger son would "go back to the people", thus keeping the aristocracy's bonds with the non-aristocratic masses[8], and six months later, he told his lunch guests that he was planning to imitate it in the slave empire he was establishing in the East[9]. However, as this book will show, any admiration Hitler may have had for the English nobility did not extend to respect for Churchill himself.

Churchill's years at school were unpromising, if not as disastrous as he implies in his memoir, *My Early Life*, and he needed three attempts to get into the Royal Military Academy at Sandhurst. Once freed from the classics-dominated English public-school world of the time, however, he began to excel. He graduated from Sandhurst eighth in his class of 150 in December 1894. Hitler was to warn that, "generally speaking, aside from cases of unusual talent, a man should not engage in politics until he is 30"[10], but by the age of 26, Churchill had been elected to Parliament for Oldham as a Conservative. After "ratting" on the Tories to join the Liberals, Churchill held his first Government office, as Under-Secretary for the Colonies, when he had just turned 31. He was, in addition, already a prolific writer. He had published six books by his 30th birthday, as well as much journalism from his military campaigns.

While Churchill was beginning to distinguish himself in Parliament and government office, Hitler was enduring his difficult teenage years. He was born in a modest *Gasthof* (inn) in Upper Austria, to a minor Austrian civil servant. As the British Empire was expanding, the Austrian Empire into which he was born was fraying at the edges. It was not yet collapsing completely, however. Though Hitler was later to describe his homeland in these years as a "corpse", the Austrian Empire kept itself together until 1918 by a shrewd policy of concessions to its non-German nationalities combined with an alliance with the flourishing German Empire. German speakers in Austria were often taken for granted by the government of the Empire when it had to make decisions, or at least felt that they were. This caused increasing resentment in the period before the First World War. The Empire nonetheless retained some vitality, and it was to endure four years of total war, helping to defeat Russia and Rumania and to hold Serbia at bay. It therefore hardly deserves to be described as dead or dying, until the middle of the First World War, which also finished off the more dynamic German Empire.

Hitler was downwardly mobile even from his relatively humble beginnings, until he discovered and developed a talent for oratory in Munich in the turbulent aftermath of the First World War. His utter incapacity for regular work is well-known, as are his attempts to avoid getting and holding a job during his four years in Vienna. According to *Mein Kampf*, he had developed a "deep hatred for the Austrian state", though this did not prevent him fraudulently living off a government pension, by claiming to be in higher education. He then painted pictures for others to sell, driving his salesman to distraction because of his idleness and unwillingness to fulfil commissions[11]. Churchill was aware of this part of Hitler's life, and indeed made gentle fun of it occasionally. As First Lord of the Admiralty at the start of the Second World War, Churchill was surprised at how little provision there was for certain professions to be promoted in the Royal Navy. He wrote to an Admiral: "If a telegraphist may rise, why not a painter? Apparently there is no difficulty about painters rising in Germany"[12].

Later during the Second World War, however, Churchill used one aspect of Hitler's family background against him. He would refer to the Nazi leader as Corporal Schicklgruber. Hitler's grandmother had brought up her son, Hitler's father, who was illegitimate. Her last name had been the comic-sounding "Schicklgruber". Hitler's father had changed his name when he was formally adopted by his mother's brother-in-law, to the shorter and more anonymous "Hitler", a different spelling of his surname "Hiedler". Hitler told his boyhood friend Kubizek that nothing his father had done pleased him as much as changing his name[13].

Churchill was not the first politician to use the name "Schicklgruber" when he wanted to ridicule Hitler, and he did so rarely, but most famously in a speech in Parliament in 1944[14]. As the context was a disparaging reference to Hitler's military judgement, Churchill clearly intended to ridicule Hitler when he used the name. He coupled the sneering mention of Hitler's last name with a reference to the commander in chief of the German armed forces, as a "Corporal". In fact, Churchill may have over-promoted Hitler by referring to him as a Corporal – at least one authority argues that the rank which he held for the entire First World War, *Gefreiter*, is more aptly translated as "Private"[15].

Childhood and adolescence

Neither Hitler nor Churchill had satisfactory family lives as children or teenagers. Churchill's parents were largely absent during his formative years. They outsourced his upbringing, firstly to a nanny, and subsequently to a series of boarding schools, as was common in the British upper classes in those days. Hitler's father was little better. His passions were bee-keeping and drinking and smoking with his companions at a *Stammtisch*† in the local pub. He died when Adolf was 13, leaving his family relatively well-provided for. Churchill's parents' neglect of him during his upbringing did not stop him from having a loving marriage once he married Clementine Hozier in 1908. Indeed, his wife told one of their daughters that the only time he deceived her during their 57-year life together was over the purchase of his country house[16]. Their letters to each other are a clear record of a close and happy marriage. Hitler, on the other hand, only married the day before he killed himself, and never had a family of his own.

A recent biographer, Sir Ian Kershaw, noted that Hitler carried a picture of his mother with him until the last days of his life in the bunker in Berlin. She died when he was 18, shortly after he left for Vienna. His only friend in those years, Kubizek, claimed that her death had a terrible impact on him[17]. Kershaw summed the young Hitler's family up as "the smothering protectiveness of an over-anxious mother in a household dominated by the threatening presence of a

---

† The German word for a particular table in a pub, unofficially reserved for a group of regulars.

disciplinarian father, against whose wrath … [the submissive mother] was helpless to protect her offspring. Adolf's younger sister, Paula Hitler, spoke after the Second World War of her mother as 'a very soft and tender person … It was especially … Adolf who challenged my father …and who got his sound thrashing every day…'"[18].

Both Hitler and Churchill thought extensively about the role of education. Both were self-taught to a considerable degree. Neither went to university, though Hitler described his prison sentence in 1924, when he read a lot, as a "university at state expense". Given Hitler's well-known incapacity for disciplined work, it is difficult to imagine him putting in years of academic toil at an institute of higher education. Churchill, too, had a spotty academic record. An early school report records him as being "a constant trouble to everybody and … always in some scrape or other"[19]. Many leading politicians would probably have echoed those comments decades later. In *My Early Life*‡, Churchill implied that his performance at school was uniformly poor, being placed in the bottom form at Harrow, the public school which he attended, and performing poorly at examinations[20]. It is clear, however, that this is an exaggeration. His performance was erratic, but by no means uniformly bad[21].

Churchill seems to have considered attending Oxford as a late entrant when he returned from service in the Army, but was discouraged by the need to learn Latin and Greek irregular verbs in particular[22]. He wrote, perhaps uncontroversially, that education should be universal, as it had been in Britain since before he was born[23]. He also argued that too much emphasis was placed on the classics in English education. In a much-quoted passage in *My Early Life*, he wrote that "I would make all [boys] learn English: and then I would let the clever ones learn Latin as an honour, and Greek as a treat. But the only thing I would whip them for is not knowing English. I would whip them hard for that"[24].

Churchill also dreaded Mathematics, describing himself as "out of my depth" when he had to study it to pass his Sandhurst exams. He describes "dim chambers lighted by sullen, sulphurous fires [which] … contained a dragon called the "Differential Calculus"". However, dread did not mean that he thought it pointless: "It is very important to build bridges and canals … I am

---

‡ Like Hitler's *Mein Kampf*, though to a lesser degree, Churchill's autobiographical writings were published while its author still had a political career in front of him, and were also supposed to make him money, and so must be taken with more than a pinch of salt.

very glad there are quite a number of people born with a gift and a liking for all of this … I hope [that they] … are well rewarded"[25].

Hitler seems to have been a bright child in the first school to which he was sent. It was in Fischlham, a small village with a handsome castle, thirty miles from the German-Austrian border. His teacher and others from those days later remembered a "lively, intelligent, and well-turned out child"[26]. At the *Realschule* (secondary school) at Linz, he was regarded as able, but idle. Some teachers and classmates subsequently claimed that Hitler did not stand out a great deal in any way at school[27]. His account of his boyhood and education in *Mein Kampf* is, for the most part, highly questionable, written as it clearly was with a view to publicising himself as a natural leader for Germany. He claimed he was top of the class in history and geography, two subjects he evidently felt were required to be a successful dictator, but his report cards show that at Linz, he received "only failing grades"[28]. He failed an examination then was granted a passing grade in the subject, but only on condition that he left the school. He was transferred to another school, fifty miles away, where he showed some improvement. He dropped out from school altogether at 16, though he passed his final exams, having re-sat his geometry examination.

Decades later, when dictator of Germany and most of Europe, Hitler repeatedly vented his spleen against schoolmasters, stating that he could not endure them[29], and that most of his were slightly mad, with the good ones being exceptional[30]. In *Mein Kampf*, he praised individual teachers, in particular his history teacher, one Dr Pötsch. After they met decades later, Hitler remarked, "you have no idea how much I owe to this old man"[31]. He had a French teacher, however, "whose whole preoccupation was to catch us out in a mistake. He was a hair-splitter and a bully"[32]. Hitler considered that the school system of his childhood produced "intellectual monsters", with society being saved from "complete decadence" only by conscription. He was not sure that it had changed much under his leadership:

> "I was shown a questionnaire, …, which it was proposed to put to people whom it was deemed desirable to sterilise. At least three quarters of the questions would have defeated my own mother … If this system had been introduced before my birth, I am pretty sure I should never have been born at all"[33].

In arguing against euthanasia, Hitler inadvertently provides perhaps the best argument in its favour.

Both men tried to educate themselves to some degree while their contemporaries were students. In Churchill's case, he read many worthy books, in particular while he was on campaign. In India in 1897, for instance, he read, Gibbon, Plato, Winwood Reade's *The Martyrdom of Man*, Hallam's *Constitutional History* and Adam Smith's *The Wealth of Nations*. He also read the *Annual Register of World Events*, beginning in 1880. These books apparently stirred in him a fleeting wish to go back to university[34]. What Hitler was reading in his teens and twenties remains unclear. His companion in Vienna, Kubizek, claims that Hitler "read prodigiously" and that he was reading a number of classics, including Ibsen, Dante, Goethe and Schiller, and that "Adolf had an especial feel for poets and authors who had something to say to him"[35]. The list of classics which Kubizek claims that Hitler read may not ring true[36]. However, Kubizek's statements that "he took care to keep a safe distance from anything which might put him to the test" and "even in his books he only found what suited him" are probably absolutely accurate[37]. As if to confirm Kubizek's opinions, Hitler himself argued in *Mein Kampf* that people should read to form and confirm their general world views[38], not, apparently to challenge or adapt views already formed.

First recognition?

It is not clear when Hitler and Churchill heard, or took notice, of each other for the first time. Interestingly, Churchill does not mention when Hitler first came to his attention in any of his many writings on the German dictator. It is possible, however, to guess when they heard of each other, from the time when both men came to international attention. According to his own, highly unreliable, account in *Mein Kampf*[39], Hitler was a voracious newspaper reader during his time in Vienna (February 1908 to May 1913), and he comments in *Mein Kampf* on the swift growth of the German battle fleet in the years before the First World War. He also opines, in his usual style combining ignorance and dogmatism, on issues of ship design and gun size which were widely debated in Germany and Britain in the years around the same time[40]. It is virtually certain that, in reading about this, he would have read about the British reaction, led, to a large extent, by the First Lords of the Admiralty. During Hitler's Vienna period and his subsequent year in Munich, these First Lords were Reginald McKenna (to 1911) and Winston Churchill (1911-1915). We can, therefore, conjecture that Hitler was aware of Churchill's existence before the First World War. Hitler does not comment, in *Mein Kampf* or anywhere else, about Austria-

Hungary's own, much smaller, naval development, but this too caused some alarm in Britain, which in turn was covered in the Austrian press. For example, the Austrian *Neue Freie Presse* referred to Churchill's statements in Parliament in declaring that Austrian naval construction had "certainly a purely defensive character" and was "not directed against England …". It returned to the subject several days later, again referring to Churchill's speech[41].

We may extend the conjecture slightly to suppose that he was aware both of Churchill's name and of his actions and policies as senior government minister for the Royal Navy. What, if anything, he thought of Churchill at this time is unrecorded. It is most likely that he was a German nationalist in Vienna. He would, therefore, have presumably opposed Churchill's efforts to maintain the Royal Navy's superiority over the Imperial German Navy. He may, however, have respected him for advancing his country's interests. Hitler later commented on how natural it had been for England to want to expand its fleet to counter the German challenge. All this, however, must remain conjecture.

It is more difficult to speculate whether Hitler was aware of Churchill before the latter's time as First Lord of the Admiralty. If he was, it cannot have been directly through Churchill's writings: Hitler spoke barely a word of English, and none of Churchill's books were published in German until his account of the First World War, *The World Crisis*, in 1924. (Hitler studied French at school, but Churchill's journalism and accounts of his adventures appeared mostly in British Empire and American newspapers). In addition, none of Churchill's "famous works" were to be found in Hitler's library after his death[42].

In *Mein Kampf*, Hitler wrote that "as a young man, in consequence of my extensive newspaper reading, I had, without myself realizing it, been inoculated with a certain admiration for the British Parliament, of which I was not easily able to rid myself. The dignity with which the Lower House there fulfilled its tasks (as was so touchingly described in our press) impressed me immensely"[43] – though his bombers were to destroy that House in May 1941. In any case, it is difficult to imagine Hitler reading to any extent about the Lower House in the decade before the First World War without reading about one of its most prominent members. Like so much else relating to his Vienna period, Hitler's reaction to Churchill's career, if any, must remain a matter for conjecture. However, Churchill attracted international attention prior to becoming First Lord of the Admiralty in a number of ways.

During the Boer War, which Hitler followed as a ten- to thirteen-year-old[44], Churchill's escape from captivity in Pretoria was publicised in the international press. As President of the Board of Trade (1908-10), Churchill, in cooperation with the Chancellor of the Exchequer, David Lloyd George, unsuccessfully opposed the Admiralty in the Navy Scare[§]. In 1911, as Home Secretary, he was responsible for ending the Siege of Sydney Street, in which armed, Latvian jewel thieves were cornered at a house in London. This dramatic operation, which involved elite troops and ended in the building going up in flames, was reported worldwide. It seems highly likely that Hitler read about at least some of these events, and about Churchill's role in them.

Churchill's domestic achievements at the Board of Trade and as Home Secretary[**] are much less likely to have attracted Hitler's attention than his time as First Lord of the Admiralty or his Boer War escapades. He created a nationwide network of labour exchanges in imitation of a system already operating in Germany, which lasts to the present day[††]. To the Prime Minister, Asquith, he went much further, advocating "a sort of Germanised network of State intervention and regulation"[45]. He humanised conditions in coal mines, forcing the management to provide baths for the miners, when few, if any, would have had private bathrooms in their own homes, and obliging the management to provide rescue and ambulance services. He assisted Lloyd George with the implementation of the National Insurance scheme in the 1909 Budget, the financing of which led directly to the tumultuous confrontation between the Liberal government and the House of Lords. He improved prison conditions and reduced the number of boys sent to prison by two-thirds. His policies reduced the numbers jailed for non-payment of fines from 100,000 in 1908/09 to 2,000 ten years later[46]. It is difficult to imagine the instigator of

---

[§] The 1909-10 Navy Estimates contained funding for the construction of six Dreadnought battleships and battlecruisers, which had been requested by the Admiralty to counter increased German construction. Churchill's and Lloyd George's counter-proposal of four battleships instead was rejected. It is impossible to resist quoting Churchill's famous summary of the outcome: "In the end, a curious and characteristic solution was reached. The Admiralty had demanded six ships; the economists offered four; and we finally compromised on eight." Winston Churchill, *The World Crisis*, Vol. 1, p.37. Britain in fact built ten Dreadnoughts in that year (though only eight were funded by Britain, the remaining two being paid for by Australia and New Zealand)

[**] Besides, perhaps, the Siege of Sydney Street.

[††] Renamed "Job Centres" in the 1960s and "JobCentre Plus" in 2002

Chapter 1

Germany's concentration and extermination camps being impressed by Churchill's liberal record on law and order. Hitler might have been more impressed with Churchill's record in upholding the death penalty: Churchill upheld 22 of the 43 death sentences on which he had to decide whether to grant clemency during his tenure, commuting the other 21[47]. Churchill evidently hated exercising the Home Secretary's responsibility in those days when deciding whether to exercise mercy in capital cases. In a Parliamentary debate on the abolition of the death penalty in 1948, he claimed that "there was no office which I was more glad to leave", though adding that he found deciding whether to commute life sentences or long prison sentences even more of an ordeal than dealing with capital cases[48].

As an anonymous dropout in Vienna and Munich prior to the First World War, and then as a junior soldier in the trenches until the end of the First World War, Hitler would not have come to Churchill's attention. It is also almost inconceivable that Churchill would have heard of Hitler when he was working for the German Army or as a rabble-rousing orator in Munich immediately following the First World War. The first mention of Hitler in the British press which I could find was in *The Times* of 18 October 1922, in a small article in the "News in Brief" section:

> "The National Socialists in Bavaria are imitating the Italian Fascisti. Under the command of a Herr Hitler, an armed body of 180 men … travelled to Allach where there was trouble between them and some workmen. Herr Hitler's men are said to be buying arms throughout the Bavarian Oberland".

In fact, we know that Churchill read several papers that day. He had just had an operation for appendicitis[49]. Martin Gilbert quotes Maurice Hankey on what happened next:

> "On coming to from his anaesthetics Churchill immediately cried, 'Who has got in for Newport? Give me a newspaper.' The doctor told him he could not have it and must keep quiet. Shortly after, the doctor returned and found Winston unconscious again with four or five newspapers lying on the bed".

One of those newspapers may well have been *The Times* of that day. However, less column space was devoted to the first mention of Adolf Hitler than the news on the same page that a hen had laid her 324th egg in a contest in California[50]. In fact, it seems unlikely that Churchill would have paid a great deal of attention to these reports of Hitler's early acts of thuggery, even if he noticed them at all. He had just had a major operation for what was, in those days, a life-threatening condition. Furthermore, British politics was then highly unstable, with Lloyd George's government collapsing the following day, and with Churchill about to find himself, in his famous words, "without an office, without a seat, without a party and without an appendix". He would have had much else on his mind.

An article in *The Times* in January 1923 on "An Army of Revenge" referred to the Nazi Party ("the so-called Fascisti of Bavaria") at some length, quoting Hitler as saying "The National Socialists were organising and recruiting an army of revenge, which in the near future would restore Germany to her former greatness"[51]. Throughout the Spring and Summer of that year, there were articles in the British press on the Nazis, with headlines such as: "The Bavarian Fascisti", and "Militarism in Germany". The *Manchester Guardian* had a long article in February which referred to Hitler as a "fanatic preacher of ruthlessness" and "the excited and muddle-headed Bohemian"[52]. However, none of these articles were particularly prominent. British and Imperial affairs were far more conspicuous in that year. Nevertheless, there was a trickle of such stories. American papers, too, had been noting the rise of the Nazis in 1923. An early example was *Time* magazine's coverage of Hitler's and Ludendorff's position in Munich politics in April of that year[53].

Hitler first made headlines around the world in the farcical but ominous Beer Hall Putsch of November 1923. His subsequent trial kept him in the British and American papers for several months thereafter. It concluded with him being sentenced to five years' imprisonment in April 1924, though in the end he was released after serving only nine months. The story was covered at length in every serious British newspaper of the time, and was picked up by the Associated Press. Much of the early coverage referred to General Ludendorff, who was involved in the *Putsch* with Hitler, as much as Hitler himself. The coverage of the trial, however, focused far more on Hitler as he stole the show in court, using it as a platform for his views. The *Manchester Guardian*, for example, had articles on "Hitler's brave words in the beer-hall" and the "Ludendorff fiasco". *The Times* contained prominent articles on the Putsch, entitled, variously, the "Ludendorff Coup", "Ludendorff Captured", "The Menace in Europe", "The Arrest of Herr Hitler", "Munich Factions", and "Hitler Confined in a Fortress"[54]. The American magazine *Time* devoted a 683-word article to the "Beer Hall Revolt"[55].

In November 1923, Churchill had many other matters on his mind. His preoccupations over the next few months were mostly British, including campaigning for a general election, which presented him with a crisis of conscience over free trade. He was also struggling with his long account of the

First World War, *The World Crisis*. He was occupied with a libel action against Lord Alfred Douglas, which went to trial the next month[‡‡]. Finally, he agreed to represent two large oil companies in a merger to the British government, though that deal eventually came to nothing. The following year was to be one of the most turbulent in British political history, with the first ever Labour government elected in December, a major espionage scandal over the forged Zinoviev letter and a landslide Conservative victory following a second general election in October 1924. Churchill's finances, too, were in an even more parlous state than usual. He had bought Chartwell, a country house on the border between London and Kent, for £5,000 in 1922, but had needed to spend four times that amount on renovating the house and grounds before occupying it for the first time in early 1924[56]. Nevertheless, it seems most unlikely that a politician like Churchill would have failed to notice front page headlines in the British and European press about the attempted revolution in Germany. When Churchill first took notice of Hitler is conjecture, but it seems most likely to have been on or just after 8-9 November 1923, when the news of the Beer Hall Putsch was broadcast around Europe and the world. This would seem to give the lie to his statement, a quarter of a century later, that in 1932, he knew little of the Nazis.

Churchill's views on Germany to 1924

While not directly related to the views and opinions of Churchill and Hitler on each other, the views they formed on each other's countries in these years are important in understanding their later opinions on each other. Churchill tried and failed to learn German[57]. It seems unlikely, however, that his failure with the language meant that he disliked the country or its people. Churchill was to argue in the 1930's, when few others in Britain would, that Germany was a menace to European peace. He seems to have had no irreconcilable dislike of the German people[§§]. When he saw a German threat to the British Empire, however, he was always ready to argue that Britain had to confront and, if

---

[‡‡] Douglas, Oscar Wilde's former lover, alleged that Churchill had been part of a Jewish conspiracy to make a fortune from releasing a false report about the Battle of Jutland in 1916. He lost the case, and was sentenced to six months in prison. Bizarrely, Douglas wrote a sonnet in praise of Churchill in 1941.

[§§] See, for example, his speech to the House of Commons on 24 October 1935, while deploring the Nazi regime, quoted in Chapter 4 below.

necessary, eliminate the peril. Likewise, his lifelong Francophilia*** was probably not caused by his relative success with the French language. During his time at school, he learned French, and spoke it with original idioms and an atrocious accent to the end of his life. In 1943, his doctor described him talking to the Turks at Adana in "his own brand of French. It isn't French and it isn't English, but something in between"[58].

Far more formative in his attitude to France and Germany was a visit he made with his father to Paris in 1883. There, he had his first experience of the results of German aggression. Sixty-three years later, he recalled being driven along the Place de la Concorde at the centre of the French capital. He noticed that one of the monuments was covered with wreaths and asked his father why. He recalled that his father replied, "These are monuments of the provinces of France. Two of them, Alsace and Lorraine, have been taken from France by the Germans … The French are very unhappy about it and hope some day to get them back". Decades later, Churchill still remembered quite distinctly thinking to himself that he hoped that the French would get them back[59]. This could of course simply be an instance of an old man projecting his current opinions back on himself as a child. However, there is another piece of evidence, this time circumstantial, that this experience left some impression on the eight-year-old boy. Seven years later, he was to write, in a poem for his school magazine, about:

> "Fair Alsace and forlorn Lorraine,
>
> The cause of bitterness and pain
>
> In many a Gallic breast, …"[60]

Churchill recognised the threat to the British Empire from growing German power in the period before the First World War - earlier than many of his countrymen - and had worked to ensure that Britain had sufficient strength to meet it. Looking back after the First World War, with the advantage of hindsight, he identified the provocative Kruger telegram as the point when British suspicions of Germany crystallised. This tactless document was sent by

---

*** "I have always been an admirer of France", he wrote in the *Strand* magazine in January 1936.

Chapter 1

Kaiser Wilhelm II in 1896 to congratulate the Boers for foiling an unofficial British raid into their territory. Churchill wrote that: "The British nation took the German Emperor's telegram as a revelation of hostile mood, and they never forgot it"[61]. Churchill had been in the Imperial presence during the Kaiser's visit to London in 1891, while still a schoolboy at Harrow, but the two men did not meet at that time[62].

In contrast to his early opposition to German rearmament in the 1930's, however, Churchill was, at first, slow in proposing British rearmament, and ambiguous about the size and nature of the German threat to Britain. Possibly from around 1903-04 (when the Entente Cordiale was concluded with France), and certainly from 1907, when a similar understanding was concluded with Russia, it seemed that Britain's only probable enemy was Germany. He seems also to have been concerned about the threat which Germany's rapid industrialisation posed to British trade, referring to "filthy Germans ... finally gaining commercial supremacy of the world"[63]. Famously, however, in one of his worst predictions, when campaigning in 1908, Churchill told audiences in Manchester and Dundee that the German threat was a figment of Tory imaginations. In the following year, he took the weaker line in opposing the building of more battleships during the Navy Scare, though he was subsequently to admit that he had been wrong[64].

However, by the following year, Churchill had begun to change his mind. In 1906, when Under-Secretary for the Colonies, he was invited to witness German army manoeuvres. He met the Kaiser, who ordered that he be shown a new artillery piece, and talked with him "about various colonial questions, including particularly the native revolt in German South-West Africa". In 1909, he was again invited, though this time he had "only one short conversation with him"[65]. Churchill began to fear the power of the German army[†††]: "I am very thankful there is a sea between that army and England", he wrote to an aunt after his first visit. To Lord Elgin, his Secretary of State, he commented, "There is a massive simplicity and force about German military arrangements which grows upon the observer ... numbers, quality, discipline and organisation are four good roads to victory"[66]. He told his wife, after his second visit that the German army "is a terrible engine ... It is in number as the sands of the sea – and with all the modern conveniences"[67]. Churchill met the Kaiser again during his second visit. A photograph exists of the relatively young English politician in military

---

[†††] It was not only the German military which impressed Churchill, however. During his 1909 visit, he observed the labour exchange at Frankfurt, and, as noted above, quickly borrowed the idea for Britain.

uniform walking and talking (for only two minutes, according to Churchill[68]) with the German emperor. Perhaps because of rapidly improving Franco-British relations, the French army manoeuvres he witnessed in September 1907 do not seem to have caused him similar dread and Churchill preferred their show to the "crude absurdities" of Germany's "theatrical display"[69]. When he reached home, though he had as yet no ministerial responsibility for the Navy, he wrote a paper on German naval expansion. The paper was gloomy on the possibility of a deceleration of the arms race. It argued that the choice lay with the German government, which would have to decide soon whether to be peaceful or bellicose[70].

In late July 1911, Churchill seems to have decided that the German threat was a national emergency for Britain, and that war was likely in the near future. He was Home Secretary during the beginning of the Anglo-German phase of the Agadir crisis. Significantly, after a preliminary chapter, he begins his own account of the First World War, *The World Crisis*, with this affair[71]. France considered that Morocco belonged to her sphere of influence. Using the excuse of an internal crisis in that African country, Germany, attempting to humiliate France, sent a gunboat to Agadir, a port on Morocco's Atlantic coast. France secured Britain's backing in the diplomatic fencing which ensued, and a war between Britain, France and Germany, probably dragging in Russia and Austria-Hungary as well, seemed likely. On 25 July, the German government replied to a British cable with what the Foreign Secretary described to Churchill as "a communication ... so stiff that [the Foreign Secretary feared that] the Fleet might be attacked at any moment". Churchill, still Home Secretary, found out that the Navy's cordite[‡‡‡] reserves were inadequately guarded: he insisted that they be watched around the clock by troops. As well as instigating military precautions, he tried to contribute to a peaceful resolution of the crisis. He attempted to impress on the German ambassador, with whom he was friendly, the British government's point of view. According to his own account, once he began thinking about the security of Britain, "it became impossible to think about anything else"[72]. In the next few months, while still Home Secretary, he wrote memoranda in which he predicted the early course of a war with Germany with considerable prescience to: the Committee on Imperial Defence; the Foreign Secretary; the Chancellor of the Exchequer (twice); the Prime Minster; and the First Lord of the Admiralty (with whom he was to swap jobs later in the year)[73].

[‡‡‡] Cordite was used as the propellant for naval shells. It is highly explosive. Without it, the Navy would have been unable to fire its big guns at all.

Perhaps in part because of these memoranda, the Prime Minister felt that Churchill's talents could be put to better use combatting the German threat. Once the Agadir crisis was resolved, Churchill was appointed First Lord of the Admiralty, a position which he held for the next three and a half years. During this time, Churchill ensured that the British fleet continued its rapid expansion and modernization, targeted explicitly against Germany. In his speech proposing the 1912-13 Navy Estimates in the House of Commons, Churchill replaced the two-power standard, which had originally been directed against France and Russia, with a one-power standard: "The actual standard of new construction … which the Admiralty has, in fact, followed during recent years, has been to develop a 60 per cent, superiority in vessels of the "Dreadnought" type over the German navy on the basis of the existing Fleet Law"[74]. He repeatedly spoke on the comparative strengths of the British and German navies throughout the rest of his time at the Admiralty[75]. Like most Britons of that era, he viewed a strong British fleet as essential to the maintenance of European civilization. After the First World War, perhaps embellishing somewhat with hindsight, he recalled his pre-war nightmare that the British fleet would somehow disappear and that "Europe [would pass] into the iron grip and rule of the Teuton and of all that the Teutonic system meant"[76].

Hitler was later to claim that "Churchill even in 1914 was one of the worst warmongers of his time"[77]. Despite the naval arms race between Britain and Germany, however, Churchill does not appear to have regarded Armageddon as unavoidable, and he made constructive suggestions to reduce the tension. His train of thought is fairly clear from his speeches at the time. For example, "I do not believe in the theory of inevitable wars … it may be that in a few years' time the democratic forces in Germany will again have greater control of their own Government, and that the landlord ascendancy which now exists will be replaced by more pacific and less formidable elements"[78]. Perhaps to assist such elements, he proposed a simultaneous freeze on construction of new battleships in both countries (his famous "Naval Holiday" idea). As with most participants in an arms race, however, he expected the other side to make the first move, writing in 1912 that "until Germany dropped the Naval challenge, her policy here would be continually viewed with deepening suspicions ... But any slackening on her part would produce an immediate detente with much good will from all England ... Anything in my power to terminate [Anglo-German antagonism and the associated arms race], I would gladly do"[79].

Churchill also proposed reducing secretiveness about naval construction, hoping that this would encourage Anglo-German understanding[80]. The Germans showed no interest in taking a Naval Holiday and the French immediately objected that Germany would enlarge her army if she did not increase her fleet.

The idea was not stillborn, but it expired fairly quickly.

The outbreak of the First World War in August 1914 did not come as a surprise to Churchill. Five months earlier, he had warned Parliament that: "the causes which might lead to a general war have not been removed and often remind us of their presence". As Europe descended into catastrophe in July 1914, Churchill made the key precautionary decision to mobilise the Royal Navy. "Everything trends towards catastrophe and collapse", he wrote to his wife, who was on holiday in Norfolk. "I am interested, geared-up and happy. Is it not horrible to be built like that?"[81] It seems, however, that he still hoped peace might be salvaged until Germany declared war on Russia on 1 August and on France two days later. On the 31 July, he wrote to his wife that there was "still hope, though the clouds are blacker & blacker"[82]. The next day, he later recalled, he had thought that "if war was inevitable, this [i.e. the German declaration of war on Russia] was by far the most favourable opportunity and the only one that would bring France, Russia and ourselves together"[83]. Three days later, however, he wrote again to his wife, that, in a world "gone mad" Britain "must look after ourselves – and our friends". On 3 August, he put into action plans already made with the French to prevent Germany sailing her fleet into the Channel and bombarding the French Channel ports or attacking French trade. The Cabinet, however, held him back from aggressive action against German warships until the expiry of the British ultimatum to Germany the following day[84].

When the Belgian government decided to resist the German invasion, which was proceeding through Belgium, Churchill concluded that war was inevitable. The Prime Minister's wife, Margot Asquith, left a small, but illuminating anecdote on Churchill's mood at this time. She wrote that, on the expiry of Britain's ultimatum to Germany, "The clock on the mantelpiece hammered out the hour … We were at war. I left to go to bed, and … I saw Winston Churchill with a happy face striding towards the double doors of the Cabinet room"[85]. Writing after the First World War, Churchill blamed Germany entirely for its outbreak. He did not even mention Austria-Hungary, which had started the whole conflagration:

> "[Britain] was guiltless of all intended purpose of war. Even if we had made some mistakes in the handling of this awful crisis, …, from the bottom of our hearts we could say that we had not willed it. Germany it seemed had rushed with head down and settled resolve to her own undoing … she had put herself hopelessly in the wrong …"[86]

Chapter 1

During the First World War, Germany and the Germans were demonised by the relatively new mass-circulation press more than any other national enemy in British history. The German army undoubtedly committed atrocities during its occupation of Belgium and part of France and in sinking British and neutral merchant ships. However, the British press published, for example, false reports of a factory near Koblenz, in Germany, where the corpses of German soldiers were allegedly recycled into pig food and other products. These atrocity stories were used deliberately to inflame opinion in Britain and neutral countries against Germany and the Germans. This propaganda later found an unlikely admirer in Hitler, who wrote: "By representing the Germans to their own people as barbarians and Huns, they prepared the individual soldier for the terrors of war, and thus helped to preserve him from disappointments"[87].

This barrage of propaganda seems to have affected Churchill, at least to some extent. In the fourth month of the war, he was referring to the German fleet as "swine"[88] in a letter to his wife. By the end of the war, he was opposing a one-day halt of bombing on Germany[89] (though more because of the effect on British morale than because of a desire to kill Germans), and proposing to use the "hellish poison"[90] of mustard gas on German troops, "Their whining in defeat is very gratifying to hear"[91], Churchill added. One of the victims of that policy was to be Hitler, who was injured by mustard gas in the last month of the war. Overall, however, his wartime correspondence and speeches are remarkable for their moderation. In Parliament, for instance, Churchill did not use the abusive word "Hun" to mean "German", unlike many other MPs[92], though he used it in private letters to his wife. When touring the front line in August 1918, Churchill passed some German prisoners. "I could not help feeling sorry for them in their miserable plight and dejection", he wrote. "… Still, I was very glad to see them where they were"[93]. In 1940, when France was being crushed and Britain's future was uncertain, he commented to one of his Generals: "I never hated the Germans in the last [First World] war, but now I hate them like … well, like an earwig"[94].

Whatever anti-German feelings Churchill had during the war cooled remarkably quickly once peace returned. On the day of the Armistice, Churchill dined with Lloyd George, F.E. Smith[§§§] and General Sir Henry Wilson. The latter recorded in his diary that Lloyd George and F.E. wanted to shoot the Kaiser, but Winston did not[95]. As soon as the war ended, he "proposed filling a dozen great liners

---

[§§§] A Conservative politician, long-time Churchill friend and subject of one of the essays in Churchill's *Great Contemporaries* (1937)

with food, and rushing them into Hamburg as a gesture of humanity"[96]. A week later, in a Cabinet memorandum, Churchill was arguing that "a permanently ruined Germany means an impoverished Britain", and he cautioned against being "drawn into extravaganzas by the fullness of ... victory"[97]. Churchill stood out against British opinion at this time. After the end of the war, there was what Churchill later called "a brief interval of absurd demands", when Britain and France made unrealistic demands that an impoverished Germany should pay the full cost of the war[98]. In a letter to a former Liberal MP, he noted that he held a reservation against the Government policy that Germany be made to pay for the war to the limit of her resources: "I do not consider that we should be justified in ... reducing ... the mass of the working class population of Germany to a condition of sweated labour"[99].

During the general election campaign which followed the Armistice, Churchill made a speech in his constituency in Dundee which may seem to be anti-German, but was in fact standard for any politician in that election:

> "No colony will be restored to Germany ... Germany must make reparation for damage done. This will cost around a thousand million pounds. People need not be alarmed lest Germany will get off lightly. Her punishment will be beyond all previous records. Practically the whole German nation has been guilty of crime, and they must suffer for it"[100].

Churchill was to argue in public, however, against squeezing Germany "until the pips squeaked", in the campaigning phrase of the time. He was heckled loudly for doing so. He was quoted in the press as saying that to recover the entire cost of the war from Germany would be impossible[101]. He wrote to a former Liberal MP: "I do not consider that we should be justified in ... reducing ... the mass of the ... population of Germany to a condition of sweated labour and servitude"[102]. He was contemptuous of the schemes for trying the Kaiser in London and exiling him to the Falkland Islands, which delighted Lloyd George[103].

At the Versailles Conference, Churchill attended the famous meeting of the British delegation which decided that the draft treaty was far too harsh on Germany and should be substantially revised[104]. The British failed to secure any significant changes to the document, however, and Churchill later told a friend that he had told Lloyd George that "he would not put his name to it for £1,000"[105]. By 1920, he was arguing for a "strong but peaceful Germany" as a bulwark against Bolshevism[106], and telling the French Minister of War that Britain "would have nothing to do with a policy of crushing Germany"[107]. In the following year, he proposed to the Imperial Conference in London that Britain should be the "friend of Germany"[108]. He "vehemently" opposed the French occupation of the Ruhr in 1923[109], and in 1925 told the President of France that his predecessor had "done great harm to British sentiments towards France" through his policy[110]. The following year, he recognised that Germany could not be kept down forever by force, as France was attempting: Germany was "a far stronger unity than France, and cannot be kept in permanent subjugation"[111]. He was also to argue, at the end of the Second World War, that demanding the abolition of the German monarchy had been a mistake. "I am of the opinion", he wrote to the British Ambassador in Brussels, "that if the Allies at … Versailles had not imagined that the sweeping away of long-established dynasties was a form of progress, and if they had allowed [the German monarchies] to return to their thrones, there would have been no Hitler"[112]. Monarchies had not saved Italy and Japan from dictatorship, and the United States had a strong form of republican democracy, but Churchill ignored this obvious counter-argument.

Any hostility which Churchill may have felt towards Germany and the Germans, then, was apparent only when Germany was an immediate threat towards Britain and the British Empire, in the period leading up to, and during, the First World War. During and after that war, he was far more moderate in his views about Germany than most other Britons. He wanted to conciliate, rather than punish, the fallen foe, and he wanted Germany to be strong, though not perhaps too strong, in order to fight the Bolshevik menace.

Churchill was to spend most of the period 1924-31 working on domestic and Imperial issues, as Chancellor of the Exchequer until the Conservatives lost office in 1929, and then as an Opposition MP. To judge from his writings and recorded conversation, he does not seem to have given Germany and the Germans much thought during these years, except for the question of reparations and war debts. As the next chapter will show, once Germany began to rearm and adopt an aggressive posture, Churchill turned his attention towards it immediately.

Hitler's views on the British Empire to 1924

Hitler never visited Britain or any part of the British Empire****. He knew essentially no English, though this did not stop him holding the opinions that "the English language lacks the ability to express thoughts that surpass the order of concrete things", and that English spelling was hopelessly unphonetic[113]. According to a Swedish businessman, Birger Dahlerus, who worked with Göring in an effort to prevent the Second World War, Hitler was "a man whose real knowledge of Britain was nil"[114]. In *Mein Kampf*, he says that, as a young boy, he thought that, in the international world of the future, "the English could supply the merchants, the Germans the administrative officials, and the Jews would [be] the owners". As mentioned above, he followed the Boer War, which took place from his tenth to his thirteenth years, and played games with his friends based on the exploits of the Boers. The first time that that he felt he had to decide whether to support the British Empire or not, he supported its enemies, though this is hardly surprising, as most of the German-speaking press and public were viciously Anglophobic throughout the conflict[††††,115].

When the First World War broke out, Hitler volunteered to serve in the Bavarian army. From the start, he seems to have regarded Britain as Germany's main enemy, though this could have been because his regiment spent most of the war facing British and Imperial troops, rather than the French and Belgians. On 20 October 1914, the young Private Hitler wrote to his landlady in Munich. "Tonight, the 20th, we are going on a 4 day train journey, probably to Belgium. I am tremendously excited. … I hope we shall get to England"[116]. On 5 February 1915, during a heavy battle, Hitler wrote to an acquaintance in Munich, describing how he looked forward to an attack on the British lines, "… tomorrow we attack the English. At last! All of us rejoiced"[117]. Later in the letter, he described with obvious relish how he was amongst "dead and wounded Englishmen… Again and again one of our shells landed in the English trench. They poured out like ants from an ant heap, and then we

---

**** In 2011, a historian put forward the theory that Hitler spent several months in Liverpool in 1912/13, but the idea has not gained widespread acceptance.

†††† Franklin Roosevelt, US President and Churchill's most important ally during the Second World War, also supported the Boers, and, according to one of the Americans present, welcomed a tired Churchill to Washington in 1941 by "needling [him] for having been on the wrong side in the Boer war" – Percy Chubb, quoted in *Road to Victory*, Martin Gilbert, p.27.

attacked...Many came out with their hands up. Those who did not surrender were mowed down"[118]. Hitler fought mostly against the British during the First World War. His position as a *Meldegänger*, or dispatch runner, was relatively privileged, though it was not free from danger. His job was to carry messages from the regimental headquarters to the front line. He was, therefore, attached to regimental headquarters, which means he was spared the worst of the mud and squalor of the trenches[119]. As a dispatch runner in his regiment, he was also much more likely to survive the war. According to Thomas Weber, one in four of those who served in his regiment were killed, and 80 per cent were casualties, while all of the dispatch runners at regimental HQ survived the war[120].

Hitler was not, however, out of danger entirely. He was involved in four of the critical battles of the First World War‡‡‡‡, each time fighting mostly against British or Imperial forces. He was seriously wounded twice, both times by the British army. On the first occasion, in October 1916, a shell burst in his dugout and injured him in the left thigh. He spent two months in a Red Cross hospital in Berlin as a result. His stay in Berlin corresponded with the early part of what the Germans came to know as the Turnip Winter (*Kohlrubenwinter*), when for weeks at a time, wheat was unavailable for making bread, and turnips were substituted. He would doubtless have realised that this was the result of the British blockade, though it may not have occurred to him that his future enemy, Churchill, had led the Admiralty which ran the blockade in the early days of the war.

Hitler was injured for the second time, as noted above, when he was caught in a British mustard gas attack in October 1918. He suffered temporary blindness, and was hospitalised for the remaining month of the war. This may have been important: he missed the dire last month of the war, when the Allies finally began to rout the German army. It may have been more difficult to believe that the Jews had betrayed the Germans if he had been fighting at the time. This, however, is conjecture, and may be wide of the mark. Hitler had a remarkable ability to close his mind to facts which did not suit his prejudices.

Inevitably, the war years affected him deeply. His armaments minister and courtier, Speer, later recalled that the "bravery and determination of the British forces had won Hitler's respect, though he would make fun of the peculiarities of the British army. He claimed, ironically, that the British were in the habit of

---

‡‡‡‡ The First Battle of Ypres in 1914, the Battle of the Somme in 1916, the Third Battle of Ypres in 1917 and *Kaiserschlacht* in early 1918.

stopping their artillery barrages at tea time, so that he, a messenger, could run his errands safely at that hour"[121]. Heavy Teutonic jokes aside, Hitler clearly had considerable respect for "England" (as he generally referred to Great Britain or the British Empire) in a number of ways. Once he became Germany's dictator, he continually tried to conclude an alliance, or at least some form of understanding, with the island nation. "If I had a choice between Italy and England", he told another courtier in 1936, "I would naturally go with the English … I know the Englishmen from the last war, they are hard fellows"[122]. His opinion of British troops apparently deteriorated during the Second World War, however: Speer recalls Hitler clinging "to the end to his preconceived opinion that the troops of the Western countries were poor fighting material"[123].

After the Armistice, Hitler remained with the Army. He was stationed in Munich, which offered an ideal setting for a rabble-rousing orator to make his mark. The city had been famous for its advanced intellectual life and tolerant atmosphere before the First World War. In the six months to April 1919, however, it had experienced perhaps the most turbulent time of any European city in history. It had lived under monarchy; extreme socialism; social democracy; Anarchism; Bolshevism; and finally a brutal counter-revolutionary dictatorship which executed at least a thousand people, and probably many more. This unhealthy, indeed murderous, political atmosphere nurtured a poisonous weed: Hitler began giving speeches to crowds of varying sizes. By 1921, his orations were drawing crowds of thousands of people. On 3 February, he spoke to an audience of 6,000 people on "Future or Ruin", denouncing the Treaty of Versailles. Three days later, he appeared (with other speakers) in front of a crowd of 20,000 in Munich's central square, the Odeonsplatz. He seems to have bombed somewhat at the latter meeting, however[124]. During the early 1920's, the most certain way to please a German crowd was not to attack the Jews or the Bolsheviks directly, but to attack the Treaty of Versailles, and this Hitler did repeatedly. In these speeches, a repeated theme was that England and France were attempting to reduce Germany to slavery, and that the Treaty of Versailles should be renounced. In 1920 and 1921, Hitler supported what became known in Germany as the Rapallo policy of alliance with Russia against the Western European powers. By December 1922, however, the outline of the foreign policy he was to try to follow for the next twenty years had formed in his mind. He was arguing that Germany should not work against England's interests. Instead, it should attack Russia with England's help, to gain living-space in the east. Then Germany should deal with France[125].

Hitler had, therefore, already begun to look on Britain more favourably than he had during, and just after, the First World War by the end of 1922. It seems, however, that the French and Belgian occupation of the Ruhr in January 1923 caused a further change in Hitler's attitude towards Britain. Germany had defaulted on reparations payments due under the Treaty of Versailles, arguing that the amounts assessed were unreasonable. The French (and the Belgians) attempted to enforce repayments by occupying the industrial Ruhr area of Germany, but, as Churchill predicted the Germans reacted with passive resistance and strikes. The occupiers only succeeded in causing the collapse of the German economy, and withdrew their troops in 1925. The British did not support the French action – as noted above, Churchill was one of those who argued that Britain should oppose the French occupation "vehemently". "I am strongly of the opinion that the Ruhr business will turn out ill for France," he wrote to his brother in January 1923[126]. Hitler's attitude towards France remained irreconcilably hostile, as this extract from a speech in May 1923 shows: "France does not want reparations; it wants the destruction of Germany, the fulfilment of an age-old dream; a Europe dominated by France". Towards Britain, however, his mood apparently continued to mellow. He made a speech in April, which deserves quotation at length for the light it casts on the distinction he began to make between Britain and France:

> "Before the war two States, Germany and France, had to live side by side but only under arms. It is true that the War of 1870-1 meant for Germany the close of an enmity which had endured for centuries, but in France a passionate hatred against Germany was fostered by every means: by propaganda in the press, in school textbooks, in theatres, in the cinemas... All the Jewish papers throughout France agitated against Berlin. Here again to seek and to exploit grounds for a conflict is the clearly recognizable effort of world Jewry.

> The conflict of interests between Germany and England lay in the economic sphere. Up till 1850 England's position as a World Power was undisputed. British engineers, British trade conquered the world. Germany, owing to greater industry and increased capacity, began to be a dangerous rival. In a short time those firms which in Germany were in English hands pass into the possession of German industrialists. German industry expands vastly and the products of that industry even in the London market drive out British goods.

> The protective measure, the stamp 'Made in Germany', has the opposite effect from that desired: this 'protective stamp' becomes a highly effective advertisement. The German economic success was not created in Essen alone but by a man who knew that behind economics must stand power, for power alone makes an economic position secure. This power was born upon the battlefields of 1870-71, not in the atmosphere of

parliamentary chatter. Forty thousand dead§§§§ have rendered possible the life of forty millions. When England, in the face of such a Germany as this, threatened to be brought to her knees, then she used the last weapon in the armoury of international rivalry - violence. Press propaganda on an imposing scale was started as a preparatory measure.

But who is the chief of the whole British press concerned with world trade? One name crystallizes itself out of the rest: Northcliffe - a Jew!***** . .. A campaign of provocation is carried on with assertions, libels, and promises such as only a Jew can devise, such as only Jewish newspapers would have the effrontery to put before an Aryan people. And then at last 1914: they egg people on: 'Ah, poor violated Belgium! Up! To the rescue of the small nations - for the honour of humanity!' The same lies, the same provocation throughout the entire world! And the success of that provocation the German people can trace grievously enough!"

Insofar as it is possible to dredge any meaning out of this rambling and inaccurate rant, Hitler seems to have thought that France and Germany were natural enemies. Anglo-German rivalry, however, was economic, and therefore perhaps avoidable. Writing in 1924-25, after the occupation of the Ruhr, Hitler discourses at some length in *Mein Kampf*, on what he thought Germany's policy towards England should be. Because his views as stated there are of such crucial importance in understanding the course of events in Europe in the 1930's, when Churchill began to take notice of, and then oppose, Hitler's policies in Germany, it is appropriate to summarise them here in some detail, despite Hitler's rambling and repetitive style.

Hitler argued that "the English nation will have to be considered the most valuable ally in the world as long as its leadership and the spirit of its broad masses justify us in expecting that brutality and perseverance which is determined to fight a battle once begun to a victorious end, with every means and without consideration of time and sacrifices; and what is more, the military armament existing at any given moment does not need to stand in any

---

§§§§ Prussian casualties in the 1870-71 Franco-Prussian war were 44,681 killed and 89,732 wounded, according to Michael Clodfelter: *Warfare and armed conflicts: a statistical reference to casualty and other figures, 1500-2000.*

***** Alfred Harmsworth, Lord Northcliffe, owner of *The Times* and the *Daily Mail* and one of the most colourful characters in the English political scene at this time, was not a Jew, nor were any of the other press barons in Britain in the early twentieth century.

proportion to that of other states"[127]. He regretted that Germany had not pursued this policy prior to 1914. He saw that Britain's traditional policy was one of maintaining a European balance of power, which had led her to confront France under Napoleon, and then Germany in the First World War. The defeat of Germany in 1918, however, had meant that France was the supreme power on the continent, so that Britain's balance of power policy had failed. England, therefore, was now a natural ally for Germany, and an enemy for France[128].

Hitler argued that it should be possible to counteract the legacy of hatred towards Germany which wartime propaganda had left, but that the "devastating Jewish influence" would make this very difficult. England's "racially unjustifiable" alliance with Japan was a natural response to her commercial rivalry with the United States, which was growing into a "new master of the world"[†††††]. Jews in England had become insubordinate, and the struggle against the world Jewish menace must therefore begin there[129]. Germany was small in relation to the British Empire, and even the French Empire, as well as the USA, Russia and China[130]. England would fight to the death to retain her Indian empire, and Germans had learned how hard it was to beat England. (Years later, he gave the British politician Lord Halifax his views on the best way to achieve this. "Shoot Gandhi", he said, and if that was not enough, "shoot a dozen leading members of Congress … until order is established")[131]. Egypt, too, would remain British. Germany should not try to take advantage of turbulence in the British Empire, and link its destiny with racially inferior oppressed peoples. An alliance with Russia against England and France was no substitute for an alliance with England. An alliance with England and Italy would give Germany the initiative in Europe[132]. Finally, and crucially, France, in occupying the Ruhr, had alienated England, and this represented an opportunity for Germany[133].

Hitler's attitude is foreshadowed in that book, written after the French occupation of the Ruhr. Before that date, he laid more stress on his view of the British Empire as Germany's enemy, and Britain's complicity with France in imposing what he regarded as the "ruinous" Treaty of Versailles on Germany. However, after the French occupation of the Ruhr, which particularly offended the Germans by using French colonial troops, he began to regard Britain as a potential ally, though he thought that gaining its friendship would be difficult. It is remarkable how, up to two decades later, Hitler's views had changed very

---

[†††††] Here, Hitler was completely wrong, as Britain had ended the alliance with Japan after heavy American pressure in 1922.

little since the publication of *Mein Kampf*. He was to retain this opinion of Britain until he realised that it would not grant him the free hand in Eastern Europe which he craved, and even then, he repeatedly stressed his ambition to come to terms with Britain. During the Second World War, the last pre-war British ambassador to Berlin, Sir Neville Henderson, wrote that Hitler "combined … admiration for the British race with envy of their achievements and hatred of their opposition to Germany's excessive aspirations"[134]. He repeatedly remarked to Albert Speer that the English were "our brothers. Why fight our brothers?"[135] He made many similar remarks to other colleagues. There is little evidence that he understood British society, politics or institutions, beyond a cursory knowledge of Parliamentary procedure, and he based many of his ideas on false information. It is hardly surprising, therefore, that his policy towards Britain ended up being a complete failure.

---

[1] *Speech to Congress*, 24 December 1941, Winston S Churchill

[2] *Churchill, A Life*, Martin Gilbert, p.459, 494, 573

[3] *The Last Attempt*, Birger Dahlerus, p.59

[4] *Hitler's Table Talk*, p.117

[5] *Albert Speer: His Battle with the Truth*, Gitta Sereny, p.217-8

[6] *Inside the Third Reich*, Albert Speer, p.286

[7] *Hitler's War*, David Irving, p.598

[8] *Hitler's Table Talk*, p.17-18

[9] *Hitler's Table Talk*, p.395

[10] *Mein Kampf*, p.61

[11] See, for instance, *I was Hitler's Buddy*, by Reinhold Hanisch, New Republic, April 13 1939

[12] *Churchill War Papers*, Vol. 1, Martin Gilbert, p.219

[13] *The Young Hitler I Knew*, August Kubizek, p.54

[14] *Hansard*, 28 September 1944

[15] *Hitler's First War*, Thomas Weber, p.53

[16] *Speaking for Themselves*, Mary Soames, p.262

[17] *The Young Hitler I Knew*, August Kubizek, p.120-131

[18] *Hitler, 1889-1936, Hubris*, Professor Ian Kershaw, p.12-13

[19] Quoted in *Churchill, A Life*, Martin Gilbert, p.6

[20] *My Early Life*, Winston Churchill, p.16

[21] For reproductions of Churchill's school reports, see the classic source for documentation of Churchill's life, the Companion Volumes to Randolph S. Churchill's and Sir Martin Gilbert's Churchill, *Winston S Churchill*, Vol I Part 1 1874-1896.

[22] *My Early Life*, Winston Churchill, p.199-200

[23] *Churchill, A Life*, Martin Gilbert, p.69

[24] *My Early Life*, Winston Churchill, p.17

[25] *My Early Life*, Winston Churchill, p.26-27

[26] Introduction to *Mein Kampf*, D.C. Watt, p.xxii

[27] *Hitler, 1889-1936, Hubris*, Professor Ian Kershaw, p.17

[28] *Hitler*, Joachim C Fest, p.18

[29] *Hitler's Table Talk*, p.168

[30] *Hitler's Table Talk*, p.356

[31] *Mein Kampf*, p.13
[32] *Hitler's Table Talk*, p.356
[33] *Hitler's Table Talk*, p.674-675
[34] *Churchill, A Life*, Martin Gilbert, p.69-70
[35] *The Young Hitler I Knew*, August Kubizek, p.180-181
[36] *Hitler, 1889-1936, Hubris*, Professor Ian Kershaw, p.41
[37] *The Young Hitler I Knew*, August Kubizek, p.182
[38] *Mein Kampf*, p.33
[39] *Mein Kampf*, p.48
[40] *Mein Kampf*, p.248
[41] *Neue Freie Presse*, quoted in the *Manchester Guardian*, 24 July 1912 and 29 July 1912
[42] *Hitler's Private Library*, Timothy Ryback, p.242
[43] *Mein Kampf*, p.69
[44] *Mein Kampf*, p.145
[45] *In Search of Churchill*, Martin Gilbert, p.22
[46] For this summary of Churchill's peacetime achievements see *In Search of Churchill*, Martin Gilbert, p. 220-221 and *Churchill*, Roy Jenkins, p.181
[47] *Churchill*, Roy Jenkins, p.183
[48] *Hansard*, 15 July 1948
[49] *Churchill*, Roy Jenkins, p.370
[50] *The Times*, 18 October 1922
[51] *The Times*, 15 January 1923
[52] *Manchester Guardian*, 8 February 1923
[53] *Time* magazine, 21 April 1923
[54] *Manchester Guardian*, 10-12 November 1923 and *The Times*, 8-15 November 1923
[55] *Time* magazine, 19 November 1923
[56] *Churchill*, Roy Jenkins, p.358-9
[57] *Churchill, A Life*, Martin Gilbert, p.24
[58] *Churchill at War, 1940-45*, Lord Moran, p.103
[59] *Never Despair*, Martin Gilbert, p.247
[60] *Churchill, A Life*, Martin Gilbert, p.25
[61] *My Early Life*, Winston Churchill, p.97
[62] *Winston S Churchill*, Randolph Churchill, Supporting Vol. 1, p.256
[63] *Churchill, A Life*, Martin Gilbert, p.89
[64] *The World Crisis*, Winston Churchill, Vol. 1, p.37
[65] *Thoughts and Adventures*, Winston Churchill, p.54
[66] *Churchill, A Life*, Martin Gilbert, p.181
[67] *Churchill, A Life*, Martin Gilbert, p.208
[68] *Churchill, A Life*, Martin Gilbert, p.208
[69] *Churchill, A Life*, Martin Gilbert, p.185
[70] *Churchill, A Life*, Martin Gilbert, p.209
[71] *The World Crisis*, Winston Churchill, Vol. 1, p.42
[72] *The World Crisis*, Winston Churchill, Vol. 1, p.50-1
[73] *Churchill*, Roy Jenkins, p.204-205
[74] *Hansard*, 18th March 1912
[75] See *Hansard*, 1912-1915, various
[76] *The World Crisis*, Winston Churchill, Vol. 1, p.119
[77] Hitler speech, 30 January 1942
[78] *Churchill, A Life*, Martin Gilbert, p.242

[79] *Winston S Churchill, Young Statesman, 1901-1914*, Randolph S Churchill, p.542

[80] *The World Crisis*, Winston Churchill, Vol. 1, p.180

[81] *Speaking for Themselves: the personal letters of Winston and Clementine Churchill*, ed. Mary Soames, p.96

[82] *Speaking for Themselves: the personal letters of Winston and Clementine Churchill*, ed. Mary Soames, p.97

[83] *The Churchill Documents, Volume 11, The Exchequer Years*, Martin Gilbert, p.560

[84] *The World Crisis*, Winston Churchill, Vol. 1, p.225

[85] *Autobiography*, Margot Asquith, p.295

[86] *The World Crisis*, Winston Churchill, Vol. 1, p.228

[87] *Mein Kampf*, p.165

[88] *Speaking for Themselves: the personal letters of Winston and Clementine Churchill*, ed. Mary Soames, p.106

[89] *Winston S Churchill*, Martin Gilbert, Supporting Vol. 4, p.319-20

[90] *Speaking for Themselves: the personal letters of Winston and Clementine Churchill*, ed. Mary Soames, p.215

[91] *Churchill, A Life*, Martin Gilbert, p.397

[92] *Hansard, 1914-1918*

[93] *Speaking for Themselves: the personal letters of Winston and Clementine Churchill*, ed. Mary Soames, p.209

[94] *The Fringes of Power*, John Colville, p.192

[95] *Winston S Churchill*, Martin Gilbert, Supporting Vol. 4, p.412

[96] *Step by Step*, Winston Churchill, p.155

[97] *Winston S Churchill*, Martin Gilbert, Supporting Vol. 4, p.418-20

[98] *Step by Step*, Winston Churchill, p.173

[99] *Winston S Churchill*, Martin Gilbert, Supporting Vol. 4, p.432

[100] *Newspaper reports*, 7 December 1918

[101] *Newspaper reports*, 2 December 1918

[102] *Churchill, A Life*, Martin Gilbert, p.403-4

[103] *Peaecemakers*, Margaret Macmillan, p.173

[104] *Peaecemakers*, Margaret Macmillan, p.479

[105] *The Churchill Documents, Volume 11, The Exchequer Years*, Martin Gilbert, p.13

[106] *Churchill, A Life*, Martin Gilbert, p.420

[107] *Speaking for Themselves: the personal letters of Winston and Clementine Churchill*, ed. Mary Soames, p.222

[108] *Churchill, A Life*, Martin Gilbert, p.439

[109] *Step by Step*, Winston Churchill, p.155

[110] *The Churchill Documents, Volume 11, The Exchequer Years*, Martin Gilbert, p.338

[111] *Churchill, A Life*, Martin Gilbert, p.464

[112] *Road to Victory, Winston S Churchill 1941-45*, Martin S Gilbert, p.1314

[113] *Hitler's Table Talk*, p.357-8

[114] *The Last Attempt*, Birger Dahlerus, p.60

[115] *Hitler, 1889-1936, Hubris*, Professor Ian Kershaw, p.15

[116] *Hitler's Letters*, Werner Maser, p.25

[117] *Hitler's Letters*, Werner Maser, p.75

[118] *Hitler's Letters*, Werner Maser, p.82

[119] On this, see Chapter 5 of *Hitler's First War*, Thomas Weber

[120] *Hitler's First War*, p.222-3

[121] *Inside the Third Reich*, Albert Speer, p.180

[122] Friedrich Wiedemann, quoted in *Hitler's First War*, Thomas Weber, p.328

[123] *Inside the Third Reich*, Albert Speer, p.418

[124] *Hitler, 1889-1936, Hubris*, Professor Ian Kershaw, p.157

[125] *Hitler, Saemtliche Aufzeichnungen 1905-1924*, Eberhard Jaeckel and Axel Kuhn, quoted in *Hitler, 1889-1936, Hubris*, Professor Ian Kershaw, p.247

[126] *The Churchill Documents, Volume 11, The Exchequer Years*, Martin Gilbert, p.15

[127] *Mein Kampf*, p.302

[128] *Mein Kampf*, p.558-566

[129] *Mein Kampf*, p.578-585

[130] *Mein Kampf*, p.588

[131] The Inner Circle, Yvonne Kirkpatrick, p.96

[132] *Mein Kampf*, p.601-607

[133] *Mein Kampf*, p.617

[134] *Failure of a Mission*, Sir Neville Henderson, p.266

[135] *Albert Speer: His Battle with the Truth*, Gitta Sereny, p.218

2
First Impressions (1925-1933)

The mid- and late-1920's were a time of peace and limited prosperity for Europe in general, and Germany in particular. Europe had finally begun to recover from the trauma of the First World War. Peace and prosperity were barren soil for the Nazis. On his release from prison on parole on 20 December 1924, Hitler had to spend the next few years rebuilding the Nazi Party, which had all but disintegrated while he had been locked up. Meanwhile, Churchill was Chancellor of the Exchequer, and, as such, his concerns were mainly domestic. While the rest of Europe was relatively prosperous, however, Britain suffered from unemployment. Churchill was, indeed, aware of the contrast, writing to a colleague in 1927 of his concern that the present trends might lead to "crushing taxation, bad trade, high unemployment and great discontent" in Britain:

> "and on the other hand Germany with no internal debt … with far lighter taxation, ever expanding trade and the contentment which comes from a sense of returning prosperity. That would be a strange combination to be produced by military victory and financial orthodoxy on the one hand, and by decisive defeat and dishonourable repudiation on the other. It is a contrast from which most misleading deductions might easily be drawn by a democratic electorate"[1].

Britain also suffered from severe industrial dislocation in these years, culminating in the General Strike of 1926. Churchill, though he had some sympathy for the miners who were at the forefront of the Strike, played a large part in ensuring its defeat. He helped to edit the *British Gazette*, the government's propaganda organ, and indeed interfered so much that the editor, a former rival, tried to have him kept out of the building while it was being printed[2].

1929 was a critical year for both men. Germany began to be hit hard by the contraction of credit from the United States, which, contrary to popular belief, was already under way before the Wall Street Crash in October of that year. These economic difficulties sent the Nazi Party's share of the vote soaring. Over the next few years, it went from strength to strength. In contrast, Churchill's fortunes waned. In May 1929, the Conservatives were defeated in a general election. Churchill lost his post as Chancellor of the Exchequer, and it was to be more than a decade before he held office again. He also lost thousands of pounds in the Wall Street Crash, meaning that he had to turn back to his writing to pay the bills. The two men's fortunes continued to diverge throughout the 1930's. After 1929 Hitler hardly experienced a significant check to his ambitions until 1940. For Churchill, on the other hand, little was to go right in his political career until that famous year.

Reformation and development of the Nazi Party to 1930

The Nazi Party was no more than a fringe movement in Germany until the 1930 elections, when it increased its number of seats in the Reichstag from 12 (in the 1928 elections) to 107, and its vote from 810,000 to 6.5 million[3]. So unexpected was the Nazi Party's success that the party leadership had not put up enough candidates, and had to scramble to find more to fill the number of seats which they had won[4]. Its membership rose only slowly in the late 1920's, from 27,000 in 1925 to 178,000 in 1929[5].

Hitler, who was not a German citizen, could not stand for election to the Reichstag, though, as argued in the previous chapter, it is difficult to imagine Parliamentary work suiting him in any case. He was banned from public speaking in states and cities across Germany. It is unlikely, therefore, that Hitler and Churchill gave each other much thought during these years, and their recorded utterances and writings contain no direct mention of each other.

In these years of hope for Germany and Europe, the Nazi Party assumed many of its distinctive characteristics. In particular, it adopted the principles that the Party was totally subordinate to Hitler's wishes and that National Socialism was whatever Hitler said it was. The Party even occasionally referred to itself as the "Adolf Hitler Party".

Hitler did not achieve this level of control without a struggle, however. Some

North German Nazis under Gregor Strasser and Paul Josef Goebbels began taking the "Socialist" component of National Socialism seriously in the mid-1920's. For a time, their calls for an alliance with Bolshevik Russia against the British and French Empires and for socialisation of the means of production appeared to pose a threat to Hitler, who had no interest in their agenda. He was much more interested in foreign and defence policy and had always hoped to attract millions of marks in funding for the Nazi Party from industry and the wealthy, which would feel threatened by any overtly socialistic programme. Though never a tool of the capitalist class, as many Marxist historians have alleged, Hitler enjoyed being popular in Munich society. He outmanoeuvred his left-wing opponents brilliantly and crushed them at a Party meeting in Bamberg in 1926. After that, his grip on the Nazi Party was never in serious doubt.

Hitler also discarded some of the early followers who had led the Party in the pre-*Putsch* days. Many of those who were subsequently to occupy important positions in the Nazi government of the German state rose to prominence in the Party for the first time. Goebbels, later Reich Propaganda Minister, joined the Party in 1924. He supported Gregor Strasser until Bamberg, but then, as a reward for supporting Hitler, was appointed *Gauleiter* (regional leader) in Berlin, and was elected to the Reichstag in 1928. Göring, amnestied in 1927 for his part in the Beer Hall *Putsch*, returned to Germany and was also elected to the Reichstag in 1928. Martin Bormann, Hitler's powerful Personal Secretary from 1941, joined the Party in 1925 following a year in prison for conspiracy to murder, and was appointed the Party's regional press officer and business manager in 1928. Heinrich Himmler, the head of the SS and perhaps the most sinister Nazi of all, was appointed to this key position in 1927.

Hitler's Second Book

Following the Party's poor performance in the Reichstag elections of 1924, Hitler considered that a sequel to *Mein Kampf* might be required, in order to update his views on foreign policy in the light of developments in the mid-1920's. Britain had become somewhat friendlier towards Germany as memories of the First World War had faded, and America was obviously growing steadily stronger in relation to the European powers. Hitler therefore dictated a book on his views on foreign policy[6], now known as his *Second Book*, also called his *Secret Book*. He dictated it to Max Amann, his publisher, in his retreat in the mountains, Obersalzberg. The book was not published at this time, apparently because of fears that it might affect sales of *Mein Kampf*, which were already poor[7]. It is illuminating in understanding his attitude towards Britain. It is not a full sequel to *Mein Kampf*, and "offers nothing new"[8]. Instead, it elaborates and updates parts of *Mein Kampf*'s foreign policy arguments. It was not published until years after Hitler's death, and has never been as well-known as *Mein Kampf*.

The *Second Book* can only be understood in the context of the foreign policy debates in Germany in the late 1920's. Italy had acquired the German-speaking province of Südtirol, or Alto-Adige, from Austria-Hungary after the First World War, under the Treaty of Saint Germain. Two decades later, Churchill was to say that "this was always held by liberal-minded folk in many lands to be one of the worst blots on the Treaty of Trianon* which was not, in itself, a model in European annals"[9]. During the late 1920's, Mussolini's government in Italy had pursued a policy of forcing German-speakers in the Südtirol to learn Italian. This was widely resented in Germany, and became an important political issue. Hitler, almost alone, argued that Germany should not confront the Italians, since it needed Italy as an ally against France. In his words:

> "the National Socialist Movement fights by unswervingly advocating an alliance with Italy against the ruling Francophile tendency. Thereby the Movement, in contradistinction to the whole of public opinion in Germany, emphatically points out that the Südtirol neither can nor should be an obstacle to this policy. This view is the cause of our present isolation in the sphere of foreign policy and of the attacks against us. Later, to be sure, it will ultimately be the cause of the resurgence of the German nation"[10].

As mentioned, the book is essentially a refinement of the foreign policy views in *Mein Kampf*, and Hitler took the opportunity to revise upwards his estimate of American power. France was still Germany's "most dangerous enemy because she alone, thanks to her alliances [with Poland and Czechoslovakia], is in a position to be able to threaten almost the whole of Germany with aircraft, even an hour after the outbreak of a conflict"[11]. In turn, the book's views on Britain are interesting. Hitler reiterates his view, which he had previously expressed in *Mein Kampf*, that pre-war German economic, colonial and naval policy was an unnecessary source of conflict with England[12]. England gathered former enemies together "out of sheer competitive envy" and tried to break German

---

* Churchill got the wrong Treaty – Saint Germain was the Treaty that concerned Austria, Trianon was with Hungary.

economic competition with economic countermeasures[†,13].

An entire chapter is devoted to the possibility of "England as an Ally". The British Empire, Hitler argued, existed because England needed an outlet for its population, sources of raw materials and markets. "The living conditions of the savages were a matter of complete indifference to the English as long, and to the extent, that they did not affect the living conditions of the English themselves". Hitler did not believe that England would oppose a dominant military power on the European continent, as long as that power limited itself to purely European goals. He considered that English statesmanship was superior to Germany's, because "[England] is not ruled by such intellectuals who can never brace themselves for an action, but by men who think naturally and for whom politics most surely is an art of the possible, but who also take all possibilities by the forelock, and really strike with them". England had no motive for being Germany's permanent enemy, as long as Germany did not pursue naval and colonial development.

However, a problem for Germany was that "world Jewry" possessed "decisive influence" in England. World Jewry would "neglect nothing to keep the old enmities alive so as to prevent a pacification of Europe from materialising, and thereby enable it to set its Bolshevist destructive tendencies into motion amid the confusion of a general unrest"[14]. In the Summary, Hitler argued that the "struggle" with "Jewry" was:

> "undecided in England. There the Jewish invasion still meets with an old British tradition. The instincts of Anglosaxondom [sic] are still so sharp and alive that one cannot speak of a complete victory of Jewry, but rather, in part, the latter is still forced to adjust its interests to those of the English. If the Jew were to triumph in England, English interests would recede into the background .... On the other hand, if the Briton triumphs, then a shift of England's attitude vis-à-vis Germany can still take place"[15].

Another chapter of the *Second Book* is devoted to the possibility of an alliance with Mussolini's Italy, whose Fascist government clearly impressed Hitler: he described Mussolini as a "brilliant statesman". Unlike Russia, Italy had none of the "living-space" which Hitler coveted for Germany, and, as mentioned above,

---

[†] In fact, Britain did nothing at all to "break" German economic competition before the First World War. She preserved her traditional policy of free trade and open markets despite the fast development of Germany's export industries in competition with her own.

he did not believe that assisting the tens of thousands of German-speakers in the Südtirol was worth foregoing the possibility of an alliance. Hitler thought that Italy, like Germany, was overpopulated, and would expand in the Mediterranean, where she must one day clash with France[16].

Churchill and Mussolini in the 1920's

Churchill, too, was interested in relations with Italy in the 1920's. Today we are accustomed to think of Mussolini, when we remember him at all, as existing very much in Hitler's shadow. This image of the Italian as the junior partner in a monstrous alliance, however, owes everything to the situation as it developed once Hitler gained power and made Germany into the greatest threat to peace in Europe. It does not come at all from the period before 1933, since in the 1920's, Mussolini was the foremost right-wing dictator in Europe. He had been appointed Prime Minister of Italy in 1922 and had consolidated his power in the following decade. In 1931, he told his generals to be ready for war in Europe within four years[17], and indeed that war nearly took place after the assassination of Alexander, King of Yugoslavia, in France in 1934. Churchill's attitude to Mussolini in the 1920's may cast some light on why he was hostile to Hitler in the early 1930's, before the latter was unmistakeably a threat to peace in Western Europe.

Churchill's first recorded comment on Mussolini, in 1923, was in response to Italy's bombardment of the Greek island Corfu, which was condemned by the League of Nations. He called the Italian dictator an "overbearing Devil" in a letter to his wife that year, and he expressed the hope that the League of Nations would call him to order[18]. "What a swine that Mussolini is", he wrote a few days later[19]. Three years later, however, he had changed his mind, writing to his wife that "No doubt [Mussolini] is one of the most wonderful men of our time"[20]. In January 1927, on his way back from a holiday in Malta, he visited Rome, and met Mussolini twice (and Pope Pius XII once). During the previous five years, Mussolini had consolidated his grip on power in Italy, though he had never been as murderously thorough as Hitler was to be throughout the life of the Third Reich. Churchill was to argue after Fascism and Nazism had been destroyed that, "as Fascism sprang from Communism, so Nazism sprang from Fascism"[21]. At the time, however, he commented at a Press conference held for Fascist newspapers on 20 January:

"I could not help being charmed, like so many other people have been, by Signor Mussolini's gentle and simple bearing and by his calm, detached poise in spite of so many burdens and dangers. Secondly, anyone could see that he thought of nothing but the lasting good, as he understood it, of the Italian people, and that no lesser interest was of the slightest consequence to him. If I had been an Italian I am sure that I should have been whole-heartedly with you from the start to finish in your triumphant struggle against the bestial appetites and passions of Leninism."

However, he did not necessarily believe that such methods were appropriate for Britain.

"But in England we have not yet had to face this danger in the same deadly form. We have our own way of doing things. But that we shall succeed in grappling with Communism and choking the life out of it - of that I am absolutely sure. I will, however, say a word on an international aspect of fascism. Externally, your movement has rendered service to the whole world. The great fear which has always beset every democratic leader or a working class leader has been that of being undermined by someone more extreme than he. Italy has shown that there is a way of fighting the subversive forces which can rally the masses of the people, properly led, to value and wish to defend the honour and stability of civilised society. She has provided the necessary antidote to the Russian poison. Hereafter no great nation will be unprovided with an ultimate means of protection against the cancerous growth of Bolshevism"[22].

People seeking to denigrate Churchill have never tired of quoting the above speech to show that Churchill approved of Fascism, and hence, by implication, Nazism. Usually, parts of Churchill's statement which qualify his admiration for Mussolini and Fascism are replaced by dots. A prime example of this technique was in Michael Foot's *The Trial of Mussolini* (1943), where the above quote was reduced to:

"If I had been an Italian I am sure I should have been whole-heartedly with you in your triumphant struggle against the bestial appetites and passions of Leninism... (Italy) has provided the necessary antidote to the Russian poison. Hereafter no great nation will be unprovided with an ultimate means of protection against the cancerous growth of Bolshevism."

Churchill's remark about Italian methods not being suitable for England was cut out, as was his comment about defending "the honour and stability of civilised society".

Churchill's comments were, indeed, as one of his biographers commented, "much too friendly" to Mussolini[23]. He had, however, an ulterior motive in being nice to Mussolini. As Chancellor of the Exchequer, he wanted to obtain an agreement from Italy to repay some of the enormous debt it owed to Britain from the First World War. Britain needed the foreign exchange to settle its debts to America[24]. In addition, diplomatic niceties and even polite hypocrisy are expected of a senior British Cabinet Minister in a foreign land. It is obvious that, selective quotation aside, Churchill was friendly, or at best indifferent, towards Italian Fascism. His friendship was due to its usefulness as an ally in stopping Communism, which he then saw as a much greater danger to what he referred to as "civilised society" than Italian Fascism. Even as late as 1938, after Mussolini had drifted towards Hitler and had invaded Abyssinia, Churchill was still to accord Mussolini some qualified greatness: "Mussolini is the greater man [than Hitler] who is on a small moke [donkey – i.e. Italy], while [Hitler] is on an elephant or a tiger [i.e. Germany]"[25].

This may shed some light on Churchill's much less strident opposition to Mussolini's Fascism compared with his consistent hatred of German Nazism. Churchill viewed German expansionism as a threat to the European balance of power, and hence as a threat to Britain. He never viewed Italian expansionism in the same light. It was directed mostly at "far away countries of which we knew little" such as Abyssinia, Greece and Albania, until Mussolini declared war on France and Britain in June 1940. It never, therefore, posed a threat to Britain and British interests comparable with Hitler's aggression or even with Russian Bolshevism. Churchill was perfectly prepared to criticise Mussolini when he broke the peace, as when Italy attacked Corfu or Abyssinia. He never, however, saw Mussolini as an existential threat to British or French civilisation in the way that Hitler or Stalin were.

Interestingly, Clementine Churchill, a lifelong Liberal, fell for Mussolini far more deeply than her husband did, and without the excuses that he had. She visited Italy in 1926 to see friends and again in 1927, on doctor's orders after a bus accident in London. During the first visit, she met Mussolini, describing him in a letter to her husband as "most impressive … has a charming smile & the most beautiful … eyes … He fills you with a sort of pleasurable awe"[26]. Churchill cautioned against relying too heavily on her impressions, however. He wrote to her, quoting another politician to the effect that "it is better to read about a world figure, than to live under his rule"[27]. In any case, on her second trip to

Italy in 1927, Clementine's Liberal principles reasserted themselves to some extent. She wrote to her husband, "I must say my *culte* for Mussolini is somewhat diminished by the ferocious poster campaign which goes on everywhere - You might think there was an Election on, tho' that is the last thing which he would allow. His photograph is everywhere, sometimes in very ludicrous attitudes"[28].

Reparations and the Young Plan referendum

The Treaty of Versailles had made Germany agree to pay war reparations, set at £6.6 billion, an unimaginable sum for the time. It also forced Germany to acknowledge responsibility for the war, in the so-called "war-guilt clause" in one of the "shame paragraphs" (*Schmachparagraphen*). Predictably, Hitler and Churchill were on opposite sides on the question of German reparations to the First World War Allies in the late 1920's, though Churchill eventually ended up rejecting the Young Plan, the settlement reached in 1929. Again, however, there is no evidence that each was aware of the other's activities. In virtually every speech he gave in the 1920's, and well into the 1930's, Hitler spoke against the Treaty of Versailles. In *Mein Kampf*, he had written that "Versailles was a scandal and a disgrace and that the dictate signified an act of highway robbery against our people"[29]. He brushed aside the arguments that it was more moderate in every respect than the Brest-Litovsk treaty that Germany had imposed on a helpless Russia; that Germany herself had demanded reparations from France in 1871; or that, had Germany won, the cost to Britain and France would have been ruinous. While his arguments had drawn enthusiastic crowds in the early 1920's, however, they failed to convince many Germans after 1925. The German population had not been converted to the justice of Versailles: it was simply that it was more difficult to agitate them when the economy was expanding and the political system was liberal and stable. The German currency was stabilized, economic growth was returning, and the French and the Belgians had withdrawn their occupation forces from the Ruhr.

Indeed, Churchill himself seems to have realised that German resentment was quiet, but still present, to some extent. He discussed the possibility of a renewal of German aggression with the President of France in 1925, saying that he thought that while "Germany would perhaps rest content with ... Versailles so far as her western frontiers were concerned ... she would never acquiesce permanently in the condition of her eastern frontier"[30]. He made similar points to the Committee of Imperial Defence and to the Cabinet at considerably greater length early in the same year. In 1928, he wrote to a colleague that "danger will arise when Germany feels herself strong enough to put pressure on France and we are reminded by France of our guarantee. I trust this day will be distant"[31].

By 1928, the Nazi Party was still floundering. Its rise over the next four years was due to two factors: the economic difficulties which became apparent from that year onwards, and a brilliant piece of opportunism by Hitler over the issue of the Young Plan. This Plan reduced the amount Germany had to pay by three-quarters, but reaffirmed the "war-guilt clause". Hitler had the Nazi Party join a right-wing group opposed to the Plan, organised by Alfred Hugenberg, a nationalist politician and owner of the big newspaper publishing company, Scherl House. Hitler demanded complete independence in waging the campaign and a great deal of money for his and his Party's expenses[32]. Hugenberg's decision to back Hitler and to instruct his newspapers to do likewise meant that Hitler's name and the Nazi Party became known all over Germany for the first time. He gained important contacts in high places in Germany, too, including various industrialists and industrial concerns. Some, such as Fritz Thyssen, had apparently been helping the Nazis as early as 1923. Prominent amongst wealthy new backers, according to the US Senate Kilgore Committee, which investigated Nazi funding after the war, were large German companies including IG Farben, DAPAG and AEG. These industrialists poured money into the party's hard-pressed coffers, which, in turn, enabled the Nazis to broadcast their message all over Germany. Nazi publicity went a good deal further than simply attacking the Young Plan.

The campaign against the Plan was a failure. When put to a referendum, the final result was a heavy defeat for Hugenberg and the Nazis, with only 13.8% of the voters supporting rejection of the Plan. The German government approved it in 1930. A tactical failure for the campaign, however, had been a strategic triumph for the Nazis, who obtained funds and priceless publicity, which they exploited brilliantly over the next two years. The famous Nuremberg rally which Hitler held in August 1929 was a harbinger of things to come. Special trains brought followers (possibly as many as 200,000) from all over Germany and Nazi marching bands and paramilitary formations disfigured the beautiful medieval walled city for days[33].

While Hitler's views on the Treaty of Versailles in general, and reparations in particular, were predictably hostile, Churchill, as Chancellor of the Exchequer, was instrumental in the collection of those reparations. Most of his role concerned the technical aspects of the question: his Department was responsible for ensuring that the money collected reached the British government. He was only indirectly concerned with whether reparations were right in principle. Churchill spoke to the House of Commons on the matter on 7 April 1925, when he proposed reforming the way in which reparations payments were collected from Germany[34]. On 23 June 1925, Churchill told the House that the cost of the British Army of Occupation in Germany had been £59 million, while the reparations payments recovered from Germany had been only £20 million[35]. Several times over the next few years, Churchill was asked about reparations payments from Germany, and the associated problems of British war-debts to the United States[36]. He was able to announce higher than expected reparations payments by 1929, as Anglo-German trade had recovered[37] and that Germany had paid £60 million[38]. One other aspect of Churchill's role on the reparations question deserves mention here. He appointed the British element of the Committee of Independent Financial Experts. This Committee investigated the future of reparations in 1929, and later issued the Young Plan, which Hitler attacked to such great effect[39].

After he had left office in 1929, Churchill did, however, oppose the Young Plan, but for reasons different to Hitler's. British policy on reparations from Germany was linked to its policy on the war debt owed to Britain by France and Italy, and the debt which it owed to the United States. Churchill was concerned that Britain was paying more to America than it was receiving from Germany, France and Italy, and that the Young Plan would entrench this mismatch[40]. However the British government ignored his objections, and approved the Plan in its entirety.

Churchill and the "Ten-Year Rule"

In 1919, the British Committee on Imperial Defence had adopted the "Ten-Year Rule", under which British defence expenditure was incurred on the basis that there would be no major war within the next ten years. The Cabinet, of which Churchill was a member, had approved it. In 1928, the Rule was debated within the Government. Churchill, with colleagues, proposed that the rule should be reviewed every year. Its aim, as he saw it, was to "check mass production [of weapons] until the situation demanded it". The Government adopted Churchill's idea to review the Rule annually. Critics of Churchill have tried to discredit his anti-appeasement stance in the 1930's by pointing to a supposed inconsistency with his support of the Ten-Year Rule in the 1920's. There is, in fact, no obvious inconsistency between the two stances. It is clear that in the late 1920's, he did not see a European war as likely in the next few years. He also felt, as he wrote several times in the 1920's, that he did "not believe Japan has any idea of attacking the British Empire, or that there is any danger of her doing so for at least a generation to come"[41]. In fact, he was strictly right to renew the

Chapter 2

Ten-Year Rule in 1928, since Britain was not to be involved in any major war in the following ten years. German sabre-rattling, however, and to a lesser degree Japanese aggression in China, meant that he changed this sanguine view completely over the following few years, and he then proposed rearming, and abandoning the Ten-Year Rule.

It is even possible to argue that the retention of the Ten-Year Rule until 1932 was beneficial to some extent. The early 1930's were a time of rapid development in critical items of military technology, in particular in the air. Had Britain rearmed in the early 1930's, it might have faced Germany and Japan in the late 1930's with large numbers of obsolescent canvas biplanes flying at 200 mph rather than with the all-metal monoplanes such as the Spitfire and the Hurricane, with maximum speeds of 400 mph. Churchill himself, however, thought little of this argument, and his reasons seem convincing:

> "If our aircraft factories had been set to work three years ago [i.e. in 1933], albeit on the old type of machines that would not have prevented the substitution of the new type for the old at the same date which is now operative. On the contrary, the effect would have been exactly the reverse. If the factories had been thrown into activity, if apprentices had been engaged, if plant and staff had been extended and developed, they would have been all the more capable of taking the new types, and the transference would have been made with far greater facilities and the deliveries would have flowed out in far greater volume at an earlier date … As a matter of fact, if you had a large stock of new machines, albeit of old pattern, you would find it a very great facility at this moment, and you would not have to draw away reserve machines from squadrons in order to assist in the business of training your rapidly expanding force"[42].

It can also be argued that the main shortage that Britain faced in the Battle of Britain was not planes, but pilots, and that an earlier and larger expansion of the RAF would have left her with more qualified fliers. Similar arguments about obsolescence can be made about tank design. However, to explore this fascinating, but largely hypothetical, argument in depth is beyond the scope of this book.

Growth of the Nazi Party after 1929 and Churchill's reaction

As highlighted above, the Great Depression of the early 1930's improved Hitler's fortunes dramatically. Partly because of its dependence on America for short-term loans, Germany was one of the worst sufferers in Europe, with 6 million unemployed by 1933 (perhaps as many as 9 million if various forms of "hidden" unemployment are included)[43]. In the 1930's, state help for those without jobs was highly limited, certainly by today's standards, and many people were desperate. Worsening unemployment increased Hitler's support: and as mentioned the Nazis went from 12 seats in the Reichstag in 1928 to 107 in 1930 and 230 in 1932. The Nazi Party became the largest single party by far, though it was still considerably short of an overall majority. They also scored notable victories in provincial elections held during these years. The miscalculations of right-wing politicians including the near-senile President, Field Marshal von Hindenburg, the head of the Catholic Centre Party, Franz von Papen[‡], and General Kurt von Schleicher, meant that Hitler was appointed Chancellor in January 1933, and was to consolidate power over the next few years. These elections and political manoeuvrings in Germany were widely reported overseas, not least by Churchill's son Randolph (see below).

In 1929, the Conservative government, whose Chancellor of the Exchequer Churchill had been, was defeated in a general election. Labour, under Ramsay MacDonald, was returned to office, despite receiving 300,000 fewer votes than the Conservatives, and Churchill, though still an MP, no longer held Government office, and was dropped from the shadow Cabinet by Stanley Baldwin. Churchill was to refer to the next few years as the "Locust Years"[44]. We know that Churchill was well aware of Hitler and the Nazi Party after the German election on 14 September 1930, because of a memorandum written by Prince Bismarck of the German Foreign Office on 20 October 1930. The Prince had dined with Churchill and others the previous Sunday. Their conversation

---

[‡] Von Papen was a colourful character, prominent and aristocratic, but utterly lacking in judgement. He had been military attaché in Washington during World War 1, and had planned to blow up bridges and railroads in the United States while America was still neutral. He was indicted in Washington in 1916 for attempting to blow up Canada's Welland Canal, but the charges were dropped when Papen was appointed Chancellor of Germany in 1932. The French ambassador to Berlin remarked that this appointment caused amazement in Berlin, as von Papen was taken seriously neither by his allies nor his enemies.

ranged widely, covering the Soviet Five Year Plan, splits within the Conservative Party and Churchill's literary efforts. Bismarck described Churchill as "extremely well informed" on recent German political developments. Churchill, his report said, "was convinced that Hitler or his followers would seize the first available opportunity to resort to armed force, despite the fact that 'Hitler had declared that he had no intention of waging a war of aggression'". Addressing the question which was to plunge Europe into war nine years later, Churchill rejected the German diplomat's argument about the "utter unsuitability of the existing Polish frontier settlement, in particular the Polish Corridor", since "Poland must have an outlet to the sea"[45].

Churchill began to argue in print and in his speeches that Hitler and the Nazis were dangerous. He made the first of many public warnings to this effect on 5 April 1931, over a minor issue. The *New York American* carried an article by Churchill which expressed support for the Austro-German customs union which had just been concluded. The French had opposed it, seeing it as a first step towards the dreaded *Anschluss*, or union of Germany and Austria, which the Treaty of Versailles had forbidden. Churchill, however, supported it on the grounds that it would help the constitutional parties within Germany and "will rob the much more dangerous Hitler movement of its mainspring"[46]. In fact, both Churchill and the French were wrong: it is doubtful whether either Hitler's or Germany's fortunes were influenced much one way or the other by this treaty.

Hitler meets Churchill's son, but refuses to meet Churchill, 1932

In 1932, at the extremely young age of 20, Churchill's son, Randolph, agreed with the press baron, Lord Rothermere, to write a series of articles for the *Sunday Graphic*, and then a weekly column for the *Daily Dispatch*. Germany was about to vote in elections for the Reichstag, which had to take place every two years. Randolph therefore decided to see for himself the political situation there[47]. According to Sir Martin Gilbert, Randolph's dispatches from Germany made him "almost the first person" to warn convincingly in the mainstream British press of the danger which Hitler's victory would bring[48]. Randolph immediately secured first-rate access to Hitler, through Hitler's press secretary, Ernst

Hanfstaengl[§]. Hanfstaengl gave Randolph extraordinary access to Hitler, even letting him ride in Hitler's private campaign plane[49].

Thirty years later, Randolph Churchill told the *Sunday Telegraph* in an interview that "Hitler considered that, as Churchill's son, I was a person to be impressed with the rightness of Hitler's purposes .... so I could go home with some 'good' impressions and report to my father". There is no evidence that Randolph did go home with good impressions, and if Hanfstaengl or Hitler hoped that this favour would gain the Nazis positive coverage in the British press, they were to be sorely disappointed. Instead of parroting the Nazi line, Randolph wrote an article which appeared on the German Election Day in Britain. It described a day in which Hitler spoke at three meetings, to hundreds of thousands of people. "Hitler speaks – quietly at first, but as he proceeds his voice becomes charged with emotion and enthusiasm and rises to a challenging note ... I can only describe the [final] meeting as a mixture between an American football game and a boy-scouts' jamboree, animated with the spirit of a revivalist meeting and conducted with the discipline of the Brigade of Guards". The conclusion is clearly hostile to the Nazis and is worth quoting at some length:

> "Nothing can delay their [i.e. the Nazis'] arrival in power ...
>
> The success of the Nazi Party sooner or later means war. Nearly all of Hitler's principal lieutenants fought in the last war ... They burn for revenge. They are determined to have an army. ... they will not hesitate to use it.
>
> ... all the time, the Nazis will attain strength and impetus, and within three years at the most Europe will be confronted with a deadly situation.
>
> Nothing except a radical revision of the Treaty of Versailles can quench the fire that burns in German breasts. The removal of the sense of injustice which the German nation feels is the most vital task that confronts European statesmanship to-day"[50].

---

§ Hanfstaengl was ironically nicknamed "Putzi", or "little chap", as he was six feet four inches tall. He had been to school and college (Harvard) in the United States and spoke English fluently, a rarity in the insular, poorly educated Nazi hierarchy. He had financed the production of two Nazi newspapers, and had therefore been appointed Hitler's press secretary. He fell out of favour with Hitler in 1937 and made his way to Switzerland, then Britain before finally settling in the United States.

Chapter 2

Throughout 1932, Winston Churchill was researching his biography of his great ancestor, John Churchill, first Duke of Marlborough. As part of his research, he decided to visit the battlefield of Blenheim, where, in 1704, the first Duke had inflicted a shattering defeat on the forces of France and its allies. The battlefield happens to be located in Bavaria, where the Nazi Party was based, and where Hitler lived. Churchill retraced the route of the British army of 1704, which had marched from Holland to the Danube through western Germany. "As we wended our way through these beautiful regions from one ancient, famous city to another, I naturally asked questions about the Hitler Movement, and found it the prime topic in every German mind. I sensed a Hitler atmosphere"[51].

Churchill decided to stop for several days in Munich. Many years later, Churchill recalled: "I had no national prejudices against Hitler at this time. I knew little of his doctrine or record and nothing of his character. I admire men who stand up for their country in defeat, even though I am on the other side. He had a perfect right to be a patriotic German if he chose. I always wanted England, Germany and France to be friends"[52].

Except for the last sentence, none of that paragraph rings true. Churchill's pleas of ignorance about Hitler, written many years later, were clearly exaggerated, if not completely wrong. They could have been intended to show that his mind was more open at this stage than was genuinely the case. He was clearly aware of Hitler's "record, doctrine and character" from at least the 1930 German election onwards, as his conversation with Prince Bismarck in that year clearly shows. It also seems almost unthinkable that he would not have read Randolph's article on Hitler's election campaign. Furthermore, what had he been asking "every German mind" about the Hitler Movement in his journey up the Rhine? We have clear evidence of earlier mentions of Hitler in Churchill's writings, including newspaper articles and private correspondence. A man as relentlessly inquisitive as Churchill would probably have made it his business to study the "prime topic in every mind" in the country in which he was travelling, even if he had to divide his time with his research. As with so much about Hitler's and Churchill's views on each other before 1933, however, this must remain speculation.

Randolph joined Churchill and his wife in Munich. He had briefly returned to England, after filing the article on Hitler's rally quoted above. Whilst in Munich, Randolph informed Hanfstaengl of Churchill's visit to Munich: "My mother and father are here and it would be awfully nice if you and your boss would come this evening to a little supper at the Hotel Continental"[53]. One version of what happened next is recorded in Hanfstaengl's memoirs, *Hitler: The Missing Years*:

"I caught up with Hitler at the Brown House [the Nazi Party's new offices] and burst into his room ... 'Mr Churchill is in Munich and wants to meet you. This is a tremendous opportunity. They want to bring you along to dinner at the Hotel Continental tonight'".

However, Hitler was not keen:

... "For God's sake, Hanfstaengl, don't they realise how busy I am? What on earth would I talk to him about?" "But Herr Hitler", I protested, "... This is one of the most influential men in England, you must meet him" ... Hitler produced a thousand excuses ... I tried one last move. "Herr Hitler, I will go to dinner and you arrive afterwards as if you were calling for me and stay to coffee." No ... we had to leave early the next day – which was the first I had heard of it as I thought we had two or three days free: "in any case, they say your Mr Churchill is a rabid Francophile".

Hanfstaengl was not so easily defeated, however.

I rang Randolph back and tried to hide my disappointment, pointed out that he had caught us at the worst possible time, but suggested, against my better knowledge, that Hitler might join us for coffee. I turned up myself at the appointed hour ... We sat down about ten to dinner ... We talked about this and that, and then Mr Churchill taxed me about Hitler's anti-Semitic views. I tried to give as mild an account of the subject as I could ... to which Mr Churchill listened very carefully, commenting: "Tell your boss from me that anti-Semitism may be a good starter, but it is a bad stayer"...

Hanfstaengl then claimed that Churchill made an important diplomatic offer, though he was out of office at the time:

... He became confidential in his tone. I can remember the scene to this day ... "Tell me", he asked, "how does your chief feel about an alliance between your country, France and England?"

I was transfixed. Damn Hitler, I thought ... I must get hold of Hitler ... Hitler had left. I rang his apartment. I lurched out of the call box into the hall and whom did I see nine or ten steps up the staircase – Hitler ... I was beside myself ... "I have too much to do, Hanfstaengl. I have to get up early in the morning" and he evaded me and walked out ... I ... went back to the party"[54].

Hitler never appeared that evening. Hanfstaengl arrived home to find a note from Hitler saying that they had to leave early the next morning for a meeting in Nuremberg with Julius Streicher, the demented editor of *Der Stürmer*, the Nazis' trashiest paper[**]. When the car turned up, Hanfstaengl persisted: "You should have been there. Among other things, Churchill sketched out the idea of an alliance, with a request you should consider it. He also wished you success in the elections". Hitler was not regretful: "In any case, what part does Churchill play? He is in Opposition and no one pays any attention to him". After Hanfstaengl retorted "people say the same thing about you", the matter seems to have been dropped[55].

The other version of this incident is to be found in Volume 1 of Churchill's *The Second World War*. Churchill's account of the evening differs from Hanfstaengl in some minor ways. Since Churchill was writing fifteen years after the events described and Hanfstaengl almost a quarter of a century later (but with the benefit of his diary), it is not clear whose account is more reliable. Both men had doubtless had plenty to drink by the end of the dinner[††], and a drunken sing-song, accompanied by the piano, was soon under way. Churchill makes no mention of proposing an alliance between England, France and Germany, though he says that he had always been in favour of friendship between them. Churchill's version of his statement on anti-Semitism is longer than Hanfstaengl's:

> "Why is your chief so violent about the Jews? I can quite understand being angry with Jews who have done wrong or are against the country, and I understand resisting them if they try to monopolise power in any walk of life; but what is the sense of being against a man simply because of his birth? How can any man help how he is born?"[56].

Churchill then said that Hanfstaengl appeared at noon the next day, and announced that the appointment which he had made to meet Hitler would not take place that afternoon. Churchill did not see Putzi again, and did not meet Hitler, though he later remarked that Hitler invited him several times when he

---

[**] "There's a man who has spirit" was Hitler's comment on Streicher in 1941.

[††] Though Churchill, according to Maurice Ashley, one of his researchers at this time, had an "excellent head" for alcohol.

became Führer: Churchill, however, let these invitations lapse[57]. Churchill's grandson believes that Hitler "had funked it"[58], and Hanfstaengl refers to Hitler "being afraid of" meeting Churchill, though it is also surely possible that Hitler was genuinely too busy, in what was a crucial year for him and his party. It could even be that Hitler realised that a meeting with anybody who would stick up for the Jews in this way would not be a meeting of minds, and therefore would probably be pointless.

What would have happened had these two remarkable men met? It could have ended in a shouting match over the Jews or foreign policy; it could have been a polite exchange of pleasantries; or it could have been a tense exchange of press statements while the two men sized each other up. It seems virtually inconceivable that one of these men would have converted or influenced the other in any significant way. Churchill was committed to peace and the status quo in Western Europe (though he was prepared to allow Germany some redress of what he saw as legitimate grievances) while Hitler was committed to ripping the Versailles settlement to pieces, violently if necessary, and to acquiring living space in the East. Hitler was a violent anti-Semite, a Francophobe and somewhat anti-American, while Churchill was a philo-Semite, a Francophile and deeply pro-American. They only agreed on the civilising influence of the British Empire in the world and the dangers of the Bolshevik peril. It seems unlikely that they could have confined their discussions to those subjects, as Churchill would have taken the first for granted, and the second was not an immediate threat to Western Europe in 1933. Some form of an argument therefore seems likely, though we cannot tell how the men would have conducted it, or how it would have ended.

Churchill's reaction to German rearmament before 1933

Even before Hitler was appointed Chancellor, Churchill had been warning of the danger of German ambitions, when backed by German rearmament and helped along by British and French disarmament. As shown above, it was in his mind even during the quiescent late 1920's. There were two principal international disarmament processes in the early 1930's: the London Naval Conference and the Geneva Disarmament Conference. The naval talks mainly concerned America, Britain and Japan, with France and Italy also taking part to some extent. Germany was not significantly involved in the naval talks, as her navy was small. However, she participated extensively in the general disarmament talks in Geneva. She had been virtually disarmed in the aftermath of the First World War, but the Treaty of Versailles explicitly stated that this was a prelude to global disarmament, which the League of Nations was meant to oversee[‡‡]. At the Geneva disarmament conference, the German government repeatedly demanded to be allowed armed forces of equal size to France's.

When in Opposition, Churchill opposed the conduct and results of the Conference and what he saw as Britain's neglect of her armed services publicly and at every turn. In 1929, while he was still in government, the British government had been warned that a new German cruiser with 11-inch guns, authorised the year before, threatened to make all British cruisers obsolete. Britain depended on cruisers to protect its world-wide trade and, as before 1914, German cruisers would most likely be intended to menace that trade. They had virtually no other conceivable purpose: Germany had no reason to quarrel with America or Japan, and wars with France, Russia and Italy would most likely be decided on land. Churchill could not, however, prevent these ships being built. They eventually became the *Deutschland*-class cruisers (referred to by the British as "pocket battleships"). They performed useful service for the German Navy before and during the Second World War, though they never seriously threatened Britain's command of the seas.

As Chancellor of the Exchequer, Churchill had repeatedly asked the Navy to reduce its requests for new cruisers. Following the Conservatives' return to Opposition in 1929, however, Churchill publicly criticised the weakness of the Navy since the 1922 Washington Treaty[59]. In 1930, before the Geneva conference had formally started, he was warning in Parliament of the "considerably reduced" state of the Royal Navy and his "deep anxiety" about the Navy's strength[60], though in this case, his concerns were justified by implied comparisons with America and Japan, rather than with Germany. In 1931, on a debate on the Disarmament Conference, Churchill referred to "the failure of all

---

[‡‡] Article 8 of the Covenant of the League of Nations stated: "The Members of the League recognise that the maintenance of peace requires the reduction of national armaments to the lowest point consistent with national safety and the enforcement by common action of international obligations.

The Council, taking account of the geographical situation and circumstances of each State, shall formulate plans for such reduction for the consideration and action of the several Governments. Such plans shall be subject to reconsideration and revision at least every ten years".

disarmament conferences which have been held up to the present time", since "Every country champions its own special interest at these conferences, and all together proclaim their high ideals". He warned the government against any weakening of the French army, and that there should not be "an approximation of military power between those two countries [France and Germany]"[61]. The following year, Germany demanded equality in armaments with France. Sir John Simon wrote the Simon Note, which said that, in Britain's view, the disarmament clauses of the Treaty of Versailles were still binding on Germany. In an article in the *Daily Mail*, Churchill argued that Sir John Simon "had done more to consolidate peace in Europe than any words spoken on behalf of Great Britain for some years… [all German parties were trying to] put up the boldest front against the foreigner"[62]. Indulging in counterfactuals after the Second World War, however, Churchill seems to have believed that offering Germany equality of armaments, together with the end of reparations, could have prevented Hitler from gaining power. "Such a settlement would of course have raised [German democratic Chancellor] Brüning's position to one of triumph … These offers had presently to be discussed with a different system [Nazism] and a different man"[63].

In a debate at the end of 1932, Churchill reaffirmed the points which he had made the previous year, and poured scorn on the differentiation which the Disarmament Conference was making between offensive and defensive weapons[64]. At the end of the year, and before Hitler had come to power (though after the German government had started to rule by decree), he referred to Germany as:

> "the same mighty Germany, which so recently withstood almost the world in arms; Germany which resisted with such formidable capacity that it took between two and three Allied lives to take one German life in the four years of the Great War; Germany which has also allies, friends and associates in her train, and a powerful nation which considers its politics as associated to some extent with hers; Germany whose annual quota of youth reaching the military age, whose annual contingent is already nearly double … the youth of France; Germany where the Parliamentary system and the safeguards of the Parliamentary system which we used to be taught to rely upon in the Great War, are in abeyance. As to Germany's Parliamentary system, I do not know where it stands to-day, but certainly military men are in control of the essentials of the position.
>
> … I am making no indictment of Germany. I have the greatest respect and admiration for the Germans and the greatest desire that we should live

on terms of good feeling and fruitful relations with her, but we must look at the facts, and I put it to you, Mr. Speaker, and to the House, that every concession which has been made — many concessions have been made and many more will be made and ought to be made — has been followed immediately by a fresh demand.

Now, the demand is that Germany should be allowed to rearm. Do not delude yourselves. Do not let His Majesty's Government believe, I am sure they do not believe, that all that Germany is asking for is equal status. I believe the refined term now is equal qualitative status, or, as an alternative, equal quantitative status by indefinitely deferred stages. That is not what Germany is seeking. All these bands of sturdy Teutonic youths, marching along the streets and roads of Germany, with the light in their eyes of desire to suffer for their Fatherland, are not looking for status. They are looking for weapons, and, when they have the weapons, believe me they will then ask for the return, the restoration of lost territories and lost colonies, and when that demand is made it cannot fail to shake and possibly shatter to their foundations every one of the countries I have mentioned, and some other countries I have not mentioned.

... I say quite frankly, though I may shock the House, that I would rather see another 10 years or 20 years of one-sided armed peace than see a war between equally well-matched Powers or combinations of Powers — and that may be the choice...

I would follow any real path, not a sham or a blind alley, which led to lasting reconciliation between Germany and her neighbours. Here at this moment if the House will permit me I would venture to propound a general principle which I numbly submit to the Government and the House, and which I earnestly trust they will ponder. Here is my general principle. The removal of the just grievances of the vanquished ought to precede the disarmament of the victors. I hope I have made that quite clear. To bring about anything like equality of armaments, if it were in our power to do so, which it happily is not, while those grievances remain unredressed, would be almost to appoint the day for another European war — to fix it as if it were a prize fight. It would be far safer to reopen questions like those of the Danzig Corridor, and Transylvania,

with all their delicacy and difficulty, in cold blood and in a calm
atmosphere and while the victor nations still have ample superiority,
than to wait and drift on, inch by inch and stage by stage, until once
again vast combinations, equally matched, confront each other face to
face"[65]

Churchill's response to Hitler's seizure of power (*Machtergreifung*)

President Hindenburg appointed Hitler as Chancellor of Germany on 30 January
1933, after Reichstag elections in which the Nazis had lost 34 of their 230 seats.
Churchill knew that Hitler had never won the majority of votes or seats in
Presidential or Parliamentary elections. During the Second World War,
presumably referring to Hitler's attempts to be President, rather than
Parliamentary elections, Churchill commented that the Germans had twice
rejected Hitler in free elections, and the second time by a bigger majority than
the first[66]. In fact, there is an element of hypocrisy in this comment. Churchill
himself had never won a general election. He had instead been appointed to his
office by the King after the resignation of its previous incumbent. Not until
1951, six years after Hitler's death, could he finally claim to have been his
people's choice.

Four days after his appointment as Chancellor, Hitler told a meeting of
Germany's military leaders that rearmament was the most important factor in
realising his aim of restoring Germany's position in Europe, and he restated this
on 9 February to his top ministers and civil servants. At first, his power was
relatively limited. Only three of twelve Cabinet Ministers were Nazis, and
Hitler had to work within the Weimar constitution and with President
Hindenburg. Over the next year and a half, however, with the Reichstag fire, the
death of Hindenburg and the purge of Hitler's political opponents, Hitler was to
become absolute dictator of Germany. In Churchill's later words, "the Corporal
had travelled far"[67].

As might be expected, Churchill was fully aware of these momentous
developments, and deeply concerned about them. On 10 March 1933, he
opposed the Government's move to reduce spending on the Royal Air Force for
the second year in a row. He spoke against requesting France to reduce the size
of its air force. He asked the Government to abandon the Ten Year Rule, though
in fact it had already been revoked the previous year. Most of all, he called on

the Government to stop encouraging the "helpless, hopeless mood" in the country[68]. As was to become usual in the 1930's, however, some of the most magnificent of Churchill's oratory was to be completely disregarded by the Government.

On 16 March 1933, in the House of Commons, Churchill asked for a debate on the German political situation and its implications for European peace, but Stanley Baldwin, for the government, refused his request[69]. A week later, a debate was held on the European situation and the Government's disarmament proposals. The House was crowded, as was the public gallery, with, according to press reports of the time, the French, German, Polish, Italian and Belgian ambassadors and various politicians from the Dominions in attendance. The Prime Minister conceded that Europe was "very unsettled", but reaffirmed his faith in disarmament. Churchill did not mention Hitler or the change of government in Germany, but attacked the Government's proposal to reduce the size of the French army: "If Europe has enjoyed peace this year, it has been under the shield of France. Be careful not to break that shield". He argued that Britain's defences and its diplomatic position had been weakened significantly in the preceding four years, and made some sarcastic comments about Ramsay MacDonald's recent trip to Rome where he had met Mussolini – somewhat hypocritically, in the light of his own visit in 1927 (see above). Though even his critics in the House admitted that the speech had been "most brilliant" and spoke of his "mastery of rhetoric" [70], the mood of the House was heavily against him.

One month later, Churchill and Austen Chamberlain, both former Cabinet Ministers, criticised Germany's rearmament and increasingly aggressive policies. The German press protested when the Foreign Secretary, Sir John Simon, associated himself with their criticisms. The German press was by this time under Nazi control. The *Börsen Zeitung*, Germany's financial newspaper, headlined its article "British offensive against Germany", and the *Deutsche Allegemeine Zeitung* criticised Parliament and the British Government for failing to criticise Poland for its mistreatment of Germans[71]. Hitler and the German foreign minister, von Neurath, authorised an official protest against Sir John Simon's speech by the German ambassador in London. This marks the first time that Hitler and Churchill confronted each other publicly, albeit indirectly.

Churchill also warned of Britain's vulnerability outside Parliament. On 23 April 1933, for example, he spoke to the Society of St. George, in an address which was broadcast over the new medium of radio: "if, while on all sides foreign nations are every day asserting a more aggressive and militant nationalism ... we remain paralysed by our own ... doctrines ..., then indeed ... our ruin will be swift and final"[72]. According to the diary of Sir Robert Bruce Lockhart, Churchill referred to Hitler as the "gangster" during a dinner in July at the House of Commons with David Lloyd George, Prince Louis Ferdinand (a grandson of the Kaiser's) and others[73]. At a garden party in Essex on 12 August 1933, he said that there was "growing reason to believe that Germany is arming or seeking to arm contrary to treaties. The fact that the French have refused to hearken to hazardous advice and weaken their splendid army is the main foundation of European peace today"[74]. In November, again addressing his some constituents in Epping, he warned:

> "In order to induce France to disarm, we are to assure her that she can count on us. If she took our advice she would be weaker, and we would be more closely bound to her, thus making the worst of both worlds - neither avoiding a Continental struggle nor having a strong ally. Every recent incident establishes the German war guilt and the dangerous character of Germany under an autocracy. Therefore, I am a consistent friend of France and an opponent of the German peril"[75].

Hitler withdrew Germany from the Disarmament Conference in Geneva in October 1933, and held a referendum in Germany the next month, in which 95% of voters expressed their approval for his actions[§§]. Churchill attacked German rearmament again at the 1933 Conservative Party Conference. In response to Lord Lloyd's motion expressing grave anxiety at the state of Imperial Defence, he said that Britain should strengthen its defences. The motion was carried unanimously, but had no direct impact on Government policy.

In November 1933, Churchill again displayed his knowledge of, and concern about, developments in Germany. He spoke at length, but with the same lack of impact, in the House of Commons. Without mentioning Hitler by name, he left the House in no doubt of his opinions on the Nazi government. He poured scorn on Government claims that the armies of the nations surrounding Germany were sufficient to mean that Germany was contained:

> "I find it difficult to believe it in view of the obvious fear which holds all the nations who are neighbours of Germany and the obvious lack of fear which apparently controls the behaviour of the German Government and a large proportion of the German people.

[§§] It was claimed that this proportion even applied amongst the prisoners in Dachau concentration camp, where more than 2,000 voted.

The great dominant fact is that Germany is re-arming, has already begun to re-arm. I have no sources of information but those of the public Press, but we read of large importations of scrap iron and nickel and war metals, quite out of the ordinary. We read all the news which accumulates of the military spirit which is rife throughout the country; we see that a philosophy of blood lust is being inculcated into their youth to which no parallel can be found since the days of barbarism. We see all these forces on the move, and we must remember that it is the same mighty Germany which fought all the world and almost beat the world; it is the same mighty Germany which took two and a half lives for every German life that was taken.... I do not know, no one knows exactly, what is the position of German armaments; all we know is that the greatest anxiety has been caused to all her neighbours by her armaments and by her doctrines.

The Leader of the Opposition said just now that he and the Socialist party would never consent to the re-arming of Germany ...But is the right hon. Gentleman quite sure that the Germans will come and ask him for his consent before they re-arm?"[76]

In his comments on the King's Speech in November, Churchill, employing exaggeration for effect, said that Britain had "almost lost the capacity to make weapons". He deplored the proposal to make Germany and Italy together stronger than France, and said that the Disarmament Conference had been a "danger to the peace of Europe". He ended with a constructive proposal: "the prudent course for us is to associate ourselves with the League of Nations to defend safety and honour by working not with three or four nations but with 12 or 14 Powers, and doing our part, and no more, in conjunction with those Powers"[77].

The mood of the country was heavily against Churchill and his warnings. The tide of opinion in Britain was overwhelmingly pacifist throughout this period. It manifested itself in diverse ways. In February 1933, for instance, the Oxford Union overwhelmingly passed perhaps the most famous resolution in its history: "That this House will in no circumstances fight for its King and Country". In the first volume of his account of the Second World War, published in 1947, Churchill argued, without producing any evidence, that this might have encouraged the dictator states in their ambitions. His son, Randolph, who had left Oxford a couple of years earlier, tried to have the resolution overturned, but was defeated even more decisively. The Manchester University Union subsequently passed a similar resolution[78]. A Labour candidate won the so called "Peace by-election" in East Fulham in October 1933 (previously a safe Conservative seat) on a platform advocating disarmament, with a huge swing of about 30%. So strong was the pacifist feeling in the country that in a speech to the Royal Naval Division Association on 14 November 1933, Churchill had to deny being a warmonger. He added that it was the Nazis who declared that war was glorious and suggested referring the disarmament question back to the League of Nations[79].

Churchill's British allies on German rearmament

Churchill had remarkably few supporters with any weight in politics during these years. The Labour, Independent Labour, and Liberal parties were staunchly pacifist in the early 1930's. The Conservative Party, in overwhelming ascendancy in Parliament between 1931 and 1945, might have been expected to be more sympathetic, but the Party in those days was more deferential towards its leaders than it is today, and Churchill was not popular with the hierarchy. It had never fully forgiven him for "ratting" on the Party by joining the Liberals in 1904 when the Conservatives moved away from free trade, despite his subsequent reconversion to the Tories. More recently, in October 1930, he had threatened to leave the Shadow Cabinet over the same issue.

The Party leadership had another grievance against him during these years. Throughout the early 1930's, Churchill was vigorously opposing Conservative policy on self-government for India. He thought that any form of home rule for the Sub-continent was impossible and likely to lead to civil war, given how diverse India was. He devoted almost as much time to this issue as to rearmament during the Locust Years. Had he not spent so much time fighting his own party over India and protectionism, it is possible, though far from certain, that he could have found a more receptive audience when he warned about the growing peril from Germany. Martin Gilbert, however, argues that his positions on India and on rearmament were of a piece, because of "[Churchill's] belief that they represented a weakening of British resolve"[80].

Churchill therefore had few supporters throughout the 1930's. Maurice Cowling has identified the non-Labour opposition to appeasement at its greatest extent as consisting of "Churchill, Sinclair, Eden, Amery and Cecil, assisted by twenty or so Conservative or National MPs inside Parliament and a handful of publicists outside"[81], in other words, not even 5% of MPs. It only reached even this extent following the resignations of Eden and Cranborne in February 1938, when it was arguably much too late to stop Hitler without a major war. For much of the 1930's, it was much smaller. Churchill was left not entirely alone, however, even at his most isolated. Other far-sighted men in British public life saw the problems caused by German rearmament and deplored British diplomatic and military weakness.

Austen Chamberlain was Neville Chamberlain's older half-brother and a former leader of the Conservative Party. Even his opponents respected what the arch-appeaser, Samuel Hoare, called "the disinterested sense of patriotism which always marked his public life"[82]. As Foreign Secretary in the 1920s, he had organised the Locarno Pact, which guaranteed Germany's western neighbours against future aggression, and had been rewarded for this achievement with the Nobel Peace Prize. He had been First Lord of the Admiralty briefly in 1931. "Unlike the Foreign Office, the Admiralty runs itself and the First Lord need not worry about it" [83], he remarked to Sir Samuel Hoare. Baldwin briefly considered reappointing him Foreign Secretary in 1935, though rejected the idea, apparently telling Chamberlain to his face that he was old (according to Baldwin) or senile (according to Chamberlain)[84]. He warned repeatedly against German aggression in Parliament, and advocated rearmament both inside and outside the House. He differed from Churchill to some extent in considering Communism less of a threat[85]. He was to die in 1937, just as the truth of his warnings became apparent.

Leo Amery had known Churchill since they were at school together. Their first encounter was unpromising, when a young Churchill pushed Amery, then Head of his House at Harrow, into the swimming pool there, though Churchill managed to dodge the painful consequences of this lèse-majesté. Amery was Secretary of State for the Colonies in the late 1920's, when Churchill was Chancellor. He was disappointed not to be given a post in the Cabinet by Neville Chamberlain in 1937. During the 1930's, he often spoke in favour of a stronger army, founding a pressure group called the Army League. He also opposed the return of colonies to Germany, establishing another pressure group called the Colonial Defence League[86]. He knew Germany well, as a director of various German metal companies. He was semi-detached from the Churchill movement throughout most of the 1930's, only moving closer around the time of the Munich crisis in late 1938[87]. During the war, Amery was to serve as Churchill's Secretary of State for India. After the war, Amery suffered a terrible blow when his son was executed for treason since he had broadcast over the radio from Fascist Italy during the war.

Admiral Sir Roger Keyes (who incidentally referred to Amery as a "very unworthy First Lord [of the Admiralty]"[88]), one of greatest naval heroes of the First World War, consistently opposed appeasement and advocated a stronger Royal Navy and Fleet Air Arm. Churchill had met Keyes when they played polo together before the First World War, and as a Commodore had proposed the operation which led to the Battle of the Bight in 1914. He had also been heavily involved in the disastrous Dardenelles campaign, which cost Churchill his political career, and the daring Zeebrugge Raid of 1918. A decade later, Keyes's advocacy of a strong Royal Navy probably cost him the job of First Sea Lord when it became vacant in 1929. He therefore took his crusade to Parliament, being elected for North Portsmouth in 1934.

Randolph Churchill was perhaps his father's staunchest supporter during these difficult years. We have already seen how he interviewed Hitler in 1932. In early 1933, Randolph attempted to secure a second interview with Hitler, but failed. In April 1933, he wrote an article which certainly could have been written by his father in which he warned that:

> "The resurgence of the German nation under Hitler sooner or later means war ... the Nazis do not merely intend to stamp out Communism. They will not be satisfied with an economic pogrom against the Jews. They will not be satisfied with equality of status. They would not even be satisfied with the return of the Polish Corridor"[89].

---

[1] *The Churchill Documents, Volume 11, The Exchequer Years*, Martin Gilbert, p.999

[2] *Churchill: A Life*, Martin Gilbert, p.476

[3] *The Rise and Fall of the Third Reich*, William Shirer, p.174

[4] *Hitler*, Joachim C Fest, p.289

[5] *The Rise and Fall of the Third Reich*, William Shirer, p.152

[6] *Hitler, 1889-1936, Hubris*, Ian Kershaw, p.291

[7] *Hitler, 1889-1936, Hubris*, Ian Kershaw, p.291

[8] *Hitler, 1889-1936, Hubris*, Ian Kershaw, p.291

[9] *Hansard*, 5 June 1946

[10] *Hitler's Secret Book*, Foreword

[11] *Hitler's Secret Book*, Chapter 11

[12] *Hitler's Secret Book*, Chapter 7

[13] *Hitler's Secret Book*, Chapter 7

[14] *Hitler's Secret Book*, Chapter 14

[15] *Hitler's Secret Book*, Chapter 16

[16] *Hitler's Secret Book*, Chapter 15

[17] *Mussolini*, Denis Mack Smith, p.201

[18] *Speaking for Themselves: the personal letters of Winston and Clementine Churchill*, ed. Mary Soames, p.274

[19] *Churchill, A Life*, Martin Gilbert, p.458

[20] *Speaking for Themselves: the personal letters of Winston and Clementine Churchill*, ed. Mary Soames, p.297

[21] *The Second World War*, Winston S Churchill, Vol. 1, p.14

[22] *Churchill Papers*, CHAR 9/82B
[23] *Churchill*, Roy Jenkins, p.412
[24] *In the footsteps of Churchill*, Richard Holmes, p.183
[25] *Winston S Churchill Companion, Volume V, Part 3, 1936-1939, The Wilderness Years*, Martin Gilbert, p.979
[26] *Speaking for Themselves*, Mary Soames, p.295
[27] *Speaking for Themselves*, Mary Soames, p.298
[28] *Speaking for Themselves*, Mary Soames, p.310-311
[29] *Mein Kampf*, p.422
[30] *The Churchill Documents, Volume 11, The Exchequer Years*, Martin Gilbert, p.339
[31] *The Churchill Documents, Volume 11, The Exchequer Years*, Martin Gilbert, p.1348
[32] *Hitler, A Study in Tyranny*, Alan Bullock, p.148
[33] *Hitler*, Joachim C Fest, p.264
[34] *Hansard*, 7 April 1925
[35] *Hansard*, 23 June 1925
[36] *Hansard*, e.g. 13 November 1925, 16 November 1926, 3 March 1927, 28 April 1927, 15 November 1927
[37] *Hansard*, 15 April 1929
[38] *Hansard*, written answer, 30 April 1929
[39] *Hansard*, 24 January 1929
[40] Newspaper reports, 4 September 1929
[41] *The Churchill Documents, Volume 11, The Exchequer Years*, Martin Gilbert, p.443
[42] *Hansard*, 20 July 1936
[43] *Hitler, 1889-1936, Hubris*, Ian Kershaw, p.318
[44] *The Second World War*, Winston S Churchill, Vol. 1, p.60, quoting Sir Thomas Inskip, paraphrasing the Bible.
[45] Winston S Churchill, Volume V, Companion Part 2, 1929-1935, The Wilderness Years, p.196-9
[46] Winston S Churchill, Volume V, Companion Part 2, 1929-1935, The Wilderness Years, p.311
[47] *His Father's Son*, Winston S Churchill, p.88-89
[48] Letter to Winston S Churchill from Martin Gilbert, 8 April 1976, quoted in *His Father's Son*, Winston S Churchill, p.91
[49] *His Father's Son*, Winston S Churchill, p.89
[50] *Sunday Graphic*, 31 July 1932, quoted in *His Father's Son*, Winston S Churchill, p.89-91
[51] *The Second World War*, Winston S Churchill, Vol. 1, p.75
[52] *The Second World War*, Winston S Churchill, Vol. 1, p.75
[53] *Hitler's Piano Player*, Peter Conradi, p.94
[54] *Hitler; The Missing Years*, Ernst Handstaengl, p.186
[55] *Hitler's Piano Player*, Peter Conradi, p.95-6
[56] *The Second World War*, Winston S Churchill, Vol. 1, p.75
[57] *The Second World War*, Winston S Churchill, Vol. 1, p.75
[58] *His Father's Son*, Winston S Churchill, p.94
[59] Newspaper reports, various, 17 June 1929
[60] *Hansard*, 17 March 1930
[61] *Hansard*, 29 June 1931
[62] *Daily Mail*, 17 October 1932
[63] *The Second World War*, Winston S Churchill, Vol.1, p.58-9
[64] *Hansard*, 13 May 1932
[65] *Hansard*, 23 November 1932
[66] *Churchill War Papers, Vol. III, The Ever-Widening War*, Martin Gilbert, p.321

[67] *The Second World War*, Winston S Churchill, Vol. 1, p.54

[68] *Quoted in Churchill: A Life*, Martin Gilbert, p.513-4

[69] *Hansard*, 16 March 1933

[70] *Hansard*, 23 March 1933

[71] Newspaper reports, 15 and 17 April 1933

[72] Quoted in *The Wilderness Years*, Martin Gilbert, p.62-63

[73] Winston S Churchill, Volume V, Companion Part 2, 1929-1935, The Wilderness Years, p.627

[74] Newspapers reports, 13 August 1933

[75] Newspaper reports, 15 November 1933

[76] *Hansard*, 7 November 1933

[77] *Hansard*, 21 November 1933

[78] *Time* magazine, 13 March 1933

[79] *Churchill: A Life*, Martin Gilbert, p.524

[80] *The Wilderness Years*, Martin Gilbert, p.77

[81] *The Impact of Hitler*, Maurice Cowling, p.224

[82] *Nine Troubled Years*, Lord Templewood, p.23

[83] *Nine Troubled Years*, Lord Templewood, p.25

[84] *Eden*, D.R. Thorpe, p.166

[85] *Winston S Churchill Companion, Volume V, Part 3, 1936-1939, The Wilderness Years*, Martin Gilbert, p.232

[86] *The Impact of Hitler*, Maurice Cowling, p.225

[87] *The Impact of Hitler*, Maurice Cowling, p.227

[88] Winston S Churchill, Volume V, Companion Part 2, 1929-1935, The Wilderness Years, p.310

[89] Daily Dispatch, 18 April 1933, quoted in *His Father's Son*, Winston S Churchill, p.97

3

Hitler Acts; Churchill Objects (1934-1936)

By the end of 1933, the rather one-sided war of words between Churchill and Hitler had settled into a rhythm. Hitler's latest aggression would be answered by Churchill, who would warn repeatedly, in any forum which would give him a hearing, that this latest move was one more stage on the road to war, and therefore that Britain should attempt to counter it, and also speed its rearmament programme. Churchill did not simply wait on events in this period, however. As we have seen in the previous chapter, he had warned about German ambitions before Hitler came to power, and would continue urging firmer British resolve and British rearmament even when Germany was relatively quiet, as was the case throughout 1937.

In the mid-1930's, Hitler consolidated his grip on Germany; murdered many of his opponents in the Nazi Party; greatly accelerated and enlarged Germany's rearmament programme, which had already started before he became Chancellor; and undermined the Treaty of Versailles. In all these policies, he was simply doing what he had said he would do, ever since he had written *Mein Kampf*. A British Cabinet paper of 1936 described Hitler's "almost unbroken success during the last three years ... in foreign affairs"[1]. Each step which Hitler took was noted by Churchill, and he warned the British (and to a lesser extent, European and American) public about them at every opportunity and in every forum to which he had access.

The other big issues on which Churchill had opposed the Conservative Party leadership in the early 1930's, Indian self-government and Protectionism, gradually faded away in the middle part of the decade. Churchill lost both those battles. Imperial Preference tariffs were introduced after the Ottawa Conference of 1932, and the India Act, which he had fought against, was finally passed in 1935. These two setbacks did not dampen his appetite for attacking his own side. He antagonised the Conservative hierarchy again when he supported his son Randolph, who stood in a by-election in Wavertree against the Conservatives. Randolph split the Conservative vote, letting the Labour candidate in. "London is seething with indignation", noted the Conservative MP, Sir Henry 'Chips' Channon[2], over what they saw as Churchill's betrayal of his party. Just when he seemed to be regaining favour with the Conservative establishment, however, Churchill championed King Edward VIII's conduct in marrying the American divorcee, Wallis Simpson. Whether or not he was right to do so, Churchill's stand on this issue lost him much of the remainder of his credibility in the Party. The estrangement came at a critical time for Britain. Until well into the Second World War, the Party's prevailing attitude towards him was one of mistrust and suspicion at his perceived unpredictability and lack of judgement. Whether he could have converted the Party and the country away from appeasement any quicker had he followed the mainstream Conservative line - on India, Protectionism and the Abdication - will, inevitably, never be known.

From 1934 onwards, Churchill concentrated his fire on British European policy and the weakness of British armed forces, particularly in the air. He had always been interested in the military application of air power, and indeed had tried to learn to fly both before and after the First World War. He had nearly been killed in the summer of 1919[3] and his wife had made him promise that he would never try again. As First Lord of the Admiralty in 1914, he had organised the first, primitive, air defences of eastern England against German attack[4] and had begun the development of the pioneering aircraft carriers. He had also sponsored the first British air raids on Germany, on Zeppelin sheds and, later, on German military targets on the Western Front. His aggressive policy did not survive his resignation. His successor, Arthur Balfour, stopped using the Naval Air Service for pre-emptive raids on Germany.

After he returned to office, however, Churchill had to deal with the domestic impact of military aviation. As Minister for Munitions in the Coalition Government later in the war, Churchill had to deal with the effects of German air raids on British armaments production, and to organise the production of aircraft to combat German machines. The end of the war did not stop Churchill's involvement with the newly-formed Royal Air Force. As Secretary of State for War, after the First World War, Churchill had had responsibility for it, as well as for the Army. Though there was now no war to fight in Europe, he used British warplanes to police Imperial trouble spots, in particular against the turbulent tribesmen on the North-West frontier of British India*.

Churchill believed that air forces would be particularly important in the coming struggle with Germany for two reasons. He thought that Germany could rearm in the air in four years, compared to ten or fifteen years at sea or on land. The Germans could reach "parity" with Britain and France much quicker by building an air force than by manufacturing tanks or warships. Also, like many people during the 1930's, he seems to have had an exaggerated view of what aerial bombing in general, and the *Luftwaffe* in particular, could achieve against enemy cities. He once told Harold Nicolson that if Britain fought against Germany, "London will be a shambles in half-an-hour"[5] – in fact, months of bombing in 1940 and 1941 failed to achieve anything like this level of damage, and much smaller German industrial cities proved harder to wreck than Churchill, or almost anyone else, had previously thought. However, he was only ten years ahead of his time. The atomic bombs of the mid-1940's could indeed have made London a shambles in half-an-hour, but, fortunately for civilisation, Nazi Germany never managed to manufacture one.

Churchill was to describe British government in the mid-1930s as "an administration more disastrous than any in our history"[6]. During the mid-1930's, he had no government office, and little support in the Conservative Party. His direct influence on government policy was therefore small. Ramsay MacDonald, Prime Minister since 1929, gradually lost control of government, and Stanley Baldwin acquired "power without responsibility" as Lord President of the Council, before becoming Prime Minister officially in June 1935. Lord Salisbury once famously described British foreign policy as "drift[ing] lazily downstream, now and again putting out a boathook to avoid a collision", and this was never truer than during the mid-1930's. Its reaction to recurrent European crises was pusillanimous and ineffective, managing to alienate allies without restraining enemies. Churchill saw this trend earlier and more clearly than any of his contemporaries, but was reduced to fuming about it impotently in public and in private. At the end of 1935, he wrote to his wife that he was still gloomy about Britain's position in Europe: "... our defences neglected, our Government less capable a machine for conducting affairs than I have ever seen. The Baldwin-MacDonald regime has hit this country very hard indeed and may well be the end of its glories"[7].

---

* What is now the still-turbulent Pakistan/Afghanistan border.

Chapter 3

Following the 1935 general election, many thought that Baldwin would offer Churchill a senior Cabinet post, but he did not do so. "Evidently B[aldwin] desires above all things to avoid bringing me in", Churchill wrote to his wife in February 1936[8]. A lesser man than Churchill might have been suspected of sour grapes, but his words were consistent with what he had been saying in public and private for years. Churchill in fact planned to write a book on Baldwin's foreign policy after he was denied office by the government in 1936. It would clearly have involved a root-and-branch criticism of every aspect of Baldwin's handling of external affairs, and particularly his appeasement of the dictator powers, and Churchill signed a publishing contract and made some notes for it. He never wrote it, however. According to David Reynolds[9], this may have been because he thought his *Evening Standard* articles would be more lucrative. In any case, he did not waste the effort. After the Second World War, Churchill used his notes to write the first volume of his mammoth war memoirs.

A good example of the relative effectiveness of British and German foreign policy in the mid-1930's was their handling of Mussolini's invasion of Abyssinia (now Ethiopia). British policy was too weak to give effective assistance to the Abyssinians, while being robust enough to offend Italy, which moved towards an alliance with Germany. According to Speer, Hitler could not at first decide how to react, and his decision was informed by his view of the English character:

> "Hitler was pacing back and forth in the garden at Obersalzberg. 'I really don't know what I should do. It is a terribly difficult decision. I would by far prefer to join the English. But how often in history the English have proved perfidious. If I go with them, then everything is over for good between Italy and us. Afterward the English will drop us and, and we'll sit between two stools'"[10].

In the end, Hitler backed Mussolini. The two Fascist dictators agreed to conclude a military pact in November. The Japanese signed a pact with Hitler (directed against the Soviet Union) a few weeks later. The new understanding with Italy allowed Hitler to bully the Austrian government into appointing two Nazis to its Cabinet. These were not the only setbacks for Britain and France in that turbulent year, however. The outbreak of the Spanish Civil War was a further complication for the democracies, and it allowed Germany and Italy to train soldiers and try out their new weaponry in combat. It also menaced Britain's position in Gibraltar.

While Churchill was warning against him, Hitler was attempting to reach an understanding with Britain along the lines he suggested in *Mein Kampf* and his *Second Book*. He thought that Germany should have a free hand in Eastern

Europe, or in his grander moments on the whole Eurasian landmass, while Britain would control the seas and her Empire. The first, and as it turned out, only, practical step towards this goal was the Anglo-German Naval Agreement of 1935 (see below). Hitler also took other, more minor, steps to influence British public opinion. In a tactic borrowed from Bolshevik Russia, the Nazis encouraged sympathetic observers from Britain and other countries to visit Germany, obviously intending that they leave with a good impression of the Nazi regime. Hitler himself met many of the more prominent visitors. Churchill himself, though invited several times, never visited Nazi Germany[11].

Hitler's salami slicing

Nazi Germany began rearming almost, though not quite, from scratch. In 1933, her armed forces were very weak, not merely when compared to Britain and France, but even, on some measures, compared to Poland and Czechoslovakia. Many of Hitler's first moves in diplomacy were directed at addressing Germany's alarming weaknesses in military matters. Britain and France dithered and protested at each stage, and at each stage, Hitler took advantage of their dithering and shrugged off their protests, which turned out to be toothless. Churchill used each move to raise awareness of Nazi aims and the nature of Hitler's regime in the House.

Beginning almost as soon as he was appointed Chancellor, Hitler ordered his military commanders to prepare for a large expansion in the army in particular, in secret at first. His tactic was to announce the steps he had taken, in effect presenting the world with a series of *faits accomplis*. In this period at least, he displayed an uncanny sense of timing, and a knowledge of what would be acceptable to European public opinion, in particular within France and Britain. After each step, he would issue reassuring statements that this demand was his last - in perfect bad faith. It is difficult not to be impressed by Hitler's low cunning and his knack of judging what he could get away with. Like most compulsive gamblers, however, he was to push his luck too far.

Hitler's first public step on the road to rearmament was relatively innocuous. On 14 October 1933, Germany withdrew from the Geneva Disarmament Conference. In the subsequent, rigged, referendum, 95% of voters approved of that decision. Rearmament now began in earnest. The Versailles Treaty had limited the German army to 100,000 men in seven divisions – Hitler increased it to 300,000 in twenty-one divisions in 1934. In 1936, he reintroduced conscription, further increasing the army to thirty-six divisions. The German

Navy was enlarged and modernised. U-boats had been designed in secret in cooperation with Finland, Sweden, the Netherlands and others since 1922. Hitler now began to build them. Germany continued to build the controversial large cruisers, or "pocket" battleships. Both these construction programmes violated the Treaty of Versailles. The Treaty had also prevented Germany from possessing military aircraft, though again it had already secretly violated this provision under the Weimar Republic. The Government promoted civil aviation which could then be converted quickly to military uses, and encouraged suspiciously large and militaristic private flying clubs. Hitler's 1935 decision to throw off the cloak of secrecy and announce the creation of an air force is covered in more detail below.

Diplomatically, too, Germany started from a weak and isolated position. France, with its huge army just across the Rhine, still regarded German rearmament as a threat. Britain was generally less hostile, but not inclined to take Germany's side against France. Poland and Czechoslovakia were friendly to France. Italy's Fascist government looked down on its German equivalent, and was more inclined to come to terms with Britain and France. Hitler's tactic, which he pursued brilliantly, was to divide and rule amongst Germany's neighbours, telling each what it wanted to hear until it was that country's turn to be knifed. A Foreign Office diplomat described Hitler's diplomatic strategy in a letter to Churchill in November 1934:

> "If Hitler were frankly aggressive the situation would be simpler, and peace ... more secure, for a frankly aggressive Germany would still unite all Europe against it. But Hitler means to achieve his objective by more subtle methods ... by playing off one Power against the other – Great Britain against France, Italy against France, Poland against Czechoslovakia, Russia against Japan, etc. – and then using the *threat* of force against each Power when it is isolated. Great Britain would probably be the last Power to be dealt with but its turn will come ..."

He clearly saw the dangers which the lack of resolve amongst the democratic powers posed to peace.

> "... The new and terrible thing [in Europe] is that the 'Have Nots' [including Germany] are growing in strength while the 'Haves' [including Britain] are growing weaker and less sure of themselves. Whereas up till recently the 'Have Nots' have been afraid of the 'Haves', it is now the 'Haves' who are beginning to be afraid of the 'Have Nots'. Here then lies the real cause of future war"[12].

Hitler seduced Poland with a Ten-Year Non-Aggression Pact in 1934 and Britain with the Anglo-German Naval Agreement in 1935. Neither of those treaties lasted as far as the end of the decade, but they served their immediate purpose well.

Despite his shrewd foreign policy, Hitler suffered some diplomatic setbacks in the summer of 1934. In July 1934, Austrian Nazis organised a coup, with a view to uniting Austria with Germany. The coup was a disaster, but Hitler's skilful reaction in disassociating himself from it avoided Italian intervention and possible humiliation. During the Night of the Long Knives [30 July 1934], he murdered hundreds of his political opponents. Many of them were well known internationally, and this first purge was very unfavourably received by European public opinion. (Europe in those days was evidently more easily shocked than today, being less familiar with the terror methods of totalitarian states). When President Hindenburg died on 2 August 1934, Hitler combined Hindenburg's office as President with his own as Chancellor. This move came as a surprise to almost everybody, but clearly showed that he was determined to be Germany's absolute ruler. Though 38 million Germans voted in Hitler's favour in the subsequent referendum, seven million - despite the likelihood of reprisals - "had the courage to vote against making that gangster autocrat for life", as Churchill wrote to his wife[13].

Hitler's successes continued in 1935. Saarland, a small, coal-rich area on the French border, had been separated from Germany by the Treaty of Versailles. In January, the inhabitants voted by 90% to rejoin Germany, which reacquired it in March. Europe viewed this as a triumph for Nazi Germany. Using the pretext of the French defensive pact with the Soviet Union, Hitler renounced the Locarno Pact of 1922, which had guaranteed France and Belgium from German invasion.

If 1935 had been successful for Hitler, 1936 was triumphant. It was the decisive year in the revival of Germany's diplomatic fortunes: she concluded an alliance with Italy and a pact with Japan, and her main opponent, France, seemed paralysed with an internal political crisis. Germany also reoccupied the Rhineland, which had been demilitarised under the Treaty of Versailles, bloodlessly, though Hitler privately ordered the Army to retreat if the French army attacked.

Chapter 3

Churchill on Hitler's Germany

Throughout these years, Churchill continued warning everyone who would give him a hearing about German rearmament, Britain's lack of preparation and the nature of the Nazi regime. He wrote four memoranda on the strengths of British and German air forces in 1936, which he circulated to the Committee of Imperial Defence[14]. They had no discernible effect on government policy. Sir Samuel Hoare claimed that "From 1931 to 1935, there was scarcely a meeting of the Committee of Imperial Defence in which disarmament was not discussed in one form or another"[15].

The Memoranda gave the basis, in greater detail, for the arguments which Churchill was making in the House of Commons throughout the mid-1930's. They clearly drew on all the sources, public, official and semi-official, to which he had access. Even today, they make a persuasive, though occasionally exaggerated, case, and a damning indictment of Government carelessness and lethargy in defending the country. Churchill knew he was fighting against majority opinion in the country, however. As Hoare noted in his defence of the Government's record twenty years later - "In cutting down the expenditure on the fighting services, we were carrying out an almost unanimous popular mandate".

Churchill continued to warn a public which did not want to hear. On January 16 1934, he warned in a radio broadcast that the British Empire faced a stark choice between safety and ruin. He proposed "building up a confederation of nations so strong and so sincere that at least no aggressor would dare to challenge it … Surely, the least we ought to do now is to have an Air Force as strong as that of the nearest Power at hand". He used economic arguments, as well as foreign policy considerations, to back his case. Disarmament would only lead to starvation and misery amongst the working classes[16]. He did not speak in the important disarmament debate in Parliament on February 6. Sir Austen Chamberlain, his ally, though nothing like as good a speaker, repeatedly questioned the Government's policy of making more and more concessions to Germany[17]. The next day, however, Churchill made a speech proposing the expansion and re-equipment of all three branches of the armed forces and significantly increased armaments production[18].

In a debate in Parliament on the Air Estimates on 8 March, the Government finally acknowledged what Churchill had been saying for years, that British air power was too weak and that further disarmament would be dangerous to the Empire's future. Churchill discussed the best methods of defence from the air in some detail, and, given what was to happen in 1940, with startling prescience.

He then commented on the nature of the Nazi regime, which was clearly already apparent to him, if not to everyone in Britain:

> "Germany is ruled — I am going to pick my words, so that there is no word of offence put in — by a handful of autocrats who are the absolute masters of that mighty, gifted nation. They are men who have neither the long interests of a dynasty to consider, for what that is worth — and sometimes it is worth something — nor have they those very important restraints which a democratic Parliament and constitutional system impose upon any executive Government. Nor have they the restraint of public opinion, which public opinion, indeed, they control by every means which modern apparatus renders possible. They are men who owe their power to the bitterness of defeat, who are, indeed, the expression of the bitterness of defeat, and of the resolved and giant strength of that mighty, that tremendous German Empire. I am not going to speak about their personalities, because there is no one in the House who is not thoroughly aware of them and cannot form his own opinion after having read the accounts of what has been happening there, of the spirit which is alive there and of the language, methods and outlook of the leading men of that tremendous community, much the most powerful one in the whole world. It is in their hands, and they can direct it this way or that by a stroke of the pen, by a single gesture.
>
> I dread the day when the means of threatening the heart of the British Empire should pass into the hands of the present rulers of Germany. I think we should be in a position which would be odious to every man who values freedom of action and independence, and also in a position of the utmost peril for our crowded, peaceful population, engaged in their daily toil"[19].

Churchill then answered those who accused him (and the Government of which he was a part) of being negligent in the 1920's, clearly and convincingly. He defended the Ten-Year Rule as appropriate at the time:

> "At any rate, as Chancellor of the Exchequer ... I shared the responsibility for what was done, or not done, in those years, and I am prepared to offer a detailed and, I trust, vigorous justification — or, I hope, vindication — if it should be desired in any quarter. But the scene has changed. This terrible new fact has occurred. Germany is arming, she is rapidly arming, no one will stop her. None of the grievances between the victors and the vanquished have been redressed. The spirit of aggressive nationalism was never more rife in Europe and in the world.

Far away are the days of Locarno when we nourished bright hopes of the reunion of the European family and the laying in the tomb of that age-long quarrel between Teuton and Gaul of which we have been the victims in our lifetime. Those days are gone, all that comfortable assurance which we felt, and which I think we felt rightly, and in which we may prove to have been right, that no major war need be anticipated for 10 years — we do not feel it now" [20].

The Government committed itself to parity with Germany in the air. Churchill was not fully placated, however. In August 1934, in a censure debate moved by Labour and criticising the Government's plans to increase the RAF by 41 squadrons, he again referred to the gravity of the European situation. In November, Churchill moved an amendment to the King's Speech, that Britain's defences were "no longer adequate to secure the peace, safety, and freedom of Your Majesty's faithful subjects". In proposing it, he made a somewhat alarmist estimate of the dangers to London of bombing from the air, saying that three or four million people would flee the city. He argued that the best defence was a large offensive capability, which would act as a deterrent to an aggressor. The Nazi regime, he said, was "now equipping itself once again, 70,000,000 of people, with the technical apparatus of modern war, and at the same time is instilling into the hearts of its youth and manhood the most extreme patriotic nationalist and militarist conceptions". He analysed German strength in the air, stating that German strength would be around double Britain's by 1937, and that her civilian planes were designed so that they could be switched to military uses very quickly. His amendment was eventually defeated by 276 votes to 35 [21].

Outside Parliament, too, Churchill argued for stronger defences and tried to alert the country to the nature of the Nazi regime and the menace posed by German aggression. In February 1934, Churchill spoke to the Oxford Union. He said, to mocking laughter, that Germany had been responsible for the outbreak of the First World War. He warned about the danger of bombing: "the hideous curse of war from the air has fallen on the world". In November, he addressed his constituents in Essex: "Germany is arming secretly, illegally and rapidly … A reign of terror exists in Germany in order to keep secret the feverish and terrible preparations. Mr. Baldwin used a formidable expression when he said in the House of Commons, 'Our frontiers are the Rhine.' Can we be sure that the men now controlling Germany will not reply, 'Our targets are the Thames?'" [22]. In an "Open Letter to a Communist" in August 1934, he attacked the hypocrisy of British Communists in objecting to censorship in Germany while saying nothing of the suppression of free speech in Russia. "Freedom of thought is equally alien to the philosophy of Marx and the creed of Hitler" [23].

The Nazi regime's internal policies clearly troubled him, if less so than its external aggression. Writing to his wife, Clementine, in March 1935, he described the "German situation" as "increasingly sombre". He was appalled by the "mediaeval gruesomeness" of Hitler's treatment of two female spies, and was alarmed that Hitler apparently felt strong enough to spurn the British Foreign Secretary, who had been due to visit Berlin[24].

Churchill did not neglect any possible avenue to warn about the danger which Hitler's regime posed to Britain. At the Conservative Party Conference in October 1935, he proposed an amendment seeking to commit the Party to greater defence. The amendment was carried unanimously, but was non-binding, and had no discernible impact on British government policy. In the *Strand* magazine of the same month, he criticized the Nazi regime, and in particular its anti-Semitism, at considerable length[25]. At a speech in Camberwell in November, he made a chilling forecast: the fate of Abyssinia, which Italy had just invaded, showed what could happen to a weak Britain. There was still time to rebuild the fleet, but a new and greater danger had arisen in the air. London was "a great, fat cow which would soon be at the mercy of the nearest foreign dictator". According to *The Times*: "Mr Churchill's speech was subjected to many interruptions, and a number of youths had to be ejected by the police". He gave the hecklers the following Churchillian retort:

> "That's just a handful of boys and girls who bring the good name of London into disrepute and have the effrontery to disturb a large public gathering … They only show the confusion, bedlam and chaos to which this country would be reduced if the people they process to represent got into power. They can shout and squeal as much as they like, but it's lucky for them there is still a British Navy or they would soon get a dose of Mussolini's castor oil or a taste of Hitler's rubber truncheons"[26].

The November 1935 edition of the *Strand* magazine contained a 4,000 word article from Churchill, entitled *The Truth about Adolf Hitler*. This article was reproduced, in a slightly altered form, as a chapter in his 1937 book, *Great Contemporaries*. The content of the 1937 section of Churchill's book is summarised in the next chapter. However, on reading the *Strand* article, the German ambassador complained to the Foreign Office and the Nazi press rounded on Churchill. The financial *Börsen Zeitung* accused Churchill of trying to restore a political reputation damaged by his campaign against the India Act at the expense of Anglo-German relations. The paper described Churchill, oddly, as "finished" – without stating why, in that case, Germany needed to react to his article.

Chapter 3

In the January 1936 issue of the *Strand* magazine, Churchill wrote a much lighter, and more humorous article, *The Truth about Myself*. He gave his views on free trade, on the Dardenelles expedition of 1915, and on making speeches ("seven or eight thousand. Isn't it awful?"). The article contained many digs against Hitler and Germany, while only once mentioning Hitler by name:

> "I know a great deal more about myself than I do about Herr Hitler ... Having been born and bred in a victorious country with a constitutional monarchy and a free Parliament, I have never been called upon to mingle in the ferocious convulsions of disaster and defeat which have gripped so many other countries. I have always been taught that 'one-man power' is odious to the British nation, and that ministers and functionaries of all kinds are servants and not masters of the state... I would not like to live under such a regime as now prevails in so many populous countries, still less would I like to be one of the grim figures who enforce it ..."

Churchill also gave his views on the appeasement which he was spending much of his time combating:

> "An insidious propaganda gains much attention. Let us give up our possessions ... Let us purchase the favours of the strong at the cost of the weak. Anything for a quiet life for a few more years. Such is the hateful theme ... I must avow myself in strong reaction against this powerful tide ... I am glad to spend what is left of my mortal span in trying to rouse the good brave people of ... Britain and of her Empire to a sense of the dangers which are closing in upon them, and to induce them to take precautions while time remains"[27].

As noted above, Germany had been prohibited by the Treaty of Versailles from having any military aviation. In fact, for years, German pilots had been training in Russia and Germany had operated an air base there. German companies also designed military aircraft through their subsidiaries in foreign countries, where the limitations of the Treaty did not apply. On 26 February 1935, however, Hitler publicly ordered Göring to establish an air force, with effect from 1 April. This move allowed pilots and planes to be brought back to Germany and gave official character to Germany's rearmament efforts. When the British government increased its defence spending in response, Hitler refused to receive the foreign secretary, who had been due to visit him in Berlin. "The German situation is increasingly sombre", Churchill wrote to his wife, "... All the frightened nations are at last beginning to huddle together"[28].

Churchill referred to Germany's new air force in the annual Parliamentary debate on Britain's Air Estimates in March 1935. He questioned the Government's complacent figures on comparative strength in the air, bemoaning German secrecy in military matters. The Government had previously pledged that it would keep up with Germany in the air. Churchill demonstrated that this pledge of "air parity" was not being kept. Britain, he maintained, was slipping behind Germany in the air and would slip further behind over the next few years[29]. He told his wife that Hitler's claim that Germany had parity in the air with Britain "vindicates all the assertions that I have made. I expect in fact he is really much stronger than we are. Certainly they will soon be at least ten times greater than we are ... Fancy if our Liberal Government had let the country down in this way before the Great War!"[30] In a sobering memorandum written in April 1935, and circulated to sixteen senior political figures in Britain, he traced the history of his warnings about British air strength, and concluded that there was "no reason to doubt the capacity of Germany to achieve an ... air force of two hundred squadrons during the ... present year, comparable in every way to the British home defence force ... of 54 squadrons, from which should be deducted the 13 auxiliary squadrons and the Fleet Air Arm"[31].

In May 1935, Churchill again attacked the Government in two debates for allowing British air strength to fall behind Germany's, contrary to its pledge to protect parity. Addressing a House of Commons, which, according to *The Times*, "can never have been more crowded"[32], Churchill was relatively hopeful about the possible collapse, or at least weakness, of the Nazi regime: "Under the grim panoply which Germany has so rapidly assumed there may be all kinds of stresses and weaknesses, economic, political and social which are not apparent, but upon which we should not rest ourselves"[33]. He advocated stronger air defence in a debate in June, without mentioning Germany or the Nazi regime by name. In two Parliamentary debates in July, Churchill criticised the Anglo-German Naval Agreement of the previous month[34]. After the summer recess, the House debated the Italian invasion of Abyssinia and other elements of the international situation. With somewhat of a leap in logic, he blamed Mussolini's aggression on German rearmament:

> "I do not, of course, suggest that German re-armament is directed against us. It may well be that we are the last people the Germans would wish to attack. Certainly it would be in their interest to have our goodwill while they decided their deep differences with other countries. There is even a theory that the Germans are re-arming only out of national self-respect and that they do not mean to hurt anyone at all. Whatever you believe, whatever you think, however it may be, I venture to submit to the House that we cannot have any anxieties comparable to the anxiety caused by

German rearmament. The House will pardon me if I continue to press that anxiety upon it. I bear no grudge, I have no prejudice against the German people. I have many German friends, and I have a lively admiration for their splendid qualities of intellect and valour, and for their achievements in science and art. The re-entry into the European circle of a Germany at peace within itself, with a heart devoid of hate, would be the most precious benefit for which we could strive, and a supreme advantage which alone would liberate Europe from its peril and its fear, and I believe that the British and French democracies, the ex-Service men, would go a long way in extending the hand of friendship to realise such a hope.

But that is not the position which exists to-day. A very different position exists to-day. We cannot afford to see Nazidom in its present phase of cruelty and intolerance, with all its hatreds and all its gleaming weapons, paramount in Europe at the present time. In the shadow of German re-armament other dangers have taken shape on the Continent. We have, for instance, this war between Italy and Abyssinia, of which the newspapers are so full and which has occupied a good deal of our attention during this Debate. It is a very small matter compared with the dangers I have just described. I do not believe that Signor Mussolini would have embarked upon his Abyssinian venture but for the profound pre-occupation of France in German re-armament, and, I must add, but for the real or supposed military and naval weakness of Great Britain"[35]

This last speech in particular annoyed the German government, especially as Sir John Simon had failed to disown Churchill's criticism of Germany's internal politics. The German ambassador sent a protest to the Foreign Office, which was promptly passed on by Churchill's ally, Ralph Wigram, to Churchill himself. The Nazi Party newspaper blamed Churchill's anti-German stance on his friendship with "the American Jew millionaire", Bernard Baruch[†]. With heavy irony, the *Deutsche Allgemeine Zeitung* claimed that Germans had learnt not to be surprised at Mr. Churchill's audacious speeches, and that it had been one of his masterpieces. It noted that the link between Italy's aggression in Africa and German rearmament was not obvious. The paper added that there had been

---

[†] Baruch was an American millionaire who had made a fortune trading sugar. He became one of Wall Street's leading financiers by 1910. He served as Chairman of the War Industries Board during the First World War, attended the Versailles Peace Conference, and assisted President Roosevelt with the New Deal. Churchill had met him during his (Churchill's) time as Minister of Munitions during the First World War.

speculation that Churchill would be appointed First Lord of the Admiralty in the Government being formed, and it called upon the Government to refute Churchill's opinions, particularly as they had not been contradicted in the House of Commons[36].

As Hitler's position improved, the critical year of 1936 was to see Churchill's fortunes at their lowest ebb in 20 years, since he had briefly contemplated suicide following the Dardenelles disaster in 1915. As Germany's rearmament continued apace, and the smaller countries of Europe saw that Britain and France would do nothing, Germany's diplomatic position improved correspondingly. Churchill continued to warn British public opinion of the menace of Hitler and his government in every forum which was open to him. In Parliament on 24 February 1936, he spoke in favour of manpower being provided for new destroyers, recalling the German submarine menace in 1915[37]. In a weighty speech on 10 March, he spoke of Germany's economic motivation for seeking war and urged the conversion of British industry for rearmament[38], noting that Hitler had spent £1,500 million on armaments, including £800 million in 1935 (compared with British defence expenditure in 1935/36 of £137 million)‡. Neville Chamberlain admitted later that Churchill's estimate of German expenditure was "not necessarily excessive"[39].

Churchill spoke, with Admiral Keyes, on the Naval Estimates in March. Most of his speech dealt with America and Japan rather than Germany, though he attacked the Anglo-German Naval Agreement once again[40]. Churchill had anticipated Hitler's next foreign policy success for some time. He had written to his wife in January that: "Rothermere who has long letters and telegrams from Hitler and is in close touch with him, believes that on 24th or it may be 21st, Hitler is going to make a most important announcement. This may well be that Germany will … reoccupy the neutral zone [of the Rhineland]"[41]. In fact, Hitler did not move until March. Recognising the overwhelming feeling in Britain against intervention, Churchill was conciliatory, despite Hitler's clear violation of the Treaty of Versailles and the Locarno Pact of 1925. He wrote in the *Evening Standard* that Hitler could "open a new era for all mankind" by a "proud and voluntary submission … to the sanctity of Treaties and the authority of public law"[42]. Later that month, Churchill praised Hitler for bringing home "trophies" for his people, while criticising the British government for not doing more to stop him. He spoke about the:

---

‡ Churchill later said that he had used £800 million, rather than £1,000 million, which was his belief, for German defence expenditure in 1935 "to be on the safe side"‡.

"... enormous triumph [that] has been gained by the Nazi regime. The German Chancellor, perhaps advised against the course he took by his military experts, nevertheless decided on ordering the violation of the Rhineland and the destruction of the Locarno Treaty. He has succeeded — it is no good blinding ourselves to it — his troops are there, and who is to say that they will be removed? He has accomplished this fact, and although the world has been alarmed and shocked, and many protests have been made, the event has occurred. And what an event. Under the brazen surface of the totalitarian State there stir and seethe all the emotions of a great, cultured, educated and once free community. The Protestant, the Catholic, the Jew, the Monarchist, the Communist, the Liberal — all these forces are there, held in suspense, held in a certain grip and vice as it were, but they are there.

Let us suppose that any one of us were a German and living there, and perhaps entirely discontented with many things that we saw around us, but thinking that here is the Führer, the great leader of the country, who has raised his country so high — and I honour him for that — able to bring home once again a trophy. One year it is the Saar, another month the right of Germany to conscription, another month to gain from Britain the right to build submarines, another month the Rhineland. Where will it be next? Austria, Memel, other territories and disturbed areas are already in view. If we were Germans, and discontented with the present regime, nevertheless on patriotic grounds there is many a man who would say "While the Government is bringing home these trophies, I cannot indulge my personal, sectional or party feelings against this regime." This country is in the presence of facts which, apart from the technical consequences of the military occupation of the Rhineland, constitute an immense blow at the League of Nations and the principle of the reign of law, and constitute an immense gain in prestige to the Nazi Government in Germany. I think that a very serious fact at the present time.

There is another reason why I feel that the Foreign Secretary was bound to make the speech that he did. We had something to do with the events which made the conditions under which the Germans acted. From the highest and most benevolent motives — and I do not dissociate myself from the general course which the Government took — we have pressed a policy of sanctions against Italy upon France that is estranging France and Italy. ….As I tried to point out to the House, the friendship between France and Italy was vital to the defence and security of every home in France, and France, out of regard for Britain and out of loyalty for the principles of the League of Nations, went very far; not so far as some enthusiasts would have wished her to go, not so far as those who did not understand how fast she was moving expected her to move; but very far did she move, and considerable injury was inevitable in the relations of France and Italy. That produced a situation in which, it seems to me, all the elements were present which led to the recent outrage upon international law and the Treaties which regulate the peace of Europe."

Churchill proposed a British alliance with France and encirclement[§] of Germany (or the "strongest and closest encirclement of Nazidom which is possible", as he expressed it in a private letter[43]). This, he felt, should be combined with a promise that no European country would invade Germany[44]. All his proposals and fulminations were entirely ineffective however: no other British politician, and very few members of the public, favoured military action to prevent Germany from reoccupying what many thought of as her own backyard. Samuel Hoare, the arch-appeaser, later described this feeling as "almost universal"[45]. On 31 March, Churchill asked the Government to ensure that no foreign loans were made to countries that were rearming[46]. He returned to the German occupation of the Rhineland in his *Evening Standard* column on 3 April and in Parliament on 6 April, when he noted that the Germans were fortifying the area, and supported the discussions which the British military was to have with their counterparts in France and Belgium.

Churchill made interventions on naval rearmament in May 1936, and enquired of the Government whether a Ministry of Supply or of Munitions (similar to the one he himself had led during the First World War) had been created. He returned to the subject on 21 May, noting the deteriorating international situation and Germany's huge rearmament programme, and again on 29 May, when he proposed accelerating the conversion of British industry to war production. In November 1936, he proposed collective security under the League of Nations. His speech which contained a memorable blast against those

---

[§] The word "encirclement" had a sinister resonance in Germany, since it reminded diplomats there of the way in which, they believed, Britain had woven alliances with countries around Germany before the First World War. From this, they would often argue that the First World War had been "forced" on the Germans. Before and during the First World War, German propaganda often referred to King Edward VII as "Edward the Encircler".

who sympathised with German fears of encirclement, argued that the main danger to Europe was Russian Communism, rather than German Nazism:

> "Germany, we are assured, is a most peace-loving country. It is true they are scraping together a few weapons, but that, we are told, is only because of the terror in which they dwell of a Russian Bolshevik invasion. Night and day the fear, we are told, of the aggression of Soviet Russia rests upon Germany. If that be their trouble it can easily be healed. Let them come into the system of collective security, and if Russia is the aggressor and the invader, then all Europe will give to Germany guarantees that they will not go down unaided. They have only to ask for guarantees for the defence of the soil of Germany, and they will find them forthcoming in the fullest measure from many nations, both powerful and small alike.
>
> What, then, is this talk about encirclement? It is all nonsense..."[47]

In July 1936, Churchill requested a Secret Session of Parliament to discuss rearmament. The Government turned his request down. He then organised an unprecedented Deputation to the Prime Minister from both Houses of Parliament, which consisted of five from the Lords and thirteen from the Commons, to urge more progress on rearmament upon Baldwin. He spoke for a long time and eloquently, repeating the points he had made many times before about German rearmament in the air and Britain's lack of preparation. The Prime Minister listened patiently, and expressed a desire to divert German expansion eastwards, in line with "that strange man's [i.e. Hitler's] programme" in *Mein Kampf*. "If there is any fighting in Europe to be done, I should like to see the Bolshies and Nazis doing it", he said. Churchill stated that he "certainly did not consider war with Germany inevitable, but I am sure that the way to make it less likely is to afford concrete evidence of our determination in setting about re-armament". The Prime Minister agreed[48], but the Deputation had no noticeable effect on policy.

Churchill's private intelligence network

All totalitarian regimes attempt to exercise complete control over information which they deem sensitive. Nazi Germany was certainly no exception here. Hitler's government exercised full control over the press, the cinema and the radio throughout his rule, and clamped down ruthlessly on the information which reached its foreign critics. Obtaining accurate information about matters which the government wished to keep secret, such as its military preparations or its plans for foreign policy surprises, was very difficult.

Until the Second World War began, however, Germany was not a closed society, like North Korea today, or the Soviet Union at the time. Apart from its military bases and concentration camps, it was open to foreign tourists and business visitors, provided that they had not previously antagonised the Nazi regime in some way. The famous Berlin Olympics of 1936 were a good example: thousands of foreign visitors were welcomed to Berlin, and the Government made considerable efforts to impress them while they were in Germany[**]. Nevertheless, the British government's own spies during this period were underfunded and its intelligence services were undermanned. They therefore found it very difficult to penetrate Nazi Germany. Britain's code breakers did not correct the deficiency which its foreign agents had left, failing to penetrate major German cyphers until the start of the Second World War.

Throughout the 1930's, Churchill attempted to obtain accurate information about German rearmament in particular, and about political developments in Germany more generally. His only official position was his membership of the Government's secret Air Defence Research Sub-Committee, from 1935 to 1939, which directed Britain's research into radar. How he found his information relating to other areas of Britain's defence preparations is a fascinating story in itself, and it is important in understanding why he, unlike so many of his countrymen, failed to be reassured by Hitler's protestations of peace. In his account of the Second World War, Churchill himself mentioned various people who helped him in this way, but he was uncharacteristically coy about what information they gave him[49].

Churchill received information from various sources, most connected in some way to British intelligence-gathering efforts in Germany. One was Major Desmond Morton, whom Churchill had met during his brief service in the trenches of the First World War. During the 1920's and 1930's, Morton worked on intelligence matters, and became an expert on the Soviet and German

---

[**] For example, Ribbentrop, Goebbels and Göring threw huge and lavish parties for foreign visitors during the Games. The government removed the "Jews not wanted" signs in Berlin. William Shirer, an American journalist in Germany, got into trouble with the Nazi regime by reporting these and similar actions. In addition, in an attempt to "clean up" Berlin, 800 Gypsies were arrested and kept in a special camp. Nazi officials also exempted foreign visitors from the criminal sanctions of Germany's anti-homosexual laws.

militaries. In 1929, he was appointed head of the Industrial Intelligence Unit of the Committee of Imperial Defence which monitored the worldwide trade in raw materials for weapons and the production of those weapons by European powers. Morton lived near Chartwell, Churchill's country estate, and was a frequent guest there. According to Gilbert, "their most frequent topic for discussion was the balance of power in Europe, for they shared the concern that Germany was aiming at rearmament"[50]. From 1933, Morton provided Churchill with information not available to the public, which Churchill used in his Parliamentary and public speeches. According to Churchill, Morton did this with the approval of the Prime Minister, Ramsay MacDonald[51].

Morton's help was crucial to Churchill's campaign throughout the mid-1930's. For example, he provided statistics about German strength in the air to Churchill before the important Commons debate on 30 July 1933. The Nazi regime clearly horrified him. In March 1934, he wrote to Churchill about a lunch he had had with some Nazi students: "They had been sent over to tell England what the Hitler movement was doing for the youth of Germany. It all sounded very unpleasant ... They make no secret of their belief that within three or four years' time Germany would be at war"[52]. Three days before another debate, on 28 November 1934, Morton supplied Churchill with a crucial, three-page analysis of German air plans[53], whose influence is clearly discernible in the speech which Churchill made in the debate.

Ralph Wigram was a senior civil servant at the Foreign Office before his somewhat mysterious death[††] in 1936 at the age of 46. He first helped Churchill in his campaign throughout the mid-1930's. On 7 April 1935, for example, he came to Chartwell with secret intelligence estimates showing that German aircraft factories were already organised "on an emergency war-time footing". A week later, he sent the Government's own most recent figures, showing that Germany's front line strength in the air had reached 800 aircraft, against Britain's 453[54]. In November 1935, Wigram sent Churchill secret despatches from the British ambassador in Berlin, in which the ambassador forecast Hitler's future territorial demands[55].

Professor Lindemann, the German-born Oxford Professor who became Churchill's favourite scientist, advised him throughout the 1930's on the best method of defence against air attack, and on many other scientific matters. One distinguished historian has described him as "the man who exercised more direct influence over him [Churchill] than any other in his adult life"[56].

[††] It remains unclear whether it was suicide or natural causes.

Churchill was to raise him to the peerage as Lord Cherwell in 1940. Lindemann, a vegetarian, non-smoking teetotaller, would eat only egg whites and stewed apples. He was, therefore, an odd companion for Churchill, the heavy drinking gourmet who smoked enormous Cuban cigars. Churchill nevertheless greatly enjoyed his company. Churchill, his children, and most of his friends and acquaintances knew Lindemann as "the Prof" and saw him as a fixture at Chartwell during the weekends and at Christmas and New Year. He managed to arrange a place for Randolph Churchill at Oxford University's Christ Church College. Churchill would sometimes make him summarise a complicated scientific idea, such as quantum theory, in five minutes, and "the Prof" would manage to shed light on the most baffling subjects.

Churchill and his family may have enjoyed his company, but Lindemann was clearly a divisive figure. Professor Maurice Ashley then Churchill's research assistant, saw Lindemann as "a bore and a toady … there was nothing he was not prepared to do to ingratiate himself with British society leaders of the time"[57]. Henry 'Chips' Channon claimed that "all Oxford loathes" him[58]. Nevertheless, Churchill was always grateful for his insights and support. As well as helping Churchill directly, he conducted his own small propaganda effort urging British preparedness. In August 1934, for example, he wrote to *The Times* (the Establishment's traditional way of communicating with itself), that leaving aerial bombardment in the hands of "gangster governments", i.e. Germany's, was unacceptable. "All decent men and all honourable governments are equally concerned to obtain security against attacks from the air, and to achieve it no effort and no sacrifice is too great"[59].

Other British civil servants and military personnel helped Churchill in this period to appreciate the form and scope of Hitler's rearmament programme. Their numbers increased throughout the 1930's as the Nazi threat became more obvious and war seemed more and more likely. Individuals with business interests in Germany also assisted him. Sir Henry Strakosch, a wealthy businessman and long-time Churchill benefactor, advised him about the financing of the German rearmament effort and the conversion of German industry to military purposes[60]. Wing Commander Charles Torr Anderson, DFC, was director of the RAF Training School. He provided Churchill with information about deficiencies in air force training[61], and in air force equipment more generally, such as the very high number of crashes of British aircraft in 1938[62].

In his history of the Second World War, Churchill also mentions information he received from three French Prime Ministers, Blum, Flandin and Deladier, and other members of the French government[63]. In 1937, for example, the French Air

Minister, Pierre Cot, sent Churchill the latest French Intelligence estimates of *Luftwaffe* strength[64], and Churchill discussed French aviation with the Prime Minister, Leon Blum, in Paris in early 1938[65]. In May 1938, he received from Deladier a detailed, seventeen page document with French estimates of German strength in the air[66]. The long-serving and shrewd Soviet ambassador to Britain, Ivan Maisky, was in contact with Churchill throughout his posting in London, This led at least one observer to conclude (wrongly) that Churchill's ancient and sincere hatred of Communism had been "buried" and that Churchill was Maisky's "bosom friend"[67]. Churchill also names Ian Colville, the Berlin correspondent of the *News Chronicle*, who had useful contacts in the German military. Finally, he mentions visits from various Germans who opposed the Nazi regime[68].

Official Britain was astonishingly tolerant about Churchill's activities. He was, after all, gathering some of the most sensitive information about Britain's defence weaknesses and Germany's strength, and he raised these matters repeatedly, both inside and outside Parliament, and in a number of memoranda to Government. The Prime Minister himself authorised British civil servants to pass some information to Churchill, apparently taking the enlightened view that Churchill's opposition to the Government should be based on facts rather than guesswork.

This official tolerance had its limits, however, as Churchill' son-in-law, Duncan Sandys, found out. Duncan Sandys was an officer in the Territorial Army. He obtained information on London's anti-aircraft defences, which he sent to the Government. Following this, he was summoned to a meeting with the Attorney-General, and later alleged that he had been threatened, in order to get him to reveal the source of that information.

The head of the Committee of Imperial Defence, Sir Maurice Hankey, with whom Churchill had worked when he had been in government, and who was Churchill's neighbour, attempted, without much success, to stop Government responses to Churchill's notes in 1936. In October 1937, Hankey sent Churchill a letter. To Churchill's astonishment, the letter ticked him off at some length for soliciting and accepting contributions from serving officers[69]. The letter evidently made a lasting impression on Churchill. Years later, he described Hankey's friendship in these years as "the caress of a worm"[70]. Hankey, for his part, evidently regarded Churchill and Lindemann as nuisances[71], though this did not prevent a mutually affectionate exchange of letters when Hankey announced his retirement from the Civil Service in 1938[72].

Hitler's diplomatic overtures towards Britain to 1936

Germany's withdrawal from the Geneva Disarmament Conference, her frantic rearmament and her internal policies all created tension in Europe throughout the mid-1930's. Hundreds of thousands of refugees, flooded out of Germany almost from the moment Hitler became Chancellor. Many of them, such as Albert Einstein, were well known. Around 80,000[73] settled in Britain[‡‡] and many thousands more around the Commonwealth. Associations were formed to help the refugees, and funds were raised. According to Richard Overy, "the details [of German persecutions] were not difficult to find since the new government in Germany made little effort to conceal them ... The plight of German Jews was also highlighted from the start, often described in the most lurid terms"[74].

Few may have doubted that the Nazi regime's internal policies were unpleasant. This did not necessarily mean, however, that it posed a threat to peace in Europe, or to the British Empire. Many felt that the threat from Soviet Communism was a greater menace, and, while Germany was relatively weak, Hitler tried to encourage this belief as much as possible. He attempted to allay British suspicions of his foreign policy intentions in 1935 and 1936, through propaganda in Britain. According to a Foreign Office note of November 1935, the German government wanted "English public men, in particular Mr Winston Churchill", to "refer to the social achievements of the German Government, to the reduction of unemployment, for example", rather than concentrating "their attention exclusively on German rearmament". It argued that depicting "the German Government as engaged solely in rearmament shows a lack of balance and sense of proportion"[75].

Hitler entrusted the task of improving Germany's relations with Britain to Joachim von Ribbentrop, who had lived overseas and whose previous job as a champagne salesman had involved travel to other European countries. This, together with a command of English and French, apparently qualified him as an international expert in Nazi circles, as most other Nazi leaders had no international experience, except for war service overseas, and diplomatic expertise was completely lacking. His other characteristics, in particular his stupidity and arrogance, raised concerns about his suitability for the job, even in Nazi Germany. The existing German Foreign Ministry regarded Ribbentrop's diplomatic skills as beneath contempt. Bizarrely, however, this counted in his

---

[‡‡] The British government started to restrict Jewish immigration to its mandate of Palestine in 1939, to placate Arab opinion there.

favour with Hitler, who despised Germany's diplomats. The professional diplomats clearly underestimated the threat to their position when Ribbentrop established a parallel foreign ministry (the *Büro Ribbentrop*) in 1933. They reacted with incredulity when Ribbentrop argued for his appointment to the powerful post of State Secretary in the same year. Ribbentrop was not a good administrator: "he had not the slightest notion of how to run a department of state" was one colleague's withering verdict[76]. The pro-appeasement British ambassador to Berlin, Sir Neville Henderson, told Ribbentrop to his face that his ignorance of British mentality and habits was "amazing"[77]. However, Hitler held him in high esteem as a committed Nazi and even during the war, after Ribbentrop had made repeated misjudgements and his Ministry had dwindled into insignificance, Hitler referred to him as "one of the greatest men we have" and "greater than Bismarck"[78],[§§].

As a diplomat, Ribbentrop had no merits. He had left school at 15, so his German spelling was poor, and his English and French writing was littered with mistakes. The official German foreign minister tried to undermine him, by forbidding subordinates from correcting spelling and grammatical mistakes in his dispatches. Ribbentrop was no more effective in face-to-face negotiation either: he would hector and harangue his hosts, and lecture them at length on the greatness of the Führer. This incompetent amateur was given the task of gaining England's friendship, or at least its neutrality, working against those, like Churchill, who were attempting to influence British opinion in the other direction.

Hitler appointed Ribbentrop as Commissioner for Disarmament Questions in April 1934, absurdly, since Germany had withdrawn from the Disarmament Conference the previous year and Hitler had no intention of disarming anyway. Ribbentrop's subsequent shuttle diplomacy to London, Paris and Rome throughout 1934, however, resulted in some positive headlines for the Nazi regime in the foreign press. His greatest triumph in the mid-1930's was the negotiation of the Anglo-German Naval Agreement in June 1935. His approach to negotiations amazed the British: he simply presented the British Government with an ultimatum upfront. Either Britain would accept the German terms in their entirety or he would walk out. These terms, which Hitler had mentioned

---

[§§] This did not stop Hitler enjoying jokes at Ribbentrop's expense, however: for his fiftieth birthday, some of his colleagues wanted to present him with copies of the treaties he had negotiated, but were embarrassed that almost all of them had already been broken by the Nazis. According to Speer, p.258, when informed of this incident, "Hitler's eyes filled with tears of laughter".

to Sir John Simon, the Foreign Secretary, in March, limited the German Navy to 35 per cent of the British Navy (except in submarines where she could build 100 per cent of England's total). The British negotiators refused, but the British Government changed its mind the next day, and agreed to Germany's demands, though these violated the Treaty of Versailles. It did so without consulting France, though Britain had promised France two months before that it would tolerate no further breaches of Versailles. Hitler described the day when the Agreement was signed as the happiest day of his life[79].

Both Hitler and Ribbentrop seem to have hoped that the Naval Agreement would be the start of an Anglo-German alliance. Churchill, on the other hand, argued against accepting such an alliance, writing to the press baron, Lord Rothermere: "... I think this would be contrary to the whole of our history. We have on all occasions been the friend of the second strongest power in Europe and have never yielded ourselves to the strongest power ... However, I think a reasonable answer to Hitler would be that his plans of an Anglo-German understanding would be most agreeable provided they included France and gave fair consideration to Italy"[80]. He had privately been "disgusted" by Rothermere's "boosting of Hitler" in his newspapers, though he thought that it was from "sincerely pacifist" motives[81]. He wrote to his wife that he thought that Rothermere was hoping to divert Hitler's aggressive urges to other European countries and trying to get Hitler to "destroy us last"[82].

In April 1936, the German ambassador to London died unexpectedly of a heart attack. Three months later, Hitler appointed Ribbentrop to replace him, on the back of Ribbentrop's success in negotiating the Anglo-German Naval Agreement and his handling of the occupation of the Rhineland. This appointment had apparently been suggested by one of Ribbentrop's enemies, who forecast: "After three months in London, Ribbentrop will be done for. They can't stand him there and we will be done with him for good and all". Göring famously said, when Hitler pointed out that Ribbentrop knew various Lords and Ministers, "Yes, but the trouble is, they know Ribbentrop"[83]. Hitler himself, however, said years later that Ribbentrop's main qualification for his appointment had been his "stubbornness". It is only fair to note that *The Times*, Britain's leading pro-appeasement newspaper, welcomed the news of his appointment: "Herr von Ribbentrop will be welcome here both for his own sake, as a man many of us have come to know and respect, and also for the policy of cooperation which he is believed to represent"[84].

Ribbentrop pursued four approaches in influencing English opinion and counteracting Churchill's efforts to persuade his countrymen of the danger they faced. First, he travelled extensively in Britain, meeting what he took for the leaders of English society. He invited those who seemed friendly to Germany - where the regime took care of them, arranging for them to meet leading Nazis, or paying their travelling expenses. Those he met in fact included Churchill, who recalled after the Second World War how the two had met "several times in society"[85]. Secondly, as Reich Commissar for Disarmament, he attempted to ensure that the world thought that Germany wanted a disarmament treaty to be agreed, while ensuring that no such treaty was ever signed. Thirdly, he attempted to assure the British government through semi-official channels of Germany's peaceful intentions.

Ribbentrop's fourth tactic, necessarily secret at the time, was large-scale bribery. As if to show his total lack of understanding of Churchill's motivations, he discussed with Hitler the possibility of bribing him. He also seems to have considered bribing someone on the British Imperial General Staff to reveal war plans. Unsurprisingly, if any such approaches were made, they seem to have failed abjectly[86]. Not everything which Ribbentrop attempted in London proved unsuccessful, and there are some factors in mitigation, such as the influence of his anti-British wife. Nevertheless, his was an appalling appointment, as can be seen by the numerous memoirs produced by his staff at the embassy[***], and by the following ditty which did the rounds in London at the end of his term:

> I think we have had a drop
> Too much of Herr von Ribbentrop
> The name by which he ought to go
> Is Herr von Ribbentrop *de trop*[87].

Despite several invitations, Churchill did not visit Nazi Germany. In his campaign to counter Nazi arguments and influence in Britain, and to convince Britain of the threat from Germany, however, he had to contend with the efforts of a long stream of English notables who visited Germany as *Ehrengäste* (honoured guests), though these visits tailed off somewhat as war loomed in 1939. Though they occasionally had minor official missions of one kind or another, these sympathetic guests should not be confused with those British politicians such as Anthony Eden and Neville Chamberlain, who visited Nazi Germany primarily on official business and who had no sympathy for its government.

British Nazi sympathisers and fellow travellers were a curious mixture of confused youths, has-beens, and people on the fringes of British political life.

[***] No fewer than six of his colleagues produced such memoirs according to Bloch, p.117

Two of the oddest were Unity Mitford and her sister, Diana Mitford, daughters of the first Baron Reesdale and cousins of Churchill's wife. They visited Nazi Germany in 1933 for the Nuremberg rally, and were captivated. Diana had deserted her first husband for Oswald Mosley, the leader of the British Union of Fascists, marrying him at the home of Joseph Goebbels in 1936, with Adolf Hitler as guest of honour. Mosley was an almost total failure in British politics, and his party never managed to win even a single Parliamentary seat. Hitler, however, thought Mosley the only Englishman to be receptive to his ideas, and, in June 1940, he told his Army adjutant that "even Churchill and Bernard Shaw were afraid of him [Mosley]", though he "could never have become a leader of the people"[88]. Diana was interned with her husband until 1943, though Churchill was arguing for her release in November 1941 as she had "now been eighteen months in prison without the slightest vestige of any charge against her, and separated from her husband"[89].

Unity Mitford returned to Germany in 1934 to go to language school in Munich, where she finally succeeded in meeting Hitler. She described him as "the greatest man of all time". Hitler clearly returned the affection, though he later remarked that she and her sister "had the typical English reserve"[90]. She wrote Churchill a letter claiming that most Austrians joyfully welcomed Germany's annexation of their country in 1938, wishing that he would visit Austria "and see how happy the recent events have made a whole people"[91]. At the end of July 1939, she dined treasonously with a German officer, who apparently thought she was related to Churchill. She assured the officer, Major Engel, that Britain was unprepared for war with Germany, and told him that London was defended by only eight anti-aircraft guns[92]. She also said that British anti-Semitism was increasing steadily. She remained in Germany until war broke out, after which she shot herself. She survived and was treated at a clinic in Munich at Hitler's expense, and then was repatriated through Switzerland in January 1940. "I'm glad to be back in England, even if I am not on your side", she reportedly remarked when she returned home. She remained a wholehearted supporter and admirer of the Nazi regime, and, at one stage, she was rumoured to be carrying Hitler's love child. Rather than being interned, like her sister and brother-in-law, Unity was released into the custody of her family[93].

David Lloyd George, the mercurial Prime Minister during the First World War, had been an associate of Churchill since their joint service in the 1906-22 Liberal and Coalition Governments. Lloyd George had argued in the early 1930's that German grievances about the Treaty of Versailles were legitimate. He visited

Chapter 3

Germany in the summer of 1936, ostensibly to study German policy on unemployment and public housing[94], meeting Hitler on 4 and 5 September at his retreat in the Bavarian Alps, Berchtesgaden. With hindsight, this two-day visit was a catastrophe for Lloyd George's reputation and damaging to his country. Colour film has been preserved, showing Lloyd George looking relaxed and obviously enjoying himself in the Bavarian sunshine, laughing and joking with Hitler, who had described him as a bungler in the handwritten notes for *Mein Kampf* a decade earlier[95]. Afterwards, Lloyd George described Hitler as the "greatest living German" and the "George Washington of Germany". In the next few years, however, as German aggression became more obvious, Lloyd George drifted away from the Nazis, though, as late as 1940, he described Hitler to Cecil King as "the greatest figure in European history since Napoleon, and possibly greater even than him". According to Hitler's photographer, Hitler revered the former British Prime Minister in his turn: "… for him, the greatest statesman of them all was Lloyd George"[96].

One statement which Lloyd George made during his visit could, possibly, have cost many thousands of Allied lives. At the very end of the Third Reich, in the Berlin Bunker, Lloyd George's (untrue) assurance that only Germany's collapse had saved the Allies in 1918 seems to have strengthened Hitler's will to fight on to the end, rather than surrender. This could have fortified Hitler's grim determination to fight on in early 1945. For his part, Churchill seems to have regarded Lloyd George's disastrous visit to Hitler as validation of his refusal to pay a similar call. According to Churchill's doctor, Lord Moran, he had been intrigued by the meeting. Moran quotes him as wanting "to find out what happened when Lloyd George saw Hitler" after the Second World War, when both Hitler and Lloyd George had died. He therefore read an account of Lloyd George's visit. "The way Lloyd George had been completely taken in and bamboozled by Hitler interested and pleased [Churchill]. He, Winston, had not fallen into the trap which Hitler had contrived"[97].

Lloyd George was the most distinguished, unofficial British visitor to Nazi Germany. The highest-born, however, was the former King Edward VIII, or the Duke of Windsor. Churchill had known him well for decades, having read the proclamation at his investiture as Prince of Wales in 1911, and had often taken his side during his frequent quarrels with his father, King George V[98]. The Duke, as he had just become, visited Nazi Germany with his wife following his abdication in 1936. The Duke and the Duchess met Himmler, Hess, Göring and Goebbels, and, on the last day of their visit, Hitler at Berchtesgaden for tea. According to Hitler's interpreter, the Duke did not discuss political questions to any great extent with Hitler, but "displayed the social charm for which he is known throughout the world"[99].

In January 1938, according to an American journalist, Vincent Sheean (writing his memoirs in 1943), Churchill, Lloyd George and the Duke and Duchess dined together with a relative of his in the South of France. The Duke praised the Nazis' social achievements to the dinner party, mentioning the impressive baths in coal mines there (a more significant social issue at the time than it sounds today). Sheean wrote: "Mr Churchill did not particularly enjoy praise of the Nazi regime, and although he had been remarkably silent throughout the meal (deferring like a schoolboy to the authority of Mr Lloyd George and the Duke) he now spoke up to say that he had proposed compulsory shower-baths at the pithead long ago"[†††],[100].

The favourable impression which the Duke made during his visit could have had dire consequences for Britain had events gone slightly differently during the Second World War. In 1940, Hitler and his henchmen hatched a bizarre plot to kidnap the Duke of Windsor in Lisbon and put him on the British throne, thereby, they hoped, ensuring peace with Britain. The plot was a miserable failure, however, and Churchill dispatched the Duke to his post as Governor of the Bahamas, far out of reach of the Nazis.

Churchill's second cousin, Lord Londonderry, Secretary of State for Air 1931-35, visited Germany in March 1936, as it was reoccupying the Rhineland. He met "all the leading people", including Hitler. Londonderry wrote to Churchill saying that when Hitler spoke of "the Communistic menace [Londonderry] found [himself] in agreement with a great deal of what he said". He cited France, where the recent formation of the Popular Front government, including Communists, meant that Communism had a foothold in Western Europe for the first time. He encouraged Churchill to "get out of your mind what appears to be a strong anti-German obsession because all these great countries are required in the political settlement of the future"[101].

Henry 'Chips' Channon, the American-born Conservative MP, was invited to watch the Olympic Games in Berlin by Ribbentrop ("looking like a jolly commercial traveller", according to Channon), after the pair spent an evening in a night club. A few weeks later, he talked to someone who "was enthralling about his visit to Germany last year, when he was received by Ribbentrop, Hitler and escorted everywhere by Storm Troopers. Honor [Channon's wife] and I can

---

††† According to Richard Toye, who quotes this anecdote from Sheean in his book, this passage was missing from the British edition of Sheean's memoirs, for unknown reasons.

now hardly wait to go"[102]. Channon clearly had an excellent time there: his diaries contain many gushing references to Berlin's "gaiety", Ribbentrop's "geniality", and the "fantastic" entertainments, though he found the Games themselves "boring"[103].

Thomas More, a former professional soldier and Conservative MP, visited Hitler in 1933, and wrote afterwards: "I can from my own experience say that peace and justice are the key points in his politics. He has a pleasant personality: artistic, visionary ... with a strong tendency towards melancholy and tenderness in his character and a marked affection for children and dogs"[104]. Sir Arthur Bryant, nationalist historian, spent much of the late 1930's urging the appeasement of Hitler[105]. He visited Germany as late as July 1939 at the invitation of the Nazi government, and urged a negotiated peace until he was at risk from internment in 1940[106]. Arnold Toynbee, another historian, met Hitler in 1936 and became convinced that the Nazi dictator posed no threat to Britain, writing to this effect to the new Foreign Secretary, Anthony Eden. He also communicated Hitler's offer to send six German divisions to help defend Britain's Far Eastern colony of Singapore[107].

The influence of this odd group on British public and government opinion, including the extent to which they counteracted Churchill's efforts, is hard to judge. It does not appear, at this distance in time, to have been large. British public opinion was broadly sympathetic, or at least indifferent, to Germany's expansion and rearmament in the early and mid-1930's. This was partly due to horror at the carnage of the First World War, partly because of a shared hatred of Russian Communism, and partly due to a belief that Germany's grievances were legitimate. Many other issues, domestic, foreign and Imperial, competed for the British public's attention in this turbulent decade, and it is only with hindsight that we can see that the German danger was the most serious. These fellow-travellers and their excessively friendly words for Hitler do not seem to have prevented British opinion from changing remarkably quickly from friendliness towards Germany to hostility against it, in the year between the annexation of Austria in 1938 and the occupation of Prague in 1939. Indeed many of them, such as Lloyd George or Ernest Tennant (a friend of Ribbentrop and founder of the Anglo-German Friendship Society), altered their opinions during these years, once the nature of the Nazi regime could no longer be denied. On balance, it seems that the time and money spent on them by the Nazi regime was largely wasted, unlike, perhaps, the far more successful courting of fellow travellers by the Bolshevik regime in Russia. This misguided group of British Nazis and Nazi fellow travellers may, therefore, be regarded as a symptom of the disease which Churchill was attempting to cure, rather than one of its causes.

---

[1] Cabinet Paper CAB/24/259

[2] *Chips – The Diaries of Sir Henry Channon*, Sir Henry Channon, p.26

[3] Thoughts and Adventures, Winston Churchill, p.147-9

[4] *First Blitz*, Neil Hanson, p.15

[5] *The Harold Nicolson Diaries, 1907-1963*, Harold Nicolson, p.163

[6] *The Second World War*, Winston S Churchill, Vol. 1, p.162

[7] *Winston S Churchill Companion, Volume V, Part 2, 1929-1935, The Wilderness Years*, Martin Gilbert, p.1366

[8] *Speaking for Themselves: the personal letters of Winston and Clementine Churchill*, ed. Mary Soames, p.412

[9] *In Command of History*, David Reynolds, p.106

[10] *Inside the Third Reich*, Albert Speer, p.117

[11] E.g. by the Gauleiter of Danzig, see (*Winston S Churchill Companion, Volume V, Part 3, 1936-1939, The Wilderness Years*, Martin Gilbert, p.1101), also *The Second World War*, Winston S Churchill, Vol. 1, p.76

[12] *Winston S Churchill, Companion Volume V, Part 2, 1929-1935, The Wilderness Years*, Martin Gilbert, p.921

[13] *Winston S Churchill, Companion Volume V, Part 2, 1929-1935, The Wilderness Years*, Martin Gilbert, p.854

[14] *Winston S Churchill Companion, Volume V, Part 3, 1936-1939, The Wilderness Years*, Martin Gilbert, p.169, p.197-99, p.251-56 and p.500-02

[15] *Nine Troubled Years*, Lord Templewood, p.24-26

[16] Newspaper reports, 17-18 January 1934

[17] *Hansard*, 6 February 1934

[18] *Hansard*, 7 February 1934

[19] *Hansard*, 14 March 1934

[20] *Hansard*, 14 March 1934

[21] *Hansard*, 28 November 1934

[22] Newspaper reports, 3 November 1934

[23] *Winston S Churchill Companion, Volume V, Part 2, 1929-1935, The Wilderness Years*, Martin Gilbert, p.859

[24] *Winston S Churchill Companion, Volume V, Part 2, 1929-1935, The Wilderness Years*, Martin Gilbert, p.1107

[25] *Strand* magazine, November 1935.

[26] *The Times*, 2 November 1935

[27] *Strand* magazine, January 1936

[28] *Speaking for Themselves: the personal letters of Winston and Clementine Churchill*, ed. Mary Soames, p.391

[29] *Hansard*, 19 March 1935

[30] *Winston S Churchill Companion, Volume V, Part 2, 1929-1935, The Wilderness Years*, Martin Gilbert, p.1129

[31] *Winston S Churchill Companion, Volume V, Part 2, 1929-1935, The Wilderness Years*, Martin Gilbert, p.1160

[32] *The Times*, 23 May 1935

[33] *Hansard*, 22 May 1935

[34] *Hansard*, 11 June and 22 July 1935

[35] *Hansard*, 24 October 1935

[36] *Deutsche Allgemeine Zeitung*, quoted in *The Times*, 26 October 1935

[37] *Hansard*, 24 February 1936

[38] *Hansard*, 10 March 1936

[39] *Hansard*, 20 July 1936

[40] *Hansard*, 16 March 1936

[41] *Speaking for Themselves*, Mary Soames, p.410

[42] *Evening Standard*, 13 March 1936

[43] *Winston S Churchill Companion, Volume V, Part 3, 1936-1939, The Wilderness Years*, Martin Gilbert, p.172

[44] *Hansard*, 26 March 1936

[45] *Nine Troubled Years*, Lord Templewood, p.201

[46] *Hansard*, 31 March 1936

[47] *Hansard*, 5 November 1936

[48] *Winston S Churchill Companion, Volume V, Part 3, 1936-1939, The Wilderness Years*, Martin Gilbert, p.265-294

[49] *The Second World War*, Winston S Churchill, Vol. 1, p.72-73

[50] *Winston Churchill, The Wildnerness Years*, Martin Gilbert, p.16

[51] *The Second World War*, Winston S Churchill, Vol. 1, p.73

[52] *Winston Churchill, The Wildnerness Years*, Martin Gilbert, p.111

[53] *Churchill, A Life*, Martin Gilbert, p.535

[54] *Churchill, A Life*, Martin Gilbert, p.543

[55] *Churchill, A Life*, Martin Gilbert, p.547

[56] *In the footsteps of Churchill*, Richard Holmes, p.178

[57] *As I Knew Him, Churchill in the Wilderness*, talk to the International Churchill Society, Dr Maurice Ashley, CBE

[58] *Chips – The Diaries of Sir Henry Channon*, Sir Henry Channon, p.133

[59] Letter to *The Times*, Professor Lindemann, 2 August 1934.

[60] *Winston S Churchill Companion, Volume V, Part 3, 1936-1939, The Wilderness Years*, Martin Gilbert, p118-122, p.152-156.

[61] *Winston Churchill, The Wildnerness Years*, Martin Gilbert

[62] E.g. *Winston S Churchill Companion, Volume V, Part 3, 1936-1939, The Wilderness Years*, Martin Gilbert, p.901,1550

[63] See also *Winston S Churchill Companion, Volume V, Part 3, 1936-1939, The Wilderness Years*, Martin Gilbert, p.65-66.

[64] *Winston Churchill, The Wildnerness Years*, Martin Gilbert, p.180

[65] *Winston Churchill, The Wildnerness Years*, Martin Gilbert, p.213

[66] *The Second World War*, Winston S Churchill, Vol. 1, p.211

[67] *Winston S Churchill Companion, Volume V, Part 3, 1936-1939, The Wilderness Years*, Martin Gilbert, p.108

[68] *The Second World War*, Winston S Churchill, Vol. 1, p.74

[69] *Winston S Churchill Companion, Volume V, Part 3, 1936-1939, The Wilderness Years*, Martin Gilbert, p.

[70] *Winston Churchill, The Wildnerness Years*, Martin Gilbert, p.184

[71] See, e.g. *Winston S Churchill Companion, Volume V, Part 3, 1936-1939, The Wilderness Years*, Martin Gilbert, p.1066-67

[72] *Winston S Churchill Companion, Volume V, Part 3, 1936-1939, The Wilderness Years*, Martin Gilbert, p.1061-63

[73] *Nineteen Weeks*, Norman Moss, p.45

[74] *The Morbid Age: Britain Between the Wars*, Richard Overy, p.281

[75] *Winston S Churchill Companion, Volume V, Part 2, 1929-1935, The Wilderness Years*, Martin Gilbert, p.1321

[76] *Hitler's Interpreter*, Paul Schmidt, p.254

[77] *Failure of a Mission*, Sir Neville Henderson, p.118

[78] *Inside the Third Reich*, Albert Speer, p.355

[79] *Hitler, 1889-1936, Hubris*, Ian Kershaw, p.558

[80] *Winston S Churchill, Volume V, Companion Part 2, 1929-1935, The Wilderness Years*, Martin Gilbert, p.1169-70

[81] *Speaking for Themselves: the personal letters of Winston and Clementine Churchill*, ed. Mary Soames, p.359

[82] *Speaking for Themselves: the personal letters of Winston and Clementine Churchill*, ed. Mary Soames, p.399

[83] *The Devil's Disciples, Hitler's Inner Circle*, p.412-3.

[84] *The Times*, August 12, 1936

[85] *The Second World War*, Winston S Churchill, Vol. 1, p.200

[86] *Ribbentrop*, Michael Bloch, p.115-16

[87] *Ribbentrop*, Michael Bloch, p.144

[88] *At the Heart of the Reich*, Major Gerhard Engel, p.93

[89] *Churchill War Papers, Vol. III, The Ever-Widening War*, Martin Gilbert, p.1457

[90] *At the Heart of the Reich*, Major Gerhard Engel, p.93

[91] *Winston S Churchill Companion, Volume V, Part 3, 1936-1939, The Wilderness Years*, Martin Gilbert, p.927

[92] *At the Heart of the Reich*, Major Gerhard Engel, p.70

[93] *Hitler's British Girl*. Channel 4. 2007.

[94] *The Times*, 3 September 1936

[95] *Hitler's Letters*, Werner Maser, p.329.

[96] *Hitler was my Friend*, Heinrich Hoffmann, p.89

[97] *Winston Churchill, the Struggle for Survival, 1940-65*, Lord Moran, p.326

[98] *Lloyd George and Churchill, Rivals for Greatness*, Richard Toye, p.323

[99] *Hitler's Interpreter*, Paul Schmidt, p.75

[100] *Between the Thunder and the Sun*, Vincent Sheean, quoted in *Lloyd George and Churchill, Rivals for Greatness*, Richard Toye, p.325

[101] *Winston S Churchill Companion, Volume V, Part 3, 1936-1939, The Wilderness Years*, Martin Gilbert, p.130-131

[102] *Chips – The Diaries of Sir Henry Channon*, Sir Henry Channon, p.69

[103] *Chips – The Diaries of Sir Henry Channon*, Sir Henry Channon, p.105-113

[104] *Der Führer ist fraglos ein grosser Mann*, Berliner Zeitung, 8 April 2000

[105] See, e.g. *Sir Arthur Bryant and national history in twentieth century Britain*, Julia Stapleton

[106] *Eminent Churchillians*, Andrew Roberts, p.303-315

[107] *The Morbid Age: Britain Between the Wars*, Richard Overy, p.271

4

Into the Maelstrom (1937-1939)

In his history of the Second World War, Churchill called the first part of this period "the Loaded Pause": "[the] two whole years ... between Hitler's seizure of the Rhineland in March 1936 and his rape of Austria in March 1938 ... was a longer interval than I expected"[1]. There was no pause in Churchill's activities, loaded or otherwise. He continued pounding away at the inadequacies of Britain's defences throughout the pre-war period, using the same tactics he had used in the mid-1930's. He acquired information from insiders and friendly foreign governments, he made Parliamentary and public speeches, and he contacted senior British government officials and ministers privately. In Parliament, for example, in 1938 alone, Churchill warned about British military weakness in no fewer than eight debates[2]. He made several major speeches as well as numerous minor interventions on the subject during that year.

Hitler himself disingenuously assured the Reichstag and the world in a speech in January 1937 that "the era of the so-called surprises" was past, though, as the British Foreign Secretary told the Cabinet, there was no evidence from his speech, or otherwise, that the "era of collaboration was about to begin"[3]. Years later, Hitler was to describe this time as a period when:

> "the clouds of a more and more menacing war danger began to gather about Germany ... When it could no longer be ignored, especially as a result of the unswervingly inciting speeches of Churchill and his following in England, that in view of the uncertain situation of the parliamentary democrats in those countries there might be a sad change of regime working against peace, I was obliged to make provision for the defence of the Reich on a large scale and as soon as possible"[4].

Chapter 4

Either Hitler's memory was playing tricks on him or he was at pains to present the war to his audience as defensive. As the last chapter argued, Hitler had been making defence "provisions" for years before, and Churchill's speeches reacted to his moves rather than anticipating them. As the British ambassador to Berlin, Sir Neville Henderson, later noted, 1937 "was for Hitler a year of intensive preparation, both diplomatic and military"[5].

The most significant international event of 1937 did not take place in Europe at all. Japan's invasion of China from Manchuria, which she had controlled since 1931, set her, and the rest of East Asia, on the disastrous road which was to lead eventually to Pearl Harbor and Hiroshima. Churchill described the invasion as "lamentable" and "not pleasant to witness nor ... agreeable to endure"[6], but he never regarded Japan as being as great a menace to British interests as he did Hitler's Germany. Events off Spain, too, gave some cause for concern, when British ships were fired upon and sunk by German and Italian submarines.

Churchill began 1937 in an optimistic mood, and indeed it was to be a relatively quiet year in European diplomacy, between the dramas of 1933-36 and the disasters of 1938 and 1939. New Year's Day found him writing to his American friend, Bernard Baruch, describing the situation in Europe as "tense", but judging that the "balance is tilting rather decidedly against Hitler. England and France have now declared what is virtually a 'defensive alliance'. Italy is by no means *'vendue a la Prusse'**. The Eastern group of states with Russia behind them are drawing together much better than I expected"[7].

While Baldwin was in power, Churchill described himself, privately, as "really the leader of the Opposition as the Labour people are so ineffectual, weak and uneducated"[8]. There are numerous anecdotes which illustrate Churchill's hostility to Baldwin. In his memoirs of the Second World War, Churchill was to write that Baldwin "was largely detached from foreign and military affairs. He knew little of Europe, and disliked what he knew"[9]. When one of Baldwin's factories was bombed by the Germans during the Second World War, Churchill couldn't resist a jibe: "very ungrateful of them". In 1941, he said that Baldwin had been one of the two most harmful influences in recent English politics[10]. After the Second World War, Churchill declined to send birthday greetings to Baldwin, saying "I wish Stanley Baldwin no ill, but it would have been much better if he had never lived"[11]. With the wisdom of hindsight, even Baldwin's allies at the time saw clearly how badly suited Baldwin had been to dealing with the rise of Hitler. According to Samuel Hoare, "Whilst he showed his wisdom

---

* French: "Sold to Prussia"

by going slow at home ... his Fabian tactics were only a sign of weakness in Hitler's eyes. The fact was that he never understood foreign countries. Like Sir Edward Grey[†], he spoke no foreign language, and had little or nothing in common with foreigners"[12].

Baldwin's replacement as Prime Minister by Neville Chamberlain in May 1937 did not lead to any significant changes in foreign policy, or to any office for Churchill, though Churchill had seconded Chamberlain for Prime Minister. He was initially somewhat sympathetic to the new Prime Minister, telling Harold Nicolson that, in his view, "never before has a man inherited a more ghastly situation than Neville Chamberlain", placing "the blame wholly on Baldwin"[13]. Whether Neville Chamberlain would have been much of an improvement, however, remained to be seen. "MacDonald was the romanticist, Baldwin the humanist and Chamberlain the analyst", according to Samuel Hoare, but none of them had any use for Churchill. "Although a man of great personal modesty, Chamberlain was not tolerant. His likes and dislikes were even stronger than Baldwin's"[14]. Chamberlain had been hostile to Churchill in the early 1920's, hoping that he would not rejoin the Conservatives in 1924, and deriding his judgement in various letters to his sisters[‡,15]. "With all his genius, Ch.[urchill] has got no judgement and that is why he will never get first place, unless he mends his ways", he had written two decades before[16].

Later in the 1920's, Chamberlain and Churchill had been Cabinet colleagues and had disagreed over various issues such as reforms to the Poor Law and to Business Rates. They had clashed more seriously in the mid-1930's when Chamberlain, as Chancellor, thought that Britain's rearmament was hurting public finances, and accordingly tried to slow the pace. Churchill destroyed Chamberlain's proposed National Defence Contribution (a tax on corporate profits) in a witty and devastating speech to the House on 1 June 1937, leading Chamberlain to refer ironically to Churchill as his "Right Honourable uncle"[17]. They had incompatible temperaments, and their relationship was never smooth. Chamberlain was entirely "obstinate", as he himself admitted, and impervious to Churchill's visionary and far-sighted arguments[18]. Many remember him as one of the "Guilty Men", who betrayed his country's interests over the Munich

---

[†] Sir Edward Grey was a Liberal politician, best known as for his time as Foreign Secretary (1905-16).

[‡] These letters are perhaps the most important sources for Chamberlain's life, since, unlike most senior British politicians, but like Stanley Baldwin, he never wrote memoirs or an autobiography.

Agreement in 1938. He had no illusions about Hitler, however, writing to his sister at this time: "Is it not positively horrible to think that the fate of hundreds of millions depends on one man and he is half mad"[19]. John Colville, then a young Assistant Private Secretary to Churchill, later described Chamberlain as "obstinate and vain"[20]. Current opinion seems more sympathetic, or at least empathetic. Richard Overy, for example, describes Chamberlain's "long struggle between a sincere and passionate longing for peace and the terrible knowledge that war might be unavoidable [which] coloured his whole premiership down to the morning of September 1939 when he found himself declaring it"[21]. Given British and Commonwealth public opinion, it is at least possible that a more active stance against Nazism before 1939 was simply not practical in any case.

However, one should not go too far in this direction: reading through Chamberlain's regular letters to his sisters, which serve in place of his memoirs since he died relatively suddenly after leaving office in 1940, one cannot help noticing that he fell for most of Hitler's propaganda offers and statements in the mid-1930s. For instance, he described Hitler's 1934 speech on disarmament as "conciliatory and pacific"[22]. In addition, and almost uniquely in Britain, he even had a (heavily qualified) good word to say for Ribbentrop. He wrote to his sister: "Ribbentrop is not I believe such a villain as you imagine; the trouble is rather that he is a mere toady of Hitler's, but he knows and understands a good deal of other countries in contrast to the Führer, Göring and Goebbels who are quite ignorant on the subject"[23].

Chamberlain also did not regard Churchill as a "team player"[24]. Indeed, at the end of 1938, over the relatively minor point of how long the House of Commons should be sent into recess, their working relationship broke down almost completely. It seems that Chamberlain was honestly convinced, in the late 1930's, that he could in some way curb Hitler's aggression, without plunging Britain into war. Churchill knew that this would be impossible to achieve, at least without allowing Hitler a free hand in Eastern Europe, which even Chamberlain, in the end, was not prepared to grant. Churchill wrote in 1937 that "we should be very wrong if we were to give Germany a guarantee that so long as she left Britain and France alone in the West, she could do what she liked to the peoples of the centre and south-east of Europe. To give such an assurance at other people's expense would not only be callous and cynical, but it might actually lead to a war the end of which no man can foresee"[25]. Between these two positions on the most important issue facing Britain at the time, compromise was clearly impossible.

Growing German hostility to Britain

Despite the temporarily calmer international scene, 1937 was the year in which Hitler seems to have accepted that his attempts to ally with Britain in return for a free hand in Central Europe had failed. In a conference on 5 November with his Chiefs of Staff and foreign minister, he rambled for four hours on Germany's foreign policy. His speech was recorded by a Colonel Hossbach, whose note has become known as the Hossbach Memorandum. Germany, he claimed, needed living space in Europe, rather than overseas colonies. He was determined to solve this problem by 1943-45 at the latest, after which Germany's armaments would begin to become obsolete. He would try to solve it earlier if Britain and France went to war with Italy. The gist of his speech was that he was prepared to risk war with Britain and France in order to acquire territory (Austria and Czechoslovakia were mentioned by name), but that France's internal situation and Britain's problems in India might mean that those countries would not be able to fight Germany.

What was new in this famous monologue was not Hitler's dislike of France, or his wishes to acquire living space in the East or to swallow Austria or Czechoslovakia, as these views can be traced back at least as far as *Mein Kampf*[26], and perhaps to his teenage monologues directed at Kubizek[27]. Hitler had clearly realised, however, that Britain was likely to be hostile to his attempts to expand Germany eastwards, even though he was willing to forget about the German colonies which the British had taken from Germany after the First World War. Accordingly, in the Memorandum's most famous phrase, he described Britain, with France, as a "hate-inspired antagonist". Hostility to Britain was tempered by a new-found indifference to the Soviet Union, however. In the Memorandum, Hitler seems far less concerned with Russia than his anti-Communist rhetoric of the last fifteen years had been.

Despite the activities mentioned in the last chapter, Ribbentrop's embassy in London had clearly not lived up to the hopes which Hitler had entertained for securing a British alliance. He had been a notably incompetent ambassador, earning the nickname "Herr von Brickendrop" because of his numerous *faux pas*. These had, in fact, started before his appointment. He had complained unofficially to the British Government about its shrewd, sceptical ambassador in Berlin, Sir Eric Phipps. Hitler did Phipps the honour of hating him, referring to him years later as a "complete thug"[28], and Ribbentrop seems to have violated diplomatic norms by showing the Foreign Office a list of Britons whom Hitler would prefer as ambassador. The stream of disasters continued after his move to the London embassy, however. At one stage, for instance, he gave the King a Nazi salute, shouting "*Heil* Hitler". In another incident, he laid a wreath with a

Nazi flag at the Cenotaph. He was just as indiscreet in private. At a dinner with Churchill, Ribbentrop had said that, in a future war with Britain, Germany would have the Italians on its side. (Churchill, referring to Italy's poor record in the First World War, responded with one of his devastating verbal flashes: "That's only fair – we had them last time"[29]).

Churchill himself met Ribbentrop at the German embassy on 21 May 1937. Churchill recorded his version of the meeting in his history of the Second World War a decade later. He said that Ribbentrop maintained that Germany still sought England's friendship and was prepared to guarantee the British Empire in exchange for a free hand in Eastern Europe. Churchill, unsurprisingly, replied that this would not be acceptable to most of British public opinion. Ribbentrop responded that "in that case, war is inevitable. There is no way out. The Führer is resolved…" Churchill warned Ribbentrop not to underestimate England: "She is a curious country, and few foreigners can understand her mind… she will bring the whole world against you, like last time"[30].

Hitler, with his usual misunderstanding of internal British politics, could have seen the abdication of King Edward VIII as an anti-German move by the British government. Ribbentrop may have encouraged Hitler in the view that the King was pro-German and anti-Semitic. There does not seem to be any basis for this idea, any more than there is for the belief that Edward VIII was "deposed by an anti-German conspiracy linked to Jews [and] freemasons"[31]. Whatever his lack of skills in diplomacy, these statements show that Ribbentrop had clearly mastered the one ability necessary to a Minister in a totalitarian dictatorship: telling his boss what he wanted to hear.

According to Churchill, Ribbentrop twice invited him to visit Germany during these years. Churchill said he would have accepted had he been head of government. He did not, however, think it appropriate to do so when he was without office:

> "[A]s a private individual, I should have placed myself and my country at a disadvantage. If I had agreed with the Dictator-host I should have misled him. If I had disagreed he would have been offended and I should have been accused of spoiling Anglo-German relations. Therefore I declined, or rather let lapse, both invitations. All those Englishmen who visited [Hitler] in these years were embarrassed or compromised"[32].

Reflecting on the failure of his embassy after the Second World War, when on trial for his life for war crimes, Ribbentrop said:

> "[Some Britons] regarded a Germany strengthened by National Socialism as a factor which might disturb the traditional British balance of power theory and policy on the Continent.
>
> I am convinced that Adolf Hitler at that time [i.e. in 1936] had no intention at all of undertaking on his part anything against England, but that he had sent me to London with the most ardent wish for really reaching an understanding with England ... I informed the Führer that in my opinion the English ruling class and the English people had a definitely heroic attitude and that this nation was ready at any time to fight to the utmost for the existence of its empire"[33].

Churchill's public campaign against Hitler to February 1938

Between the occupation of the Rhineland in March 1936 and Hitler's "rape" of Austria in March 1938, Churchill continued to warn, officially, semi-officially and unofficially about the great danger which Hitler, in particular, posed to Britain and the Empire, and the necessity of improving the armed forces, in particular the air force, but also the army and the navy. Churchill had a regular column in the *Evening Standard*, and then in the *Daily Telegraph*, of which Hitler's aggression was frequently the subject. His articles were later published as a book, *Step by Step*[§]. He contributed to numerous other British and American newspapers, and his articles were syndicated widely in Britain and around Europe.

Churchill also lobbied the Government, focusing his attention in particular on Anthony Eden, foreign secretary from December 1935 until his resignation in February 1938. Churchill privately opposed Eden's appointment, writing to his wife that "Austen [Chamberlain] would have been far better", and that "the greatness of his [Eden's] office will find him out"[34]. He changed his opinion,

---

[§] On reading *Step by Step* in 1941, Goebbels, Hitler's Minister of Propaganda, wrote in his diary, "If he had come to power in 1933, we would not be where we are today. And I believe he will give us a few more problems yet. But we can and will solve them. Nevertheless, he is not to be taken as lightly as we usually take him".

however, and came to regard Eden as the most courageous member of the government[35]. The Germans on the other hand, according to the British ambassador to Berlin, regarded Eden as a *Deutschenfresser*[36] (roughly a German-eater). A decade later, Churchill was to describe Eden as the "one strong young figure standing against … dismal … tides of draft and surrender"[37]. In one meeting, to "loud and prolonged cheers, Churchill called for "all support to our Foreign Secretary … a message of encouragement and good cheer from the whole of the Conservative Party""[38]. This view of Eden was justified by events: in an *Evening Standard* article, entitled "A Plain Word to the Nazis", Churchill drew attention to the alleged activities of Nazis in Britain, and compared them to those of the Communist International. The German embassy complained to the Foreign Office, to no avail. Eden minuted: "Certainly we can do nothing to stop Mr Churchill, with whose point of view I have personally a considerable measure of sympathy"[39].

At the Leeds Chamber of Commerce in January 1937, Churchill compared Nazism and Communism: "I repudiate both, and will have nothing to do with either. As a matter of fact, they are as like as two peas. Tweedledum and Tweedledee were violently contrasted compared with them … You leave out love and you substitute hate". He gave his usual warning about German rearmament and the need for Britain and the League of Nations to resist the dictators[40]. At the Iron and Steel Federation in February, Churchill abandoned temporarily his usual support for free trade, welcoming the moderate protective tariffs placed on imports of iron and steel, which had caused a revival in the production of those commodities in Britain: "essential in present times in case war should come upon us"[41]. A few days later, Churchill highlighted the threat from the Nazis as a reason to oppose extreme left-wing candidates in the upcoming London County Council election[42].

Churchill broadcast on BBC Radio on the Responsibilities of Empire on 30 April 1937. His was the third contribution in a multi-part series, the first of which had been given by the Prime Minister, Stanley Baldwin. He spoke mostly about the position of the Empire in the Far East, but again referred to the necessity of Britain being armed, and acting in accordance with the Covenant of the League of Nations[43].

Churchill spoke to the Czech Society of Great Britain on 26 April 1937, praising Czechoslovakia for remaining calm despite campaigns against her in neighbouring countries (i.e. Germany). He proposed a strong tribunal linked to the League of Nations[44]. A month later, on May 25, he delivered an address to the New Commonwealth Society, of which he was the President, at the Dorchester hotel. In front of various foreign ambassadors and British dignitaries, he reiterated the case for a strong, well-armed British Empire, and called on Hitler to agree to limit bombing from the air and on all nations to join together to end the Spanish Civil War.

On 15 June 1937, Churchill wrote an essay on Marxism and Communism, which was not published at the time. He observed that:

> "the Nazi and Communist creeds seek to divide the world between them by hurling the democratic nations at one another in ferocious conflict. At home, a secret police continually spies on and threatens the safety and life of every citizen ... Rather than submit to such oppression there is no length to which the people of Britain will not go. Communism and Nazism both worship 'One Man Power' ... a thing odious, pernicious and degrading to man ... We must arm ourselves so that the good cause may not find itself at a hopeless disadvantage against the aggressor"[45].

At the Conservative Party Conference in October, however, Churchill was more complimentary to the British Government's policy. While mentioning the sinking of British ships in the Mediterranean by Italian submarines, and noting that Britain faced "a time of great anxiety, Churchill welcomed the progress being made in rearmament and the increasing sympathy for Britain's position which he saw in America"[46].

In a debate on the third reading of the Defence Loans Bill in March 1937, to a "thinly attended" house, Churchill expressed for the first time some degree of satisfaction with British rearmament. He also warned against complacency, and said that the Government must be prepared to impinge on private trade[47]. He returned to this theme on 11 March, expressing satisfaction at the Government's very large programme of naval construction, which would see 148 warships under construction by the end of 1937[48]. On 22 March, however, he expressed his unhappiness with the speed of expansion of the Royal Air Force, saying that only 31 new squadrons, instead of the 71 planned, had been formed. On 27 July, too, during a debate on civil defence, he was reproaching the Government for complacency, giving his opinion that defence from aerial attack would be possible "within ten years", an estimate which proved mercifully too long. In November, he supported a bill setting out and funding air raid precautions.

In a debate on foreign affairs on 21 December 1937, Churchill, in "sparkling form" according to *The Times*, attacked Mussolini. To "growing cheers", he called on Italy to leave the League of Nations, and implied that Italy had been behind piracy in the Mediterranean[49]. On 5 January, he, Lloyd George and

Anthony Eden had lunch on the French Riviera, where they were holidaying separately. Eden recorded in his diary that "Both [Lloyd George and Churchill were] strongly opposed to any recognition of the Italian conquest of Abyssinia. I told them something of our efforts to ensure co-operation with the U.S. Both seemed impressed with the progress that had been made"[50].

In a letter to Ludwig Noe, a German living in Danzig, in January 1938, Churchill claimed that he was not anti-German so much as opposed to German aggression: "England is seeking nothing from Germany except that the Germans should live in a happy contented manner in their own country without attacking any of their neighbours. As long as Germany does not embark upon a policy of aggression there can be no possible quarrel between our two countries, though of course it is painful to every country to see the cruel persecution of the Jews, Protestants and Catholics and the general suppression of Parliamentary life"[51]. Churchill's estimate of the probability of a peaceful resolution of European problems decreased further the following month. In February 1938, following the dismissal of two German generals, which cemented Hitler's grasp on the German army (the only force in Germany capable of challenging the Nazi regime) Churchill argued to a correspondent that this made war more likely, as the "whole place is in the hands of violent party men"[52].

Great Contemporaries – "Hitler and his Choice"

In 1937, Churchill published a collection of essays, *Great Contemporaries*, on men who had been prominent in British and European politics since about 1890 (and one, added in later editions, on Franklin Roosevelt). He had written the essay on Hitler in 1935 and published it (illustrated with pictures of Hitler) in the November edition of the *Strand* magazine. The essay sought to answer the portentous rhetorical question it asked towards the end: "What manner of man is this grim figure who has performed these superb toils and loosed these frightful evils?" The version published in 1937 was toned down somewhat from the *Strand* article, apparently at the request of the Foreign Office. Such censorship was felt very important when dealing with prickly foreign dictators – Churchill removed the essays on Trotsky and Savinkov in the 1941 edition, apparently to please Stalin. For the 1941 edition he retained his essay on Hitler and did not add to it substantially or seek to change its tone, despite the German invasions of Austria, Czechoslovakia, Poland and the outbreak of the Second World War.

The essay clearly shows that in the mid-1930's, Churchill was to some extent reserving judgement on Hitler, despite all the atrocities, crimes and threats of which Hitler had already been guilty. The first sentence denies that it is possible "to form a just judgement of a public figure who has attained the enormous dimensions of Adolf Hitler until his life work as a whole is before us". Churchill hoped that Hitler would mellow, and turn into "a gentler figure in a happier age".

Reading the essay with the expectation that Churchill's opinion of Hitler in 1935 and 1937 was the same as that in 1942, when the Nazi regime had occupied two dozen countries, torpedoed hundreds of British ships and unleashed terror bombing on British cities, the numerous favourable or neutral comments can seem surprising. Churchill mentions the possibility that Hitler may be regarded as one of the "great figures whose lives have enriched the story of mankind", and that he may "go down in history as the man who restored honour and peace of mind to the great Germanic nation, and brought it back, serene, helpful and strong, to the forefront of the European family circle". He refers to Hitler's "courage, perseverance and vital force", and the "patriotic ardour" of the Nazis. He mentions the impressions of those who had met Hitler, whom he quotes as finding "a highly competent, cool, well-informed functionary with an agreeable manner, a disarming smile, and ... a subtle personal magnetism" [53].

The earlier version of the article, published in the *Strand* magazine in November 1935, contained Churchill's reflections on the Night of the Long Knives in the previous year, when Hitler had executed many of his followers: "The history of the world is full of gruesome, squalid episodes of this kind, from the butcheries of ancient Rome and the numberless massacres which have stained the history of Asia ... But in all its ups and downs mankind has always recoiled in horror from such events; and every record which has pretended to be that of a civilized race has proclaimed its detestation of them. ... It is true that he explained that many more people were murdered – for I call the slaughter of a human being in peace without trial murder – who were not on his list" [54]. Churchill removed this discussion of the Night of the Long Knives from the 1937 book.

However, the essay lists many of Hitler's other crimes, and there can be no doubt that Churchill himself, never having met Hitler, was entirely unaffected by his agreeable manner or his personal magnetism. Churchill describes Hitler's "stern, grim and even frightful methods", and his ruthless treatment of his opponents. He criticises Hitler's treatment of the Jews, though the horrors of *Krystallnacht* and the Final Solution were still in the future in 1937: "The twentieth century has witnessed with surprise, not merely the promulgation of these ferocious doctrines, but their enforcement with brutal vigour ... No past services ... could procure immunity for persons whose only crime was that their parents had brought them into the world". He mentions Hitler's persecution of religion and of the liberals, socialists and Communists, and spends two pages on German rearmament.

Two other chapters in *Great Contemporaries* refer to Hitler. The essay on Hindenburg mentions his appointment of Hitler as Chancellor[55]. Though critical of the decision, Churchill excuses Hindenburg, saying that Hindenburg "had become senile. He did not understand what he was doing". However, the appointment had opened "the floodgates of evil upon German, and perhaps upon European, civilisation". Churchill also referred to Hitler in his chapter on Roosevelt. He rejected any comparison between Roosevelt's economic and social policies and Hitler's[**]:

> "To compare Roosevelt's effort with that of Hitler is to insult not Roosevelt but civilisation. The petty persecutions and old-world assertions of brutality in which the German idol has indulged only show their smallness and squalor compared to the renaissance of creative effort with which the name of Roosevelt will always be associated"[56].

Churchill was gratified to receive approval from Brüning, Germany's Chancellor between 1930 and 1932, who wrote to Churchill that he "admired very much" the essay on Hitler. Brüning denied that significant rearmament had taken place during the years of the Weimar Republic, said that Hindenburg had "detested" Hitler, and that Hitler had drawn together the heads of the Army in 1932, to tell them that he would "re-introduce a big front-line Army". In reply, Churchill regretted that it had not been possible to incorporate Brüning's comments in his text[57].

Interestingly, Goebbels, Hitler's propaganda chief, read the original, 1935, article in March 1945, just as the Red Army was about to capture Berlin. He wrote in his diary:

> "I have had submitted to me an essay by Churchill written about the Führer in 1935. The essay is extraordinarily characteristic of Churchill. He evinces great admiration for the Führer's personality and achievements but forecasts that whether he can retain his fame in history will depend on his further measures (from 1935 onwards)"[58].

[**] Many, for instance the impeccably liberal John Kenneth Galbraith, have noted the similarities between Roosevelt's and Hitler's stimulus programmes and martial rhetoric in this period.

Goebbels had quite a record of reading what he wanted to read into articles and books, and, despite the favourable comments referred to above, the "great admiration" which he detects for Hitler's personality is simply not there.

Anschluss – the 'rape' of Austria

1937 had been a relatively quiet year in European politics. On 10 September, Churchill felt able to cable to Bernard Baruch "on basis no major war this year"[59], though he wrote two weeks later that he was full of foreboding for 1938, which would "see Germany relatively stronger to the British Air Force and French Army than now ... we shall certainly need to be ready by then"[60]. He was right to be concerned: 1938 was to be the most turbulent year in Europe since the end of the First World War, two decades before. Germany began to prepare for war against Britain, with secret Navy and *Luftwaffe* exercises taking place from February 1938 onwards[61]. But she turned her fire first against Europe's smaller nations.

The union of Austria with Germany had been forbidden under the Treaty of Versailles. Hitler had always proclaimed his wish to join the two countries, for instance on the first page of the first chapter of the first volume of *Mein Kampf*, but a premature attempted coup by the Austrian Nazis in 1934 had been blocked by Mussolini. After two months of growing tension, Hitler and Göring sent troops into Austria on 11 March 1938. Churchill had foreseen that this was likely as early as March 1936, when, after the occupation of the Rhineland, he had asked the House of Commons whether Austria would be next[62]. In October 1937, he wrote to his second cousin, Lord Londonderry, that Germany would "devour Austria and Czechoslovakia as a preliminary to making a gigantic middle-Europe bloc"[63].

Churchill had no doubt which way events were going as early as 22 February 1938. The previous day, Lord Halifax had replaced Anthony Eden as Foreign Secretary. Halifax had visited Germany the previous year, and indeed had visited Nazi Germany and said that he "liked all the Nazi leaders, even Goebbels" and described himself as "much impressed, interested and amused by the visit"[64]. He was widely assumed to be much more pro-German than Eden. Churchill regarded Eden as the Government's "only popular figure"[65] and had admired his relatively robust attitude towards Germany and Italy. In a speech to the Constitutional Club said he "deplored very deeply" Eden's resignation and the attendant circumstances[66]. In the *Strand* magazine the following year, he criticised the Conservative Party's treatment of Eden bitterly[67]. Doubtless remembering his opposition to their invasion of Abyssinia, the Italian press rejoiced at Eden's resignation, "his mind poisoned with venom against our country", according to one Italian newspaper[68].

Following the German occupation of Austria, a motion was tabled in the Commons, expressing no confidence in the Government's handling of foreign affairs. Churchill, though a government backbencher, abstained, having spoken in the Commons. After addressing Anglo-Italian relations, he turned to Hitler:

> "This last week has been a good week for dictators – one of the best they ever had. The German dictator has laid his heavy hand upon a small but historic country, and the Italian dictator has carried his vendetta to a victorious conclusion against my right hon. Friend the Member for Warwick and Leamington (Mr. Eden) …
>
> Austria has been laid in thrall, and we do not know whether Czechoslovakia will not suffer a similar attack. Let me remind hon. Members when they talk about Germany's desire for peace, that this small country has declared that it will resist, and if it resists that may well light up the flames of war, the limits of which no man can predict"[69].

When the German army marched against Austria, Ribbentrop, Chamberlain and Churchill were dining at Downing Street, as Ribbentrop was just finishing his tour at the London embassy. Churchill wrote about the occasion years later. According to his account, a message was brought in, and the Prime Minister seemed agitated and wished to bring the evening to an end after dinner. Ribbentrop and his wife, either not noticing the Prime Minister's preoccupation or wishing to keep him busy, continued talking to the Prime Minister and Mrs Chamberlain for half an hour, until the Prime Minister abruptly made his excuses. At one moment, Churchill expressed a wish for continued Anglo-German friendship. "Be careful you don't spoil it", was her charmless reply. Churchill ended his account of this event as follows: "That was the last I saw of Herr von Ribbentrop before he was hanged [at Nuremberg in 1946]"[70].

Following Germany's occupation of Austria, at the House of Commons debate on 14 March, Churchill condemned Hitler's action in his least compromising language yet. His speech was welcomed in the remaining democratic countries of Europe, in particular, France. He clearly foresaw that war with Germany was likely in the near future, though he did not explicitly say so:

> "Europe is confronted with a programme of aggression, nicely calculated and timed, unfolding stage by stage, and there is only one choice open,

not only to us, but to other countries who are unfortunately concerned — either to submit, like Austria, or else to take effective measures while time remains to ward off the danger and, if it cannot be warded off, to cope with it. Resistance will be hard, yet I am persuaded — and the Prime Minister's speech confirms me — that it is to this conclusion of resistance to overweening encroachment that His Majesty's Government will come, and the House of Commons will certainly sustain them in playing a part, a great part, in the effort to preserve the peace of Europe and, if it cannot be pre-served, to preserve the freedom of the nations of Europe. ...

Where are we going to be two years hence, for instance, when the German Army will certainly be much larger than the French Army, and when all the small nations will have fled from Geneva to pay homage to the ever waxing power of the Nazi system, and to make the best terms that they can for themselves? We cannot leave the Austrian question where it is. We await the further statement of the Government, but it is quite clear that we cannot accept as a final solution of the problem of Central Europe the event which occurred on 11th March. The public mind has been concentrated upon the moral and sentimental aspects of the Nazi conquest of Austria, a small country brutally struck down, its Government scattered to the winds, the oppression of the Nazi party doctrine imposed upon a Catholic population and upon the working classes of Austria and of Vienna, the hard ill-usage of persecution which indeed will ensue, which is probably in progress at the moment, of those who, this time last week, were exercising their undoubted political rights, discharging their duties faithfully to their own country...

Churchill clearly realised which countries were now in danger from Hitler's aggression:

"... Rumania has the oil, Yugoslavia has the minerals and raw materials. Both have large armies, both are mainly supplied with munitions from Czechoslovakia. To English ears, the name of Czechoslovakia sounds outlandish. No doubt they are only a small democratic State, no doubt they have an army only two or three times as large as ours, no doubt they have a munitions supply only three times as great as that of Italy, but still they are a virile people, they have their rights, they have their treaty rights, they have a fine of fortresses, and they have a strongly manifested will to live, a will to live freely"[71].

Churchill proposed an alliance of countries bordering Germany with Great Britain and France. He made a similar proposal in more depth in an article in the *Evening Standard* on 18 March, in which he pressed the Government to join France in guaranteeing Czechoslovakia from Nazi aggression. Commenting on this, the Foreign Secretary, Lord Halifax, wrote, in a cabinet memorandum, that such a course might provoke Germany to invade Czechoslovakia in the meantime[72], naively ignoring the probability that Hitler would invade as soon as he could in any case. Chamberlain dismissed the idea in a letter to his sister: "nothing that France or we could do could possibly save Czecho-Slovakia from being overrun by the Germans if they wanted to"[73]. In a debate on 24 March, he referred for the first time to the "rape" of Austria, and again expressed his fear that Czechoslovakia was next in the frame:

> "Under the Covenant of the League, we are not obliged to go to war for Czechoslovakia. But we are obliged not to be neutral, in the sense of being indifferent, if Czechoslovakia is the victim of unprovoked aggression.
>
> Do not let anyone suppose that this is a mere question of hardening one's heart and keeping a stiff upper lip, and standing by to see Czechoslovakia poleaxed or tortured as Austria has been. Something more than that particular kind of fortitude will be needed from us. It is not only Czechoslovakia that will suffer".

Churchill returned to the theme of the "rape of Austria" in a Daily Telegraph article in July 1938. The Nazis had begun their usual persecutions as soon as they arrived in Austria, and Churchill's article drew especial attention to the plight of Vienna's 300,000 Jews[74].

During the late 1930's, Churchill was in intermittent contact with the senior members of the German opposition to Hitler. He often agreed to meet them when they came to England, but his lack of an official position and the difficulties he had with many of the opposition's demands meant that the meetings he held generally ended in frustration for both sides, and nothing came of them, either in the short or the long run. In April 1938, for example, Churchill met the former German Chancellor Brüning, who demanded extra territory for Germany as a price for the overthrow of Hitler, a concession which Churchill was neither willing nor able to make. Churchill also told Brüning that he doubted, correctly, that the Chamberlain government would be able to make any concessions in this area[75].

The turn of Czechoslovakia

Hitler destroyed Czechoslovakia in two stages: in the autumn of 1938, he absorbed the German-speakers in the frontier provinces (the so-called Sudetenland), and in March 1939, he occupied the remainder of what is today the Czech Republic. Tensions began rising in May 1938, when a Czech official shot dead two Sudeten Germans. A full scale crisis ensued, though Hitler seems to have believed that the Germans would not be ready for war for another six months, and backed down, temporarily as it turned out. During that momentous May, Churchill met Konrad Henlein, the leader of the Sudeten Nazis, at the Foreign Office's suggestion. They discussed a settlement which would give the Germans in Czechoslovakia a considerable measure of autonomy, while keeping them in Czechoslovakia[76], and the two men remained optimistic that a peaceful outcome to preserve Czechoslovakia could be achieved as late as July[77]. In fact, his diplomatic efforts could have been counter-productive: a correspondent wrote to Churchill, warning him that the Germans were misusing his appeals for compromise, claiming to have his support against the Czechs[78].

That summer, Churchill thought the situation in Europe so serious that he cancelled a lucrative lecture tour of the United States which had been planned for the autumn. He wrote to the Foreign Secretary proposing two moves to deter "violent action by Hitler", but stopping short of a full guarantee: a joint declaration by Britain, France and Russia, and a partial mobilisation of the Fleet[††]. Lord Halifax sent a brush-off reply, but this does not seem to have deterred Churchill. According to Sir Samuel Hoare's diary entry for 11 September 1938, after a Cabinet meeting:

> "we found Churchill waiting in the hall. He had come to demand an immediate ultimatum to Hitler. He was convinced it was our last chance of stopping a landslide, and according to his information, which was directly contrary to our own, both the French and the Russians were ready for an offensive against Germany".

[††] The Fleet was, in fact, mobilised by the First Lord of the Admiralty, Alfred Duff Cooper, who was to resign shortly afterwards in protest at the Munich agreement. Churchill congratulated him on the mobilisation in the anonymous Londoner's Diary column in the Evening Standard on 28 September 1938.

Chapter 4

Churchill met the Foreign Secretary and the Prime Minister on the same day, where he conveyed the same message[79]. In his regular column in the *Telegraph*[‡‡] on 15 September 1938, he wrote that the Nazis could not be reasoned with, and proposed a joint declaration with France and Russia of action if Czechoslovakia were attacked[80].

Unlike his attempt to put pressure on the British Cabinet, Churchill's meeting with Ewald von Kleist Schmenzin in August 1938, who had already been imprisoned by the Nazis, at least produced a positive result. Churchill subsequently wrote to him, drawing attention to the Foreign Secretary's speech in the Commons which said Britain and France would probably act together in the event of a German attack on Czechoslovakia, without giving an explicit guarantee[81]. Once the world was assured of a peaceful tolerant and law-abiding government (i.e. a non-Nazi government) in Germany, questions between the two countries could be resolved. Churchill wrote a letter to Wilhelm Canaris, the anti-Nazi head of the intelligence organisation - the Abwehr - which stressed Britain's opposition to a German attack on Czechoslovakia, and advised Germany to think carefully before she started a European war. He concluded by looking forward to Anglo-German friendship in the future and "the true reunion of our countries on the basis of the greatness and freedom of both"[82]. This letter does not seem to have had much effect in causing Hitler's downfall, though, unfortunately, it sealed Kleist's fate when he came under suspicion in 1944. It was found in his desk by the Gestapo and he was arrested and later executed.

When Hitler proposed a conference in Munich with Britain, France and Italy, and Chamberlain dramatically accepted, during the course of a speech in the House of Commons, Churchill shook Chamberlain's hand publicly, and wished him "God speed". He was less than happy with the result, however. According to Oliver Harvey's diary, Churchill described Chamberlain's visit to Munich to broker the surrender of the German-speaking parts of Czechoslovakia to Hitler as "the stupidest thing that has ever been done"[83]. When Chamberlain returned after the Munich Agreement, the House of Commons held a marathon, four-day debate, during which the Opposition parties and a few Conservatives attacked Chamberlain's handling of the issue. In one of his best and most memorable speeches, Churchill summed up the results of the Munich agreement:

[‡‡] The *Evening Standard* had ended Churchill's column earlier in the year, because their editorial stance differed from the opinions he was expressing. The *Daily Telegraph* had taken him on almost immediately.

"If I do not begin this afternoon by paying the usual, and indeed almost invariable, tributes to the Prime Minister for his handling of this crisis, it is certainly not from any lack of personal regard. ...

I will, therefore, begin by saying the most unpopular and most unwelcome thing. I will begin by saying what everybody would like to ignore or forget but which must nevertheless be stated, namely, that we have sustained a total and unmitigated defeat, and that France has suffered even more than we have...

£1 was demanded at the pistol's point. When it was given, £2 were demanded at the pistol's point. Finally, the dictator consented to take £1 17s. 6d. and the rest in promises of good will for the future.

...They were varying forces, those of a military character which declared that Germany was not ready to undertake a world war, and all that mass of moderate opinion and popular opinion which dreaded war, and some elements of which still have some influence upon the German Government. Such action would have given strength to all that intense desire for peace which the helpless German masses share with their British and French fellow men, and which, as we have been reminded, found a passionate and rarely permitted vent in the joyous manifestations with which the Prime Minister was acclaimed in Munich...

All is over. Silent, mournful, abandoned, broken, Czechoslovakia recedes into the darkness. She has suffered in every respect by her association with the Western democracies and with the League of Nations, of which she has always been an obedient servant. She has suffered in particular from her association with France, under whose guidance and policy she has been actuated for so long...

I venture to think that in the future the Czechoslovak State cannot be maintained as an independent entity. You will find that in a period of time which may be measured by years, but may be measured only by months, Czechoslovakia will be engulfed in the Nazi regime..."[84].

Chapter 4

The *Observer* described Churchill's speech as "both bitter and eloquent"[85]. Nevertheless, it was to cause him trouble in his constituency, where a move was soon afoot to deselect him. The Unionist Association said that it felt "increasingly uneasy at Mr Churchill's growing hostility to the Government"[86]. As Churchill's former colleague Arthur Balfour said in 1909, "I would no more consult [the Conservative Party] on a matter of high policy than I would my valet"[87]. The move was ultimately defeated, though it caused him some anxiety.

Churchill would always believe that Munich had been a disastrous mistake. He wrote to Paul Reynaud in France after the conclusion of the Munich debate that "the magnitude of the disaster [in Munich] leaves me groping in the dark. Not since the loss of the American colonies has England suffered so deep an injury. France is back to … 1870"[88]. In a broadcast to the United States in October, he listed all the advances which the dictator states had made, and said that a resolute guarantee by Britain and France, allied to moderate elements in Germany, would have prevented the crisis with Czechoslovakia[89]. A decade later, in his history of the Second World War, he allowed himself some speculation as to what might have happened had Britain and France fought Germany in 1938, rather than 1939. He admits that Britain would have had to do without many of the fighter aircraft and much of the radar equipment that enabled it to prevail (barely) in the summer of 1940. It would also, most likely, have had to fight without the support of the Dominions, though Churchill does not mention this. Nevertheless, he argued that Britain was damaged by the year's delay, as British and French military expenditure was far lower in 1938-9 than Germany's, and the Germans would have had fewer tanks in 1938. He makes the highly questionable statement that "the German armies were not capable of defeating the French in 1938 or 1939"[90]. In the nature of counter-factuals, we will never know whether he was correct.

Churchill did not confine himself to carping from the sidelines. Though this was clearly a gloomy time for him, he tried to offer positive suggestions. During the Munich negotiations, he twice issued press releases in which he referred to the possibility of joint action between Britain, France and Russia, the "one good chance of preserving peace"[91]. He also made a dramatic visit to France, meeting opponents of appeasement, in an attempt to rally support. This personal initiative won him no thanks in official Britain, however. Maurice Hankey described this visit as "most improper"[92].

German propaganda launches its counter-offensive against Churchill

By the end of 1937, Churchill's consistent campaign against Hitler and the Nazi regime had begun to provoke the German Government into replying, though its responses were slow at first. Churchill's hostile articles in the British and foreign press were clearly being read and taken seriously by the Nazis, and he was regarded as one of their most effective and influential foreign critics. On 6 September 1937, Hitler arrived in Nuremberg for the annual Nazi rally. The chief of the Reich Press Organisation, Dr Otto Dietrich, told foreign journalists (without irony) that Nazism could not be grasped intellectually. He went on: "When, a few days ago, Mr Winston Churchill began his articles in the newspapers of numerous countries with the phrase 'National-Socialist Germany is an enigma to the world', he might have found the explanation of the enigma at Nuremberg if he were as full for the fanatical desire for truth and knowledge as he is of aggressive feeling against us"[93]. For a Nazi to criticise someone else for their "aggressive feeling" is richly ironic.

Germany expelled its 20,000 Polish Jews in the autumn of 1938. This atrocity led a 17-year-old Jew, Herschel Grynsban, to murder the German consul, Ernst vom Rath, in Paris. Apparently to inflame its domestic audience, the German press accused Churchill, without evidence, of being complicit in the murder. Though it had done much to highlight German persecutions in the early years of the Hitler regime, *The Times* had advocated British appeasement of Germany in the mid-1930's and commented, in an editorial entitled "A Black Day for Germany":

> "... A semi-official German newspaper, the *Angriff*, devoting itself to the provocation of the disorders which have since occurred, published in a prominent position a monstrous attack on Mr Churchill under the headings: 'The work of the instigator-international. A straight line from Churchill to Grynsban.' 'It is no coincidence,' the article began. Grynsban 'took the same line as is pursued by Messrs. Churchill, Eden, Duff Cooper and their associates'. ... This attempt to implicate British politicians in the murder of Herr Vom Rath is not the work of an obscure sheet, but of a journal controlled by the Minister of Propaganda, Dr Goebbels. It is much worse than merely ludicrous. It is wholly intolerable. It demands official notice, and should receive it without delay"[94].

Hitler himself counterattacked, mentioning Churchill by name. As Churchill noted in his subsequent press release, it is very unusual for a head of state to attack a foreign, backbench politician in a public speech, but Hitler was to attack

Chapter 4

Churchill in no fewer than three speeches that autumn. In Saarbrücken on 9 October 1938, Hitler made a survey of the foreign situation, in the course of which he said:

> "Opposite us are statesmen who - that, we must believe of them - also want peace. However, they govern in countries whose internal construction makes it possible for them at any time to be supplanted by others who do not aim at peace. These others are there in England, it merely is necessary that instead of Chamberlain, a Duff Cooper or an Eden or a Churchill gain power. We know that the aim of these men would be to start a war. They do not attempt to hide it. That obligates us to be on the watch to think of the protection of the Reich.
>
> …
>
> I have, therefore, decided to continue construction of our fortifications in the west with increased energy as already indicated in my Nuremberg speech. ... That will be done for the protection of the Reich".

In the second speech, at Weimar on 6 November 1938, Hitler attacked both disarmament and democracy in an unusually forthright way, before devoting several hundred words to demolishing Churchill's arguments:

> "It is very fine to talk of international peace and international disarmament, but I am mistrustful of a disarmament in weapons of war so long as there has been no disarmament of the spirit.
>
> ....
>
> Mr. Churchill had stated his view publicly, namely that the present regime in Germany must be overthrown with the aid of forces within Germany which would gladly co-operate. If Mr. Churchill would but spend less of his time in émigré circles, that is with traitors to their country maintained and paid abroad, and more of his time with Germans, then he would realize the utter madness and stupidity of his idle chatter. I can only assure this gentleman, who would appear to be living in the moon, of one thing: there is no such force in Germany which could turn against the present regime.
>
> I will not refuse to grant to this gentleman that, naturally we have no right to demand that the other peoples should alter their constitutions.

But, as leader of the Germans, I have the duty to consider this constitution of theirs and the possibilities which result from it. When a few days ago in the House of Commons the Deputy Leader of the Opposition declared that he made no secret of the fact that he would welcome the destruction of Germany and Italy, then, of course, I cannot prevent it if perhaps this man on the basis of the democratic rules of the game should in fact with his party in one or two years become the Government.

But of one thing I can assure him: I can prevent him from destroying Germany. And just as I am convinced that the German people will take care that the plans of these gentlemen so far as Germany is concerned will never succeed, so in precisely the same way Fascist Italy will, I know, take care for itself! …

So long as the others only talk of disarmament, while they infamously continue to incite to war, we must presume that they do but wish to steal from us our arms, in order once more to prepare for us the fate of 1918-19. And in that case, my only answer to Mr. Churchill and his like must be: That happens once only and it will not be repeated!"

Churchill issued a statement expressing surprise that a Head of State would attack a British MP without office. He denied that he, Eden, Duff Cooper or others had ever dreamed of an attack against Germany. He continued:

"I have always said that if Great Britain were defeated in war, I hope we should find a Hitler to lead us back to our rightful position. I am sorry, however, that he has not been mellowed … The whole world would rejoice to see the Hitler of peace and tolerance….

He is mistaken in thinking that I do not see Germans of the Nazi regime when they come to this country … Let this great man search his own heart and conscience before he accuses anyone else of being a war-monger.

…

If Herr Hitler's eye should fall upon these words, I trust he will accept them in the spirit of candour in which they are uttered"[95].

Chapter 4

In the third speech, on 8 November 1938 in his annual address to the survivors of the 1923 Beer Hall *Putsch*, Hitler returned to the attack:

> "What precisely is democracy? Has the good Lord handed over the keys to democracy to Mr Churchill or Mr Duff Cooper? ...Today I have the complete approval of the German people – let Mr Churchill doubt this if he pleases. I did not eliminate two democracies this year – rather I destroyed two dictatorships ...
>
> The gentlemen of the British Parliament are no doubt at home in the British Empire but not in Central Europe ...
>
> ... I differ from Messrs Churchill and Eden who are the advocates of the whole world. I am only the representative of my people and I do here what I think necessary. When Mr Churchill says to me, "How can the Head of State cross swords with a British Member of Parliament", I answer him, "Mr Churchill, don't you feel honoured? You can see from the fact that in Germany even the Head of State is not afraid to cross swords with a British Member of Parliament the high esteem in which British Members of Parliament are held.
>
> ...
>
> Mr Churchill and these gentlemen are deputies of the English people and I am a deputy of the German people. The difference is only that Mr Churchill received but a fraction of British votes and I represent the whole German people..."

In January 1939, Hitler again attacked Churchill, both indirectly and by name, in a long speech to the Reichstag to celebrate the sixth anniversary of his appointment as Chancellor. The main theme of the speech was Germany's need for more territory, and he pressed for the return of Germany's colonies. He said that he wanted a long peace between Britain and Germany, but he took issue with many prominent Englishmen and Americans (Churchill being half-English and half-American) who had criticized Germany in recent months. In some democracies, it appeared to be one of the prerogatives of political life to attack totalitarian states. However, when the totalitarian states defended themselves against such "agitators" as Mr Duff Cooper, Mr Eden, Mr Churchill, Mr Ickes[§§]

[§§] Harold Ickes was the US Secretary of the Interior between 1933 and 1946.

and the rest, their deed was announced as an encroachment on the rights of the democracies. Given the political structure of the democracies, such men could be in government at any time, and therefore the German people should know the truth about them in good time. The German people had nothing against Britain, France or America, but those nations were being stirred against Germany. In the future, German propaganda would reply to all of their attacks. With truly breathtaking effrontery, Hitler said sarcastically that the democratic world oozed sympathy with the Jewish people, but would do nothing to help them – ignoring the fact that he and his government were the sole cause of their troubles.

A few days later, Churchill spoke in his constituency. He rose above Hitler's gibes of a few days previously, welcoming Hitler's statement that he expected a long period of peace. "It is certainly within his power to bestow that inestimable blessing upon mankind… What we want to see are not only words which indicate a desire for peace"[96]. In fact, Hitler was already planning his next aggression, against the rump of Czechoslovakia. He had pointedly failed to guarantee the independence of the rest of that country, despite promising to do so at Munich. On 14 March, Churchill addressed his constituency association. He predicted the end of Czechoslovakia, which indeed was to take place the next day: "I pointed out that Munich sealed the ruin of Czechoslovakia… The Czechoslovak Republic is being broken up before our eyes. Their gold is stolen by the Nazis. The Nazi system is to blot out every form of internal freedom… Disturbances have been fomented in Slovakia, I have no doubt at Herr Hitler's instigation … They are being completely absorbed, and not until the Nazi power has passed away from Europe will they emerge again in freedom"[97].

It was not only Hitler who was troubled by Churchill's attacks on the Nazi regime in Germany. The British ambassador to Berlin, Sir Neville Henderson, quoted Göring as asking: "What guarantee had Germany that Mr Chamberlain would remain in office and that he would not be succeeded by 'a Mr Churchill or a Mr Eden' Government? That was Germany's main preoccupation"[98]. Hitler himself seems to have regarded a war with England as more and more likely after Munich, and even, intermittently, to have relished the prospect. "I don't give a damn if it takes ten years, I am going to rub them down", Walter Ansel has him saying, though arguing against Admiral Raeder in 1939, Hitler thought that his diplomacy could reduce the chance of such a war to only one percent[99].

The Fascist General Franco's defeat of Republican Spain in early 1939 increased Britain's insecurity, and Hitler's occupation of the remainder of the Czech lands*** destroyed most of the remaining goodwill towards his regime in Britain. Sir Neville Henderson wrote later that "on those Ides of March, [Hitler] defiantly hoisted the skull and crossbones of the pirate and appeared under his true colours as an unprincipled menace to European peace and liberty"[100]. The previously pro-Appeasement "Chips" Channon wrote in his diary: "No balder, bolder departure from the written bond has ever been committed in history … I can never forgive him … The country is stirred to its depth and rage against Germany is rising"[101].

Following the occupation of Prague, a revolution occurred in British foreign policy. The nature of the Nazi regime and of Hitler's insatiable desire for conquest dawned even on Neville Chamberlain. "In those conditions [i.e. in the Commons after Hitler's occupation of Prague] one could only make the briefest and most objective statement but as soon as I had time to think I saw that it was impossible to deal with Hitler, after he had thrown all his own assurances to the winds"[102], Chamberlain wrote to his sister. In a speech in Birmingham on 17 March 1939, he signalled unmistakably that Britain would now oppose future Nazi aggression, even at the risk of war: "No greater mistake could be made than to suppose that, because it believes war to be a senseless and cruel thing, this nation has so lost its fibre that it will not take part to the utmost of its power in resisting such a challenge if it ever were made". He had clearly relished the Birmingham speech, writing to his sister that it "gave me a great opportunity to speak to the world"[103]. Churchill wrote to Chamberlain guessing that Hitler "must be under intense strain at this moment … With such a man anything is possible. The temptation to make a surprise attack on London, or on the aircraft factories … would be removed if it was known that all was ready"[104]. Accordingly, he proposed manning the anti-aircraft defences.

The Cabinet Minutes of the next day record Chamberlain as saying that "no reliance could be placed on any of the assurances given by the Nazi leaders[105]. Chamberlain issued a British guarantee to Poland on 31 March, protecting its "independence", though not its specific boundaries. This guarantee infuriated Hitler, who replied in a ranting speech against England and British statesmen (though this time he did not mention Churchill by name) at Wilhelmshaven the next day, distorting history and current circumstances and incidentally threatening to tear up the Anglo-German naval agreement of 1935. Further British guarantees were issued to Romania and Greece the following month. The guarantees failed in their purpose: they did not prevent war breaking out

---

*** Germany did not directly occupy Slovakia, which instead became a German protectorate.

some months later, but they were a crucial warning to Hitler, and equally important, perhaps, in reconciling much of British public opinion to the probability of war.

These momentous events were of huge importance to Churchill, as he was now confronting only his country's enemies, rather than his country's government as well[ttt]. He himself had no doubt about their significance: as he said in Parliament in April, "For the first time Great Britain has taken the initiative against the Nazi aggression"[106]. The clamour for Churchill's inclusion in the Government grew greater with each passing week. "What Price Winston?" posters appeared all over London, and in the first week of July 1939 most national newspapers contained editorials urging Chamberlain to bring Churchill into the Cabinet. Concerning this possibility, on 8 July 1939, a Lieutenant-Colonel Gray wrote to Lord Halifax of a conversation with the member of the German opposition, Count Schwerin:

> "I asked him what he thought the effect would be if Winston were included in the Cabinet. He said – there would be a tremendous outcry in Germany: but Hitler thinks that Churchill is the only dangerous Englishman, and it might perhaps do good, because it might perhaps *make* him realize that Great Britain really intends to fight if there is any further aggression"[107].

A week later, Chamberlain wrote to his sister that "There are more ways of killing a cat than strangling it and if I refuse to take Winston into the Cabinet to please those who say it would frighten Hitler it doesn't follow that the idea of frightening Hitler, or rather of convincing him that it would not pay him to use force, need be abandoned"[108]. Chamberlain's irritation at Churchill is also evident from a letter he wrote to his sister at this time, telling her that:

> "…it doesn't make things easier to be badgered for a meeting of Parliament by the two Oppositions and Winston who is the worst of the lot, telephoning almost every hour of the day. I suppose he has prepared a terrific oration which he wants to let off. I know there are a lot of reckless people who would plunge us into war at once but one must resist them until it becomes really inevitable"[109].

[ttt] Though he and Chamberlain were to clash again in Parliament over the question of whether Britain could have deterred Germany's annexation of the Sudetenland in August 1939.

Chapter 4

The two Fascist invasions of the spring of 1939 (Italy occupied Albania in April and Germany annexed a small sliver of territory in Lithuania, called Memeland) simply made the British government and public more aware that war was likely, and sooner rather than later. Hitler later claimed that Chamberlain had told him through a third party when he took possession of Memeland "that he understood very well that this step had to be taken, even though he could not approve of it publicly" because "at this period [he] was being fiercely attacked by the Churchill clan"[110].

Poland and war

On 22 December 1938, Churchill wrote to his wife that "Everything goes to show that our interests are declining throughout Europe, and that Hitler will be on the move again in February or March, probably against Poland ... It is part of the price we pay for Munich"[111]. He was wrong: Hitler did indeed move in March, but against Czechoslovakia again, rather than Poland. Poland's turn would come later in the year. Churchill spent much of January out of the country on his last pre-war vacation in southern Europe. He met the Duke and Duchess of Windsor (the former King Edward VII and Wallis Simpson) in their villa at Antibes, after dinner one evening "declaring flatly that the nation stood in the gravest danger of its long history"[112]. He continued to warn about Nazi aggression through the spring and summer of 1939. In Parliament on 5 April, he denied again that he was proposing the encirclement of Germany:

> "If Herr Hitler fears that he will be overrun by Russia, that he will be fallen upon by Poland, that he will be attacked by Belgium, Holland or Switzerland, that he will be browbeaten by Denmark, he has only to declare his anxiety open to the world in order to receive the most solemn international guarantees. We seek no security for ourselves that we do not desire Germany to enjoy as well".

He poured his usual scorn on Hitler and his regime:

> "The men at the head of Germany are not restrained by any scruples. They have risen to their power by violence, cruelty and murder. Herr Hitler plumes himself particularly upon the lightning character of the blows which he strikes. These are men in the path of whose ambition it is very dangerous to stand, and we have taken up our stand right in their path" [113].

The Italian attack on Greece prompted Churchill to make another long speech, ending with a warning that "some new stroke" was about to fall[114]. In a debate on conscription, Churchill recommended that Britain ignore Hitler's words in a speech he was due to give the next day:

> "If Herr Hitler utters words of menace, that will not make the situation any worse than it appears on the actual facts. If he utters reassurances I, for one, shall not believe them until they are confirmed by deeds. If he utters mere abuse, why should we pay any attention to that? We pay too much attention to the speeches of dictators and give too little study to the marshalling of their forces and the strength of their authority, which is continually going on"[115].

In April, President Roosevelt appealed to Hitler to guarantee 35 named countries against German aggression. Hitler answered Roosevelt, in what some consider his best speech on foreign policy. He expressed his admiration for the British Empire at some length, and incidentally formally tore up two international treaties: the Anglo-German Naval Agreement and Germany's Non-Aggression Pact with Poland. In a broadcast to the United States on 28 April 1939, Churchill said that:

> "The character and quality of Herr Hitler's speech shows a certain improvement ... Any improvement in Herr Hitler's declaration is ... due to the revival in Europe of a system of mutual aid against aggression, and to the active formation of a peace bloc of nations ... Finally, it is due to the consolidation of France and to the rearmament of Britain... The denunciation of the Anglo-German Naval Agreement need excite no regrets or alarm. The British Navy cannot be overtaken by any efforts which Nazi Germany may make... The denunciation of the Non-Aggression Pact with Poland ... must be regarded as the most serious feature of the speech and as a new cause for anxiety".

Churchill saw clearly how Hitler had sought to succeed during the 1930's.

> "The Hitler method has always been to take one step at a time and, while reassuring others, to get one country shut up with him alone. There are many passages in Herr Hitler's speech which would seem designed to induce Great Britain to abandon her precautions ... They will not have any effect upon the now thoroughly awakened British population ..."

He also analysed the roots of Hitler's grievances, which he saw lay in the end of the First World War.

> "It is quite natural that Herr Hitler should not like the way in which the Great War ended. He would rather it had ended in a German victory … In the German view, which Herr Hitler shares, a peaceful Germany and Austria were fallen upon in 1914 by a gang of wicked designing nations … Germany has sought … to forge a hideous apparatus of slaughter to hold the world to ransom or subject it to servitude"[116].

One of Churchill's friends said of the impact of this speech: "I hear that your name is on every tongue in England and America"[117].

Churchill's time in May and June was taken up mainly with his literary efforts (he was attempting to finish his *History of the English-Speaking Peoples*), though he still found time to advocate an Anglo-Russian alliance in Parliament[118], and to oppose handing over £6 million of Czech gold reserves kept at the Bank of England to Nazi Germany "which only wishes to use it, and is only using it, as it does all its foreign exchange, for the purpose of increasing its armaments"[119]. He also received the German opposition leader von Goerdeler in May, though as ever, nothing concrete came of their discussions. At the end of June, he spoke to businessmen in the City about the recently passed Conscription Act. He advocated an alliance with Russia. By July, however, it was obvious that Hitler would move next against Poland over the Danzig Corridor, which was a piece of Polish and international territory which split Germany in two. As Churchill wrote to the press baron Lord Rothermere on 19 July, "Evidently a great 'crunch' is coming, and all preparations in Germany are moving forward ceaselessly to some date in August"[120].

Churchill went to France in August, where he was conducted around the French Army's defences (the formidable but infamous Maginot Line) by General Georges. He had always admired the French Army. During the First World War, according to Margot Asquith, "Mr Churchill asked [Lord Kitchener] which he would rather have under his command, English, French or German troops: Kitchener said that after the English, he thought the Germans were the best soldiers: Winston said he thought the French were superior"[121]. As a result of his visit, Churchill went home and wrote a prescient memorandum, drawing attention to the possibility of Germany invading France through Belgium. Churchill argued that the likeliest date for Hitler to strike would be "the first fortnight of September [1939]", though Churchill thought he would attack in the west and then deal with Poland "before the mud period" of the late autumn[122]. He also wrote a memorandum to the Secretary of State for Air, on the speculative subject of atomic weapons. The memo had the unfortunate forecast that a nuclear explosion "might be as good as our present day explosives, but it is unlikely to produce anything very much more dangerous"[123]. The Molotov-Ribbentrop Pact, which was publicly a non-aggression pact between Germany and Russia, was announced on 23 August 1939. It secretly provided for Nazi-Soviet occupation of Poland and the Baltic States. Even the public pact, however, obviously meant war over Poland would come soon. Churchill had, in fact, foreseen the possibility that "if Germany were driven back on Russian support, Poland in the end would be crushed between them" fifteen years before, and told the Polish ambassador of his forebodings[124]. However, the Poles had not been able to avoid the danger.

On 1 September 1939, after all the crises and disasters of the inter-war years, Germany invaded Poland. Churchill apparently knew before the British War Office did[125]. Two days later, Britain declared war on Germany. Hitler had been hoping against hope that Britain would pull back from the brink, but was "more disappointed than surprised" when the declaration of war came[126], though another source has him saying, "Now my whole work falls to pieces. My book [i.e. *Mein Kampf*] has been written in vain"[127]. Churchill, whose real work was just beginning, reacted with characteristic defiance. His detective, W.H. Thompson, later recalled Churchill's reaction:

> "Within a few minutes [of the declaration of war], the air raid sirens sounded over London. Churchill went outside and stood staring into the sky … It was with difficulty that we prevailed upon him to enter an air-raid shelter. He only agreed to go when it was pointed out that it was up to him to set an example.
>
> Down we went into a basement, the Old Man with a bottle of brandy under his arm. There he paced up and down …"[128]

A German neighbour of the Churchills recalled seeing Churchill in the shelter that day "in a great state of indignation, stamping his foot, complaining that there was no telephone and no portable wireless, and saying that the Germans would have much better organised air-raid shelters … The all-clear was sounded a few minutes later"[129]. Unlike his reaction to the outbreak of war a quarter of a century before (see Chapter 2), no-one reported Churchill having a "happy face". However, it seems his neighbours may have had such expressions. "Everyone [in the air-raid shelter] was cheerful and jocular, as is the English manner when about to encounter the unknown", Churchill later remembered[130]. Clearly he tired of sitting in a shelter fairly quickly. He ran up to the roof of his block of flats and stood there, apparently looking for aircraft in the cloudless sky.

He was immediately appointed to the War Cabinet as First Lord of the Admiralty. It had been almost a decade since he left government, and almost a quarter of a century since he had resigned as First Lord of the Admiralty. "Once again", he wrote after the war, "we must fight for life and honour against all the might and fury of the valiant, disciplined and ruthless German race. Once again! So be it"[131]. The famous signal, if it ever existed‡‡‡, had already been flashed to every ship in the Royal Navy:

"WINSTON IS BACK".

---

[1] *The Second World War*, Winston S Churchill, Vol. 1, p.190

[2] *Hansard*, 7 February, 7 March, 17 March, 21 March, 24 March, 12 May, 25 May, 3 December

[3] Cabinet minutes, 3 February 1937, CAB/23/87

[4] Hitler speech, 12 February 1942

[5] *Failure of a Mission*, Sir Neville Henderson, p.100

[6] *Winston S Churchill Companion, Volume V, Part 3, 1936-1939, The Wilderness Years*, Martin Gilbert, p.755

[7] *Winston S Churchill Companion, Volume V, Part 3, 1936-1939, The Wilderness Years*, Martin Gilbert, p.521

[8] *Chips – The Diaries of Sir Henry Channon*, Sir Henry Channon, p.122

[9] *The Second World War*, Winston S Churchill, Vol. 1, p.199

[10] *Jock Colville diary*, 26 January 1941 quoted in *Churchill War Papers, Vol. III, The Ever-Widening War*, Martin Gilbert, p.140

[11] *In Search of Churchill*, Martin Gilbert, p.106

[12] *Nine Troubled Years*, Lord Templewood, p.26-35

[13] *The Harold Nicolson Diaries, 1907-1963*, Harold Nicolson, 16 March 1938, p.163

[14] *Nine Troubled Years*, Lord Templewood, p.26-38

[15] *The Neville Chamberlain Diary Letters*, Vol.2, p.214

[16] *The Neville Chamberlain Diary Letters*, Vol.1, p.354

[17] *Hansard*, 1 June 1937

[18] *Winston S Churchill Companion, Volume V, Part 3, 1936-1939, The Wilderness Years*, Martin Gilbert, p.1345

[19] *The Neville Chamberlain Diary Letters, Volume 4*, Neville Chamberlain, p.342

[20] *The Fringes of Power*, Sir Jock Colville, p.79

[21] *The Morbid Age: Britain Between the Wars*, Richard Overy, p.342.

[22] *The Neville Chamberlain Diary Letters, Volume 4*, Neville Chamberlain, p.52

[23] *The Neville Chamberlain Diary Letters, Volume 4*, Neville Chamberlain, p.181

[24] See, e.g. Camrose, quoted in *Winston S Churchill Companion, Volume V, Part 3, 1936-1939, The Wilderness Years*, Martin Gilbert, p.1544-45

---

‡‡‡ Sir Martin Gilbert searched for the signal in the Admiralty's archives and failed to find it.

[25] *Step by Step*, Winston Churchill, p.157-8

[26] *Mein Kampf*, e.g. p.1

[27] *The Young Hitler I Knew, p.91*

[28] *Hitler's Table Talk*, p.488

[29] *Time* magazine, 25 June 1945

[30] *The Second World War*, Winston S Churchill, Vol. 1, p.201

[31] *Hitler, 1936-1945, Nemesis*, Ian Kershaw, p.24

[32] *The Second World War*, Winston S Churchill, Vol. 1, p.224

[33] *Nuremberg Trial Proceedings*, Volume 10, p.238

[34] *Speaking for Themselves, the personal letters of Winston and Clementine Churchill*, p.402

[35] *The Second World War*, Winston S Churchill, Vol. 1, p.218

[36] *The Eden Memoirs, The Reckoning*, Anthony Eden, p.6

[37] *Winston S Churchill, Volume V, 1922-1939*, Martin Gilbert, p.903

[38] *The Times*, 8 October 1937

[39] *Winston S Churchill Companion, Volume V, Part 3, 1936-1939, The Wilderness Years*, Martin Gilbert, p.749

[40] *The Times*, 26 January 1937

[41] *The Times*, 19 February 1937

[42] *The Times*, 23 February 1937

[43] *The Times*, 1 May 1937

[44] *The Times*, 29 April 1937

[45] *Winston S Churchill Companion, Volume V, Part 3, 1936-1939, The Wilderness Years*, Martin Gilbert, p.704-05

[46] *The Times*, 8 October 1937

[47] *The Times*, 5 March 1937

[48] *The Times*, 12 March 1937

[49] *The Times*, 22 December 1937

[50] *Anthony Eden diary*, Eden papers, 5 January 1938, quoted in *Eden*, D.R. Thorpe, p.201

[51] *Winston S Churchill Companion, Volume V, Part 3, 1936-1939, The Wilderness Years*, Martin Gilbert, p.880

[52] *Winston S Churchill Companion, Volume V, Part 3, 1936-1939, The Wilderness Years*, Martin Gilbert, p.906

[53] *Great Contemporaries*, Winston S. Churchill, p.261

[54] *The Truth About Hitler, Strand* magazine, Winston S Churchill, November 1935

[55] *Great Contemporaries*, Winston S. Churchill, p.120

[56] *Great Contemporaries*, Winston S. Churchill, p.374

[57] *Winston S Churchill Companion, Volume V, Part 3, 1936-1939, The Wilderness Years*, Martin Gilbert, p.755

[58] *Goebbels diaries*, 29 March 1945

[59] *Winston S Churchill Companion, Volume V, Part 3, 1936-1939, The Wilderness Years*, Martin Gilbert, p.764

[60] *Winston S Churchill Companion, Volume V, Part 3, 1936-1939, The Wilderness Years*, Martin Gilbert, p.767

[61] *Hitler confronts England*, Walter Ansel, p.13

[62] *Churchill: A Life*, Martin Gilbert, p.553

[63] *Churchill: A Life*, Martin Gilbert, p.581

[64] *Chips – The Diaries of Sir Henry Channon*, Sir Henry Channon, p.141

[65] *Step by Step*, Winston Churchill, p.207

[66] *The Times*, 25 February 1938

[67] *Winston S Churchill Companion, Volume V, Part 3, 1936-1939, The Wilderness Years*, Martin Gilbert, p.923 note 1

[68] Quoted in *The Times*, 22 February 1938

[69] *Hansard*, 22 February 1938

[70] *The Second World War*, Winston S Churchill, Vol. 1, p.242-43

[71] *Hansard*, 15 March 1938

[72] *Winston S Churchill Companion, Volume V, Part 3, 1936-1939, The Wilderness Years*, Martin Gilbert, p.947

[73] *Winston S Churchill Companion, Volume V, Part 3, 1936-1939, The Wilderness Years*, Martin Gilbert, p.953

[74] *Daily Telegraph*, 6 July 1938

[75] *The Unnecessary War*, Patricia Meehan, p.123-4

[76] *Winston S Churchill Companion, Volume V, Part 3, 1936-1939, The Wilderness Years*, Martin Gilbert, p.1023-4

[77] See his article in the Daily Telegraph on 26 July 1938, his interview with Herr Foerster, *Winston S Churchill Companion, Volume V, Part 3, 1936-1939, The Wilderness Years*, Martin Gilbert, p.1100-02

[78] *Winston S Churchill Companion, Volume V, Part 3, 1936-1939, The Wilderness Years*, Martin Gilbert, p.1112-13

[79] *Winston S Churchill Companion, Volume V, Part 3, 1936-1939, The Wilderness Years*, Martin Gilbert, p.1155-56

[80] *Daily Telegraph*, 15 September 1938

[81] *Winston S Churchill Companion, Volume V, Part 3, 1936-1939, The Wilderness Years*, Martin Gilbert, p.1120

[82] *The Unnecessary War*, Patricia Meehan, p.143

[83] *Winston S Churchill Companion, Volume V, Part 3, 1936-1939, The Wilderness Years*, Martin Gilbert, p.1162

[84] *Hansard*, 5 October 1938

[85] *Observer*, 9 October 1938

[86] *Winston S Churchill Companion, Volume V, Part 3, 1936-1939, The Wilderness Years*, Martin Gilbert, p.1239

[87] Quoted in *Churchill, A Life*, Roy Jenkins, p.531

[88] *Winston S Churchill Companion, Volume V, Part 3, 1936-1939, The Wilderness Years*, Martin Gilbert, p.1208

[89] *Winston S Churchill Companion, Volume V, Part 3, 1936-1939, The Wilderness Years*, Martin Gilbert, p.1216-27

[90] *The Gathering Storm*, Winston S Churchill, p.301-304

[91] *Winston S Churchill Companion, Volume V, Part 3, 1936-1939, The Wilderness Years*, Martin Gilbert, p.1171, 1177

[92] *Winston S Churchill Companion, Volume V, Part 3, 1936-1939, The Wilderness Years*, Martin Gilbert, p.1196

[93] *The Times*, 7 September 1937

[94] *The Times*, 11 November 1938

[95] *Winston S Churchill Companion, Volume V, Part 3, 1936-1939, The Wilderness Years*, Martin Gilbert, p.1260

[96] *The Times*, 2 February 1939

[97] *Winston S Churchill Companion, Volume V, Part 3, 1936-1939, The Wilderness Years*, Martin Gilbert, p.1390

[98] *Winston S Churchill Companion, Volume V, Part 3, 1936-1939, The Wilderness Years*, Martin Gilbert, p.1374

[99] *Hitler confronts England*, Walter Ansel, p.14-5

[100] *Failure of a Mission*, Sir Neville Henderson, p.210

[101] *Chips – The Diaries of Sir Henry Channon*, Sir Henry Channon, p.186

[102] *The Neville Chamberlain Diary Letters*, Vol.4, p.393

[103] *The Neville Chamberlain Diary Letters*, Vol.4, p.393

[104] *The Second World War, Volume 1, The Gathering Storm*, Winston Churchill, p.312

[105] Cabinet minutes, 18 March 1939

[106] Hansard, 3 April 1939

[107] *Winston S Churchill Companion, Volume V, Part 3, 1936-1939, The Wilderness Years*, Martin Gilbert, p.1556

[108] *The Neville Chamberlain Diary Letters*, Vol.4, p.428

[109] *The Neville Chamberlain Diary Letters*, Vol.4, p.403

[110] *Hitler's Table Talk*, p.254

[111] *Winston S Churchill Companion, Volume V, Part 3, 1936-1939, The Wilderness Years*, Martin Gilbert, p.1323

[112] Vincent Sheean, quoted in *Winston S Churchill Companion, Volume V, Part 3, 1936-1939, The Wilderness Years*, Martin Gilbert, p.1349

[113] *Hansard*, 3 April 1939

[114] *Hansard*, 13 April 1939

[115] *Hansard*, 27 April 1939

[116] *Winston S Churchill Companion, Volume V, Part 3, 1936-1939, The Wilderness Years*, Martin Gilbert, p.1478-80

[117] *Winston S Churchill Companion, Volume V, Part 3, 1936-1939, The Wilderness Years*, Martin Gilbert, p.1481

[118] *Hansard*, 19 May 1939

[119] *Hansard*, 26 May 1939

[120] *Winston S Churchill Companion, Volume V, Part 3, 1936-1939, The Wilderness Years*, Martin Gilbert, p.1569

[121] *Autobiography*, Margot Asquith, p.323

[122] *Winston S Churchill Companion, Volume V, Part 3, 1936-1939, The Wilderness Years*, Martin Gilbert, p.1593-96

[123] *The Second World War*, Winston S Churchill, Vol. 1, p.345

[124] *The Churchill Documents, Volume 11, The Exchequer Years*, Martin Gilbert, p.501

[125] *Winston S Churchill Companion, Volume V, Part 3, 1936-1939, The Wilderness Years*, Martin Gilbert, p.1602

[126] *At Hitler's Side*, Nicolaus von Below, p.33

[127] *Hitler Privat*, Albert Zoller, p.156

[128] *Winston S Churchill Companion, Volume V, Part 3, 1936-1939, The Wilderness Years*, Martin Gilbert, p.1609

[129] *Winston S Churchill Companion, Volume V, Part 3, 1936-1939, The Wilderness Years*, Martin Gilbert, p.1610

[130] *The Second World War, Volume 1, The Gathering Storm*, Winston Churchill, p.364

[131] *The Second World War, Volume 1, The Gathering Storm*, Winston Churchill, p.365

5

"Winston is Back" (1939-1940)

The coming of war changed Hitler's routine. His public speeches became much less frequent (and eventually ceased altogether), and he spent more time in Spartan, dismal bunkers with his cronies and his generals, directing military operations. When he made a big, set-piece speech, however, he would often use it to pour scorn on Churchill. One of the greatest contrasts between the two men as leaders is in their public appearances during the war. Churchill went out of his way to be seen in public, using the force of his personality and his matchless eloquence to inspire the people of Britain and its Empire, as well as Occupied Europe, to fight on, even when, as after Dunkirk, he had no idea how victory might be achieved. He visited bombed areas during the Blitz, while Hitler never visited devastated streets in Germany personally, even as its cities were reduced to rubble. He allowed his cronies, in particular Goebbels, to appear in public and attempt to boost morale. Hitler's private conversations, too, mentioned Churchill more and more, though still less often than Churchill referred to him. "The Führer has nothing but contempt for current English policy. He finds my attacks on Churchill particularly gratifying", Goebbels noted in his diary in October 1939[1].

Between Churchill's reappointment to the Admiralty at the outbreak of war in Europe and the German invasion of the West in May 1940, the nature of the confrontation between himself and Hitler changed completely. From being an MP without government office - warning from the sidelines about Nazi aggression - Churchill became, like Hitler, the leader of a great country at war. He was clearly determined to end his opponent's hold on power, if not yet to have him killed. His rhetoric was an important tool to this end, especially after the fall of France, when the British army had lost its arms and heavy equipment at Dunkirk. In confronting Hitler in 1940, Churchill gave some of the most memorable political speeches ever made. He certainly never underestimated the effect of his own rhetoric, often taking days to prepare a speech, and saying after the war ended: "… we had much the best of the speeches in the last war, that fellow Hitler wasn't up to much in that respect"[2].

On the other hand, Churchill's regular columns in the press, which he had used to warn against the Nazis in the mid- and late-1930's, ceased, as they had when he had accepted high office thirty years before. He wrote the last such article in May 1939, on the question of Britain's diplomatic relations with Turkey[3], crucial to the Imperial position in the Middle East. As First Lord of the Admiralty, and then as Prime Minister, he could clearly no longer spare the time for writing a 1,000 word article each fortnight. He had finished his 1.5 million word book about the life of Marlborough the previous year. Extraordinarily, he continued to work on his *History of the English-Speaking Peoples* while First Lord of the Admiralty, in "every spare half hour"[4], until he became Prime Minister in May 1940, when the book was put on hold – as it turned out, for more than a decade[5].

As First Lord of the Admiralty in a country at war, Churchill no longer had to alert the country about the Nazi menace in general. He therefore spoke less about the dangers of German aggression than he had in previous years. His speeches in Parliament were largely concerned instead with Admiralty business, such as the convoy system which protected British merchant ships and the sinking of major warships such as the aircraft carrier, *Courageous*, or the battleship, *Royal Oak*.

Even when Prime Minister, Churchill mentioned Hitler in private conversations much less often than he had when he was trying to alert friends, colleagues and opponents to the Nazi menace before the outbreak of war. This may, at first, be surprising, but during the war, Churchill had to convince very few in Britain of the threat from Germany. What counted now were war production and strategy, and relations with allies and neutrals. Hitler certainly intruded into these areas, but figured in Churchill's private conversations much less often than President Roosevelt or Stalin, and hardly more frequently than General de Gaulle.

Hitler's offers of peace refused

During the campaign in Poland, Hitler had devoted considerable effort to minimising confrontation in the West. Partly this was because he did not want to fight on two fronts at once, but he also seems to have wanted to end the war with his Western enemies once Poland had been smashed by a compromise peace. He did not want to provoke Britain or France into continuing the war by inflicting large numbers of casualties. He therefore refused Göring's pleas to be allowed to bomb the British fleet at Scapa Flow[6], despite the political damage that serious losses might have caused Churchill.

Following the destruction of Poland by Germany and the Soviet Union, Hitler made a triumphant entry into Danzig. After thanking his generals for the victory, at the Führer conference on 30 September, General Halder recorded him as being "prepared for peace. Utmost determination"[7]. At a speech in the former Free City, now incorporated into the German Reich, he referred back to his claim in his 1938 speeches in Saarbrücken and Wilhelmshaven (see Chapter 4) that he feared democracy because men like Churchill could be in government at any time. He also said:

> "It is said in England that this war, of course, is not for Poland. That is only secondary. More important is the war against the regime in Germany. And I receive the honour of special mention as a representative of this regime. If that is now set up as a war aim, I will answer the gentlemen in London thus:
>
> It is for me the greatest honour to be thus classed. On principle I educated the German people so that any regime which is lauded by our enemies is poison for Germany and will therefore be rejected by us. If, therefore, a German regime would get the consent of Churchill, Duff Cooper and Eden it would be paid and kept by these gentlemen and hence would be unbearable for Germany. That, certainly, is not true with us. It is, therefore, only honourable for us to be rejected by these gentlemen. I can assure these gentlemen only this: If they should praise, this would be a reason for me to be most crestfallen. I am proud to be attacked by them.
>
> But if they believe they can thereby alienate the German people from me, then they either think the German people are as lacking in character as themselves or as stupid as themselves. They err in both. ... By their ridiculous propaganda the German people will not be undermined. Those bunglers will have become our apprentices for many years before they can even attempt propaganda"[8].

Hitler addressed the Reichstag at the start of October. He proposed peace to England, on the basis that he would keep the half of Poland which Germany had conquered, and all of the Czech lands which it had annexed the previous year.

Chapter 5

Again he spent part of his speech denouncing Churchill:

> "Mr. Churchill and his companions may interpret these opinions of mine [on the futility of war against France and Britain] as weakness or cowardice if they like. I need not occupy myself with what they think; I make these statements simply because it goes without saying that I wish to spare my own people this suffering.
>
> If, however, the opinions of Messrs. Churchill and followers should prevail, this statement will have been my last.
>
> Then we shall fight. Neither force of arms nor lapse of time will conquer Germany. There never will be another November 1918 in German history. It is infantile to hope for the disintegration of our people.
>
> Mr. Churchill may be convinced that Great Britain will win. I do not doubt for a single moment that Germany will be victorious"[9].

Once news of this speech reached England, Churchill wrote a note to the Cabinet, arguing that no negotiations should begin until Germany had offered reparation to the conquered nations, and that "no confidence can be placed in any assurance by Herr Hitler or by the Nazi Party which is identified with him"[10]. In a covering note sent to Chamberlain, he wrote that it was "no use holding discussions with Herr Hitler until he showed by his actions that his policy had changed"[11]. Churchill always saw the removal of Hitler as a precondition for any peace negotiations. He refused to accept leaving Hitler even "a ceremonial and honourable position", arguing, unrealistically, that, given British firmness, "the Germans themselves may disintegrate"[12]. Chamberlain evidently agreed. He wrote to his sister "to my mind, it is essential to get rid of Hitler. He must either die or go to St Helena or become a real public works architect, preferably in a 'home'"[13]. Chamberlain rejected the peace proposals a few days later in the Commons, in terms so firm that Churchill predicted "a violent reaction from Herr Hitler", and ordered various dockyards to be particularly vigilant[14]. On hearing of this rejection, Hitler remarked to von Brauchitsch, the commander in chief of the German Army, that "the British will be ready to talk only after a beating"[15].

Four days after Hitler's speech, he was telling his generals in private his plans for war in the west, in case he had to continue hostilities[16]. Making his annual speech on the anniversary of the 1923 Beer Hall *Putsch* in Munich in November 1939, Hitler referred to Churchill's record during the First World War:

"… The lies come from the same people, who lie again today, because they are the same warmongers since Churchill and Co. took part in the previous war. In that way everything is the same. Only something has changed: when Churchill fomented war then, there was a weak government in Germany. Today Churchill foments war again, but there is a different government in Germany. And the government of today confronts the English! And it has no more respect than one needs to have for other soldiers: not the slightest feeling of inferiority, but on the contrary, the feeling of superiority …

… Then it was often said: … we, the Churchills, Chamberlains and so on, are not fighting against the German people. We are only fighting against the regime which is oppressing the German people … We want free trade over the whole world. That is also a lie – as Herr Churchill remarked at that time…"

In neither of Hitler's speeches, in which he mentioned Churchill several times, did he mention Chamberlain, or any other member of the British government, or any French politicians at all, either directly or indirectly. It is clear that, right from the start of the war, he regarded Churchill as his main enemy in Britain, even though Churchill was not yet Prime Minister, and indeed had only just returned to office, after almost a decade's exile.

Hitler finished making his speech and left the beer cellar. Minutes later, one of the two nearly successful attempts on his life occurred. A bomb exploded, killing nine people. The Nazis tried, frantically but unsuccessfully, to prove that the bomber, Johann Georg Elser, had been working for the British. However, he was working alone, and he had embarrassed the vaunted Nazi security apparatus by coming very close to killing the dictator. Not until the war was obviously lost, in 1944, would another assassination attempt come so close to success.

Even the smallest sign of trouble for Churchill was relayed to Hitler by Goebbels, whose job it was to keep an eye on the foreign press. In October 1939, Goebbels wrote in his diary that the Führer was "much amused" by a few quips by George Bernard Shaw against Churchill[17]. The next day, as noted above, Goebbels wrote that Hitler found his "attacks on Churchill particularly gratifying"[18]. In December, at a lunch with Goebbels, Hitler launched "a strong attack on Churchill. The man is living in the sixteenth century and has absolutely no understanding of his compatriots' real needs"[19]. Why Hitler thought that he, knowing very little about Britain, understood its needs better than Churchill did, is unrecorded.

Chapter 5

On 30 January 1940, Hitler celebrated the seventh anniversary of his appointment as Chancellor with a speech to the Reichstag. After a long, ranting criticism of Britain's history, he "praised" Churchill sarcastically, for speaking openly on what he claimed Chamberlain was thinking: he wanted the dissolution of Germany; the destruction of Germany and the extinction of the German people. (In fact, as *The Times* pointed out, Churchill had never called for the dissolution or destruction of Germany, and had indeed specifically stated that this was not a British war aim[20]). After outlining the progress of the war to date, Hitler claimed that Churchill "could not wait" for the second phase of the war to begin. "Through his middlemen, and personally too, he hopes that at last the bombing war will begin. And they cry to the heavens that this war will not of course stop short at women and children – when did Britain ever stop short at women and children?"

In private, to Goebbels, Hitler compared Churchill to the German conservative and monarchist politician Oldenburg-Januschau, "bare-faced but with no capacity for thought"[21]. Speaking in Munich on 24 February, he returned to his sarcastic way of "thanking" Churchill, in this case for the "compliment" that Churchill had paid him in hating him. He grouped Churchill in with Duff Cooper, Chamberlain, and the "eternal Jew", the British Minister of War, Leslie Hore-Belisha, though in fact Hore-Belisha had been dismissed from the Government the previous month.

While the war of words between their leaders continued, the first few months of the war were quiet for the British and French armies, which faced the German army across the Rhine. Chamberlain apparently "saw no need to *fight* a war, however definitive the declaration"[22]. 'Chips' Channon asked himself, in his diary, "Is [Hitler] trying to bore us into peace?"[23] Some Britons apparently referred to this period as the "Bore War"[24], American journalists dubbed it the "Phoney War", the Germans know it as *"Sitzkrieg"* (the sitting war – as opposed to *Blitzkrieg*, the lightning war). Churchill himself later borrowed Chamberlain's term, "The Twilight War"[25].

There was, however, no phoney war either in Poland, which was crushed by the Nazis and the Soviets, or at sea, where the liner *Athenia* was torpedoed within 12 hours of Britain's declaration of war on Germany, with the loss of 112 lives. As First Lord of the Admiralty, Churchill announced the "outrage" of the sinking of the *Athenia* to the Commons[26], saying that the sinking breached a naval treaty by which Germany had promised to abide. At first, Hitler seems to have been told by his admirals that there had been no German submarines nearby. He learned the truth soon after. The German press, directed by Goebbels and Hitler, farcically attempted to claim that Britain had placed a bomb on its own ship, to inflame neutral opinion against Germany, though they convinced few who did not want to be convinced. Goebbels noted in his diary that "My attack against Churchill is approved by the Führer. We shall respond with new material during the next few days. Churchill has named four German passengers on the *Athenia*. But these were Jewish émigrés. The response to my speech in the editorial pages of the German press has been enormous"[27]. After releasing an even more fantastic story, that Churchill had sunk the *Athenia* by having holes bored into its bottom, Goebbels received instructions from Hitler on "how to handle the case of Churchill. [Hitler] … believes that we may succeed in causing his downfall. That would mean more than the sinking of two battleships"[28].

Indeed, as Churchill announced to Parliament on 8 November, during the first two months of the war, the Royal Navy had lost more men than the remainder of the Allied armed forces combined (he presumably did not include Polish forces in his calculation of the Allied totals)[29]. The losses included one battleship, the *Royal Oak*, which was sunk by a U-boat in the main British naval harbour, Scapa Flow, with the loss of 800 of her crew, and one large fleet aircraft carrier, the *Courageous*.

During October 1939, the Nazi press launched frequent attacks on Churchill, approved by Goebbels, over such matters as the sinking of the battleship *Royal Oak* (true) and the aircraft carrier *Ark Royal* (false, as it had only been damaged)[30]. Goebbels noted in his diary that: "Our Stukas' [dive bombers'] attacks on the English fleet have been very successful. The effect on world opinion has been tremendous. Churchill is continuing to lie his heart out. But now we have him. He will not escape us. We shall not pause or rest until he is a beaten man"[31]. In fact, as this account has argued, it was the Nazis who were doing most of the lying.

Throughout the early months of the war, and in the absence of any move once Poland was crushed, Churchill attempted to speculate on what Hitler's strategy would be. As early as the middle of September, Churchill predicted in a letter to Chamberlain that the Germans would probably not "attempt an offensive in the West at this late season". He argued that Hitler should "make good his Eastern connections and feeding-grounds during these winter months, and thus give his people the spectacle of repeated successes"[32]. He advocated an idea to which he was to return frequently during the war: building up a South-Eastern European front against Germany, through the involvement of Hungary, Rumania, Bulgaria and Turkey. The whole effort of Britain and France should be concentrated on "smashing Hitlerism". He foresaw the likely events of the spring of 1940, forecasting "a major attack on the western front, probably through Belgium, collecting Holland on the way ... when at least thirty divisions have been concentrated opposite Belgium and Luxemburg" [33].

Churchill's oratory nevertheless served him well in the early months. Harold Nicolson, a Conservative MP and diarist, recorded his impression of a debate in Parliament in September 1939:

> "The Prime Minister gets up to make his statement ... One feels the confidence and spirits of the House dropping inch by inch ... [Then] Winston Churchill ... gets up. He is greeted by a loud cheer from all the benches ... He began by saying how strange an experience it was for him after a quarter of a century to find himself once more in the same room ..., fighting the same enemy ... His face then creases into an enormous grin and he adds ... "I have no conception how this curious change in my fortunes occurred". The whole House roared with laughter and the Prime Minister had not the decency to raise a sickly smile ... [Churchill's] delivery was amazing. Once could feel the spirit of the House rising with every word ... Old Parliamentary hands confessed that never in their experience had they seen a single speech so change the temper of the House" [34].

Despite the press of official business, Churchill managed to make fairly frequent swipes against Hitler and the Nazi regime. On the day war was declared, he referred to "the pestilence of Nazi tyranny" [35]. Two months later, Churchill had:

> "the sensation, and also the conviction, that that evil man over there and his cluster of confederates are not sure of themselves, as we are sure of ourselves; that they are harassed in their guilty souls by the thought and by the fear of an ever-approaching retribution for their crimes, and for the orgy of destruction in which they have plunged us all ..."

He seemed confident that the Allies would eventually prevail:

> "The whole world is against Hitler and Hitlerism. Men of every race and clime feel that this monstrous apparition stands between them and the forward move which is their due ... Even in Germany itself there are millions who stand aloof from the seething mass of criminality and corruption constituted by the Nazi regime" [36].

Even Churchill's relations with Neville Chamberlain mellowed to some degree: in November 1939, they and their wives dined at Admiralty House. Chamberlain told Churchill the story of his unsuccessful, five-year attempt to grow sisal on a barren islet in the Caribbean, at his father's instructions. This was, apparently, the only intimate social conversation between the two successive Prime Ministers in nearly twenty years of shared political life[37]. (Churchill's wife, Clementine, was less impressed by the hardship of Chamberlain's posting than Churchill was).

Churchill continued to attack Hitler at every opportunity, both in Parliament and outside. Moving the Naval Estimates in February 1940, Churchill commented on the Nazi response to the arming of merchant ships, drawing attention to Hitler's inconsistent attitude towards international law:

> "Thousands of guns of all sorts and sizes are being issued to our merchant and to our fishing fleets. The Nazis have retorted by saying that this entitles them to break all the conventions which they had already broken many times over. They may, of course, apply their methods on a larger scale, but they have not for some time been able to descend to any new levels of cruelty and disgrace.
>
> I suppose the House realises that Herr Hitler and his Nazis have quite definitely exceeded the worst villainies which Imperial Germany committed in the late war. This brings me to a point that I should like to put to the House. One of the most extraordinary things that I have ever known in my experience is the way in which German illegalities, atrocities, and brutalities are coming to be accepted as if they were part of the ordinary day-to-day conditions of war. Why, Sir, the neutral Press makes more fuss when I make a speech telling them what is their duty than they have done when hundreds of their ships have been sunk and many thousands of their sailors have been drowned or murdered, for that is the right word, on the open sea"[38].

One crucial contribution which the Admiralty, under Churchill's direction, made to the British war effort in the early months of the war was the defeat of the Germans' magnetic mine. This device sunk metal ships by exploding an explosive charge once it detected their magnetic field. Though expecting that a solution would be found "in time", Churchill described these to the War Cabinet as "a grave menace which might well be Hitler's 'Secret Weapon'"[39]. It was the first of several weapons to be thus identified during the war. The severe losses which it caused to British merchant shipping in the North Sea caused the War Cabinet considerable anxiety in November and December 1939.

In fact, thanks to the Admiralty's scientists, it was neutralised by the end of the year: a relatively simple demagnetising procedure in effect rendered ships invulnerable to the danger. Hitler's subsequent secret weapons were not to be so easy to defeat.

Scandinavian diversions

The first major land campaign between Germany and the Western Allies occurred not in the area between France and Germany, but in Scandinavia. Germany's successful invasion of Norway in April 1940 eventually resulted in the fall of Chamberlain and his replacement by Churchill, just in time for Churchill to have to deal with the German onslaught in the West. This came as a climax to six months' growing tensions in northern Europe. Germany desperately needed the iron ore from Sweden which came through Norway, though it was her intention to keep Norway neutral unless "England threatens Norway's neutrality"[40]. Churchill thought that stopping this trade was "worth all the rest of the blockade" combined[41].

Attempts to stop the trade using diplomatic means failed. The Scandinavian countries understandably, but unrealistically, wanted to be left alone to trade with whomever offered them the best terms. In a broadcast in January 1940, Churchill warned about "the lot of the unfortunate neutrals. Whether on sea or on land, they are the victims upon whom Hitler's hate and spite descend. Look at the group of small but ancient and historic states which lie in the North … Every one of them is wondering tonight which will be the next victim on whom the criminal adventurers of Berlin will cast their rending stroke" [42]. Or, he observed more succinctly, "each [neutral country] hopes that if he feeds the crocodile enough, it will eat him last". This speech, with its unforgettable comparison of Hitler and Nazi Germany to a crocodile, reminded the neutrals of their vulnerability. It caused an uproar in the few free countries left in Europe. Goebbels noted in his diary that "Churchill's speech threatening the neutrals has aroused a huge response. The old fox has made another serious mistake"[43]. A day later, however, and presumably echoing Hitler's words, as he so often did, Goebbels made Churchill's point for him in the privacy of his diary: "Have no intention of helping out these tiny dwarf-like states. They deserve to disappear", he wrote[44].

War had, in fact already spread to Scandinavia. The Red Army invaded Finland in November 1939. The Russians wanted to annex some Finnish territory which guarded the approaches to Leningrad. Finland put up a magnificent resistance during the four months of the so-called Winter War, before surrendering to the overwhelming numbers of the Red Army in March 1940. One of the few matters on which Churchill and most Germans agreed was that Finland was in the right over her struggle with the Soviet Union. During the Winter War, there had been talk in both Britain and France of sending help to the Finns. For Churchill, military help for Finland would be a golden opportunity to cut one of Germany's lifelines: the supply of Swedish iron ore through the Norwegian port of Narvik. He heaped praise on their "superb, nay sublime – in the jaws of peril" performance in the Winter War[45].

The Germans, however, had to swallow their sympathy for Finland in order to avoid antagonising the Soviet Union, which was supplying Germany with priceless raw materials. Hitler wanted the war to end as quickly as possible, and certainly did not want to intervene[46]. Both Hitler and Churchill admired Finland's struggle, however. In 1941, when Finland was at war with Britain's ally, Russia, Churchill wrote to the Finnish President that "it would be most painful to the many friends of your country in England if Finland found herself in the dock with the guilty and defeated Nazis"[47]. In 1942, Hitler said that after the Winter War, "the Finns applied to me, proposing that their country should become a German protectorate. I don't regret having rejected this offer … the heroic attitude of this people … deserves the greatest respect. It is infinitely better to have this people of heroes as allies than to incorporate it in the Germanic Reich"[48].

German intelligence picked up some hints from Churchill at a press conference on 2 February that he was considering military operations in Norway[49]. Churchill's first military intervention in Scandinavia occurred when the Royal Navy stopped the German tanker, *Altmark*, which was carrying British prisoners in Norwegian waters. Whether this action was legal under international law was, and remains, unclear. Churchill, however, had no doubts. In the House of Commons, he poured scorn on the very idea that the Nazis could appeal to international law when they had themselves repeatedly violated it:

> "Apparently, according to the present doctrine of neutral States, strongly endorsed by the German Government, Germany is to gain one set of advantages by breaking all the rules and committing foul outrages upon the seas, and then go on and gain another set of advantages through insisting whenever it suits her, upon the strictest interpretation of the International Code she has torn to pieces"[50].

After months of dithering, Britain finally mined the Norwegian coast to prevent coast-hugging traffic, including Germany's iron ore supplies, in March 1940.

Chapter 5

The Germans promptly invaded both Denmark and Norway. Planning had already been taking place, but it seems to have been Hitler's reaction to an intercept of a conversation between Churchill, the French and the Finns which caused him to accelerate preparations for the invasions[51].

Hitler later placed much of the blame on Churchill, saying that "if Churchill and Reynaud had kept quiet, I might not have invaded Norway"[52]. Churchill, speaking with what the *Daily Mail* described as "firm confidence"*, used irony and scorn to mock Hitler's actions:

> "The Nazi German Government is accustomed to spreading through its channels a continuous flow of threats and rumours. These are put forth by all their agents in neutral countries, by the "hangers-on" of their legations and by their sympathisers and backers, wherever they may be found. ... All these countries have been threatened, and as the German Government are not restrained by law or scruple, and as they have an obvious preference for striking at the weak rather than the strong, all the small countries on their borders were, and still are, in a high state of alarm. Even those neutrals who have done the most to placate Germany, and have been the greatest aid to her, could not feel any sense of security that they would not be attacked without any reason or without any warning, swiftly overrun, reduced to bondage and pillaged of all their property, especially all eatables...
>
> In the small hours of Monday morning we learned that Norway and Denmark had drawn the unlucky numbers in this sinister lottery. Denmark, of course, had special reason for apprehension, not only because she was the nearest and the weakest of Germany's neighbours, but because she had a recent treaty with Germany guaranteeing her from all molestation and because she was engaged in active commerce both with Germany and Great Britain, the continuance of which in time of war had been foreseen by Germany, and was guaranteed by special trade arrangements between the German and Danish Governments. This, obviously, placed her in a position of peculiar danger"[53].

Churchill expressed sympathy at the Norwegians having to risk a German invasion, while managing to deplore their lack of judgment in failing to consult Britain and France on a military response to a Nazi attack:

---

* Though Harold Nicolson described it as a "lamentable ... feeble, tired" speech

"I here must say a word about Norway. We have the most profound sympathy with the Norwegian people. We have understood the terrible dilemma in which they have been placed. Their sentiments, like those of every other small country, were with the Allies. They writhed in helpless anger while scores of their ships were wantonly sunk and many hundreds of their sailors cruelly drowned. They realise fully that their future independence and freedom are bound up with the victory of the Allies. But the feeling of powerlessness in the ruthless grip of Nazi wrath made them hope against hope until the last moment that at least their soil and their cities would not be polluted by the trampling of German marching columns or their liberties and their livelihood stolen away by foreign tyrants. But this hope has been in vain. Another violent outrage has been perpetrated by Nazi Germany against a small and friendly Power, and the Norwegian Government and people are to-day in arms to defend their hearths and homes...

But what an example this Norwegian episode is to other neutral countries. What an example it is of the danger of supposing that friendly relations with Germany, or friendly assurances from Germany, or treaties of any kind, or friendly offices rendered to Germany, or advantages given to Germany — what a danger to suppose that any of these are the slightest protection against a murderous onslaught the moment it is thought by Germany that any advantage can be gained by such action. If the Norwegian Government had not been so very strict and severe in enforcing their neutrality against us and in leaving their corridor open to German operations and machinations, and if they had entered into confidential relations with us, it would have been very easy to give them more timely and more opportune support than is now possible. It is not the slightest use blaming the Allies for not being able to give substantial help and protection to neutral countries if they are held at arm's length by the neutral countries until those countries are actually attacked on a scientifically prepared plan by Germany, and I trust that the fact that the strict observance of neutrality by Norway has been a contributory cause of the sufferings to which she is now exposed and in the limits of aid which we can give her will be meditated upon by other countries who may to-morrow, or a week hence, or a month hence find themselves the victims of an equally elaborately worked out staff plan for their destruction and enslavement"[54].

Churchill ended his hour-long speech by arguing that Hitler had made a grave strategic blunder in attacking Norway in particular. He was to repeat this line subsequently in private correspondence and in a broadcast. He seemed to be somewhat clutching at straws when he celebrated the occupation of the Faroe Islands:

> "In my view, ... Herr Hitler has committed a grave strategic error in spreading the war so far to the North and in forcing the Scandinavian people, or peoples, out of their attitude of neutrality. We have suffered from nothing in our blockade policy so much as the denial of the Norwegian coast, and that cursed corridor is now closed for ever. Hitler has effected with his Germans lodgments of various strengths at many points of the Norwegian coasts, and he has felled with a single hammer blow the inoffensive Kingdom of Denmark, but we shall take all we want off this Norwegian coast now, with an enormous increase in the facility and in the efficiency of our blockade. We are also at this moment occupying the Faroe Islands, which belong to Denmark and which are a strategic point of high importance, and whose people showed every disposition to receive us with warm regard...
>
> In the upshot, it is the considered view of the Admiralty that we have greatly gained by what has occurred in Scandinavia and in Northern waters in a strategic and military sense. For myself, I consider that Hitler's action in invading Scandinavia is as great a strategic and political error as that which was committed by Napoleon in 1807 or 1808, when he invaded Spain. Hitler has violated the independence and soil of virile peoples dwelling in very large and expansive countries capable of maintaining, with British and French aid, prolonged resistance to his soldiers and his Gestapo. He has almost doubled the efficiency of the Allied blockade. He has made a whole series of commitments upon the Norwegian coast for which he will now have to fight, if necessary, during the whole summer, against Powers possessing vastly superior naval forces and able to transport them to the scenes of action more easily than he can. I cannot see any counter-advantage which he has gained except the satisfaction of another exercise of the brutal lust of unbridled power".

History has not borne out this particular argument of Churchill's. The occupation of Norway was not a serious drain on Hitler's forces, and it ensured his iron ore supplies for the rest of the war. It was nevertheless fortunate for Britain that Hitler did invade these countries. The political crisis which Britain's lacklustre response caused was to propel Churchill into Downing Street a few weeks later. However, his argument, made to the Cabinet on 11 April, that Hitler's cruiser force had been "almost destroyed" and that Hitler had "sacrificed his Navy", indicating that it was "only the prelude to more serious operations designed to finish the war", looks rather better, with hindsight[55]. When the Germans considered invading Britain in the summer, they found their naval forces totally inadequate for the task.

With his usual knack of completely misreading British politics, Hitler had thought it unlikely that Chamberlain's government would fall. According to Halder, Hitler remarked in conference on 5 May that "Chamberlain's Cabinet will not be overthrown at the present moment. Only when Britain will have to bear the brunt of the war set off by him, will an anti-war party rise in the country"[56]. The German invasion of Norway and Britain's late response, led to one of the most famous Parliamentary events in British history – the so-called "Norway debate".

According to Eden, writing years later, the mood in the House was of "sour disillusionment with undertones of bitterness"[57]. Churchill, a member of the Government, voted for the Government and spoke in its defence. He defended the Government's handling of the Norway campaign, though it had ended in disaster. He was willing, by this time, to admit that "Hitler's sudden overrunning of Norway has had astonishing and unwelcome effects, nevertheless, the advantages rest substantially with us"[58]. Not only had Hitler blockaded himself, Britain could now use the Norwegian and Danish merchant fleets. The Labour benches repeatedly heckled Churchill, and he gave as good as he got. One observer thought that his speech "did not ring entirely true"[59], and another commented, "how much of the fire was real, and how much *ersatz*, we shall never know"[60].

Churchill's accomplices in advocating British rearmament, Sir Roger Keyes and Leo Amery, both made crucial interventions in this debate. Keyes famously appeared in the full uniform of an Admiral of the Fleet and made a devastating speech blaming the lack of political leadership for the defeat in Norway. Amery's speech was subsequently credited with persuading several Conservative MPs to vote against the Government. At the end, he decided spontaneously to quote Oliver Cromwell's famous line to the Government: "You have sat too long here for any good you have been doing. Depart, I say, and let us have done with you. In the name of God, go!"

Chamberlain went, despite winning the vote at the end of the debate. His majority was only 81, rather than the 200 or so which he should have had. 33 Conservatives voted with the Opposition and 60 abstained. Given the narrowness of the Government's victory, he decided that an all-Party coalition must be formed. As Labour refused to serve under him, this meant, effectively, that the choice of Prime Minister was between Churchill and Lord Halifax, the

Chapter 5

Foreign Secretary. As King George VI later improperly told Halifax, he would have been glad to have him as Prime Minister[61]. As Halifax was a peer, however, and knew nothing about military matters[†], the King sent for Churchill, with whom he had differed on the Abdication and Appeasement[62]. Churchill's account is suspect, as he got the day and time of the interview wrong, and could have made it more melodramatic than it was. According to him, the King quipped, "I suppose you don't know why I have sent for you?" "Sir, I simply couldn't imagine why", replied Churchill. "I want to ask you to form a Government" came the reply[‡]. Churchill was now Prime Minister[63].

After the interview Churchill was joined by his bodyguard, who remarked to him that his task was enormous. "Tears came into his eyes as he answered gravely, 'God alone knows how great it is. I hope that it is not too late. I am very much afraid that it is. We can only do our best'"... Then he set his jaw and with a look of determination ... he began to climb the stairs of the Admiralty"[64]. This brief display of insecurity could have been for show, however. In 1947, he recalled that, on being appointed Prime Minister, "I had no feeling of personal inadequacy, or anything of that sort. I went to bed at three o'clock, and in the morning I said to Clemmie, 'There is only one man [who] can turn me out and that is Hitler'"[65].

The German wireless, no doubt on the orders of Goebbels after consulting Hitler, announced the news. It commented: "Thus the post ... is taken over by Churchill, most brutal representative of the policy of force, the man whose programme is to dismember Germany, this man whose hateful face is well known to all Germans"[66]. The Italian government was less impressed. Mussolini's foreign minister, Ciano, wrote in his diary that "Churchill replacing Chamberlain is seen here with complete indifference. The Duce views it with irony"[67].

[†] Halifax's ignorance of, and poor judgement, on military affairs is shown by his statement to the War Cabinet that Hitler would not attack on the Western Front, a few weeks before the attack was launched (CAB/65/56)

[‡] The King's account, in his diary, differs somewhat from Churchill's as to what was said.

The fall of France

Now Prime Minister, Churchill could determine Britain's policy towards Hitler's Germany. Throughout the spring and summer of 1940, he was to repeat publicly and privately, that there would be no yielding to Nazi Germany[§]. 26 May saw him telling the King of the Belgians, who was about to surrender, that "England will never quit the war whatever happens till Hitler is beat or we cease to be a state". He told the French Prime Minister over lunch that Britain "would rather go down fighting than be enslaved to Germany"[68]. These could have been mock-heroic statements to stiffen the morale of wavering allies, but they were of a piece with all his other utterances at this time. At War Cabinet, Churchill was just as defiant. He said that "Herr Hitler thought he had the whip hand. The only thing to do was to show him that he could not conquer this country". If, as Reynaud had told him, France was beaten, Britain must go on alone[69].

As France was obviously collapsing, on Sunday 26 May 1940, and it was still uncertain whether the British Expeditionary Force could be repatriated successfully, Churchill made perhaps his only, and certainly his most significant, remark, to the effect that he might consider accepting peace terms from Hitler, along the lines of those that the Führer was likely to offer. His remark at that meeting, which covers two and a half lines of a seven page note of the session, has offered those wishing to decry Churchill's bulldog spirit their strongest piece of evidence. The context is worth exploring in some detail. Lord Halifax, the Foreign Secretary, had met the Italian Ambassador the previous day, to discuss Anglo-Italian relations. The Italian had raised the possibility of a peace conference. The War Cabinet the following day discussed this overture. Halifax offered to approach Hitler and ask for terms which would safeguard British independence. In response, the minutes attribute the following sentence to Churchill: "If Herr Hitler was prepared to make peace on the terms of the restoration of German colonies and the overlordship of Central Europe, that was one thing". However, as the next sentence makes clear, Churchill did not think that this was in prospect: "But it was quite unlikely that he would make any such offer"[70].

[§] Though refusing to surrender his country to the Nazis, Churchill hated ordering troops to fight to the last man. According to General Ismay, when Churchill told Brigadier Nicholson that his troops could not be withdrawn from Calais and that he must fight it out to the bitter end, "he was unusually silent during dinner that evening, and he ate and drank with evident distaste. So we rose from the table, he said, 'I feel physically sick'." There is no record of any similar compassion from Hitler for the hundreds of thousands of men he condemned to death with similar orders to fight to the last man.

Chapter 5

Some consider this statement as evidence that the Second World War could perhaps have been ended at this point, had events run slightly differently, since Hitler would conceivably have entertained a peace on these terms. Hitler's assistant von Etzdorf was saying, on 21 May, that Germany was "seeking to arrive at an understanding with Britain on the basis of a division of the world"[71]. In mid-June, Ciano, the Italian foreign minister, compared Hitler to "the gambler, who, having made a big win, would like to leave the table, risking nothing more"[72]. However, at that same meeting, Churchill also told the War Cabinet: "it was impossible to imagine that Herr Hitler would be so foolish as to let us continue our rearmament. In effect, his [peace] terms would put us completely at his mercy. We should get no worse terms if we went on fighting, even if we were beaten, than were open to us now. If, however, we continued the war and Germany attacked us, no doubt we should suffer some damage but they also would suffer severe losses"[73]. At a meeting later that evening with ministers who were not in the War Cabinet, Hugh Dalton recorded Churchill as being "quite magnificent". He quoted Churchill in his diary as saying "if at last the long story [i.e. British history] is to end, it were better it should end, not through surrender, but only when we are rolling senseless on the ground"[74].

We must bear in mind three factors in assessing Churchill's comments at the War Cabinet concerning the possibility of asking Nazi Germany for peace. First, they are isolated and very different from what he said both before and after that meeting. Second, he had around the Cabinet table many ministers from the Chamberlain regime, several of whom would probably have been glad of peace with Hitler. Refusing to entertain any offer whatsoever would have isolated himself from large parts of his own government. As it was, he managed to carry the War Cabinet with him, but only just. Finally, though Churchill may have been prepared to grant Hitler "overlordship of Central Europe", Hitler might have wanted to keep control of France and the Low Countries, which would probably have been unacceptable to Britain.

In any case, if Churchill's resolve did briefly falter, he never wavered to the extent of asking Hitler for terms: later in that same meeting, he refused to do so. His period of irresolution, if that is what it was, did not last for more than a few hours. He told the War Cabinet at a further meeting that evening, i.e. 26 May, that they should wait to see how many British troops could be rescued from the beaches of Dunkirk. As the success of the evacuation became clearer over the next few days, it became more obvious that Britain was not yet decisively beaten. Three days later, on 29 May, Churchill sent a note around his Government ordering that "... whatever may happen on the Continent, we cannot doubt our duty and we shall certainly use all our power to defend the Island, the Empire and our Cause"[75]. A month later, after France had fallen, Churchill was still dauntless. On 24 June, he insisted to the Prime Minister of Canada, Mackenzie King, that "I shall myself never enter into any peace negotiations with Hitler"[76]. On 28 June, he instructed Lord Halifax, his foreign secretary, to make it clear to the Papal Nuncio, "that we do not desire to make any enquiries as to terms of peace with Hitler, and that all our agents are strictly forbidden to entertain any such suggestion"[77].

Churchill took this line because he believed that Hitler would only offer Britain terms which would, in effect, leave it at Hitler's mercy. He was not prepared to concede that at any rate, while there was any chance of victory, or even of a stalemate. It was of particular importance that America be convinced that Britain intended to fight on, so Churchill assured President Roosevelt of this several times throughout June and July 1940. In public, Churchill consistently spat defiance at Hitler. In his immortal "fight on the beaches" speech, he scorned (rightly, as it turned out) Hitler's ability to invade Britain, making the Dunkirk evacuation seem almost a victory: "We are told that Herr Hitler has a plan for invading the British Isles. This has often been thought of before. … Napoleon … was told by someone, 'There are bitter weeds in England'. There are certainly a great many more of them since the British Expeditionary Force returned"[78]. In his equally famous "Battle of Britain" speech, he delivered a broadside which should have told even the Führer that a separate peace was out of the question while Churchill remained in power:

> "What General Weygand called the 'Battle of France' is over. I expect that the battle of Britain is about to begin. Upon this battle depends the survival of Christian civilisation. Upon it depends our own British life and the long continuity of our institutions and our Empire. The whole fury and might of the enemy must very soon be turned on us. Hitler knows that he will have to break us in this island or lose the war. If we can stand up to him, all Europe may be free …. But if we fail then the whole world … will sink into the abyss of a new dark age, made more sinister, and perhaps more prolonged, by the lists of a perverted science. Let us therefore brace ourselves to our duty and so bear ourselves that if the British Commonwealth and Empire lasts for a thousand years, men will still say, 'This was their finest hour'"[79].

While his British opponent was spitting defiance at every opportunity, Hitler reverted to the pro-British ideology in *Mein Kampf* and his *Second Book*. Goebbels' diary records that Hitler refused to respond to Churchill, "who is trying to provoke us"[80]. According to Ribbentrop, talking to an amazed Ciano in

June, Hitler did:

> "... not desire the destruction of the British Empire. He asks only that
> England renounce [the former German colonies] and accept [German
> dominance in Europe]. On these conditions, Hitler would be prepared to
> come to an agreement ...If England chooses peace, the Führer will be
> happy to cooperate in the reconstruction of Europe"[81].

Hitler asked Ribbentrop to draft a speech along these lines, offering peace to
Britain. Believing that the war would be over very soon, the German people
enjoyed the coffee and silk which their army had plundered from France[82]. In
the ten days that Ribbentrop took to write the speech, Hitler had turned
indecisively against Britain. Ciano noted in his diary in early July his impression
of the Germans' attitude: "[Hitler] is rather inclined to continue the struggle and
to unleash a storm of wrath and steel upon the English. But the final decision
has not been reached, and it is for this reason that he is delaying his speech, or
which, as he himself puts it, he wants to weigh every word"[83]. He had already
mentioned the possibility of invasion to his army commander, von Brauchitsch,
who had mentioned casually that it might be necessary to invade Britain if she
would not make peace.

"Hitler agreed", noted his *Luftwaffe* adjutant later, "but preferred to see how
things turned out in the short run. Britain's war policies, [Hitler] said, amounted
to an expression of Churchill's personal ambitions. These could only be realised
through war. Accordingly, Churchill had been beavering away since the mid-
1930's in the hope of engineering a war and had now found an ally in his
endeavour – Roosevelt ... Churchill had organised feeling against Germany in
the English-speaking world with allegations that Hitler wanted war with the
West. If a German invasion of Britain succeeded, it would then be at least
questionable whether Britain would be able to carry on the fight from her
outposts of Empire as Churchill was now promising in Parliament"[84].

On 16 July, Hitler gave orders for the invasion of Britain. The Directive was
intercepted by British intelligence, and was on Churchill's desk within hours.
Its implementation clearly posed a deadly threat to Britain. Nevertheless, its
ambiguous wording displays Hitler's considerable reluctance to come to grips
with his last remaining enemy:

"TOP SECRET

Führer Headquarters

❧

16 July 1940

Since England, despite her hopeless military situation, still shows no sign of wanting to come to terms, I have decided to prepare a landing operation and, if necessary, to carry it out.

The aim of this operation is to eliminate the English homeland as a base for ... the war against Germany, and if necessary to occupy it altogether."

He discarded Ribbentrop's speech[85], and gave a rambling, 90-minute oration of his own to the Reichstag, on 19 July. In the middle of this oration, he created twelve new field marshals and appointed Göring, who was already a field marshal, a Reichsmarschall**. An American journalist in Berlin, and subsequently a distinguished historian of Nazi Germany, William Shirer, described the occasion as a "fantastic show" and noted that Hitler had a gift "for using his face and eyes ... and the turn of his head for irony, of which there was considerable in tonight's speech, especially when he referred to Churchill"[86]. Hitler made an unsubtle reference to Churchill's speech the previous month, which had talked about the continuation of the war from Britain's empire, were Britain to be occupied:

"From Britain, I now hear only one cry – not of the people but of the politicians – that the war must go on... [British politicians] declare that ... even if Great Britain should perish, they would carry on from Canada ... Presumably only those gentlemen interested in the continuation of the war will go there ...

** The first of this rank in more than two centuries and only the second in history. As so often with Göring, his pretensions struck everybody else as ridiculous, but he revelled in the opportunity to wear a new uniform with new insignia.

Believe me, gentlemen, I feel a deep disgust for this type of unscrupulous politician who wrecks whole countries."

The unscrupulous Nazi politician, who was destined to wreck a score of countries, including his own, before his career was over, continued with an even more direct *ad hominem* attack on Churchill:

"Mr Churchill will no doubt be in Canada already where the money and children of those principally interested in the war have already been sent. For millions of their people, however, great suffering will begin.

…

In this hour I feel compelled, standing before my conscience, to direct yet another appeal to reason in England. I believe I can do this as I am not asking for something as the vanquished, but rather, as the victor, I am speaking in the name of reason. I see no compelling reason which could force the continuation of this war.

I can see no reason why this war needs to continue.

…

Mr Churchill ought, for once, to believe me when I prophesy that a great world empire will be destroyed, a world empire which I never had the ambition to destroy or as much as harm. Alas, I fully am aware that the continuation of this war will end only in the complete shattering of one of the two warring parties. Mr. Churchill may believe this to be Germany. I know it to be England".

According to Shirer, Hitler's speech left the deputies in the Reichstag cold: "no applause, no cheering, no stamping of heavy boots. There was silence. And it was tense"[87]. It left the British even colder. A BBC journalist called Sefton Delmer completely rejected all of Hitler's proposals without waiting for the Government's decision. The War Cabinet agreed that nothing in the speech required a response from the Government[88]. The only overt response came from Churchill, who ordered an air raid on Germany that night. The war would continue, though Goebbels reported that Hitler still had some difficulty in accepting this, noting in his diary that Hitler was "still minded to wait awhile. After all, he appealed to the British people, not Churchill".

"Britain at bay"

With the fall of France, and the escape of most of the British Army back to England from the beaches of Dunkirk, neither Hitler nor Churchill was certain what to do next. This was disastrous for the Germans: as General von Manstein later noted, "when Hitler conceived the plan (without actually making up his mind) to tackle Britain by invasion, no practical preparations whatever had been taken to this end. In consequence we threw away our best chance of taking immediate advantage of Britain's weakness"[89]. Whatever the General may have said, it is difficult to see what Hitler could have done even had he started preparing the year before, as the Royal Air Force was still active, and the Royal Navy was vastly stronger than its German counterpart.

Hitler and Churchill devoted some time over the summer to speculating on the other's next move. As David Irving wrote, "Winston Churchill's resistance in the summer of 1940 overthrew the very basis of Hitler's calculations"[90]. According to his *Luftwaffe* adjutant, "[Hitler] did not imagine for one moment that Churchill would be ready for peace negotiations … in the next Reichstag session, he [Hitler] would make a fresh offer to Britain even though he did not think it was likely to be successful"[91]. Churchill wondered whether Hitler would soon invade Spain, musing that Hitler might shrink "from becoming embroiled in a war with the Spanish people"[92], though in fact the Germans were trying to work with the Spanish government, which they thought "determined not to come in until Britain was defeated"[93]. Hitler was acknowledging defeat in this endeavour by 1 November, calling General Franco a "Jesuit swine"[94]. More accurate, as it turned out, was a note by Anthony Eden. It suggested that Hitler might attempt to conquer Egypt if he could not invade or starve Britain[95].

Churchill realised that Hitler was a far more dangerous opponent now that he controlled most of Europe. In his famous Battle of Britain speech, he told the House of Commons that "if Hitler can bring under his despotic control the industries of the countries he has conquered, this will add greatly to his already vast armament output"[96]. In a letter to Reynaud during the Battle of France, Churchill had refused to send most of the Royal Air Force to help the defeated French, forecasting that "Hitler will break his air weapon in trying to invade us". He made a similar prediction to his old friend the South African General Smuts the next day. In telegrams to Smuts and Beaverbrook, Churchill forecast, correctly, that, if Britain could frustrate Hitler, Hitler would probably "recoil eastwards. Indeed he may do this even without trying invasion"[97].

By July, Hitler saw that peace with Britain was extremely unlikely, if not impossible, while Churchill was still Prime Minister, though he may, briefly, have believed that attacks by the *Luftwaffe* on Britain's shipping would bring Churchill to the conference table[98]. He advised his Field Marshals to wait to see what the *Luftwaffe* could do, and also watch for a possible general election[99]. He seems to have been unaware that general elections had been suspended in Britain for the duration of the war. He sent a German lawyer to the British embassy in Sweden with proposals for peace, but Churchill ordered that the staff there not to meet him.

Singeing Hitler's beard

Throughout this period, Churchill sought opportunities to take the war to the enemy. Even before he became Prime Minister, he had urged heavy bombing of Germany's cities, in order to disrupt German war production and lower morale. The RAF should, he thought, sow explosive mines in the River Rhine, which was extremely important to the German economy. Britain's navy and merchant fleet had suffered heavily from German mines and this was one of the few options open to it after the fall of France. Churchill told Beaverbrook that one thing could stop Hitler –"an absolutely devastating, exterminating attack by very heavy bombers from this country upon the Nazi homeland. We must be able to overwhelm them by this means, without which I do not see a way through" [100]. This was the genesis of the bombing offensive which was to turn most of Germany's major cities to rubble, damage her war industries and communications and cost perhaps half a million civilian lives. As Churchill argued, "even if Hitler was at the gates of India, it would profit him nothing if at the same time the entire economic and scientific apparatus of German war power lay shattered and pulverised at home"[101].

While Hitler was resting after the defeat of France in late June 1940, Churchill kept up British bombing raids on Germany. Goebbels wrote in his diary that "Churchill is just trying to provoke us. But the Führer does not intend to respond, yet"[102]. At this stage in the war, however, Britain did not have the heavy bombers or enough of the big bombs necessary to devastate German industry or German cities. Churchill did not want to confine bombing to Germany. Even during the autumn of 1940, when Britain expected invasion imminently, Churchill ordered the bombing of Italy, which had just attacked Greece, though he was talked out of it by the War Cabinet[103].

Churchill also set up the Special Operations Executive, with a mission to "set Europe ablaze" through acts of sabotage in German-occupied countries. Its operations were often daring, such as the assassination of Himmler's deputy,

Heydrich, in Prague in 1942, and sometimes bizarre, as when German prisoners of war were trained to act as British spies and dropped into Germany in the hope that the Germans would capture them and think that there was a large resistance movement in the Reich itself. The SOE's operations make for exciting reading, but, though some of them undoubtedly damaged Germany's war effort, they do not seem to have had a decisive influence on the course of the war, compared to the Red Army's advance through Eastern Europe or the Anglo-American heavy bombing offensive after 1943.

Churchill was repeatedly over-optimistic about the likelihood of Britain invading, or raiding, Nazi or Vichy French possessions. The attack on the Vichy French port of Dakar in September 1940, a minor target isolated from support by hundreds of miles, was a complete disaster, and a raid on Dieppe in 1942 was a bloody fiasco. The German defenders killed more than 3,000 of the original force of 5,000 Canadians. One crucial success was achieved in July 1940, and was to have lasting consequences in both Germany and the United States. Churchill, though regretting the action, felt obliged to attack part of the French fleet at anchor at Oran in Algeria, to prevent it from going over to the Germans. More than a thousand French sailors were killed, but "the transference of these ships to Hitler would have endangered the security of both Great Britain and the United States", he declared in a radio broadcast to the French. "The peoples of Europe will not be ruled for long by the Nazi Gestapo", he added "nor will the world yield itself to Hitler's gospel of hatred, appetite and domination"[104]. Later in the war, Churchill argued to Harry Hopkins, the President's emissary, that Oran had been "the turning point in our fortunes: it made the world realise that we were in earnest in our intentions to carry on"[105]. However, as Chips Channon noted in his diary, "…how ironical that our first victory in the war should have been over our Allies"[106]. The attack at Oran clearly made Hitler realise that Churchill intended to continue the war, and further confirmation was provided by the British Ambassador to Moscow, Sir Stafford Cripps: "who was heard to explain in Moscow that Britain could not make peace 'because Germany would without doubt demand the entire British fleet to be handed over to her'"[107].

On 12 July, Churchill reflected after dinner at Chequers at length on the future course of the war. He argued that Hitler was likely to "take the other children's candy", i.e. to steal food from Occupied Europe, before he would allow the Germans to go hungry. He also thought that if the British undertook "butcher and bolt" raids on the continent, Hitler would "find himself hard put to it to hold 2,000 miles of coastline"[108] (in fact, as mentioned above, the only large raid undertaken, at Dieppe in 1942, was to be an ignominious and disastrous failure).

173

Chapter 5

The next day, over lunch, Churchill referred to "that man" (as, according to Colville, he always called Hitler – this became "that bad man" in a telegram to Roosevelt in August). He said that Britain, having attained "bombing supremacy" would make Germany "a desert, yes a desert". Hitler could "do anything he liked where there was no salt water to cross, but it would avail him nothing if he reached the Great Wall of China and this Island remained undefeated". Hitler "must be driven to attempt invasion … and he would not succeed" [109]. Over that weekend, Churchill kept repeating that "Hitler must invade or fail" [110].

On the same day, and with his usual complete lack of understanding for other people's points of view, Hitler was telling General Halder that he was:

> "greatly puzzled by Britain's persisting unwillingness to make peace. He sees the answer, (as we do) in Britain's hope on Russia, and therefore counts on having to compel her by main force to agree to peace. Actually that is much against his grain. The reason is that a military defeat of Britain will bring about the disintegration of the British Empire. This would not be of any benefit to Germany. German blood would be shed to accomplish something that would benefit only Japan, the United States and others" [111].

On 22 July, Halder recorded that, though Britain's position was "hopeless", she continued the war because of hopes of aid from Russia and America [112], though Hitler noted that Russia was not giving Britain any cause for hope in the Stalin-Cripps negotiations which there then taking place, because "the Russians are afraid of compromising themselves in our eyes; they don't want war" [113]. A week later, Churchill was refusing to answer Hitler's latest peace proposals, "not being on speaking terms with him" [114]. This had not stopped him answering previous speeches, but this time he clearly felt that the imperative for showing the world that Britain was not seeking peace despite the disasters of the spring was overwhelming. To the "ignominious" King of Sweden, who had offered to mediate at the start of August, Churchill retorted that the Government's intention was "to prosecute the war against Germany by every means in their power until Hitlerism is finally broken". He then listed all the countries whose neutrality Hitler had violated [115]. At the end of July, as Hitler was telling his generals, entirely correctly, that "Britain's hope lies in Russia and the United States" [116], Churchill wrote to Roosevelt to ask for destroyers to escort convoys in the North Atlantic, where U-boats were beginning to take a serious toll on British merchant shipping. It was vital to convince Roosevelt that Britain meant business, and had a realistic chance of staying in the war. Churchill therefore claimed that Britain was "hitting that man hard, both in repelling attacks and in bombing Germany"[117].

The Battle of Britain[tt]

"Discussion [with Hitler] of basis for warfare against England", General Halder noted in his diary on 1 July 1940 in his usual laconic style. "Prerequisite is air superiority"[118]. Three weeks later, Hitler was saying that "Britain must be reduced by the middle of September, at the time when we make the invasion"[119]. The first decisive battle in the air was fought between early July and 15 September 1940, ending in a form of stalemate which, in practice, was a strategic victory for the British, and Hitler's first defeat. The all-out German offensive against the Royal Air Force began on Eagle Day, 13 August. Three days earlier, Churchill had been arguing that Hitler's aircraft position must be less good than the British had supposed. Otherwise why would he delay an all-out onslaught on Britain?[120] When the attack came, he was quick to recognise its importance. In the fourth of his great speeches of 1940, he referred to the pilots of Fighter Command, delivering the immortal line: "never, in the field of human conflict, was so much owed by so many to so few".

Churchill had no illusions about the importance of this novel battle: "It is quite plain that Herr Hitler could not admit defeat in his air attack on Great Britain without sustaining the most serious injury"[121]. In mid-August, as the Battle of Britain raged in the skies above southern England, Churchill was at rifle practice with his son. "The whole time he talked of the best method of killing Huns. Soft-nose bullets were the thing to use and he must get some. But, said Randolph, they are illegal … to which the PM replied that the Germans would make very short work of him if they caught him, and so he didn't see why he should have any mercy on them"[122]. By mid-September, however, he was broadcasting that "there is no doubt that Herr Hitler is using up his fighter force at a very high rate, and that if he goes on for many more weeks he will wear down and ruin this vital part of his Air Force"[123].

[tt] In his June 1940 speech, Churchill clearly meant the phrase "the Battle of Britain" to signify more than the series of engagements between Fighter Command and the Luftwaffe in the summer of that year. He also meant to include the naval battles, British bombing raids on German-occupied Europe and the ground defence of the British Isles. However, the term has since been attached to the struggles of Fighter Command against the *Luftwaffe* in the late summer of 1940 and I see no reason to depart from this convention.

Chapter 5

Invasion

As noted in Chapter 2, Hitler relished the thought of taking part in an invasion of England in 1914. A quarter of a century later, he was to get the chance to put his hope into practice, as a Supreme Commander rather than as a private soldier. Churchill knew that the only way for the Germans to win the war swiftly was to conquer the British Isles. For his part, he seems to have regarded the possibility of an invasion with less concern than many of his countrymen. In July 1940, when Germany had just crushed France in six weeks and Britain had hardly any well-equipped land forces left, he wrote a paper for the War Cabinet in which he argued that an invasion in the near future was very unlikely to succeed[124], though this did not of course mean that it would not be attempted. As late as mid-October, when the stormy weather in the Channel was starting to make an invasion impossible, and with German barges assembled, he was arguing that it was "premature to suppose that the danger of invasion had passed"[125]. He never had the slightest doubt that it was to the twenty-mile stretch of water that England owed its deliverance. His doctor quotes him musing in 1952: "If the Almighty were to rebuild the world and he asked me for advice I would have English Channels round every country. And the atmosphere would be such that anything which attempted to fly would be set on fire"[126].

Hitler agreed with Churchill. He remarked to General Halder in July that a "positively decisive result can be achieved only by invasion of Britain"[127], and in mid-September that a "successful landing followed by occupation would end the war in short order"[128]. However, on 21 July, the Nazi dictator told his Generals that he considered an invasion of Britain to be "very risky"[129]. He did not share the overconfidence of his foreign minister, who told his Italian counterpart on 19 September that "the invasion will take place as soon as there are a few days of fine weather... A single German division will suffice to bring about a complete collapse"[130]. In fact, the Germans had already begun to dismantle the airborne component of their invasion force in such a way that it was very unlikely that they could mount an invasion that year. Again, the codebreakers at Bletchley Park told Churchill of the German action almost as soon as Hitler had issued the order, and Churchill immediately realised its significance. According to the code-breaker who gave him the news:

> "... the conference knew that the dismantling of the air-loading equipment meant the end of the threat ... There was a very broad smile on Churchill's face now as he lit up his massive cigar and suggested that we should all take a little fresh air. As we surfaced, the air raid was at its height. Winston stood alone in front ... his chin thrust out, the long cigar

in his mouth … It was a moment in history to remember".

He quotes Churchill's angry voice:

"by God, we'll get the B's [sic] for this"[131].

The German Ordnance Office had apparently always been told that an invasion of England was not being considered[132].

Writing after the war, Churchill declared that he was always confident that Britain could defeat any invasion attempted, and described invasion as "the kind of battle which … one ought to be content to fight"[133]. He clearly took the possibility of invasion seriously, however, even if he was aware from his experience with the Dardanelles fiasco in the First World War how difficult successful invasions were. Throughout September 1940, rumours of an invasion reached Churchill. It was clear that invasion barges were being moved to Channel ports, where they were repeatedly and successfully attacked by the RAF. On 7 September 1940, the pre-arranged codeword "Cromwell" was actually sent out to the army to indicate "Invasion Imminent". The signal was somehow copied to the Home Guard, and disseminated widely. The wider population seems to have taken it to mean that the Germans had actually started to move across the Channel. Church bells were rung as an invasion signal, but no invaders appeared.

One telling detail shows how far Churchill was prepared to go to defeat an attack by Hitler's forces. In the event of an invasion of the English south coast, he was prepared to sanction the use of poison gas on German troops. He even thought that Hitler might pre-empt him, and wanted to be prepared. Asking General Ismay about British gas masks, Churchill also speculated that Hitler had "some gas designs on us"[134]. In the event he was wrong. The Germans never used poison gas against British troops during the Second World War, but this was a possibility about which it was clearly better to be safe than to be sorry.

Had Britain been successfully invaded in the summer of 1940, the Nazis would have attempted to arrest 2,820 people on a list compiled by Walter Schellenberg of the German Secret Service, the SD. With the element of farce that was often present in the Nazi invasion plans in the summer of 1940, the document was handed to the man who was to be in charge of the arrests on the day that the invasion was stood down indefinitely[135]. Unsurprisingly, Churchill headed the list. It is inaccurate in many places, including people who had already died, such as Sigmund Freud. For reasons that are not clear, Churchill and some others on the list were to be handed over to Amt VI (Foreign Intelligence), rather than Amt IV (the *Gestapo*), which was charged with the detention of most of the prisoners. What Hitler would have done with Churchill had he been captured is not certain. Based on the fate of hostile foreign statesman whom the Nazis captured, Churchill's execution was almost certain, but it is not clear whether Hitler would have organised a show trial, to humiliate his arch rival and provide a semblance of legality.

The Blitz

During the First World War, Germany had bombed England repeatedly. Plans for destroying London with incendiary bombs were about to be implemented when the Armistice intervened. The total number of British civilians killed in German raids during the First World War, however, was less than an average day's loss of life on the Western Front. At least since the start of the Second World War, Hitler had envisaged bombing England and Speer later remembered:

> "his [Hitler's] reaction to the final scene of a newsreel on the bombing of Warsaw in the autumn of 1939. We were sitting with him and Goebbels in his Berlin salon watching the film. Clouds of smoke darkened the sky; dive bombers tilted and hurtled towards their goal … Hitler was fascinated. The film ended with a montage showing a plane diving toward the outlines of the British Isles. A burst of flame followed and the island flew into the air in tatters. Hitler's enthusiasm was unbounded. 'That is what will happen to them' he cried out, carried away. 'That is how we will annihilate them'"[136].

After the British attacked Berlin, Hitler bombed British cities. At a conference on 14 September, Hitler gave his air force "a free hand in attacking residential areas"[137]. "Churchill had brought [the Blitz] upon himself by his pathetic air raids on Berlin that summer"[138]. The man whose air force had rained terror upon Guernica in Spain, Rotterdam, Warsaw, Coventry and London told the Germans in his New Year message in 1941 that "Herr Churchill was the man who suddenly discovered unrestricted air raids as the great secret for victory. This criminal has been bombing German cities by night … for three and a half months". Somewhat hypocritically, given his wish to attack Germany with a destructive bombing campaign, Churchill said in a broadcast on 11 September 1940 that:

"These cruel, wanton, indiscriminate bombings of London are, of course, a part of Hitler's invasion plans. He hopes, by killing large numbers of civilians, and women and children, that he will terrorise and cow the people of this mighty imperial city … Little does he know the spirit of the British nation, or the tough fibre of the Londoners … This wicked man, the repository and embodiment of many forms of soul-destroying hatred, this monstrous product of former wrongs and shame, has now resolved to try to break our famous island race … What he has done is to kindle a fire in British hearts … which will glow along after all traces of the conflagration … have been removed…"[139]

Churchill correctly foresaw that the Blitz would "fail", as he wrote to the Prime Minister of Canada as early as 6 October 1940[140]. He even made light of its effects in the House of Commons on 8 October: "A month has passed since Herr Hitler turned his rage and malice on to the civil populations of our great cities … Statisticians may amuse themselves by calculating that … it would take 10 years at the present rate, for half the houses of London to be demolished … Quite a lot of things are going to happen to Herr Hitler and the Nazi regime before 10 years are up"[141]. In a letter to Sir Samuel Hoare, he went even further, saying that Britain had "got Hitler beat and … his doom is certain"[142]. By November, surveying the course of the war, Churchill saw "no reason to regret that Herr Hitler tried to break the British spirit by the blind bombing of our cities and our countryside"[143].

Though he belittled their effects, Hitler's attacks on Britain's civilian population clearly roused Churchill to an even greater level of fury in his attacks on the Nazi dictator. In July, he had already envisaged German air raids on London being answered by British raids on Berlin[144]. In a broadcast to France on 21 October, he attacked Hitler and Mussolini in the strongest terms yet:

"Herr Hitler … has managed to subjugate for the time being most of the finest races in Europe [with] his little Italian accomplice … trotting along hopefully and hungrily… this evil man, this monstrous abortion of hatred and defeat, is resolved on nothing less than the complete wiping out of the French nation … By all kinds of sly and savage means he is plotting and working to quench for ever the fountain of characteristic French culture … All Europe, if he had his way, will be reduced to one uniform Bocheland, to be exploited, pillaged and bullied by his Nazi gangsters…

Chapter 5

He was already looking ahead to punishing Hitler and his cronies after the war:

> "…All these schemes and crimes of Herr Hitler's are bringing upon him and upon all who belong to his system a retribution which many of us will live to see. We are on his track …
>
> … We seek to beat the life and soul out of Hitler and Hitlerism"[145].

Given his well-known indifference to personal danger, it was perhaps inevitable that Churchill would watch at least some of the bombing, however much his lack of concern for his own safety horrified his staff. Hitler studiously kept himself out of danger during the Second World War, but Churchill stood with his bodyguard "on the roof of the No. 10 Annexe watching the German bombers attacking London. Later, [Churchill] remarked firmly, 'I must take the same chance as the rest'"[146]. In early 1941, he refused to have an air raid shelter built at his country seat, Chartwell, though this was apparently because of a Ministry of Works estimate that it would cost £700[147]. He continued to pour scorn on his German opponent. By December, Churchill was refusing to compare Hitler and Napoleon since he "did not wish to insult the dead"[148]. In Parliament, Churchill also refused to compare Hitler and Napoleon, saying that he "always deprecate[d] comparisons"[149]. Four days later, however, Churchill made a similar comparison of his own: in a broadcast to the Italians, Churchill did, however, refer to Hitler as an "Attila over the Brenner Pass with his hordes of ravenous soldiery and his gangs of Gestapo policemen"[150].

---

[1] *The Goebbels Diaries, 1939-41*, p.24

[2] *Never Despair*, Martin Gilbert, p.589

[3] *Step by Step*, Winston Churchill, p.

[4] *Finest Hour, 1939-41*, Martin Gilbert, p.56

[5] *Hitler and Churchill*, Andrew Roberts, p.164-65

[6] *Hitler's War*, David Irving, p.6

[7] *The Private War Journal of Colonel General Franz Halder*, Vol. 1, p.94

[8] Hitler's speech in Danzig, 19 September 1939

[9] Hitler's speech in Danzig, 6 October 1939

[10] *Churchill War Papers*, Vol. 1, Martin Gilbert, p.226

[11] *Finest Hour, 1939-41*, Martin Gilbert, p.57

[12] *Churchill War Papers*, Vol. 1, Martin Gilbert, p.322-3

[13] *The Neville Chamberlain Diary Letters*, Vol.4, p.467

[14] *Churchill War Papers*, Vol. 1, Martin Gilbert, p.235

[15] *The Private War Journal of Colonel General Franz Halder*, Vol. 1, p.106

[16] *The Private War Journal of Colonel General Franz Halder*, Vol. 1, p.100

[17] *The Goebbels Diaries, 1939-41*, p.23

[18] *The Goebbels Diaries, 1939-41*, p.24

[19] *The Goebbels Diaries, 1939-41*, p.64

[20] *The Times*, 1 February 1940
[21] *The Goebbels Diaries*, 1939-41, p.107
[22] *The Impact of Hitler*, Maurice Cowling, p.352
[23] *Chips – The Diaries of Sir Henry Channon*, Sir Henry Channon, p.224
[24] *The Fringes of Power*, Sir Jock Colville, p.28
[25] *The Second World War*, Winston Churchill, Vol. 1, Ch XXII
[26] *Hansard*, 4 September 1939
[27] *The Goebbels Diaries*, 1939-41, p.33
[28] *The Goebbels Diaries*, 1939-41, p.26
[29] *Into Battle*, Winston Churchill, p.138
[30] *The Goebbels Diaries*, 1939-41, p.20-22
[31] *The Goebbels Diaries*, 1939-41, p.23
[32] *Churchill War Papers*, Vol. 1, Martin Gilbert, p.98
[33] *Churchill War Papers*, Vol. 1, Martin Gilbert, p.148
[34] *The Harold Nicolson Diaries*, Harold Nicolson, p.202
[35] *Into Battle*, Winston Churchill, p.128
[36] *Into Battle*, Winston Churchill, p.146
[37] *The Second World War*, Winston Churchill, Vol. 1, p.445
[38] *Hansard*, 27 February 1940
[39] Cabinet papers 65/2/3
[40] *The Private War Journal of Colonel General Franz Halder*, Vol. 1, p.166
[41] *Churchill War Papers*, Vol. 1, Martin Gilbert, p.553
[42] *Churchill War Papers*, Vol. 1, Martin Gilbert, p.670
[43] *The Goebbels Diaries*, 1939-41, p.101
[44] *The Goebbels Diaries*, 1939-41, p.102
[45] *Churchill War Papers*, Vol. 1, Martin Gilbert, p.671
[46] *The Private War Journal of Colonel General Franz Halder*, Vol. 1, p.183
[47] *Churchill War Papers, Vol. III, The Ever-Widening War*, Martin Gilbert, p.1520
[48] *Hitler's Table Talk*, p.399-400
[49] *Hitler's War*, David Irving, p.93
[50] *Hansard*, 27 February 1940
[51] *Hitler's War*, David Irving, p.85-86
[52] Diary of Ambassador Hewel, 6 July 1941
[53] *Hansard*, 11 April 1940
[54] *Hansard*, 11 April 1940
[55] *Churchill War Papers*, Vol. 1, Martin Gilbert, p.1011
[56] *The Private War Journal of Colonel General Franz Halder*, Vol. 1, p.342
[57] *The Eden Memoirs, The Reckoning*, Earl of Avon, p.96
[58] *Hansard*, 8 May 1940
[59] *Churchill War Papers*, Vol. 1, Martin Gilbert, p.1252
[60] *Chips – The Diaries of Sir Henry Channon*, Sir Henry Channon, p.246
[61] *King George VI*, John Wheeler-Bennett, p.446
[62] *King George VI*, John Wheeler-Bennett, p.445
[63] *The Gathering Storm*, Winston Churchill, p.525
[64] *Beside the Bulldog*, Walter Thompson, p.84-5
[65] *Winston Churchill, Struggle for Survival*, Lord Moran, p.324
[66] *Churchill War Papers*, Vol. 1, Martin Gilbert, p.1287
[67] *Ciano's diary 1937-1943*, Ciano, p.350
[68] *Churchill War Papers*, Vol. 2, Martin Gilbert, p.151
[69] *Churchill War Papers*, Vol. 2, Martin Gilbert, p.156-58

[70] *War Cabinet Minutes*, 27 May 1940

[71] *The Private War Journal of Colonel General Franz Halder*, Vol. 1, p.413

[72] *Ciano's diary 1937-1943*, Ciano, p.363

[73] *Churchill War Papers*, Vol. 2, Martin Gilbert, p.180-81

[74] *Churchill War Papers*, Vol. 2, Martin Gilbert, p.182-83

[75] *Churchill War Papers*, Vol. 2, Martin Gilbert, p.187

[76] *Churchill War Papers*, Vol. 2, Martin Gilbert, p.409

[77] Minute of 28 June 1940: Churchill Papers, 20/13, quoted in *Finest Hour, Winston S Churchill, 1939-41*, Martin Gilbert, p.607

[78] *Hansard*, 4 June 1940

[79] *Hansard*, 18 June 1940

[80] Goebbels diaries, 29 June 1940

[81] *Ciano's Diplomatic Papers*, p.373

[82] *Hitler Confronts England*, Walter Ansel, p.3

[83] *Ciano's diary 1937-1943*, Ciano, p.369

[84] *At Hitler's Side*, Nicolaus von Below, p.64

[85] *Ribbentrop*, Michael Bloch, p.310-311

[86] *Berlin Diary*, William L Shirer, p.455

[87] *Berlin Diary*, William L Shirer, p.453

[88] War Cabinet Minutes, 24 July 1940 CAB 65/8/23

[89] *Lost Victories*, Field Marshal Eric von Manstein, p.157

[90] *Hitler's War*, David Irving, p.152

[91] *At Hitler's Side*, Nicolaus von Below, p.63

[92] *Churchill War Papers*, Vol. 2, Martin Gilbert, p.566

[93] *The Private War Journal of Colonel General Franz Halder*, Vol. 1, p.565

[94] *The Private War Journal of Colonel General Franz Halder*, Vol. 1, p.670

[95] *The Eden Memoirs, The Reckoning*, Earl Avon, Appendix B

[96] *Hansard*, 18 June 1940

[97] *Churchill War Papers*, Vol. 2, Martin Gilbert, p.269-71

[98] *Göring, A Biography*, David Irving, p.292

[99] *Hitler's War*, David Irving, p.158

[100] *Churchill War Papers*, Vol. 2, Martin Gilbert, p.429, 492

[101] *Hansard*, 18 August 1940

[102] Goebbels diaries, August 1940

[103] *Finest Hour, Winston S. Churchill, 1939-41*, Martin Gilbert, p.876

[104] *Churchill War Papers*, Vol. 2, Martin Gilbert, p.517

[105] *The Fringes of Power*, Sir Jock Colville, p.335

[106] *Chips – The Diaries of Sir Henry Channon*, Sir Henry Channon, p.260

[107] *Hitler's War*, David Irving, p.143

[108] *The Fringes of Power*, Sir Jock Colville, p.192

[109] *The Fringes of Power*, Sir Jock Colville, p.194

[110] *The Fringes of Power*, Sir Jock Colville, p.195

[111] *The Private War Journal of Colonel General Franz Halder*, Vol. 1, p.506

[112] *The Private War Journal of Colonel General Franz Halder*, Vol. 1, p.515

[113] *The Private War Journal of Colonel General Franz Halder*, Vol. 1, p.518

[114] *The Fringes of Power*, Sir Jock Colville, p.200

[115] *Churchill War Papers*, Vol. 2, Martin Gilbert, p.603

[116] *The Private War Journal of Colonel General Franz Halder*, Vol. 1, p.533

[117] *The Fringes of Power*, Sir Jock Colville, p.205

[118] *The Private War Journal of Colonel General Franz Halder*, Vol. 1, p.487

[119] *The Private War Journal of Colonel General Franz Halder*, Vol. 1, p.516
[120] *The Fringes of Power*, Sir Jock Colville, p.177
[121] *Hansard*, 18 August 1940
[122] *The Fringes of Power*, Sir Jock Colville, p.219
[123] *Churchill War Papers*, Vol. 2, Martin Gilbert, p.801
[124] CAB 66/9/44, 10 July 1940
[125] CAB 65/9/33, 15 October 1940
[126] *Winston Churchill, The Struggle for Survival*, Lord Moran, p.366
[127] *The Private War Journal of Colonel General Franz Halder*, Vol. 1, p.531
[128] *The Private War Journal of Colonel General Franz Halder*, Vol. 1, p.583
[129] *At Hitler's Side*, Nicolaus von Below, p.69
[130] *Ciano's diary 1937-1943*, Ciano, p.383
[131] *The Ultra Secret*, FW Winterbotham, p.58-60
[132] *The Private War Journal of Colonel General Franz Halder*, Vol. 1, p.488
[133] *The Second World War*, Winston Churchill, p.397
[134] *Churchill War Papers*, Vol. 2, Martin Gilbert, p.516
[135] *The Rise and Fall of the Third Reich*, William Shirer, p.937
[136] *Inside the Third Reich*, Albert Speer, p.317-8
[137] *The Private War Journal of Colonel General Franz Halder*, Vol. 1, p.585
[138] *At Hitler's Side*, Nicolaus von Below, p.77
[139] *Churchill War Papers*, Vol. 2, Martin Gilbert, p.802-03
[140] *Churchill War Papers*, Vol. 2, Martin Gilbert, p.905
[141] *Churchill War Papers*, Vol. 2, Martin Gilbert, p.913
[142] *Churchill War Papers*, Vol. 2, Martin Gilbert, p.969
[143] *Hansard*, 5 November 1940
[144] *Finest Hour, Winston S. Churchill, 1939-41*, Martin Gilbert, p.673
[145] *Churchill War Papers*, Vol. 2, Martin Gilbert, p.981
[146] *Beside the Bulldog*, Walter Thompson, p.94
[147] *Churchill War Papers, Vol. III, The Ever-Widening War*, Martin Gilbert, p.73
[148] *Hansard*, 21 December 1940
[149] *Hansard*, 19 December 1940
[150] *Churchill War Papers*, Vol. 2, Martin Gilbert, p.1287

6

Germany on Top (1941)

At the start of 1941, Germany seemed invincible. Britain had no immediate prospect of liberating the countries which Germany had conquered in 1939 and 1940. Nevertheless, Germany's hopes for the summer, that the war would be over quickly, had been disappointed. Hitler's New Year message to the German armed forces blamed: "the will of the warmongering democrats, and of their capitalist and Jewish allies for the continuation of the war"[1]. Hitler also argued, incredibly, that Britain's war aim was "to dominate the Continent [of Europe]". He "was convinced that Churchill was waiting for either the United States or the USSR to enter the war against Germany"[2], and he was not the only person thinking along these lines.

In fact, Hitler had already decided to do exactly what his enemy wanted. In December 1940, he had signed the directive for the invasion of Russia, one of the great misjudgements that were to seal his fate. In doing so, he was to give Churchill the one thing the British Prime Minister craved above all: a mighty ally. Churchill was not to know of Hitler's decision for several months. The country had survived the trials of the Battle of Britain and the first part of the Blitz, and would continue to defy Germany. If the invasion of Russia was eventually to seal Hitler's doom, this did not mean that Churchill was able to lessen his efforts. During the first few months of the year, Britain had to deal with a Nazi stranglehold on her oceanic lifeline, the Italian invasion of Egypt and nightly bombing of her cities by the *Luftwaffe*.

Looking back after the war, Churchill wrote that he could not "recall any period when its stresses ... bore more directly on me and my colleagues than the first half of 1941"[*]. However, even at this dark time, he seems never to have doubted the eventual outcome of the struggle against "the only enemy who matters - Hitler"[3], as long as Britain's oceanic lifelines to the New World and to its oil supplies in the Middle East could be kept open. In this, he was no doubt encouraged to hear from Roosevelt's close advisor, Harry Hopkins. After a long Churchillian speech on freedom, Hopkins commented: "I don't think the President will give a dam' for all that ... You see, we're only interested in seeing that that Goddam sonofabitch, Hitler, gets licked"[4].

In June 1941, Churchill wrote two letters in this vein. He told his son, Randolph, that he felt "more sure than ever that we shall beat the life out of Hitler and his Nazi gang"[5]. He wrote to the Prime Minister of Yugoslavia, who had just refused passage to German troops which were going to help the Italians in Greece, "Your Excellency, the eventual total defeat of Hitler and Mussolini is certain"[6]. In writing this appeal, he ignored the inconvenient fact that America's only real resolve was to keep out of the war, and in any case, he would of course have wanted to present an optimistic face to a wavering neutral. This appeal nevertheless corresponds to his resolute words in public and in private. "My one aim is to extirpate Hitlerism from Europe", he remarked in a speech in Glasgow in January 1941[7]. Two months later, Churchill declared in a broadcast that no prudent and far-seeing man could doubt that the eventual and total defeat of Hitler and Mussolini was certain. However, even his eloquence could not prevent the Yugoslavs from signing an alliance with Hitler two days after he sent the appeal, and the fact was that without American and Russian intervention, Britain's prospects of liberating Europe and overthrowing Hitler, as opposed to simply surviving, were slim.

Churchill constantly looked for opportunities to engage the Germans on the continent of Europe. He also tried to guard against any sudden moves Hitler might make. In December 1940, before the War Cabinet, Churchill had argued that Hitler's most likely next move was towards Spain and the North African coast[8], though he considered that it would be dangerous for Germany to do so. In fact, Hitler had tried and failed to involve Spain in the war. Churchill recognised this in January 1941: "it is becoming increasingly unlikely that the Spanish Government will give Hitler passage or join the war against us"[9], he wrote to the Chiefs of Staff Committee. Spain and Turkey were the dogs that never barked during the Second World War. Both countries resisted persistent

---

[*] Though in fact he seems to have nominated September and October 1942 for the most stressful of the war in conversation with his doctor in 1953. *Struggle for Survival*, Moran, p.71

attempts from both sides to involve them in the conflict. Spain remained neutral throughout the war, and Turkey did so until her participation was too late to affect the outcome.

Churchill's attitudes towards the Germans in general and Nazis in particular were hardening during this period. At a lunch with Charles Eade, the editor of the *Sunday Dispatch*, on 6 March 1941, Mrs Churchill said that the English people were unable to hate their enemies. Churchill replied that before the war was over, they would be hating their enemies all right[10]. Reports of Nazi atrocities in Occupied Europe clearly strengthened his views. "Surely more stir ought to be made about Hitler shooting the Norwegian Trade Unionists...?" he wrote in response to reports of one atrocity[11]. While Churchill was concentrating on the darker side of Nazi-occupied Europe, Hitler and Goebbels were drawing political conclusions from Churchill's private behaviour. Goebbels noted, in May 1941, "A book on Churchill reports that he drinks too much and wears pink silk underwear. He dictates messages in the bath or in his underpants; a startling image which the Führer finds most amusing. He sees the English Empire as slowly disintegrating. Not much will be salvageable"[12]. Five days later, however, Goebbels at least was having second thoughts: "I study Churchill's new book, *Step by Step*. Speeches from 1936-39, and essays. This man is a strange mixture of heroism and cunning. If he had come to power in 1933, we would not be where we are today. And I believe that he will give a few more problems yet. But we can and will solve them. Nevertheless, he is not to be taken as lightly as we usually take him"[13].

Invasion

With the wisdom of hindsight, it is clear that the danger of a direct invasion of Britain by the Germans was over by the end of 1940, if indeed it had ever existed. Mussolini visited Hitler in January 1941, and reported back to his foreign minister that he had:

> "found a very anti-Russian Hitler, loyal to us, and not too definite on what he intends to do in the future against Great Britain. In any case, it is no longer a question of landing in England. Hitler said that the undertaking would be extremely difficult and that if it failed the first time it could not be attempted again. Added to this there is the fact that while England now fears the loaded pistol of invasion, after a failure she would know that Germany holds only an empty pistol".

Chapter 6

Ciano's counterpart was even more pessimistic: "Ribbentrop … sees no possibility of [the war] ending before 1942"[14]. Nevertheless, Hitler was demanding that preparations for the invasion continue during the winter of 1940-41[15]. He had realised that the operation was too risky (describing it to his generals as a "crime" in early 1941[16]), and had made up his mind to attack the Soviet Union instead. Churchill, however, seems to have believed that "Herr Hitler's need to starve or crush Great Britain is stronger than it has ever been … Therefore the task of preventing Invasion … must in no way be compromised for the sake of any other objective whatsoever"[17], as he wrote in early 1941.

A German directive of 12 October said that "preparation for the landing in England was "to be maintained merely as measures of political and military pressure"[18]. Hitler still wanted to "give England the k.o. – … only so we can live at peace with her, and the Englishman can only respect somebody who has knocked him out"[19]. But the means were lacking. "We cannot knock out England with a landing operation"[20], Halder quotes Hitler as saying on 16 January 1941. The *Luftwaffe* had failed to gain mastery of the skies over southern England by day; the German Navy was utterly inadequate for the task of controlling the English Channel even for the few days which an invasion would require, and the enormous numbers of suitable landing craft which an invasion would require were not available. The Straits of Dover, which are so narrow that it is possible to see one side from the other, frustrated Hitler as surely as they had frustrated Phillip II of Spain, Louis XIV and Napoleon. At a time when Britain's army could not have begun to cope with its German counterpart in Europe, Hitler was nonetheless arguing that he "must be so strong on the Continent that this aim will never be attained"[21], and was starting to fortify the northern French coast, the most likely spot for an invasion from Britain.

Churchill was also aware that a frontal assault might not be the only way for Hitler to win the war. In January, he wrote to the Earl of Selborne: "That bad man [Hitler] may as you say try Ireland and the mad policy of [Irish Prime Minister Eamonn] de Valera makes it difficult to ward off the first lodgement. However, we are watching very carefully and will do our best"[22]. Hitler had in fact asked his staff to investigate the possibility of an invasion of Ireland in late 1940, but Admiral Raeder, the head of the German Navy, demonstrated that in the face of Britain's vastly more powerful fleet, such an operation was "quite out of the question"[23].

With an invasion impossible, Hitler continued to hammer Britain with the *Luftwaffe*. He had never been to London and seems to have thought that a few raids would destroy the sprawling city. As noted in Chapter 4, many Britons, including Churchill, had expressed similar views during the 1930s. With his usual ignorance of British history he ranted at a supper in 1940 that "a single source of fire would destroy the whole city, as happened once before, two hundred years ago[†]". As Churchill wrote, however, "the assault upon our lives and homes ... failed utterly in its purpose of breaking the British spirit"[24]. On the contrary, there is even evidence from Cabinet papers that morale was highest where bombing was heaviest[25].

In any case, Hitler's attention had turned towards the steppes of Russia, which he wanted, and away from England, which he had never coveted. Churchill was aware that this could happen at some point. In January 1941, he wrote to Roosevelt that "it would be natural for Hitler to make a strong threat against the British Isles in order to occupy us here and cover his Eastern designs. The forces at his disposal are, however, so large that he could carry out both offensives at the same time"[26]. As early as 31 July 1940, Hitler remarked in conference with his generals that:

> "All that Russia has to do is to hint that she does not care to have a strong Germany and the British will take hope, like one about to go under, that the situation will undergo a radical change within six or eight months.
>
> <u>With Russia smashed, Britain's last hope would be shattered...</u>
>
> <u>Decision: Russia's destruction must therefore be made a part of this struggle. Spring '41".</u> [Halder's emphasis]"[27].

However, the British of 1940 were not of course aware of German military thinking, and Churchill referred throughout that year, both in public and in private, to the possibility of some form of invasion. Though he later described invasion as "the kind of battle which ... one ought to be content to fight"[28], he clearly felt that the success of an invasion, while unlikely, could not be ruled out entirely. Admiral Forbes suggested at the Defence Committee that Hitler should be lured into attempting an invasion, since his chances of success were so remote. At this distance, we cannot tell whether this suggestion, which seems too clever by half, was meant seriously. Churchill, however, wisely refused to consider this plan, as it would have courted disaster[29].

[†] In fact the Great Fire had occurred almost three hundred years previously. Though it had destroyed the wooden City, it could not consume the brick and stone buildings further west.

189

Chapter 6

In a speech on 31 January 1941, Churchill said that an invasion by Hitler would be more difficult than in July the previous year. However, "that bad man has never had so great a need as he has now to strike Great Britain from his path. He is master of a great part of Europe. His armies can move almost where they will upon the Continent. He holds down eight or ten countries by force … Therefore it is for Herr Hitler a matter of supreme consequence to break down the resistance of Great Britain, and thus rivet effectively the shackles he has prepared for the rest of Europe … My one aim is to extirpate Hitlerism from Europe. The question is such a simple one"[30].

On 8 April, Churchill again alluded to the possibility that Hitler "may at any time attempt the invasion of this island … At the present moment he is driving South and South-East through the Balkans, and at any moment he may turn upon Turkey. Once we have gained the Battle of the Atlantic … then, however far Hitler may go … he may be sure that, armed with the sword of retributive justice, we shall be on his track"[31]. On 25 June 1941, after Germany had invaded Russia, he told the House of Commons that "in a few months, or even less, we may be exposed to the most frightful invasion the world has ever seen"[32].

In July 1941, Churchill was warning that "the invasion season is at hand. All the Armed Forces have been warned to be at concert pitch by 1st September and to maintain the utmost vigilance meanwhile. We have to reckon with a gambler's desperation. We have to reckon with a criminal"[33]. How exactly Hitler was to spare the huge air and land forces which he would require for the invasion of Britain when Germany had devoted all its strength to attacking Russia, Churchill did not say. Even as late as 15 October, he remarked that "he had not put out of his mind the thought that Hitler might still attempt an invasion of the British Isles … 'Hitler's revised plan undoubtedly is now – Poland '39, France '40; Russia '41; England '42 and, '43, maybe America'", and to the War Cabinet in November, he "had to keep a sufficient air force in this country to assist in repelling any invasion Germany might make next spring. Hitler had great need to invade this country"[34].

In seeking to keep the British on their toes, Churchill was helped by Hitler. Hitler had chosen to continue to prepare to invade partly to put political and military pressure on Britain but without any intention of invading. By the end of 1940, however, the invasion preparations were chiefly intended as a cover plan for the invasion of Russia[35]. When the Russians expressed concerns about the dozens of German divisions massing in Eastern Europe, the Germans would respond that they had moved the armies so far east so that British intelligence could not monitor them. Stalin's gullibility in these months was truly remarkable.

There was an amusing postscript to the rumours of an invasion in the spring of 1941. In order to cover Hitler's planned invasion of Russia, the Germans planted numerous rumours that they were likely to invade Britain in June 1941. One such rumour involved Goebbels writing an article (corrected by Hitler) about the invasion of Crete, "Crete as an Example", which attempted to show how paratroopers could be used to invade England. Once the Germans were sure that the article had reached the foreign press, copies were seized, too late to prevent it appearing in the American papers the following day. To give the impression that he had committed a *faux pas*, Goebbels placed himself in sham "disgrace" for the next few days. If this was an attempt to deceive Britain, it does not seem to have worked. British Intelligence consistently and correctly predicted an invasion of Russia throughout early 1941, and advised Stalin of the exact date on which the invasion would take place. Stalin utterly failed to act on these warnings.

Even as late as November 1941, Churchill thought it unwise to send fighters from Britain to Singapore, despite the steadily increasing Japanese menace, and the inadequate air defences there. He believed that the only way that Hitler could win the war was to invade and conquer Britain. "Above all", he told the Cabinet, "we had to keep a sufficient air force in this country to assist in repelling any invasion Germany might make next spring. Hitler had great need to invade this country. It would be possible for him to contain the Russian front, and to move sufficient forces to the West and stage an operation on such a scale as had never been attempted before, and regardless of losses. The key to repelling such an attempt lay in fighter superiority over the enemy"[36].

Throughout the remainder of the war, Churchill would occasionally use the German threat of invasion in 1940-1 in his private conversation, to prove whatever point he was making at the time. In August 1942, for example, Stalin was pressing Churchill to invade France as early as possible. Churchill was resisting, fearing that a premature invasion would be a fiasco. He asked Stalin "why Hitler did not come to England in 1940, when we had only 20,000 trained troops, 200 guns and 50 tanks; and when Hitler had everything he needed … The fact was that Hitler was afraid of the operation"[37].

Chapter 6

The Battle of the Atlantic

Both Hitler and Churchill knew that the outcome of the Battle of the Atlantic would decide whether Britain would survive or not. "If there should be war [with Britain]", Hitler ranted just before it started, "I shall build U-boats, U-boats, U-boats, U-boats, U-boats"[38]. Churchill himself later confirmed that this strategy was correct. "The only thing that ever really frightened me during the war", he wrote in his history of the war, "was the U-boat peril ... our life-line was endangered"[39]. "How willingly would I have exchanged a full-scale invasion for this shapeless, measureless peril, expressed in charts, curves and statistics"[40], he later wrote.

Churchill always believed in preparing the British people for the worst. Anticipating Hitler's strategy, he warned in no uncertain terms: "we must therefore expect that Herr Hitler will do his utmost to prey upon our shipping and reduce the volume of American supplies entering these islands".

> "[British General] Sir John Dill ... has warned us all that Hitler may be forced, by the strategic, economic and political stresses in Europe, to try to invade these islands in the near future. That is a warning which no one should disregard ... we are far stronger than we ever were before, incomparably stronger than we were in July, August and September ... I drop one word of caution. A Nazi invasion of Great Britain last autumn would have been a more or less improvised affair. Hitler took it for granted that when France gave in we should give in; but we did not give in ... An invasion now will be supported by a much more carefully prepared ... equipment ... We must be prepared to meet gas attacks, parachute attacks, and glider attacks with constancy, forethought and practised skill.
>
> ... In order to win the war, Hitler must destroy Great Britain. With every month that passes, the many proud and once happy countries he is now holding down by brute force and vile intrigue are learning to hate the Prussian yoke and the Nazi name ..."[41]

The U-boat war was at the forefront of Churchill's mind throughout the Second World War. On 18 March 1941, clearly hoping to draw the United States closer to the war, he returned to this theme in a speech at the Savoy: "but anyone can see how bitter is the need of Hitler and his gang to cut the sea roads between Great Britain and the United States, and, having divided these mighty powers, to destroy them one by one"[42]. In August, he told the War Cabinet that President Roosevelt had told him that Roosevelt "would wage war, but not declare it, and that he would become more and more provocative. If the Germans did not like it, they could attack American forces … It might suit us, in six or eight weeks' time, to provoke Hitler by taunting him with this difficult choice"[43]. He wrote to the South African politician Smuts, in September 1941, that Hitler would "have to choose between losing the Battle of the Atlantic or coming into frequent collision with United States ships and warships"[44]. Churchill would never tolerate complacency, however. He warned Parliament in September that the "very great improvement [i.e. decrease] in our losses at sea" should not mean "vain talk about the Battle of the Atlantic having been won …war is inexhaustible in its surprises, and very few of those surprises are of an agreeable character"[45].

Churchill addressed the House of Commons three days later. He used the speech to attempt to sow suspicion of Hitler in Spain and Russia, while attacking Hitler:

> "Some have compared Hitler's conquests with those of Napoleon. It may be that Spain and Russia will shortly furnish new chapters to that theme. It must be remembered, however, that Napoleon's armies carried with them the fierce, liberating and equalitarian winds of the French Revolution, whereas Hitler's Empire has nothing behind it but racial self-assertion, espionage, pillage, corruption and the Prussian boot".

He claimed that Hitler feared America, as he had not yet declared war on them, and had been surprised at Britain's resistance: "little did Herr Hitler know, when in June 1940 he received the total capitulation of France … that 10 months later … he would be appealing to the much-tried German people to prepare themselves for the war of 1942"[46]. Churchill won the subsequent vote of confidence by 447 votes to 3.

Hitler and Goebbels discussed this speech two days later. Goebbels thought it contained "excuses and very little information". The pair saw it as "the product of desperation. [Churchill] is out on his feet [sic]. But what can England do? The Empire will be ruined when all this is over"[47].

Mutual intelligence

The Battle of the Atlantic would have been much closer run, or even lost altogether, without the invaluable work of the British codebreakers. As is now well known, during most of the Second World War, the Allied war effort benefited hugely from Britain's interception and decryption of German radio messages which had been encrypted using the famous Enigma machines. The decrypts, codenamed "Ultra", played a crucial role at various times during the War. They also granted Churchill insights into Hitler's mind and strategy which he would otherwise have been denied. They enabled him, for instance, to warn Stalin of the impending German invasion, though, as noted above, the Soviet tyrant did not act on what should have been priceless information.

What is less well known is that German intelligence was intercepting and decoding much Allied signals traffic throughout the war. German intelligence broke the code used by Britain's merchant fleet until 1943, so that U-boats could be steered into the paths of convoys which had been rerouted to avoid them. It also managed to intercept many messages sent by Churchill himself. The German Post Office, for instance, managed to break into the only radio-telephone link between London and Washington, and decrypt the conversations between top American and British military planners, and even between Roosevelt and Churchill themselves. Hitler eagerly devoured the decrypts he was sent, and they played an important role in many decisions he took during the Second World War, for example to invade Norway or to continue the war in the hope that the British and Americans would fall out with the Russians. At one point, he even managed to joke about the help he was receiving from intercepted American messages with his heavy Germanic humour: "Let's hope that the American legation in Cairo continues to keep us so excellently informed of British military plans with its badly enciphered cables"[48]. Frustratingly, few of the intercepts survive, so we do not know what was contained in them, and the air of secrecy surrounding decrypted signals traffic means that we can only guess Hitler's reaction to reading Churchill's thoughts.

Setting the Balkans ablaze

In a broadcast early in February, Churchill had asked:

> "What has that wicked man whose crime stained regime and system are at bay and in the toils – what has he been preparing during these winter months? What delivery is he planning? What new small country will he overrun or strike down? What fresh form of assault will he make upon our Island home and fortress; which let there be no mistake about it is all that stands between him and the dominion of the world?"[49]

Churchill listed a number of possible new fronts which Hitler could establish.

He did not have to wait long to find out which ones the Nazi tyrant had chosen. Mussolini had invaded Greece, but the Greeks had thrown the Italians back into Albania, and, as usual, the Italians needed German help to avoid humiliation. Churchill was anxious to avoid giving the Germans a pretext to intervene: "it would indeed be a diplomatic error to aid Hitler to found his aggression nominally upon an admission of this kind [that Britain was sending an army to Greece] by us", Churchill wrote to Eden[50]. Hitler was reluctant to destroy the Greeks, against whom Germany had no claims. "I am fighting a war against Britain, not against these little countries", the man who had destroyed a dozen "little countries" remarked to a Hungarian diplomat. He regarded Britain, here as elsewhere, as the cause of the aggression which he unleashed[51]. As usual, one Briton in particular provoked his ire. According to Goebbels, "Churchill has made a speech, crowing about Yugoslavia. The Führer is outraged. In Belgrade, they are trying to defuse the situation"[52].

Hitler invaded Yugoslavia and Greece, delaying the attack on Russia, codenamed *Barbarossa*, by six weeks, to 22 June 1941. When the Greek campaign ended in disaster for the Greek, British and Imperial forces, who had tried to defend it from the Nazis, Hitler taunted Churchill in the Reichstag on 4 May 1941:

> "Just as he did after Norway and Dunkirk, Mr. Churchill – he also began this campaign – is trying to say something that he might yet be able to twist and distort into a British victory. . . Mr. Churchill may be able to lay down a smokescreen before his fellow-countrymen, but he cannot eliminate the results of his disasters".

Goebbels in his diary noted this particular aspect of his speech: "The Führer speaks… Tough against Churchill and his incompetence"[53]. Hitler continued that Churchill's appeal three days before to the German people to desert their Führer was explicable only as the fevered outburst of a paralytic or the delirious shout of a chronic drunkard. Churchill's brain had bred the ill-conceived Balkan expedition as a vain attempt to set south-eastern Europe ablaze. The *Manchester Guardian* reported that "Hitler's Reichstag speech was particularly notable for its violent attacks on the Premier [Churchill]"[54]. Inconveniently for Hitler, however, Churchill survived this further disaster. From sources in Lisbon, Hitler heard that Churchill was very popular in Britain, but that Anthony Eden was blamed for the disaster in the Balkans[55].

The flight of Rudolf Hess

On 11 May 1941, Hitler's stupid and confused deputy, Rudolf Hess, took it into his head to fly to Britain to attempt to contact the British government and arrange a separate peace. What now seems an intriguing but ultimately unimportant event in the global catastrophe of the Second World War was profoundly embarrassing for the Nazi regime at the time. It was also troubling to Hitler personally: "I do hope that Hess will die in England", he told his Munich housekeeper, "so that I will be spared passing judgement on him. It would be the hardest thing for me"[56]. He feared what Churchill would say, confiding to his adjutant Schaub, "If Hess really gets there just imagine: Churchill has Hess in his grasp! What lunacy on Hess's part. . . They will give Hess some drug or other to make him stand before a microphone and broadcast whatever Churchill wants"[57]. His Army and his *Luftwaffe* adjutants both thought him "furious"[58]. Goebbels considered it a "hard, almost unbearable blow". He had to stop his gloating at the latest "inferno" in London, which seemed "almost meaningless" in comparison[59]. He wanted the affair to "blow over quickly", while waiting to see if the British "and most of all Churchill – took him [Hess] seriously"[60].

The initiative struck Churchill, who was about to watch a film with some of his friends, as "fantastic" until he found out that it was true[61]. He did not seem in any immediate hurry to talk to Hitler's deputy. A film had been scheduled for that evening, and Churchill was determined to see it. "Hess or no Hess", he said, "I am going to see the Marx Brothers". He seems briefly to have considered whether to "run the line that he [Hess] has quarrelled with Hitler"[62]. In the end, however, at the urging of Eden, Beaverbrook and others, he decided to "let the Press have a good run for a bit and keep the Germans guessing"[63]. He ordered that Hess be confined "in the strictest seclusion", considering that "the public will not stand any pampering except for intelligence purposes with this notorious criminal"[64], though quite how the public were to find out about the terms of Hess's confinement, given the strict secrecy of his imprisonment and Britain's heavily censored and self-censored wartime press, is not clear. If Churchill wanted to confuse Hitler, he succeeded: a month later, twelve hours before the invasion of Russia, Hitler was pacing up and down the drawing room in his Chancellery asking Goebbels "why was Mr. Churchill still systematically playing down Hess and his peace mission?" Hitler took no chances when informed that another senior Nazi Party figure, Gauleiter [a Regional Party Leader] Karl Roever, was about to fly to Britain a year later: the Gauleiter died a mysterious death two days after his intentions had become known to Hitler's office[65].

Churchill wrote an illuminating report on Hess's arrival to Roosevelt. He described Hess's offer of peace in exchange for a free hand for Germany in Eastern Europe as "the old invitation to us to desert all our friends in order to save temporarily the greater part of our skin". Hess was, however, "a potential war criminal whose fate must ultimately depend upon the decision of the Allied governments"[66]. During the war, Churchill would occasionally tease Hitler, by revealing fragments of what he claimed Hess had told his captors. "In the various remarks which … Hess has let fall from time to time, nothing has been more clear than that Hitler relied upon the starvation attack [i.e. U-boats] … to bring us to our knees", he told the Commons in November 1941[67]. His last word on Hess, in his memoirs, referred to him as "a medical and not a criminal case", and Hess escaped with his life at the Nuremberg trials in 1946[68].

Hess's flight was clearly a trauma for the Nazi regime. Hitler's furious reaction attests to that, as does a passage in Goebbels's diary almost a year later: "We [Goebbels and Göring] talked at some length about Hess … Had Churchill actually succeeded in discrediting our fidelity to our Allies, the war might conceivably have taken an entirely different turn. All of us were quite justified in being extremely worried"[69]. He was right to be worried that his allies would be concerned. For example, Ciano wrote in his diary that the affair was the "first real victory for the English"[70], for some reason ignoring their naval victories, the Battle of Britain and their spectacular triumphs against the Italians in North Africa. Perhaps the only significant effect of the affair on the Allied side was the impression it made on Stalin. It certainly heightened his suspicions about Britain's will to resist Hitler, and it may have caused him to disregard the warnings he received from British intelligence about Hitler's intention to attack Russia. According to Sir Martin Gilbert, while the British Commonwealth was winning its only solo large success against the Germans on land during the Second World War at El Alamein, Stalin accused the British no fewer than five separate times in two days of intending to use "its unexpected visitor, Rudolf Hess, for a negotiated peace with Hitler"[71]. It is impossible to know whether Stalin actually believed this. In any case, it was completely untrue.

Churchill and Hitler's invasion of Russia

"If you hold out alone long enough, there always comes a time when the tyrant makes some ghastly mistake", Churchill said years later, when the war was plainly won, "… Hitler hurled himself on Russia"[72]. Since Hitler's triumphs in the summer of 1940, relations between Germany and the Soviet Union had been deteriorating sharply. Hitler had hoped that he could "bring Russia into the anti-British front"[73], and to that end, the Soviet Foreign Minister, Molotov, was invited to Berlin in November. "A slap in the face for England", Goebbels wrote in his diary. "Will do Churchill no good"[74]. Molotov, however, not only refused to join in the war against Britain, but raised concerns about Germany's actions in Scandinavia and the Balkans. The visit seems to have confirmed Hitler's previous decision to attack Russia while Britain was undefeated. Churchill had been urging Russia to act against Germany. A memorandum to this effect from Churchill to Stalin in July 1940 was passed by the Russians to Berlin. In it, Churchill told his ambassador in Moscow, Cripps, that "What we want them [the Russians] to realise is that Hitler intends to attack them sooner or later, if he can"[75].

The contents of Churchill's memorandum were clearly influential in Hitler's statement that at the end of July 1940 that "Russia is the factor by which England sets the greatest store … If Russia is beaten, England's last hope is gone … Russia must be dealt with. Spring 1941"[76]. Hitler had seen Eden's appointment as Foreign Secretary, replacing Lord Halifax, as a sign that Churchill was trying to woo Stalin. He had seen Eden, mistakenly, as pro-Soviet. Justifying his invasion to his generals, on March 30 1941, he argued that Britain only fought on because of the influence of the Jews and of the Churchill clique. Now Britain was hitching her fortunes to the United States and Russia, declared Hitler. He was not afraid of the United States. But Russia must be defeated now[77].

Hitler had used similar reasoning in a speech to his generals on 30 March 1941. He identified two reasons for Britain continuing the war, "the influence of the Jews and of Britain's international financial involvements, and the dominant influence of the Churchill clique". Churchill's amazing ability to present Dunkirk almost as a victory still clearly irked him: "although [Britain] had demonstrably lost four hundred thousand tons of shipping at Dunkirk, she had camouflaged the rout as a victorious retreat"[78]. Britain was now hitching her hopes to America and Russia.

In his meeting with Mussolini on 2 June 1941, Hitler speculated that Lloyd George would replace Churchill[79]. "Then we must see what possibility there is of settling our differences". He did not mention his decision to invade Russia to his major ally, however, and indeed he did not tell the Italians at all until his troops were crossing the Russian frontier. In his letter to Mussolini, justifying the invasion, Hitler claimed that the attack on Russia was in fact aimed at England. A week after the invasion, Hitler speculated to his generals about the "possibility of Churchill's overthrow by Conservatives with a view to forestalling a Socialist-Communist revolution in the country". David Lloyd George and Sir Samuel Hoare were mentioned, presumably either as leaders of that revolution, or as possible Prime Ministers after Churchill had been deposed. The return of German East Africa, which the British had taken from the Germans during the First World War, was "desirable, but not essential"[80].

Hitler thought that Churchill would not oppose the attack on the Soviet Union. Goebbels recorded him saying, just before the attack, "The Bolshevik poison must be eliminated from Europe. It will be difficult for Churchill or Roosevelt to say anything against that"[81]. One of his bodyguards, Misch, remembered Hitler talking "about England so often; he always thought they would come in with us, against the Russians. 'Churchill is no communist,' [Hitler] said"[82]. One of Hitler's senior officials argued, however, that for Britain to come to an agreement with Germany after the invasion of Russia, it would be necessary for Churchill to be overthrown, as he relied on the support of the Labour Party, which would want to continue the war against Germany[83]. Right up to the invasion, Hitler was arguing that "Russia's collapse would induce England to give in"[84].

Churchill anticipated Hitler's views, just as he predicted the attack. He wrote later that the movement of troops in Poland in March 1941, which had been detected by intelligence, "illuminated the whole Eastern scene like a lightning flash". It could "only mean Hitler's intention to invade Russia in May"[85]. He wrote to Roosevelt a week before the invasion that he did not "expect any class political reactions here"[86]. At dinner with Anthony Eden, John G. Winant - the American ambassador, and others two days before the German invasion, Churchill said that a German attack on Russia was certain. According to Colville, he thought "that Hitler is counting on enlisting capitalist and right-wing sympathies in this country and the US. PM says he is wrong; he will go all out to help Russia". Later, Churchill told Colville that "he had only one single purpose – the destruction of Hitler, and his life was much simplified thereby. If Hitler invaded Hell, he would at least make a favourable reference to the Devil"[87]. In one of his less happy predictions, Churchill forecast that night that Russia would be defeated, although he was merely following the advice from his ambassador in Moscow, who had told the War Cabinet a few days before that "The prevailing view in diplomatic circles in Moscow was that Russia could not hold out against Germany for more than three or four weeks"[88]. He had also predicted to Marshal Smuts that "Hitler is going to take what he wants from Russia, and the only question is whether Stalin will attempt a vain resistance"[89].

Throughout early 1941, no fewer than eighty warnings were sent to Stalin, many but not all from Britain, predicting the attack. "Let them come", Stalin replied to one warning with incredible, and completely misplaced, smugness. "We will be ready for them"[90]. Churchill told Marshal Smuts that an attack was likely as early as 15 May: "It looks as if Hitler is massing against Russia ... Nobody can stop him doing this, but we hope to blast the Fatherland behind him pretty thoroughly as the year marches on. I am sure that with God's help we shall beat the life out of the Nazi regime"[91]. Stalin, however, ignored the warnings. When the Germans attacked, Russian forces were taken by surprise all along the front. As Hitler had predicted to Misch, Churchill had no problem at all in allying with Russia, despite his impeccable anti-Communist credentials. His adjutant, von Below, claimed that "Hitler had expected nothing else from him", apparently contradicting Misch's account, cited above, that Hitler thought that Churchill would not be able to oppose him once he invaded Russia (though Misch was referring to England, while von Below was talking about Churchill)[92]. In a radio broadcast on the day the Germans invaded Russia, Churchill noted that Hitler had employed:

> "All his usual formalities of perfidy ... with scrupulous technique. A non-aggression treaty had been solemnly signed and was in force between the two countries. No complaint had been made by Germany of its non-fulfilment... Then suddenly, without a declaration of war, without even an ultimatum, German bombs rained down from the air upon the Russian cities ...

He had plenty of choice words of abuse against the Nazi dictator.

> Hitler is a monster of wickedness, insatiable in his lust for blood and plunder. Not content with having all Europe under his heel ... he must now carry his work of butchery and desolation among the vast multitudes of Russia and of Asia ...

> So now this bloodthirsty guttersnipe must launch his mechanised armies upon new fields of slaughter, pillage and devastation. Poor as are the Russian peasant, workmen and soldiers, he must steal from them their daily bread...

Nor was the Nazi government immune from Churchill's barbs.

> The Nazi regime is indistinguishable from the worst features of Communism. No one has been a more consistent opponent of Communism than I have for the last twenty-five years. I will unsay no word that I have spoken about it ... But all this fades away before the spectacle which is now unfolding before us ...

Any man or state who fights on against Nazidom will have our aid. Any man or state who marches with Hitler is our foe"[93].

This last group clearly included Finland, who attacked the Soviet Union along with the Germans, in order to regain the territory which the Russians had taken from them the year before. "There is no need to declare war", Churchill wrote to his Foreign Secretary, "but it seems to me they [the Finns] should have much the same treatment as if they were at war"[94]. Churchill's eagerness to extend help to the Soviets caused Hitler to mock the spectacle of "Churchill, Stalin and Roosevelt as fighters for freedom"[95]. However, the German dictator did not necessarily regard this alliance as permanent. He mused to Goebbels on 18 August 1941 that quite suddenly peace might be declared: he might accept peace terms from Stalin, or Churchill might be deposed. Neither in the end happened, though Stalin seems to have come close to offering the Germans peace during the summer of 1941[96].

Shortly after the invasion of Russia, Churchill's line if anything hardened against the Nazis, with him telling the War Cabinet that "we were not prepared to negotiate with Hitler at any time on any subject"[97], though he later told them that "he thought it would be going too far to say that we should not negotiate with a Germany controlled by the Army. It was impossible to forecast what form of Government there might be in Germany at a time when their resistance weakened and they wished to negotiate"[98]. This is clearly far different from his May 1940 position that he would consider a peace offer from Germany, and would even be prepared to restore some colonies in exchange for peace (see the previous chapter).

Churchill's injunction that the past should fade away also clearly refers to Russia's appeasement of Nazi Germany. He wrote to Stafford Cripps that:

> "they [the Russians] brought their own fate upon themselves when, by their pact with Ribbentrop, they let Hitler loose on Poland and so started the war. They cut themselves off from an effective second front when they let the French Army be destroyed. ... We did not however know till Hitler attacked them ... what side they would be on. We were left along for a whole year while every Communist in England, under orders from Moscow, did his best to hamper our war effort. If we had been invaded or destroyed ... they would have remained utterly indifferent‡ ... If they

---

‡ According to Gilbert, Churchill originally wrote at this point 'only have laughed', but deleted this phrase at Eden's suggestion.

harbour suspicions of us it is only because of the guilt and self-reproach in their own hearts"[99].

In a broadcast on 24 August 1941, Churchill again compared Hitler to Napoleon: "… Napoleon's armies had a theme … But Hitler, Hitler has no theme, naught but mania, appetite and exploitation"[100].

Hitler was still intending to take the fight to the British Empire, once Russia had been destroyed, unless the British came to terms in the meantime. On 6 July 1941, he talked to his generals about keeping tanks back from Russia for operations against "the British land route in the Middle East", and to safeguard Spain from a British attack. Where the Germans were actually fighting the British, however, in North Africa, Hitler would confine himself to reinforcing the German divisions there[101]. He regarded Churchill's position as far from secure, telling Ambassador Hewel on 10 July, that: "Churchill will topple all at once, quite suddenly. Then in Britain an immense anti-Americanism will arise, and Britain will be the first country to join the ranks of Europe in the fight against America"[102]. Hitler did not think the British could give effective assistance to the Russians in time. In October 1941, he remarked to his dinner companions that: "the only palpable relief for Russia would be if Britain could force us to withdraw tanks and aircraft from the eastern front, and this she can only do by invading the Continent. Churchill has warded off this Stalin demand by arguing that the invasion danger increases with the approach of dull and foggy weather again, and that he needs his forty-five divisions to defend the British Isles"[103].

Hitler still appealed to the British people over Churchill's head from time to time. In his speech of 3 October 1941 at the *Sportspalast*, for instance, in which he declared that Russia "was broken and would never rise again", he referred to "all the years I tried to achieve understanding whatever the cost, there was Mr. Churchill who kept on shouting, 'I want war!' Now he has it". He even told a Colonel Speidel that he had rejected French offers of collaboration because it would stand in the way of a future understanding with Britain[104]. He had heard, however, that Churchill was hoping for an approach from him, so that he could ridicule it in public. By late 1941, he had finally realised that peace with Britain was most unlikely. He remarked that what irritated him most was that "that cretin Churchill" was interrupting him in his mighty task of cultural reconstruction[105].

By the end of 1941, the Germans had received their first checks in their invasion of Russia. Plans for their thrust towards Moscow had been revealed to Churchill by the intelligence services, and Churchill sent Stalin eight warnings of the impending attack[106]. The advance was slowed by the autumn rains and ground to a halt entirely just short of Moscow in December. In Washington just before Christmas, Churchill paid tribute to the Russians. "Hitler prophesised that he would take Moscow in a short time … Now his armies are joggling backwards over this immense front, wondering where he can find a place to winter"[107]. A revealing anecdote, however, shows that even at this early stage, the British government was worried about Soviet intentions in post-war Europe. In 1950, Eden told the Commons about his visit to Moscow in late 1941:

> "One night, after our discussions about the immediate situation were over and we were conversing more discursively, we spoke of Hitler. After all, the German armies were then about 40 miles from Moscow. We discussed his character and I remember that Marshal Stalin made this comment, 'We should not underrate Hitler. He is a very able man, but he made one mistake. He did not know when to stop' …
>
> I suppose I smiled. At any rate Marshal Stalin turned to me and observed, 'You are smiling, and I know why you are smiling. You think that if we are victorious, I shall not know when to stop. You are wrong. I shall know.'[108]

The Communist North Koreans had just invaded South Korea with Stalin's backing when Eden made that speech. He clearly hoped that Stalin still knew when to stop.

The invasion of Russia clearly opened a new chapter in Nazi savagery against the Jews. Churchill was, from the outset, in possession of decrypted German Police messages which showed the extent of the atrocities. While referring to Russian patriots rather than Jews, he referred to these murders in a broadcast: "As his [Hitler's] armies advance, whole districts are being exterminated. Scores of thousands … of executions in cold blood are being perpetrated by the German police-troops upon the Russian patriots who defended their native soil"[109]. On 14 November 1941, in a letter to the *Jewish Chronicle*, Churchill observed how "none has suffered more cruelly than the Jew the unspeakable evils wrought on the bodies and spirits of men by Hitler and his vile regime. The Jew bore the brunt of the Nazi's first onslaught upon the citadels of freedom and human dignity"[110].

At a dinner with Hugh Dalton, and others, Churchill asked the Australian Prime Minister Sir Robert Menzies, who was also present, "Hitler says that 16 million Jews ought to go and live in Australia. What do you say to that?"[111] Menzies made no reply, and did not mention this episode in his diary. Hitler, as well as identifying British and American opposition to him with the Jews, seems to have thought that anti-Semitism could develop in Britain. "The English are engaged in the most idiotic war they could wage", he told his dinner guests on 5 November 1941. "If it turns out badly, anti-Semitism will break out amongst them – at present it's dormant"[112].

After a dinner a week later with Menzies, where the Chief of the Imperial General Staff, Sir Alan Brooke, was also present, Churchill sent for his rifle and gave the Empire's most senior soldier a demonstration of his prowess with a bayonet. "This was one of the first occasions on which I had seen Winston in one of his real light-hearted moods", Brooke recalled years later. "I was convulsed [with laughter] watching him give this exhibition of bayonet exercises with his rifle ... I remember wondering what Hitler would have thought of this demonstration ..."[113]

North Africa

British and Imperial troops had fought the Italians, with stunning success, in North Africa in 1940. In Libya a much smaller force had captured almost forty thousand Italians, including four generals, in exchange for approximately a hundred casualties. The tremendous British victories there and in Somaliland had given a significant boost to British morale. Churchill recognised, however, that German intervention would be another matter entirely. "I cannot believe Hitler will not intervene soon", he wrote to his commander, General Wavell, on 5 January 1941[114]. According to Harry Hopkins' note to Roosevelt, Churchill recognised that "Hitler will permit Mussolini to go only so far downhill", and would therefore intervene in Greece and North Africa[115]. Hitler, in the person of Major-General Rommel, appeared in Libya in February 1941. Hitler's bizarre briefing for Rommel in Berlin had included showing him British and American magazines to show him what his enemies would look like![116]

In fact, German intervention in 1941 was enough to prevent Britain from routing the Italians completely, but was never enough to drive Britain out of the Middle East entirely. This probably reflects Hitler's obsession with Russia and his fundamental lack of interest in the North African desert. He declared to his staff in early 1941 that the loss of Italian North Africa would mean little militarily, but politically the consequences for his Italian ally would be devastating[117].

Naval and military prowess

Throughout 1941, Hitler and Churchill poured scorn on the other's military abilities. Given the disastrous course of the war for Britain so far, and the German army's triumphant conquest of most of Europe, Hitler would seem to have had the greater reason to gloat. To some extent, Churchill agreed. "I feel very doubtful", he wrote to General Sir John Dill in January 1941, "of our ability to fight the Germans anywhere on the mainland of Europe"[118]. Nevertheless, he managed to find some crumbs of comfort. He believed that Hitler had "blurted out in January and February" his plans for attacking British shipping, and that this "certainly proved helpful to us"[119], though it was hardly surprising that the Germans planned to attack the convoys in the North Atlantic. By the end of the year, he saw that "Hitler's weakness is in the air … Hitler has not enough air [forces] for the simultaneous support of the operations open to his armies"[120]. Churchill said that Hitler might use poison gas on the British[121], but this did not in fact happen during the Second World War.

Hitler also poured scorn on his opponent's military abilities. Churchill "will end by reducing the empire to ruin"[122], Hitler predicted to Goebbels in May 1941. The sinking of the new German battleship the *Bismarck* in May was a bad blow to the small German Navy, and to Nazi pride. Both Churchill and Hitler had been involved in the nail-biting chase, which saw the *Bismarck* sink the British battlecruiser *Hood*, and almost escape from the British several times. On 10 June 1941, in the course of asking the Commons for understanding given the weight of his responsibilities, Churchill taunted Hitler in the Commons over this naval epic. "I have not heard … that Herr Hitler had to attend the Reichstag and tell them why he sent the *Bismarck* on her disastrous cruise". In the same speech, he taunted his opponent when he noted that the massive U-boat offensive which Hitler had forecast in January for March had not taken place[123].

The Greek campaign was the first direct clash of British and German armies since Dunkirk, and the British, with a much smaller army and without air support, came off second best. In the debate in the Commons once the campaign was lost, Churchill managed a gibe against Hitler: "Hitler has told us that it was a crime … on our part to go to the aid of the Greeks. I do not wish to enter into arguments with experts. This is not a kind of crime of which he is a good judge"[124].

But the Russian war was the biggest of Hitler's military blunders in 1941, and Churchill saw this early, though, as he wrote, "neither Great Britain nor the United States have any part to play in this event"[125]. Churchill saw that Hitler had made a mistake as soon as his troops crossed the Russian border. He repeatedly rubbed Hitler's nose in it. "In Hitler's launching of the Nazi campaign upon Russia we can already see, after less than six months of fighting, that he made one of the outstanding blunders of history, and the results so far realized constitute an event of cardinal importance in the final decision of the war"[126]. Churchill believed that Stalin hated "Hitler, which he certainly did not in 1935, with cold fury"[127]. In a broadcast on 24 August, he noted that "for the first time Nazi blood has flowed in a fearful torrent"[128], though failing to mention the far greater numbers of their enemies whom they had killed. In a speech to the Commons in September, he argued that "Hitler's hopes of a short war with Russia will be dispelled"[129]. Churchill recognised Hitler's defeat on the outskirts of Moscow in December as "little short of a disaster", and foresaw a possible "military catastrophe" for Hitler in the East[130].

The Germans, meanwhile, thought that "Churchill is forming a gang of bitter-enders, and is governing against the moderates and also against Labour"[131]. According to David Irving, in October 1941, "Hitler made fun of the British suggestion that he had not spoken in recent months as he had nothing cheerful to tell the German people. 'Over this period Churchill has admittedly made almost a dozen speeches, but if you compare actions and achievements, then I am quite content to stand before history as I am.' His table companions laughed heartily; two days later they recognized that Hitler had just tried out his next big speech on them"[132].

In a confused memorandum from the OKW, and approved by Hitler, in September 1941, the Germans foresaw the strengthening of the British position in Libya, and a British-Russian link-up in Iran. They did not think it was likely that Britain would be able to invade the Continent, however, and "Britain's situation becomes hopeless immediately ... France, Spain and Turkey ... would join the war against England". "Adequate air forces for a siege of Britain will not be available until the Eastern campaign is substantially concluded". "Our goal, as before, is to defeat and force Britain to sue for peace". However, "the collapse of Russia is our immediate and paramount objective"[133]. There was no mention of Britain's internal political situation, or of Churchill.

Churchill, Hitler and the Japanese/American war

For years, Churchill had attempted to alert the American public and its President to the menace of Nazi Germany. He had used any means at his disposal, including broadcasts, newspaper articles and approaches to senior figures in American politics. The story of these efforts is fascinating in itself, though there is not enough space here to detail it in full. The culmination of these efforts was the Lend-Lease programme, which allowed America to supply Britain with war materials without any payment, provided American naval help against U-boats in the North Atlantic, and which brought about the joint declaration of war principles known as the Atlantic Charter. When Hitler was informed about the latter, and particularly the section which promised "the final elimination of the National Socialist tyranny", he flew into "a passion of rage... He said that was something they would never achieve"[134].

Hitler always viewed his alliance with the Japanese as an expedient, ultimately preferring to come to terms with England. "If the English are smart", he told his dinner guests six weeks before Pearl Harbor, "they will ... make an about turn – and they will march on our side. By getting out of the war now, the English would succeed in putting their principal competitor, the United States, out of the game for thirty years"[135]. Hitler had admired Japan since the Russo-Japanese war of 1904-5[136] and as already noted, in *Mein Kampf*, he had called the British alliance with Japan of 1902 "racially indefensible"[137]. However, while the British were hostile, he thought that the Japanese were keeping the British Empire occupied in Asia[138]. His conversation is riddled, however, with contemptuous references to America, a "decayed country"[139]. He thought that "America's rearmament will not reach its peak until 1945"[140]. Despite the examples of the American Civil War and the First World War, when America had mobilised huge armies and kept them supplied, he utterly underestimated its war-making potential, for example refusing to believe that it could replace Russia's losses in 1941[141]. He also argued that "Germany is the biggest industrial nation in the world"[142], though it lagged far behind the United States. He also believed that America and Britain were natural enemies, and that the United States was plotting to inherit the British Empire. Once it became clear that Britain would continue to resist, however, the Germans attempted to persuade the Japanese to attack Britain's Far Eastern Empire, with Ribbentrop urging them to take Singapore[143]. But Hitler did "not want to be pressing, so as to avoid the impression that we need the Japanese"[144].

Churchill always saw Germany, rather than Japan, as Britain's major enemy. However, he saw the unity of purpose between the two nationalist dictatorships. He wrote to the Chinese leader, Chiang Kai-Shek, who had been fighting the

207

Japanese since 1937, that "Hitler's madness has infected the Japanese mind, and that the [German] root of the evil and its [Japanese] branch must be extirpated together"[145]. Churchill hoped to prevent Japan attacking Britain or Russia in the East. He tried to bluff Japan against attacking several times during 1941, for example writing to her Government a series of questions which were meant to show that Britain and America were stronger than Japan[146], and also sending two capital ships to East Asia. He also tried conciliation, closing the Burma Road to anti-Japanese war supplies to the Chinese in early 1941. However, he knew that if war came, Britain would have no choice but to join in, and promised to declare war immediately if Japan attacked the United States. On 23 August 1941, Churchill received a decryption of a Japanese message which showed him that Hitler had said that he would attack the United States if Japan did. Churchill immediately recognised this mistake, and urged that the message be shown to the Americans, only to be told that the Americans had already seen it[147].

While Churchill knew that the entry of the Americans into the war would ensure victory for the Allies, he knew that an unprovoked American declaration of war was exceedingly improbable, if not impossible. As he wrote to his son, to his annoyance, Hitler would "give no help in bringing things to a head, by attacking American ships …"[148] In his speeches, however, he did what he could to provoke American suspicions and dislike of Hitler. "If Hitler has not yet declared war upon the United States, it is surely not out of love for American institutions … the real reason is, I am sure, to be found in the method to which he has so faithfully adhered and by which he has gained so much … One by one … that is the trick by which he has enslaved so large a portion of the world"[149]

There is no truth in the persistent rumour that Roosevelt or Churchill knew of the Japanese attack on Pearl Harbor before it happened[150], and it appears to have come as a shock to Hitler too. On the night of the attack, Churchill was dining with the American Ambassador and Averell Harriman. According to Harriman, he seemed tired and depressed[151]. When the Japanese attack on Pearl Harbor was announced on the radio, however, Churchill immediately wanted to declare war on the Japanese. "Good God", said the American ambassador, "You can't declare war on a radio announcement"[152]. So confirmation was sought and obtained from Washington, and war declared almost immediately thereafter. Churchill saw at once what it meant for the war against Hitler, writing to Eden a few days later that "the accession of the United States … with time and patience will give certain victory"[153].

Bizarrely, Hitler also appears to have thought that Pearl Harbor meant that victory would be his. When told about Pearl Harbor, he apparently slapped his thighs in delight and shouted: 'the turning point!' "He bounced out of the bunker and ran through the darkness, hatless and unescorted, to show the news bulletin to Keitel and Jodl., telling Ambassador Hewel, "Now it is impossible for us to lose the war: we now have an ally who has never been vanquished in three thousand years, and another ally,' referring to the Italians, 'who has constantly been vanquished but has always ended up on the right side'"[154]. Nor was this only a spur of the moment reaction: a month later, he told a lunch guest that Japan's entry into the war had been "an immense relief … I'll never believe that an American soldier can fight like a hero"[155]. The Germans in fact had wanted Japan to attack Russia, rather than the United States. Hitler, however, hastened to declare war on the Americans three days after Pearl Harbor. The Tripartite Pact only bound him to declare war on Japan's enemies if they attacked her, but Hitler does not seem to have understood the implications of American entry into the war. It was the worst misjudgement of his life.

In addition to attacking the Americans, the Japanese had also attacked the British and Dutch Empires in South East Asia, and the independent country of Thailand. The British Empire's defences in the Far East collapsed astonishingly quickly. In conversation with Ambassador Hewel, Hitler noted a paradox which was to bother him increasingly over the next few months: "Strange, that we are destroying the positions of the white race in East Asia with the help of Japan, while Britain has joined the Bolshevik swine in the fight against Europe!"[156]. With his racial view of the world confounded by events, Hitler adopted an I-told-you-so attitude to the British. During one of his monologues at lunch on 18 December 1941, he claimed: "what is happening in the Far East is … by no will of mine. For years I never stopped telling all the English I met that they'd lose the Far East if they entered into a war in Europe. They didn't answer, but they assumed a superior air. They're masters in the art of being arrogant!" He wrongly forecast that the Japanese would manage to seize Australia, and that the "white race" would "disappear from those regions" [157].

At the end of this turbulent but promising year, Churchill could indeed argue that "Hitler and his Nazi gang have sown the wind; let them reap the whirlwind". He was gratified that the "United States War Administration … were clearly resolved … to crush Hitler, our main enemy"[158]. His promise of the "total and final extirpation of the Hitler tyranny, the Japanese frenzy and the Mussolini flop"[159] seemed a good deal more realistic in December than it had in January. His doctor, Lord Moran, accompanied him to America at the end of the year. He commented on the change in Churchill's mood: "He is a different man since America came into the war. The Winston I knew in London frightened me … And now … a younger man has taken his place … suddenly, the war is as good as won and England is safe"[160].

Hitler was still "hoping to come to terms with Britain at the expense of France", according to a diplomat, Hasso von Etzdorf[161]. According to an Admiral, in November 1941, "the Führer would be glad for Britain, once the eastern campaign is over, to show signs of common-sense (*not* that the Führer expects it of Churchill) even if it meant that Germany could not win further ground than she already occupies"[162]. Even at the height of the war, Hitler found time to study his enemy, if never as thoroughly as Churchill studied him. He and Goebbels both read Churchill's secretary's memoirs, published in 1941. These described Churchill's high consumption of alcohol and his habit of dictating memos in his bath[163].

[1] Hitler broadcast, 31 December 1940

[2] *At Hitler's Side*, Nicolaus von Below, p.83

[3] *Churchill War Papers, Vol. III, The Ever-Widening War*, Martin Gilbert, p.1391

[4] *Churchill War Papers, Vol. III, The Ever-Widening War*, Martin Gilbert, p.69

[5] *Churchill War Papers, Vol. III, The Ever-Widening War*, Martin Gilbert, p.768

[6] *Churchill War Papers, Vol. III, The Ever-Widening War*, Martin Gilbert, p.383

[7] *Churchill War Papers, Vol. III, The Ever-Widening War*, Martin Gilbert, p.90

[8] CAB/65/16/13, 15 December 1940

[9] *Churchill War Papers, Vol. III, The Ever-Widening War*, Martin Gilbert, p.41

[10] *Churchill War Papers, Vol. III, The Ever-Widening War*, Martin Gilbert, p.321

[11] *Churchill War Papers, Vol. III, The Ever-Widening War*, Martin Gilbert, p.1212

[12] *Goebbels diaries, 1939-41*, p.346

[13] *Goebbels diaries, 1939-41*, p.354

[14] *Ciano Diaries*, Count Ciano, p.415

[15] *The Private War Journal of Colonel General Franz Halder*, Vol. 1, p.674, 704

[16] *Hitler's War*, David Irving, p.196

[17] *Churchill War Papers, Vol. III, The Ever-Widening War*, Martin Gilbert, p.44

[18] *Hitler Confronts England*, Walter Ansel, p.304

[19] *Hitler's Table Talk*, p.12

[20] *The Private War Journal of Colonel General Franz Halder*, Vol. 1, p.751

[21] *The Private War Journal of Colonel General Franz Halder*, Vol. 1, p.751

[22] *Churchill War Papers, Vol. III, The Ever-Widening War*, Martin Gilbert, p.73

[23] *Hitler's War*, David Irving, p.185

[24] *Churchill War Papers, Vol. III, The Ever-Widening War*, Martin Gilbert, p.936

[25] E.g. CAB/66/11/39, 5 September 1940

[26] *Churchill War Papers, Vol. III, The Ever-Widening War*, Martin Gilbert, p.145

[27] *The Private War Journal of Colonel General Franz Halder*, Vol. 1, p.533

[28] *The Second World War*, Winston Churchill, p.397

[29] *Churchill War Papers, Vol. III, The Ever-Widening War*, Martin Gilbert, p.56

30 *Churchill War Papers, Vol. III, The Ever-Widening War*, Martin Gilbert, p.164
31 *Churchill War Papers, Vol. III, The Ever-Widening War*, Martin Gilbert, p.470
32 *Hansard*, 25 June 1941
33 *Churchill War Papers, Vol. III, The Ever-Widening War*, Martin Gilbert, p.1013
34 *Churchill War Papers, Vol. III, The Ever-Widening War*, Martin Gilbert, p.1413
35 *Hitler Confronts England*, Walter Ansel, p.305
36 CAB/65/24/2
37 *Road to Victory*, Martin Gilbert, p.177-8
38 *The Last Attempt*, Birger Dahlerus, p.62
39 *The Second World War*, Winston Churchill, p.397
40 *The Second World War*, Winston Churchill, vol 3, p.100-1
41 Churchill broadcast, 9 February 1941
42 *Churchill War Papers, Vol. III, The Ever-Widening War*, Martin Gilbert, p.365
43 *Churchill War Papers, Vol. III, The Ever-Widening War*, Martin Gilbert, p.1081
44 *Churchill War Papers, Vol. III, The Ever-Widening War*, Martin Gilbert, p.1215
45 *Hansard*, 9 September 1941
46 *Hansard*, 7 May 1941
47 *Goebbels diaries*, 1939-41, p.355
48 *Hitler's War*, David Irving, p.400
49 Churchill broadcast, 9 February 1941
50 *Churchill War Papers, Vol. III, The Ever-Widening War*, Martin Gilbert, p.353
51 *Hitler's War*, David Irving, p.226
52 *The Goebbels Diaries, 1939-41*, 29 March 1941
53 *The Goebbels Diaries, 1939-41*, 5 May 1941
54 *Manchester Guardian*, 5 May 1941
55 *Hitler's War*, David Irving, p.230
56 Interrogation of Anni Winter by Captain Norden, November 1945
57 *Hitler's War*, David Irving, p.386
58 *At the Heart of the Reich*, Major Gerhard Engel, p.112 and *At Hitler's Side*, Nicolaus von Below, p.98
59 *Goebbels diaries*, 1939-41, p.363
60 *At the Heart of the Reich*, Gerhard von Engel, p.112
61 *Churchill War Papers, Vol. III, The Ever-Widening War*, Martin Gilbert, p.648
62 *Churchill War Papers, Vol. III, The Ever-Widening War*, Martin Gilbert, p.651
63 *Churchill War Papers, Vol. III, The Ever-Widening War*, Martin Gilbert, p.678
64 *Churchill War Papers, Vol. III, The Ever-Widening War*, Martin Gilbert, p.676
65 *Hitler's War*, David Irving, p.250
66 *Churchill War Papers, Vol. III, The Ever-Widening War*, Martin Gilbert, p.678
67 *Hansard*, 12 November 1941
68 *The Second World War, Volume 3, The Grand Alliance*, Winston Churchill, p.49
69 *The Goebbels diaries*, 1942-43, p.143
70 *Ciano's diary 1937-1943*, Ciano, p.424
71 *Road to Victory, Winston S Churchill 1941-45*, Martin S Gilbert, p.243
72 *Speeches*, Winston Churchill, Vol.VII, p.7160
73 *The Private War Journal of Colonel General Franz Halder*, Vol. 1, p.670
74 *The Goebbels Diaries, 1939-41*, p.169
75 *Churchill War Papers, Vol. III, The Ever-Widening War*, Martin Gilbert, p.447
76 *Inside Hitler's Headquarters*, W Warlimont, p.113-4
77 *Hitler's War*, David Irving, p.222
78 *Hitler's War*, David Irving, p.222

[79] *Hitler, 1936-1945, Nemesis*, Ian Kershaw, p.383

[80] *The Private War Journal of Colonel General Franz Halder*, Vol. 2, p.991

[81] *The Goebbels diaries, 1939-41*, p.414

[82] *Albert Speer, His Battle with Truth*, Gitta Sereny, p.522

[83] *The Private War Journal of Colonel General Franz Halder*, Vol. 2, p.965

[84] *The Private War Journal of Colonel General Franz Halder*, Vol. 2, p.958

[85] *The Second World War, Volume 3, The Grand Alliance*, Winston Churchill, p.319

[86] *Churchill War Papers, Vol. III, The Ever-Widening War*, Martin Gilbert, p.807

[87] *The Fringes of Power*, John Colville, 20 June 1941, p.350

[88] CAB 65/22/26

[89] *Churchill War Papers, Vol. III, The Ever-Widening War*, Martin Gilbert, p.817

[90] *Hitler's War*, David Irving, p.234

[91] *Churchill War Papers, Vol. III, The Ever-Widening War*, Martin Gilbert, p.676

[92] *At Hitler's Side*, Nicolaus von Below, p.105

[93] *Churchill War Papers, Vol. III, The Ever-Widening War*, Martin Gilbert, p.836-7

[94] *Churchill War Papers, Vol. III, The Ever-Widening War*, Martin Gilbert, p.898

[95] *Hitler's War*, David Irving, p.284

[96] *The Goebbels diaries, 1939-41*, 18 August 1941

[97] War Cabinet minutes, 7 July 1941

[98] *Churchill War Papers, Vol. III, The Ever-Widening War*, Martin Gilbert, p.1513

[99] *Churchill War Papers, Vol. III, The Ever-Widening War*, Martin Gilbert, p.1384

[100] *Churchill War Papers, Vol. III, The Ever-Widening War*, Martin Gilbert, p.1103

[101] *The Private War Journal of Colonel General Franz Halder*, Vol. 2, p.1017

[102] *Hitler's War*, David Irving, p.283-4

[103] *Hitler's War*, David Irving, p.319

[104] *Hitler's War*, David Irving, p.335

[105] *Hitler's War*, David Irving, p.339

[106] *Churchill War Papers, Vol. III, The Ever-Widening War*, Martin Gilbert, p.1238

[107] *Churchill War Papers, Vol. III, The Ever-Widening War*, Martin Gilbert, p.1670

[108] *Hansard*, 5 July 1950

[109] *Churchill War Papers, Vol. III, The Ever-Widening War*, Martin Gilbert, p.1102

[110] *Churchill War Papers, Vol. III, The Ever-Widening War*, Martin Gilbert, p.1454

[111] *Churchill War Papers, Vol. III, The Ever-Widening War*, Martin Gilbert, p.301

[112] *Hitler's Table Talk*, p.117

[113] *Churchill War Papers, Vol. III, The Ever-Widening War*, Martin Gilbert, p.335-6

[114] *Churchill War Papers, Vol. III, The Ever-Widening War*, Martin Gilbert, p.27

[115] *Churchill War Papers, Vol. III, The Ever-Widening War*, Martin Gilbert, p.60

[116] *Hitler's War*, David Irving, p.200

[117] *Hitler's War*, David Irving, p.199

[118] *Churchill War Papers, Vol. III, The Ever-Widening War*, Martin Gilbert, p.126

[119] *Hansard*, 30 September 1941

[120] *Churchill War Papers, Vol. III, The Ever-Widening War*, Martin Gilbert, p.1379

[121] *Churchill War Papers, Vol. III, The Ever-Widening War*, Martin Gilbert, p.60

[122] Unpublished Goebbels diary, quoted in *Goebbels, Mastermind of the Third Reich*, David Irving, p.390

[123] *Hansard*, 10 June 1941

[124] *Hansard*, 7 May 1941

[125] *Churchill War Papers, Vol. III, The Ever-Widening War*, Martin Gilbert, p.1633

[126] *Hansard*, 11 December 1941

[127] *Churchill War Papers, Vol. III, The Ever-Widening War*, Martin Gilbert, p.1325

[128] *Churchill War Papers, Vol. III, The Ever-Widening War*, Martin Gilbert, p.1011

[129] *Churchill War Papers, Vol. III, The Ever-Widening War*, Martin Gilbert, p.1193

[130] *Churchill War Papers, Vol. III, The Ever-Widening War*, Martin Gilbert, p.1625

[131] *The Private War Journal of Colonel General Franz Halder*, Vol. 2, p.1222

[132] Hitler's War, David Irving, p.319

[133] *The Private War Journal of Colonel General Franz Halder*, Vol. 2, p.1228-33

[134] *At Hitler's Side*, Nicolaus von Below, p.110

[135] *Hitler's Table Talk*, p.93

[136] *Hitler's Table Talk*, p.35

[137] *Mein Kampf*, p.582

[138] Hossbach memorandum

[139] *Hitler's Table Talk*, p.188

[140] *The Private War Journal of Colonel General Franz Halder*, Vol. 1, p.583

[141] *Hitler's Table Talk*, p.26

[142] *The Private War Journal of Colonel General Franz Halder*, Vol. 1, p.751

[143] *The Private War Journal of Colonel General Franz Halder*, Vol. 2, p.818

[144] *The Private War Journal of Colonel General Franz Halder*, Vol. 2, p.1222

[145] *Churchill War Papers, Vol. III, The Ever-Widening War*, Martin Gilbert, p.1584

[146] *Churchill War Papers, Vol. III, The Ever-Widening War*, Martin Gilbert, p.439-440

[147] *Churchill War Papers, Vol. III, The Ever-Widening War*, Martin Gilbert, p.1095

[148] *Churchill War Papers, Vol. III, The Ever-Widening War*, Martin Gilbert, p.1132

[149] Churchill broadcast, 24 August 1941

[150] See, e.g. http://www.winstonchurchill.org/learn/myths/myths/he-knew-of-pearl-harbour-attack for a convincing refutation of the silly conspiracy theory

[151] *Finest Hour*, Martin Gilbert, p.1267

[152] *Finest Hour*, Martin Gilbert, p.1267

[153] *Finest Hour*, Martin Gilbert, p.1274

[154] *Hitler's War*, David Irving, p.352

[155] *Hitler's Table Talk*, ed. Hugh Trevor-Roper, p.181

[156] Diary of Ambassador Walther Hewel, quoted in *The Secret Diaries of Hitler's Doctor*, David Irving, p.88

[157] *Hitler's Table Talk*, ed. Hugh Trevor-Roper, p.150

[158] War Cabinet Paper 8 of 1942, quoted in *Road to Victory, Winston S Churchill 1941-45*, Martin S Gilbert, p.43

[159] *Churchill War Papers, Vol. III, The Ever-Widening War*, Martin Gilbert, p.1711

[160] *Winston Churchill, The Struggle for Survival*, Lord Moran, p.9

[161] *The Private War Journal of Colonel General Franz Halder*, Vol. 2, p.1341

[162] *Hitler's War*, David Irving, p.335

[163] *Goebbels, Mastermind of the Third Reich*, David Irving, p.390

7

The Turning Point (1942)

During 1942, the Axis powers lost the strategic initiative in the war, which they were never to regain. The year actually began badly for the Allies, with Germany stabilizing its position in Russia and Japan rampant in the Far East. By the end of 1942, however, Germany had suffered decisive defeats in North Africa and many of its finest soldiers were pinned down in Stalingrad. For Hitler, indeed, the year began as it ended, with a crisis on the Russian front. Hitler saw in the New Year with a three hour telephone conversation with one of his generals, ordering him to stand fast in Russia[1].

Indeed, the contrast between the men's respective activities in the first few hours of the year is instructive. At the same time as Hitler was ordering his general not to retreat, Churchill was in Ottawa, about to travel to Washington, DC, where he approved a declaration of war aims drafted by the Americans, and ultimately signed by 26 countries[2]. During the remainder of the war, Hitler was to spend more and more time ordering his generals not to retreat, especially on the Eastern Front, while Churchill was to devote much of those three and a half years to managing his mighty allies, trying to ensure that Britain did not end the war completely in their shadows.

The war of words between Hitler and Churchill reflected the changing fortunes of their respective countries during 1942. Churchill had no reason to doubt the ultimate outcome, since, as he told his War Cabinet on his return from Washington, "the United States Administration ... were clearly resolved ... to crush Hitler"[3]. Nevertheless, the Allies faced severe short term difficulties on all fronts. By the end of the year, however, the British Empire had turned the Nazi tide back at El Alamein, the Russians were about to destroy the German Sixth Army at Stalingrad, and the Americans had invaded North Africa. The Anglo-

Chapter 7

American bombing offensive against Germany, which was to end by pulverising most of her cities, got underway in earnest with the first thousand bomber raid, on Cologne. Japan's Navy received a series of staggering blows, most decisively at the Battle of Midway, and Britain managed to hold the Japanese Army at the gates of India. It was, however, a spectacular year for the U-boats, during which they sank more than seven million tons of Allied shipping, though by the end of the year, the tide was starting to turn there too. Lord Moran noted how this peril weighed upon Churchill:

> "One day when things at sea were at their worst, I happened to go into the Map-room. There I found the PM. He was standing with his back to me, staring at the huge chart with the little black beetles representing German submarines. 'Terrible', he muttered … He knows that we may lose the war at sea in a few months and that he can do nothing about it"[4].

Hitler seems to have realised, at least subconsciously, that the war which he had started might no longer be won. He started casting around for people to blame, and there was one obvious suspect:

> "Before I entered upon this war, I had begun a gigantic program of social, economic, cultural work, in part already completed. But everywhere I had in mind new plans, new projects.
>
> When, on the other hand, I look at my opponents, what have they really done, now? They could rush easily enough into war. War did not rob them of a peaceful state, for they have accomplished nothing. This prattler, this drink-bold Churchill, what has he in reality accomplished in his life? This perfidious fellow is a lazybones of the first order.
>
> If this war had not come, the centuries would have spoken of our generation and also of all of us and also of myself as the creator of great works of peace. But if this war had not come, who would speak of Churchill? Now he will one day be spoken of, to be sure, but as the destroyer of an empire, which he and now we destroyed. One of the most pitiful phrase-mongering natures of world history, incapable of creating anything, of accomplishing anything, or of performing creative acts, capable only of destroying"[5].

Not that Hitler thought Churchill solely responsible for the war. There was clearly more than enough blame to go around. 27 September 1942 found him dictating a letter to the writer Sven Hedin, in which he blamed Roosevelt, who in fact had despatched peace missions to Europe to try to stop the war: "No doubt the one man responsible for this war … is none other than the American President, Roosevelt"[6]. According to one of Hitler's secretaries, Christa Schroeder, when he was dictating a letter to her, "as soon as he started talking about Bolshevism, he would get infuriated. That also happened when he mentioned Churchill or Roosevelt. He wasn't one to mince words! He would rant about the Whiskyquaffer (Churchill) and the Bloodhound (Stalin) and I would just write this. Remarkably, he never said anything about this when he made corrections, this is how real his annoyance was" [7]. Indeed the proliferation of enemies caused problems for Hitler's propaganda: "Many people in a quandary as to whether they ought to hate [Roosevelt] or Churchill more", noted Goebbels in his diary in January 1942[8].

During 1942, Hitler realised that the American entry into the war, and Britain's recovery from the disasters of 1940, meant that Germany would probably have to face an invasion of her French colony from across the English Channel at some point. He had warned the Italians in November 1941, before America entered the war, about British intentions to invade southern Europe. In early November, Ciano recorded that he had Mussolini had received a "long letter from Hitler … He fears English landings in Corsica, Sicily and Sardinia …"[9] Churchill realised, however, how long it would take to prepare such a huge and hazardous expedition. "No attempt is to be made at large scale landings on the Continent", he wrote in December 1941, "until Germany is reduced to very great weakness by night air bombing"[10]. To increasing American and Russian annoyance, he insisted that a number of preconditions be met before the invasion would take place. He undoubtedly intended to invade at some point, however, unless Germany surrendered. He even had in mind a D-Day. In November 1942, he wrote to the Chiefs of Staff Committee that he thought that "12 July 1943 should be fixed as the target date" for an invasion of France, because "it does not look as if Hitler will be able to bring back any large force from the east to the west"[11].

This did not prevent Britain from attempting a small-scale raid on the Continent in 1942. In August of that year, the British and Canadians launched a large raid on the French town of Dieppe. The raid ended in disaster, around 60% of the invading force being killed or captured. For a few days after the raid, Churchill apparently allowed himself to be persuaded that it had been a success, or at least not a complete failure, but his position became gloomier over the next few months as more information about the raid came in[12]. Hitler had foreseen something of the sort, telling a Balkan diplomat three days before the raid: "As lunatics like that drunkard Churchill and Maccabeans and numskulls like that brilliantined dandy Eden are at the helm we've to be prepared for just about anything!"[13] In his speech on 30 September, he returned to this theme, pouring scorn on Churchill's military abilities:

> "I shall not say, though, that we have done nothing to prepare for a second front*. When Mr. Churchill says: 'We wish now to leave it to the Germans to ponder in their anxiety where and when we shall open it'. I can say to Mr. Churchill merely: 'So far you have never caused me any anxiety'.

> But he is right in saying that we must ponder. If I had an opponent of stature, of military stature, then I could calculate pretty closely where he would attack. But when one faces military idiots, one cannot know, one cannot know where they will attack. It may be the craziest sort of undertaking, and that is the one unpleasant thing - the fact that in the case of these mentally sick or perpetually drunk persons one never knows what they are really up to.

> For this reason we must naturally be prepared everywhere, and I can give Mr. Churchill assurance - whether or not he chose with cleverness and military shrewdness the first spot at which he wished to start the second front; opinions in England are already divided on this, and that will be evident on all sides from now on that it does not matter where he is looking for the next spot. He can call it good luck anywhere if he can remain on land for nine hours"[14].

Taunts

Knowing Churchill's state of mind and thinking at any point in the war is rarely a problem. He was one of the most open of men, very bad at hiding anything, and his thoughts are in any case exhaustively (though sometimes inaccurately) chronicled in the six volumes of war memoirs which he wrote after he was victorious. Most of his friends and colleagues, too, published memoirs and

---

* Both Hitler and Churchill, as well as many others, used the phrase "second front" to refer to the Western Allies' liberation of France, even though there were several other fronts in existence, including the North African theatre, the U-boat war and the air offensive against Germany. As Churchill told the Commons in March 1943, "I do not want to discourage the use of [the term 'Second Front'], because our good friends, fighting so hard, know very well what they mean by it."

records of him after the war. One can choose between the writings of several of his secretaries, his bodyguard, his doctor and literally dozens of his generals and fellow politicians to know what Churchill was saying during these turbulent years.

Knowing the state of Hitler's mind at any given time, on the other hand, presents a problem. He did not survive the war, so published no memoirs, though from time to time he would express a wish to write them. Even his closest admirers found him inscrutable. Von Ribbentrop, for example, confessed to his interrogators in 1945 that he hardly knew Hitler better after working with him for two decades than he did when they first met. For 1942, however, we are much better informed than for most years of Hitler's life, because we have a 700-page record of his *Table Talk*, dinner conversations recorded by an official at his secretary's command. Notes were kept from 1941 to 1944, and again briefly in February 1945 (see Chapter 9), but about two-thirds of them record conversations in the first nine months of 1942. It is an extraordinary insight into the vulgar and brutal mind of the dictator of most of Europe at the height of his power. As might be expected from such a record, it rambles over every subject under the sun, from the national character of the Hungarians[15] to leather shorts[16] to linguistics[17].

As a historical source, Hitler's *Table Talk* needs to be treated with care, however. Hitler did not drink alcohol, so would have been sober when he made the remarks recorded, but would probably have been tired for at least some of the time. It is also possible that the official writing the notes might have omitted some of his remarks, or made mistakes. We cannot know what was said at the dinners, but not recorded. The note-taker's writings were submitted to Hitler's factotum, Martin Bormann, who edited them. As Bormann was a devoted Nazi, he would presumably have omitted anything which might cast Hitler in an unfavourable light.

A further problem with Hitler's *Table Talk* is more generic with historical documents. From written records such as these, one can rarely tell if the speaker is being facetious, ironic or serious. It is difficult to know, for instance, if Hitler's comment, after a rambling and erroneous discussion about economics, that "for the next ten years, the essential thing is to supress all the chairs of political economy in the universities"[18] was meant to be taken literally. Nevertheless, the remarks recorded in this book are as close as we are likely to get at this remove in time to peering into the mind of the Führer while he was relaxing during arguably the most critical year in his fortunes, when everything started to go wrong for him.

Hitler's *Table Talk* contains many mentions of Hitler's greatest opponents, and it refers more often to Churchill than to Roosevelt and Stalin combined. Besides references to Churchill connected to specific events during the war, which are covered in other parts of this book, there are a number of general indications of Hitler's private opinion of Churchill. Churchill was a "puppet of the Jewry that pulls the strings"[19], who had managed to get England involved in the war. He was "a bounder of a journalist"[20], an "impostor"[21], a "drunkard"[22] and "the most guilty man of all [presumably guilty of starting the war]"[23]. "I never met an Englishman who didn't speak of Churchill with disapproval", he remarked in January 1942. "Never one who didn't say he was off his head"[24]. Hitler did not pause to ask himself how, in that case, Churchill had become Prime Minister, or whether the Englishmen he met had been unrepresentative.

On February 18 1942, Hitler gave his dinner guests, including Rommel, the benefit of his views on Churchill. He was "the very type of a corrupt journalist. There's not a worse prostitute in politics. He himself was written that it's unimaginable what can be done in war with the help of lies. He's an utterly amoral, repulsive creature". Hitler then speculated on what Churchill might do if he lost the war. "I'm convinced that he has his place of refuge ready beyond the Atlantic. He obviously won't seek sanctuary in Canada. In Canada he'd be beaten up. He'll go to his friends the Yankees" [25]. Quite what made Hitler think he understood Canadian public opinion so thoroughly is unclear.

Occasionally, Hitler refers to Churchill and Roosevelt together, as in early January 1942, when he remarked, "There's nobody stupider than the Americans … In any case, neither of the Anglo-Saxons is better than the other. One can scarcely see how they find fault with each other. Churchill and Roosevelt, what impostors!"[26] He also speculated that the Americans may have bribed Churchill somehow: "The fact that America is insisting on England's abandoning the Far East will obviously never bring about any change in Churchill's attitude towards America: the man is bought"[27]. During the Spring, Hitler seems to have speculated on whether the British political system could survive. According to a bugged conversation by one of his generals, who had been captured by the British, "The Führer is personally convinced that the country in Europe which is nearest to communism is England", though why he thought that is not clear. The general who reported that remark thought that it was "a sign that the man has never been out in the world" [28].

Churchill spent a good part of 1942 travelling. In January 1942, Hitler divined a possible source of hope from this. He thought that "The opposition to Churchill is in the process of gaining strength in England. His long absence has brought it on him"[29]. By September, however, once Churchill had won two votes of confidence in Parliament overwhelmingly, these hopes had retreated. Hitler still made fun of him for travelling so much, however. He spoke in September of "he who can travel around the world for weeks at a time, with a broad sombrero on his head, wearing a white silk shirt here, and some other outfit there"[30]. He thought that the eight-day duration of Churchill's "negotiations" with Roosevelt meant that there had been difficult because "[w]hen two people are in general agreement, decisions are swiftly taken"[31]. In fact, assuming that Hitler was referring to Churchill's most recent visit to Washington in June 1942, his negotiations with Roosevelt had lasted only five days, though he was in America for about a week. Churchill arrived at Roosevelt's estate at Hyde Park on 19 June, and left Washington on 23 June to inspect American troops in South Carolina[32]. There were indeed many points for the two men and their staffs to discuss, in particular the prospects for British and American landings in Europe and North Africa in 1942. However, reading the participants' reports of the negotiations today, they do not seem to have been particularly difficult. Indeed, the flinty, no-nonsense British Chief of the Imperial General Staff, Sir Alan Brooke, commented after the war about those negotiations that the British and Americans "were always able … to walk out arm-in-arm and go to lunch together still exactly the same friends"[33].

Hitler was more accurate a few days later in his comments on the British political situation, however. The loss of Tobruk, and, more generally, the almost unbroken series of disasters which Britain had suffered in the war to date, had led Churchill's opponents to move a vote of no confidence in the government's conduct of the war. On 1 July, Hitler commented to his lunch guests that:

> "For Churchill and his supporters, therefore, the loss of Egypt must inevitably give rise to fears of a considerable strengthening of the popular opposition. One must not lose sight of the fact that to-day there are already twenty-one members of Parliament who openly oppose Churchill; and even though the discipline of the voting system is invoked to silence them, it is not by methods such as these that Churchill will succeed in remaining in office. Only if he succeeds by the successful handling of public opinion in turning popular attention from Egypt … will he be able to oppose with any chance of success a tremendously increased opposition"[34].

Hitler was almost spot on about the number of Members of Parliament who opposed Churchill. At the vote of confidence, the government was opposed by twenty-five MPs, rather than twenty-one. However, he was entirely wrong about Churchill's handling of public opinion. Churchill's political position was saved by Britain's triumph in Egypt, and by the Allied landings in North Africa, later that year, so, far from turning popular attention from the Egyptian campaign, Churchill was saved by it.

Churchill's political position continued to intrigue Hitler. On 2 February 1942, he told his lunch guests that "Churchill is like an animal at bay. He must be seeing snares everywhere. Even if Parliament gives him increased powers, his reasons for being mistrustful still exists. He's in the same situation as Robespierre on the eve of his fall. Nothing but praise was addressed to this virtuous citizen, when suddenly the situation was reversed. Churchill has no more supporters". Later in that same lunch, Hitler referred to Churchill as "the most guilty man of all"[35].

One of the more bizarre of Hitler's comments about Churchill in his *Table Talk* concerns Churchill's family. At dinner on 27 June 1942, Hitler commented that "[b]y far the most interesting problem of the moment is, what is Britain going to do now? She has already made herself look ridiculous in the eyes of the world by declaring war when quite inadequately armed ... At the moment, the British are trying to wriggle out of their difficulties by spreading the most varied and contradictory of rumours". But the best way of finding out what England wanted to do "would be by means of a little flirtation with Churchill's daughter". Which of Churchill's three daughters he meant is not clear, even assuming he knew that Churchill had more than one. However, since the other two were then married, it was probably the then nineteen-year-old Mary (now Lady Soames), who was serving in anti-aircraft batteries in London at the time. However, for some reason, Hitler's "gentlemanly diplomats consider such methods beneath their dignity, and they are not prepared to make this agreeable sacrifice"[36]. There is no evidence at all that Churchill told his daughter his strategic plans, and but in any case, Hitler's scheme does not seem to have been put to the test. Decades later, Andrew Roberts was informed by Lady Soames "that to her certain knowledge no such honey-trap operation was mounted against her"[37].

Hitler often speculated on British politics in the 1930s. He would vent his anger at the British people's failure to fulfil the role he had assigned to them, of allowing Germany to conquer Eastern Europe. "It's a queer business, how England slipped into this war", he told his dinner guests in October 1941. "The man who managed it was Churchill, that puppet of Jewry who pulls the strings", though in fact Churchill had been out of office until after Britain's declaration of war. "Next to him, the bumptious Eden", who had also been out of office for more than a year when war was declared, "the Jew ... Hore-Belisha ... and after that some Jews and business men"[38]. He also discussed Churchill's position in British domestic politics. Again and again throughout 1942, he expressed the hope that Churchill might be dismissed. In January 1942, he told his dinner guests that, "on his return to England [from America] Churchill will have no difficulty in getting round the House of Commons – but the people who whose fortunes are in India won't let the wool be pulled over their eyes"[39]. For the fourth time that month, he speculated on the likelihood of Britain withdrawing from the war to spite the United States, a possibility that seems to have obsessed him, but which was never seriously considered by the British government. "A change of government in England", he speculated on 24 January 1942, "would be associated, in England, with the decision to abandon Europe. They'll keep Churchill in power only as long as they still have the will to pursue the struggle here … This would result in the collapse of the American economy, and also the personal collapse of Roosevelt. Simultaneously, America would have ceased to be a danger to England"[40].

Three days later, with the sinister SS chief Himmler as his special guest, he gave a long speech to his dinner companions on Churchill's political position, which revisited many of the themes he had discussed with them previously. In the context of his ideas about the English class system, he remarked: "If Chamberlain, on his return from Munich, had based elections on the choice between war and peace, he'd have obtained a crushing majority in favour of peace … At this period, Chamberlain was being fiercely attacked by the Churchill clan. If he'd had the presence of mind to organise an election, he'd have been saved. In similar cases, I've always made arrangements for a plebiscite to be held. It produces an excellent effect, both at home and abroad"[41].

Four days later, Hitler hoped that there would appear "amongst the English, at the last moment, a man capable of any lucidity of mind [who would] … immediately try to make peace, in order to save what can yet be saved". He wanted an MP to stand up and say to Churchill, "so that we may at last have some good news for the Empire, have the kindness to disappear". He thought that English Parliamentarians were too cowardly to do so, however. He argued that the secret sessions undermined Churchill's prestige, but that Churchill would not be driven from office until a successor appeared. Churchill was relying on the patriotism of the English people to see him through. The English, who were behaving as if they were stupid, "owe all that's happening to one man, Churchill"[42].

At the end of March 1942, Stafford Cripps, a senior Labour politician, went on an official mission to India, to present proposals for Dominion status to Indian politicians. This led to another lecture on English politics by Hitler to his lunchtime guests. "One thing is indisputable", he began, "in Stafford Cripps, and as a counterpart to Churchill, England has found a statesman whose influence is not negligible … There is, doubtless, a state of crisis in England, and we must reckon with it". After drawing various erroneous historical parallels, Hitler thought that Churchill's replacement by Cripps would not be welcome. "A Socialist England would be a permanent danger in the European space … I hope, therefore, that Cripps will be sunk by the fiasco of his mission to India … Between Churchill and Cripps, I have no hesitation in choosing. I prefer a hundred times the undisciplined swine who is drunk eight hours out of every twenty-four to the Puritan". This was partly based on his knowledge of Churchill's personal habits. "A man who spends extravagantly, an elderly man who drinks and smokes without moderation, is obviously less to be feared than the drawing-room Bolshevist who leads the life of an ascetic. From Churchill, one may finally expect that in a moment of lucidity – it's not impossible – he'll realise that the Empire's going inescapably to its ruin, if the war lasts another two or three years. Cripps, a man without roots, a demagogue and a liar, would pursue his sick fancies although the Empire were to crack at every corner"[43]. In a bizarre form of transference, Hitler managed to blame Cripps, who had been British ambassador to Moscow, for the German attack on Russia. He even thought that "it is possible that Moscow is using Churchill as a puppet. The British hate and despise the Bolsheviks and one day the break must come … Stalin is the arch-blackmailer – look at the way he tried to extort things from us"[44]. It is hard to think of anyone less likely to have been a puppet of Communist Russia than the fiercely anti-Communist, utterly straightforward Churchill.

In August 1942, Hitler remarked to his dinner guests that "If Churchill goes to see Stalin, the latter will tear the hide off him! He'll say to Churchill, 'I've lost ten million men and it's all thanks to your Mr Cripps. If he had kept his mouth shut, the Germans would never have attacked'". Unfortunately, the reasoning behind this leap of logic is not in the written record[45]. He expressed the opinion that "Churchill's visit to Moscow has done him a lot of harm … It was the most futile stupidity he could have committed … He has pleased no one [in British politics] – for one side he has gone much too far, for the other he has not gone nearly far enough"[46]. Later that same month, he hoped that Britain was not "going Left; if she did, it would be catastrophic. For as long as the war lasts, Churchill will remain". He continued that "Opinion in the Conservative Party is against Churchill. The man who … may well play a leading role is Beaverbrook. He at least can say 'I told you so!'"[47]

The benefit of Hitler's final attempt to read British politics that summer was given to his long-suffering guests at the start of September 1942. "We must persist in our assertion that we are waging war, not on the British people, but on the small clique who rule them... If I give Churchill grounds for declaring that Britain is fighting for her survival, then I immediately close the ranks for him", he commented. Hitler argued that the ruling clique in Britain would fight on until they saw that the war could no longer be won, and realised that stopping the fighting would not destroy the British Empire[48].

The Pacific War

Hitler appreciated how Japan's entry into the war had complicated Churchill's position. "For years I never stopped telling all the English I met that they'd lose the Far East if they entered into a war in Europe", he told Himmler at dinner in December 1941. "They didn't answer, but they assumed a superior air. They are masters in the art of being arrogant"[49]. New Year's Eve had the arrogant Nazi dictator remarking that "it would have been possible to hold the Far East if the great countries of the white race had joined in a coalition for the purpose"[50].

As argued in the previous chapter, the British and the American government (though not many Americans) both viewed the Germans, rather than the Japanese, as the main enemy. The perpetual fear of many British that the Americans would devote most of their war effort to the defeat of Japan at the expense of the war in Europe never materialised. "Once Germany is defeated, the collapse of Italy and the defeat of Japan must follow", the American Chiefs of Staff minuted in December 1941[51], and they stuck to this policy until Germany had surrendered. Both Britain and America suffered terrible blows in the Far East in 1942, however. Britain lost Hong Kong, Singapore, Malaya and Burma, while America lost the Philippines and Guam. The disintegration of Britain's defences in South-East Asia caused Churchill to demand a vote of confidence from the House of Commons, which he won on 29 January 1942 by 464 votes to 1. The debate happened before the fall of Singapore two weeks later. During the debate, however, he had to defend the decisions he had made, particularly when it came to the Far Eastern campaign. He continued to hold out the possibility that Hitler might invade Britain, though he told the House that the presence of American troops in Britain would be an important deterrent:

> "… the advantage, not only to Britain but to the Empire, of the arrival of powerful American Army and Air Forces in the United Kingdom … the presence in our Islands of a Force of heavy but unknown strength, and the establishment of a broader bridgehead between us and the New World, constitutes an important additional deterrent to invasion at a time when the successful invasion of these Islands is Hitler's last remaining hope of total victory"[52].

Hitler clearly read the speech, and regarded it, according to Goebbels, as "exceptionally weak and wearisome". Goebbels noted in his diary on 30 January that Hitler did not think that Churchill would fall from power:

> "…[Hitler], too, does not believe that Churchill is any longer sitting on top of the world, but on the other hand he sees no possibility of an early collapse of the Churchill regime…

> Churchill by the way remarked in his speech that Hess had really flown to England in order to unseat Churchill and bring about a suitable peace. That he made this remark is a proof of his nervousness …"

Goebbels speculated, as he often did, on British politics from a position of almost total ignorance:

> "The Tories are no doubt playing a decisive role behind the scenes in England. Churchill has never been a friend of the Tories. He was always an outsider … The Führer recalled that all Englishmen whom he received before the outbreak of war were in agreement that Churchill was a fool. Even Chamberlain said so to the Führer"[53].

Like the rest of the world, the Germans were amazed at how quickly the Japanese overcame the British, American and Dutch defences in South-East Asia. Hitler was far from overjoyed about the collapse of the European empires in the East. "The Führer profoundly regrets the heavy losses sustained by the white race in East Asia, but that isn't our fault", Goebbels wrote in his diary at the end of January[54]. A few days later, the imminent fall of Singapore was the cause of further reflection on the strength of Churchill's position. Goebbels noted in his diary that "The Führer regards the fall of Singapore as a very serious thing for the English. He believes a crisis may possibly arise for the British Empire. Churchill's position may be badly shaken. I am not prepared as yet to believe it. Churchill is already trying to minimise these events, and as the English know very well that Churchill's fall would provoke a most serious crisis for the British war spirit, they will shrink from this last measure for settling scores with the arch liar"[55].

Two days later, after his conversation with Goebbels, as Singapore's fall loomed, Hitler changed his opinion about the safety of Churchill's position:

> "Week by week the Tories are becoming more and more distrustful of the Churchill policies. This distrust has been especially fed by the silly declarations of Cripps. The Führer agrees that Cripps is a real treasure for us, to be guarded carefully"[56].

Goebbels himself had a preferred candidate for British Prime Minster, however. He wrote in his diary in February 1942 that: "It is claimed that Hore-Belisha and Cripps intend to found a new anti-Churchill party. It would be best, of course, if Churchill were defeated and Hore-Belisha took his place. Today we would most heartily welcome a Jew as Prime Minister"[57].

Hitler continued to have mixed feelings towards the disasters which were unfolding for the British Empire in East Asia. He does not seem ever to have reconciled himself entirely to having Japan, rather than Britain, as an ally. Even after Singapore had fallen, Hitler refused to gloat publicly at what was the worst disaster ever to befall British arms. When Ribbentrop drafted a press release gloating at Britain's defeat, according to his secretary, "Hitler shook his head, and advised Ribbentrop: 'We have to think in terms of centuries. Who knows, in the future the Yellow Peril may well be the biggest one for us.' He tore the document in half"[58].

Another, much lesser, disaster for Britain occurred on 13 February, when two German battleships, the *Scharnhorst* and *Gneisenau*, broke through the Straits of Dover in daylight from France to the safety of Germany, despite attacks from British warships and planes. Since Britain had claimed mastery of the English Channel for centuries, it was a severe blow to her pride. Hitler had asked that the ships be moved to Norway because of something Churchill had said. According to his naval adjutant, "Since Churchill has stated that the British still have the bloodiest sacrifices to bear, he considers an invasion of Norway quite likely"[59]. (At Churchill's request, the British Chiefs of Staff investigated the possibility of such an invasion in June, but ruled it "unacceptable")[60]. According to Goebbels, Hitler was delighted at his success, and was certainly aware of the extent of consternation in Britain:

> "Lunch with the Führer and Quisling. The Führer is naturally very happy that our warships succeeded in breaking through. He believes we gained enormously in prestige while the British lost prestige

correspondingly. He is still of the opinion that Churchill has been manoeuvred into a dangerous position and that his fall may possibly be expected.

Singapore too has weakened his position very much. As the crisis extended it would exhaust the energies of the English public more and more and someday a catastrophe would result. Although I am not so optimistic in these matters as the Führer, I believe, nevertheless, it may be assumed that Churchill's position has been weakened and that he must watch his step"[61].

Today the so-called "Channel Dash" appears an irrelevance. However, coming on top of the fall of Singapore it could have been a serious blow to Churchill's leadership. The Commons debate on 17 February on the fall of Singapore with 85,000 prisoners devoted as much time to the Channel Dash as to the war in South East Asia.

Churchill fought back in two ways: in a broadcast to the public, and in Parliament. He broadcast to the British people on 15 February about the fall of Singapore. He acknowledged that it was a severe blow, however he listed the advances the Allies had made over the last few months. In particular, the defeat of the German Army outside Moscow had "broken the Hitler legend" for the first time[62].

Churchill also defended his handling of the escape of the warships in the Commons, and announced a secret inquiry. He argued that the German warships would be less of a threat to British ships than they had been in the Atlantic, and that the British bombers could now target Germany instead. Their near-misses would hit German, rather than French, houses[63]. In fact, as he had found out from the Enigma decrypts, both ships had been damaged by British aircraft, and it would be some months before they were operational again[64]. Had he been able to make this information public, the Channel Dash could have been much less damaging to his Government. He survived the subsequent storm of protest in Parliament. Goebbels, no doubt echoing Hitler's thoughts, found a crumb of comfort in the failure of the opposition to unseat Churchill. He wrote in his diary on 17 February 1942:

"For the further progress of the war, we cannot possibly think of a prime minister who would be better for us than Churchill. Aside from the fact that we are accustomed to his personality and his policies, it must not be overlooked that Churchill's strategy is so short-sighted that he will certainly lead the Empire from one reverse into another. Let us therefore rejoice that he continues at the head of the world empire. If the empire is to be laid to eternal rest anyway, it is comforting to have an experienced gravedigger to hand"[65].

Russia

During 1942, and indeed throughout the rest of the war, Hitler's great preoccupation was the land fighting in Russia. This titanic conflict caused around four-fifths of all the losses suffered by the German Army during the Second World War. Churchill recognised its importance from the start. "I am sure that [Stalin] is entirely with us against Hitler", Churchill had written to Eden in December 1941[66]. He had no sympathy at all for the Communist regime, but was entirely aware of the irony that he was now trying to preserve it.

Churchill wrote years later that, while flying to Moscow to meet Stalin in August 1942, "I pondered on my mission to this sullen, sinister, Bolshevik State I had once tried so hard to strangle at its birth, and which, until Hitler appeared, I had regarded as the mortal foe of civilised freedom"[67]. According to Martin Gilbert, he was aware of Hitler's boast in March 1942 that Russia would soon be "annihilatingly defeated"[68], and British intelligence's warning of a large German spring offensive indicated that this was not just rhetoric. In any event, he clearly recognised how important the year's events in Russia would be to Britain. "All now depends", he wrote to Roosevelt in April 1942, "upon the vast Russo-German struggle"[69].

Hitler enjoyed speculating on the meaning of Churchill's visit to Moscow in the summer of 1942. "Stalin is an anarchist educated in an ecclesiastical college! Our newspapers ought to ask whether he and Churchill sang psalms together in Moscow!" He thought it might be connected with the disaster which had overtaken a British convoy, carrying supplies to Russia: "I cannot help connecting in my mind Churchill's visit to Moscow with the affair of the last convoy. That they had some big project in mind I am convinced; otherwise why should they have sent the Mediterranean Fleet to sea?"[70]

As Churchill knew, it was a struggle to which Britain could contribute only indirectly, though he had written in December 1941 that it was vital to send Stalin the supplies promised "without fail and punctually"[71]. This aid manifested itself in some surprising ways: for example, Churchill told Stalin that he would use Britain's "immense store" of poison gas on the Germans if they used it in Russia[72]. (He warned the Germans publicly of this possibility in a broadcast in May 1942). "We have built a great plan here for bombing Germany, which is the only way in our power of helping Russia", Churchill told his deputy, Attlee on 16 April 1942[73]. He remarked in a broadcast in February 1942: "It seemed our duty ... to do everything in our power to help the Russian people to meet the prodigious onslaught which had been launched against them. It is little enough we have done for Russia, considering all she has done to beat Hitler and for the common cause"[74]. As noted above, he saw the long-term psychological implications of the German defeat in the snowy hell outside Moscow the previous December. The advance of the Russian army following its rout of the Germans had "broken the Hitler legend"[75].

Churchill clearly saw that it had been a great mistake for Hitler to invade Russia, and once the Russians had survived the first winter of the Nazi-Soviet war, he could say so. Such an opportunity to taunt Hitler could not, of course be lost:

> "Even a Hitler makes mistakes sometimes. In June last, without the slightest provocation and in breach of a pact of non-aggression, he invaded the lands of the Russian peoples.
>
> ...
>
> Then Hitler made his second grand blunder. He forgot about the Winter. There is a Winter, you know, in Russia. For a good many months the temperature is apt to fall very low. There is snow; there is frost and all that.
>
> Hitler forgot about this Russian Winter. He must have been very loosely educated. We all heard about it at school, but he forgot it. I have never made such a bad mistake as that.
>
> So Winter came and fell upon his ill-clad armies, and with the Winter came the valiant Russian counter-attacks. No one can say with certainty how many millions of Germans have already perished in Russia and its snows"[76].

Churchill realised that it was important to reassure the Russians as often as possible that Britain would not make a separate peace with the Germans. In May, Churchill told Molotov that, even if the Germans defeated the Russians, Britain would continue to fight. After the fall of France, "Great Britain had stood alone for a whole year with but a handful of ill-equipped troops between her and Hitler's victorious and numerous divisions"[77]. By October, Churchill knew that the worst of the danger had passed. Based on information from the Enigma decrypts, he wrote in a telegram to General Wavell that "it looks as if Hitler's campaign against Russia in 1942 will be a great disappointment to him"[78]. As another winter was starting, Churchill taunted "Corporal Hitler's" management of the war in the East:

> "The jaws of another Russian winter are closing on Hitler's armies. One hundred and eighty German divisions, many of them reduced to little more than brigades by the slaughters and privations they have suffered, together with a host of miserable Italians, Rumanians and Hungarians dragged from their homes by a maniac's fantasy – all these, as they reel back from the fire and steel of the avenging Soviet armies, must prepare themselves with weakened forces and with added pangs for a second dose of what they got last year. They have of course the consolation of knowing that they have been commanded and led not by the German General Staff but by Corporal Hitler himself"[79].

However, even from a distance, Churchill thought that he could influence the course of the battle to some extent. He telegraphed unsolicited advice to Stalin about the safety of Russia's oil supplies, "when Hitler despairs of taking Baku, he will try to wreck it by air attack". In reply, Stalin thanked Churchill, and assured him that he had the situation under control[80].

The titanic struggle at Stalingrad, which absorbed much of Hitler's and Stalin's attention, unfolded in late 1942 and early 1943. Churchill recognised its importance, and watched it with "breathless attention"[81], but it was far too far away from British and American bases for there to be any question of direct intervention. Hitler thought that "perhaps the fall of Stalingrad may compel him [Churchill] to make a complete *volte face* ... When once the terms we offered to Great Britain are made public there will be an uproar throughout the Kingdom". He offered a suggestion for any successor to Churchill: "If a change of leadership occurs, the first thing the new man should do would be to release all those who had been incarcerated by Churchill ... These people would soon settle accounts with the Jews!"[82] In fact, as noted previously, Churchill himself was unhappy with keeping political prisoners in jail without trial or even charge, and released them as soon as he safely could. Their release during the second half of the war had no measureable effect on public order in Britain.

Chapter 7

North Africa

British and Commonwealth forces confronted the Germans on land and without allies during only one major campaign in the Second World War: the war in Egypt and Libya. It was as near as Churchill and Hitler came to fighting a duel by proxy on land (the Americans being present in Normandy), but to Hitler, it was always a secondary front. It was the Italians, not the Germans, who first attacked the British Empire in Egypt. There were no vital German interests in the sands of North Africa. Hitler only intervened to assist Mussolini and embarrass the British; he thought, the "man-in-the-street" regarded Egypt as "one of the most important props of British prosperity"[83]. By the time the Germans began to arrive in Africa in February 1941, Hitler had already turned his attention to the attack on Russia. In January 1942, he told his dinner guests that "British military prestige has been re-established by the conquest of Benghazi. It was the psychological moment to put an end to the war. But Churchill had Russia at the back of his mind – and he didn't see that, if Russia were to triumph over Germany, Europe would at once come under the hegemony of a great power"[84].

Churchill, however, always regarded the war in North Africa much more seriously. "Egypt must be held at all costs", he wrote to his Minister Resident in the Middle East[85]. Goebbels may have mocked him for the interest he took, describing him in early 1942 as "a collector of deserts"[86]. However, unlike Germany, the British Empire had vital interests in the Middle East: the oil of Arabia and the Suez Canal, the lifeline to India and a (limited) supply route to Russia. From the time the Italians attacked, there was no question but that British interests would be robustly defended. "We are determined to fight for Egypt … as if it were the soil of England itself", Churchill told journalists in Cairo in August 1942[87]. At his conference with Roosevelt in December 1941, Halifax, by then British ambassador to Washington, noted that there was "general agreement that if Hitler was held in Russia he must try something else". British success in North Africa might make "Hitler want if he could to get hold of Morocco as quickly as possible". It was therefore "vital to forestall the Germans in North West Africa and the Atlantic Islands"[88]. The meeting therefore agreed to invade French North-West Africa.

Though regarding it as a secondary front, Hitler had high hopes for the campaign in North Africa in 1942. "If we succeed in neutralising Malta and getting new tanks to Africa, Rommel will be able to recapture the operational initiative", he remarked in early January. For the first nine months of 1942, the initiative in North Africa lay broadly with the Axis, to Churchill's increasing frustration. They surged into Egypt and besieged a 35,000 strong British and

Commonwealth garrison at the desert fortress of Tobruk. The fall of this town on 21 June 1942 was a big victory for the Germans and a huge blow to the British. Churchill, talking with Roosevelt in Washington when he heard the news, described it as "a bitter moment", while a delighted Hitler promoted Rommel to Field Marshal. "I am so ashamed", Churchill later told Lord Moran, "I cannot understand why Tobruk gave in. More than 30,000 of our men put up their hands. If they won't fight…" and he broke off[89]. He had another explanation: "I fear we have not very good generals", he told Eden[90]. In fact, and despite his triumphs in the desert, Hitler thought that Rommel's reputation was exaggerated: some of it, he remarked, was due to British praise: "The British themselves, as Dr Goebbels rightly says, have given Rommel enormous publicity, because, by writing up his exceptional military capabilities, they hoped to make more palatable to their own people the defeats suffered at his hands"[91]. "Between them", Hitler argued after Tobruk, "Churchill and the Duce have caused the name of Rommel to be hallowed among the primitive races of North Africa and the Middle East with a prestige which it is impossible to exaggerate. This shows how dangerous it is for a responsible person to portray his opponent in the manner in which Churchill is portraying Rommel"[92]. He himself thought that the British made good soldiers, or, at least, much better than Americans, referring to "the opinion of the Japanese, who consider that the Englishman is a much better soldier than the American"[93].

In June and July, Hitler was dangerously overconfident about German prospects in the desert. "The capture of Tobruk is a victory as great as it was inconceivable", he told his dinner guests on 27 June, "and at the moment it comes as a real stroke of fortune for the German people"[94]. Hitler seems to have thought that the victory might have had some effect on Spain, though if it did, it was too small to affect the Spanish policy of neutrality. Five days later, he remarked to his dinner guests that German propaganda should "trumpet … that for Egypt the day of freedom has at last dawned". He thought that the German foreign office should encourage the King of Egypt to withdraw from British protection[95]. According to one historian, "Hitler agreed with Keitel's prediction that 'when the Germans captured Alexandria the *entire* British public would be thrown into a far greater rage than at the surrender of Singapore'. It would stir them up against Churchill. 'Let's hope that the American legation in Cairo continues to keep us so excellently informed of British military plans with its badly enciphered cables'". He even hoped that British morale would be undermined so heavily that, after his upcoming offensive in Russia, Britain would make peace[96].

Chapter 7

That summer, as Hitler was overconfident about the position in North Africa, Churchill was so concerned about the British position after Tobruk that he took the considerable risk of flying to Cairo twice in August 1942 to see the situation there for himself. The American General Douglas MacArthur proposed that he be awarded the Victoria Cross for those flights[97] (though in fact Churchill, as a civilian, would only have been ineligible for the Military Medal). In fact, the British, Commonwealth and American reinforcements which poured into the theatre in the summer and autumn, the new commanders that Churchill appointed and the strangulation of Rommel's supply lines turned out to be decisive. The Eighth Army held Rommel's offensive at the Battle of Alam Halfa, really the first battle of El Alamein, in August. Three months later, they delivered their knockout punch. The decisive British and Commonwealth victory at El Alamein in November 1942 rewarded Churchill's perseverance and judgement to the full. It was the start of the long German retreat in North Africa, which ended in Tunisia in May 1943. Had Britain lost this battle and had the landings in Algeria also been a disaster, it is difficult to see how Churchill could have remained Prime Minister. Certainly, he seems to have been extremely worried. He had told Eden and Attlee on 1 October 1942 that, if the landings failed, "then I'm done for and must go and hand over to one of you"[98] (because of the overwhelming Conservative majority in Parliament, it probably would have been Eden, rather than the Labour leader).

On October 23, the British and Commonwealth forces attacked, and ten days later, after much hard fighting, they had routed Rommel, who retreated, while apparently allowing Hitler to believe that he had stood fast. Celebrating the "great victory in the Battle of Egypt, which is a British victory of the first order", Churchill ordered the church bells to be rung, though many in Britain at the time thought that this was tempting fate. In fact, the bells were marking his own political survival, as well as the victory in North Africa. It was a turning point of the duel between the two men, and Churchill felt able to insult Hitler. At the Mansion House in the City of London, he made one of his most famous speeches:

> "Now, this is not the end. It is not even the beginning to the end. But it is, perhaps, the end of the beginning. Hitler's Nazis will be equally well armed and, perhaps, better armed. But henceforward they will have to face in many theatres that superiority in the air which they have so often used without mercy against others and of which they boasted all around the world that they were to be masters and which they intended to use as an instrument for convincing all other peoples that all resistance to them was hopeless"[99].

As the Germans were being routed at El Alamein, an Anglo-American force had invaded French North Africa. Churchill used his Mansion House speech to gloat at Hitler's expense. "Hitler knew that something was brewing, but what, he could not guess. He naively complained of "military idiots" and drunkards—he is quite uncivil from time to time—the working of whose tortuous minds he and his staffs were unable to discern. In fact, however, while he was thus wondering, the largest amphibious operation ever conceived was about to sail…" Churchill had foreseen the strategic implications of the Allied victory in North Africa for the future course of the war. "If we could end the year in possession of North Africa", Churchill remarked to Stalin in August 1942, "we could threaten the belly of Hitler's Europe"[100]. Two days later, he remarked to Stalin that success in North Africa would "create much difficulty for Hitler and Vichy"[101].

Later in November 1942, Hitler invaded Vichy France. "I never had the slightest doubt myself that Hitler would break the Armistice, over-run all France and try to capture the French fleet at Toulon", commented Churchill[102]. This gave Churchill yet another opportunity to taunt his German enemy: "To-day the news reaches us that Hitler has decided to overrun all France, thus breaking the Armistice which the Vichy Government had kept with such pitiful and perverted fidelity, at a horrible cost, even sacrificing their ships and sailors to fire upon American rescuing troops as they arrived. Even while they were doing that for the sake of this Armistice they have been stricken down by their German taskmasters" [103].

Carpet bombing

"If need be", Churchill told Stalin in Moscow in August 1942, "we [hope] to shatter almost every dwelling in almost every German city"[104]. 1942 was the first year in which the British were in a position to launch the annihilating bombing raids on German cities for which Churchill had long called. The British had been attacking since 1940, and had begun using two-ton Blockbuster bombs (much heavier than the German bombs dropped on London during the war) in April 1941[105]. They started to drop four- and eight-ton bombs in 1942. These raids were to be the most controversial part of Britain's war effort, and a particularly divisive example was the attack on the medieval wooden city of Lübeck on 28 March 1942, which destroyed or damaged around 60% of the buildings in the town. According to the head of Britain's Bomber Command, Arthur "Bomber" Harris, Lübeck had been chosen because it had some importance as a port and there were U-boat factories near it[106]. Its high proportion of wooden buildings meant that it would be particularly vulnerable to the incendiary bombs which the RAF wanted to use. Hitler, however, apparently believed that Churchill himself had chosen the target because it was a historic city. In one of his more bizarre decisions, he ordered the *Luftwaffe* to target British cities of historic or cultural importance (reputedly selected from the German Baedeker guidebooks). "It was an unedifying sight – the two opposing leaders, well-bunkered in their respective capitals, trading blows at each other's innocent citizenry"[107], though Churchill at least made an effort to see the damage to his own country, and was sometimes booed for doing so, while Hitler did not.

The fury and consternation which the British raid on Lübeck caused in Germany, however, was as nothing compared to that which gripped the Nazi leadership after the first "thousand-bomber" raid on Germany, on Cologne at the end of May 1942. Several hundred died and 45,000 were made homeless. According to David Irving:

> "The local *Gauleiter* reported that the damage was vast. Göring, however, comfortably holidaying at his castle outside Nuremberg, claimed that since his air defences had destroyed nearly forty of the bombers and "only seventy or eighty" had actually attacked, the occasion had been an overwhelming *Luftwaffe* victory. Hitler believed the *Gauleiter* in preference to Göring—the more so when Churchill announced that a thousand bombers had taken part in the bombing; even Churchill could hardly get away with exaggerating by a multiple of ten, reasoned Hitler. He said that Churchill may have sent three hundred over as a sop to Stalin"[108].

In April 1942, Hitler made the amazing statement that Churchill had started the bombing, conveniently forgetting that he himself had begun the practice in Guernica in 1937 and Warsaw in September 1939:

> "But if in England the idea should prevail of carrying on air warfare against the civilian population with new methods, then I should like right now to state the following to the whole world: Mr. Churchill began this warfare in May, 1940. For four months I warned him and waited. Then the time came in which I was compelled to act. The person who was alone responsible for this kind of fighting began to complain. Even now my waiting is no weakness. Let this man not complain and whine again when I find myself compelled to give an answer which will bring very much suffering upon his own people"[109].

Hitler thought that, for their own strategic interests, the British were aiming at the wrong targets. "Were he Stalin or Churchill, he said, he would risk anything to knock out those nickel mines: within a few months no more German tanks or shells could be produced"[110]. He could only offer vague hopes to the German people who were suffering the greatly intensified British bombing:

> "In May, 1940, Mr. Churchill sent the first bombers against the German civilian population. I warned him at that time and for almost four months but of course in vain. Then we struck and indeed so thoroughly did we strike, that he suddenly began to cry and declared, it was barbarism and it was terrible. England would take revenge for it. The man who has all of this on his conscience! If I take no note of the war-monger general of this war, Roosevelt - the one to blame for all of this - he (Churchill) was the one who then dared to represent himself as innocent.

> Again today they are conducting this warfare and I would like to express one thing here: The hour will come this time also in which we will answer. May both of the chiefs of this war and their Jewish backers not begin to squirm and whine if the end for England is more horrible than the beginning"[111].

Submarine war

For the Germans, the brightest feature of the war in the West in 1942 was the enormous destruction of Allied shipping in the North Atlantic. It was a danger which constantly worried Churchill. According to his doctor, "I have been finding out that wherever he goes, he carries in his head the monthly figures of all sinkings … [so that] nothing he says could discourage anyone"[112]. Hitler intended to give Churchill plenty of worry during 1942. In May, Goebbels noted in his diary: "In the course of the next month we are going to put into service one and a half times as many submarines as are at present on the firing line … In the Führer's opinion we shall here strike at an especially sensitive nerve of the enemy. If Churchill and Roosevelt a few months ago were hopeful that the German submarine danger was eliminated, the hard facts of the situation will convince them of the opposite. They are going to get so many unexpected blows in this submarine war that all their loud-mouthed boasts of being able to cover the losses easily by new construction will be relegated to the realm of fantasy"[113].

The Germans had decided to change the design of the Enigma machine in [February], effectively blinding the Allied code-breakers for the year. The

Admiralty could no longer steer Allied convoys away from the positions of U-boats. Partly as a result, and also because of the incompetent, Anglophobe American Admiral Ernest King's decision to delay implementing convoys in the American part of the North Atlantic, the Germans sunk massive numbers of Allied ships. During one week in June 1942, 400,000 tons of shipping were lost, "a rate unexampled in either this war or the last, and … beyond all existing replacement plans", as Churchill wrote to Roosevelt[114]. Sinkings continued throughout the rest of the year: in November 1942, 721,700 tons of shipping were sunk, the worst monthly total during the Second World War. Fortunately, the British broke the new German cipher in December, so that the convoys could be steered away from the waiting U-boats again. Together with new long range aircraft which could now escort convoys all the way across the Atlantic, this meant that the U-boats were to be much less effective in 1943.

Hitler repeatedly drew attention to Churchill's overconfident boast that the British had mastered the submarine menace, making several speeches during the war along these lines:

> "During the winter of 1939-1940 a certain Mr. Churchill stated: "The submarine danger is eliminated. Hitler is finished." He has destroyed two, three, five submarines daily. At that time, he destroyed more than we even had then. He was exhausted. He had destroyed nothing, for then I again committed a very great error. The error was: I had only a very small number of our submarines fighting and held back the greater part of the submarines in order to train the crews for the new submarines being launched."[115]

Churchill was to have the last laugh in the second half of the war, when Allied counter-measures and the overwhelming pace of American construction meant that the U-boats were no longer a serious danger to Britain's lifelines. However, the battle was never completely won, and the sinking of Allied ships continued until the end of the war.

Hitler, Churchill and the Holocaust

Nazi Germany had subjected Jews under its rule to terrible indignities already, but most historians accept that the orders for the extermination of all of the Jews in Nazi-occupied Europe were given in early 1942, and that the process began in earnest later that year. By the end of the year, information about the on-going genocide had reached the British government from several sources, in particular the Polish *émigré* government in London. Churchill was certainly aware of the atrocities which Hitler's Reich was committing. He attempted to alert others to the terrible disaster which was taking place in Europe. On 29 October, he wrote to the Archbishop of Canterbury about "the systematic cruelties to which the Jewish people ... have been exposed [which] are amongst the most terrible events of history, and place an indelible stain upon all those who perpetrate and instigate them"[116].

On 7 December, Eden reported to the Cabinet "reports of further atrocities against the Jews in Poland". The War Cabinet resolved to explore the possibility of a Joint Declaration on the subject. A week later, the War Cabinet discussed the matter briefly. "Any confirmation of story of wholesale massacre? By mass electrical methods", Churchill asked Eden according to the abbreviated notes. "Nothing direct, but indications that it may be true", Eden responded. "Can't confirm the method. Know that Jews are being withdrawn e.g. from Norway and sent to Poland for some such purposes evidently. Agreement reached on declaration ... This commits us to punishing those responsible"[117]. On 23 December, the War Cabinet committed Britain to accommodating Jewish refugees who managed to escape from Nazi-occupied Europe[118]. A week later, Churchill proposed an indirect step to assist the Jews and Poles. He suggested that Berlin should be bombed, and leaflets should be scattered during the raids, to make it clear to the Germans that the air raids were reprisals for Nazi atrocities in Occupied Europe[119].

Hitler regarded Churchill as dominated by the Jews, though perhaps less so than Roosevelt. On listening to Roosevelt talk in January 1942, Hitler described the American President's brain as "sick", and noted, oddly, that "the noise he made at his press conference was typically Hebraic"[120]. He seems to have thought that Churchill, who was perpetually hard up, was receiving money from shadowy Jewish conspirators, rather than from his literary efforts and his Prime Ministerial salary. "The campaign of antagonism against Germany was organised by Churchill on the orders of his Jewish paymasters, and with the collaboration of Eden, Vansittart and company", Hitler told his dinner guests in August 1942[121]. Hitler thought that Churchill's policy of the balance of power was "to nobody's interest ... but that of the Jews ...What is that Moroccan Jew whom Great Britain named a Minister of War [Hore-Belisha]? The generals finally broke him"[122].

Chapter 7

Prospects for the future

Both Churchill and Hitler quite clearly saw the turning point which 1942 represented. "If North Africa were won this year we could make a deadly attack upon Hitler next year", Churchill told Stalin in August 1942. "Our aim was to pretend that we were going to strike at the Pas de Calais [instead of North Africa] … It was of the utmost importance that nothing should be said or done to indicate that we were not going to attack Hitler in France"[123]. At the end of the conference, Churchill and Stalin pledged to continue the war until the complete defeat "of Hitlerism and any similar tyranny"[124] (though presumably not the Communist despotism in Russia). After the Allied victory at El Alamein and the success of the landings in North Africa, Churchill telegraphed to a colleague that "an entirely new view must be taken of possibilities of attacking Hitler in 1943"[125]. Churchill had seen since Pearl Harbor the year before that the allies would win. His speeches refer more and more often to ultimate victory.

> "Our enemies have been more talkative lately. Ribbentrop, Göring, and Hitler have all been making speeches which are of interest because they reveal with considerable frankness their state of mind. There is one note which rings through all those speeches. It can be quite clearly heard above their customary boastings and threats - the dull, low, whining note of fear. They are all the speeches of men conscious of their guilt and conscious also of the law.

> …

> Evidently, something has happened in these two years to make these evil doers feel that aggression, war, and bloodshed, the trampling down of the weak may not be after all the whole story. There may be another side of the account. It is a long account, and it is becoming pretty clear that the day is coming when it will have to be settled.

> The most striking and curious part of Hitler's speech was his complaint that no one pays sufficient attention to his victories. "Look at all the victories I have won," he exclaims in effect. "Look at all the countries I have invaded and struck down. Look at all the thousands of kilometres that I have advanced into the lands of other people. Look at all the booty I have gathered and all the men I have killed and captured. Contrast these exploits with the performances of the allies. Why are they not downhearted? How do they dare to keep up their spirits in the face of my great successes and their many misfortunes?"

That in fact - I have not quoted his actual words but I have given their meaning and their sense - that is his complaint. That is the question which puzzles him and angers him. It strikes a chill into his marrow because in his heart he knows that with all his tremendous victories and vast conquests his fortunes have declined.

His prospects have darkened to an immeasurable degree in the last two years, while at the same time Britain, the United States, Russia, and China have moved forward through tribulation and sorrow, steadily forward, steadily onward from strength to strength.

He sees with amazement that our defeats are but the stepping stones to victory and that all his victories are stepping stones to ruin. It was apparent to me that this bad man saw quite clearly the shadow of slowly and remorselessly approaching doom, and he railed at fortune for mocking him with the glitter of fleeting success"[126].

Churchill was, however, far too optimistic in the euphoria caused by victory at El Alamein. A paper he submitted to the Chiefs of Staff in December 1942 proposed a schedule for operations in Europe and North Africa. It foresaw the clearance of North Africa by the end of January 1943, compared with an actual date of May 1943, and an invasion of France in the summer of 1943, compared with an actual date of June 1944[127]. By the end of December, his mood had cooled notably, and he recognised that German strength in Europe, and the weakness of American forces in Britain, made a cross Channel invasion unlikely in 1943[128].

For Hitler, on the other hand, the prospects had darkened considerably. According to David Irving, writing about the summer of 1942, "Whether Hitler expected a full-scale Second Front soon is uncertain. He believed that Churchill's recent visit to Washington had been to advise against such an invasion until 1943 and that Stalin was consequently being advised to stave off defeat until then. In the west, therefore, Churchill might find his hand forced over a Second Front — anything was possible"[129].

---

[1] *Hitler's War*, David Irving, p.364
[2] *Road to Victory, Winston S Churchill 1941-45*, Martin S Gilbert, p.35
[3] *Road to Victory, Winston S Churchill 1941-45*, Martin S Gilbert, p.43
[4] *Winston Churchill, The Struggle for Survival*, Lord Moran, p.32

[5] Hitler speech, 30 January 1942

[6] Hitler's Letters, Werner Maser, p.188

[7] *Er war mein Chef*, Christa Schroeder, p.78-9

[8] The Goebbels Diaries, 1942-43, p.45

[9] *Ciano's diary 1937-1943*, Ciano, p.460

[10] Premier papers, 3/499/2, quoted in *Road to Victory, Winston S Churchill 1941-45*, Martin S Gilbert, p.21

[11] *Road to Victory, Winston S Churchill 1941-45*, Martin S Gilbert, p.266

[12] *Road to Victory, Winston S Churchill 1941-45*, Martin S Gilbert, p.211-2

[13] *Hitler's War*, David Irving, p.409

[14] Hitler speech, 30 September 1942

[15] *Hitler's Table Talk*, p.654

[16] *Hitler's Table Talk*, p.317-8

[17] *Hitler's Table Talk*, p.356-8

[18] *Hitler's Table Talk*, p.129

[19] *Hitler's Table Talk*, p.72

[20] *Hitler's Table Talk*, ed. Hugh Trevor-Roper, p.187

[21] *Hitler's Table Talk*, p.179

[22] *Hitler's Table Talk*, p.421-2

[23] *Hitler's Table Talk*, p.276

[24] *Hitler's Table Talk*, ed. Hugh Trevor-Roper, p.186

[25] *Hitler's Table Talk*, ed. Hugh Trevor-Roper, p.318

[26] *Hitler's Table Talk*, p.179

[27] *Hitler's Table Talk*, ed. Hugh Trevor-Roper, p.186

[28] *Tapping Hitler's Generals*, Soenke Neitzel, p.69-70.

[29] *Hitler's Table Talk*, ed. Hugh Trevor-Roper, p.187

[30] Hitler speech, 30 September 1942

[31] *Hitler's Table Talk*, p.537

[32] *Road to Victory, Winston S Churchill 1941-45*, Martin S Gilbert, Chapter 8

[33] Papers of Lord Alanbrooke, 9/3/8, quoted in *Masters and Commanders*, Andrew Roberts, p.201

[34] *Hitler's Table Talk*, p.546

[35] *Hitler's Table Talk*, ed. Hugh Trevor-Roper, p.274-6

[36] *Hitler's Table Talk*, p.539

[37] *Hitler and Churchill, Secrets of Leadership*, Andrew Roberts, p.118

[38] *Hitler's Table Talk*, ed. Hugh Trevor-Roper, p.72

[39] *Hitler's Table Talk*, ed. Hugh Trevor-Roper, p.207

[40] *Hitler's Table Talk*, ed. Hugh Trevor-Roper, p.237

[41] *Hitler's Table Talk*, ed. Hugh Trevor-Roper, p.254

[42] *Hitler's Table Talk*, ed. Hugh Trevor-Roper, p.299-301

[43] *Hitler's Table Talk*, ed. Hugh Trevor-Roper, p.367-9

[44] *Hitler's Table Talk*, ed. Hugh Trevor-Roper, p.684

[45] *Hitler's Table Talk*, ed. Hugh Trevor-Roper, p.620

[46] *Hitler's Table Talk*, ed. Hugh Trevor-Roper, p.680

[47] *Hitler's Table Talk*, ed. Hugh Trevor-Roper, p.684

[48] *Hitler's Table Talk*, ed. Hugh Trevor-Roper, p.687

[49] *Hitler's Table Talk*, p.150

[50] *Hitler's Table Talk*, p.159

[51] General Marshall and Admiral Stark Minute of 22 December 1941, quoted in *Road to Victory, Winston S Churchill 1941-45*, Martin S Gilbert, p.25

[52] *Hansard*, 29 January 1942

53 *Goebbels Diary*, 30 January 1942

54 *The Goebbels Diaries, 1942-43*, 30 January 1942

55 *The Goebbels Diaries, 1942-43*, 11 February 1942

56 *The Goebbels Diaries, 1942-43*, 11 February 1942

57 *The Goebbels Diaries, 1942-43*, 13 February 1942

58 *Hitler's War*, David Irving, p.373

59 *Hitler's War*, David Irving, p.368

60 *Road to Victory, Winston S Churchill 1941-45*, Martin S Gilbert, p.116

61 *The Goebbels Diaries, 1942-43*, 13 February 1942

62 *Road to Victory, Winston S Churchill 1941-45*, Martin S Gilbert, p.58

63 *Hansard*, 17 February 1942

64 *Road to Victory, Winston S Churchill 1941-45*, Martin S Gilbert, p.56-7

65 *The Goebbels Diaries, 1942-43*, 17 February 1942

66 *Road to Victory, Winston S Churchill 1941-45*, Martin S Gilbert, p.8

67 *The Second World War*, Volume 4, Winston S Churchill, p.428.

68 *Road to Victory, Winston S Churchill 1941-45*, Martin S Gilbert, p.75

69 *Road to Victory, Winston S Churchill 1941-45*, Martin S Gilbert, p.83

70 *Hitler's Table Talk*, ed. Hugh Trevor-Roper, p.631

71 *Road to Victory, Winston S Churchill 1941-45*, Martin S Gilbert, p.9

72 *Road to Victory, Winston S Churchill 1941-45*, Martin S Gilbert, p.76

73 *Road to Victory, Winston S Churchill 1941-45*, Martin S Gilbert, p.92

74 Churchill broadcast, 15 February 1942

75 *Road to Victory, Winston S Churchill 1941-45*, Martin S Gilbert, p.58

76 Churchill broadcast, 10 May 1942

77 *Road to Victory, Winston S Churchill 1941-45*, Martin S Gilbert, p.111

78 *Telegram of 7 October 1942, Churchill papers 20/88*, quoted in *Road to Victory, Winston S Churchill 1941-45*, Martin S Gilbert, p.237

79 Churchill broadcast, 29 November 1942

80 Prime Minister's personal telegram, 7 November 1942, quoted in *Road to Victory, Winston S Churchill 1941-45*, Martin S Gilbert, p.255

81 *Road to Victory, Winston S Churchill 1941-45*, Martin S Gilbert, p.266

82 *Hitler's Table Talk*, ed. Hugh Trevor-Roper, p.684

83 *Hitler's Table Talk*, ed. Hugh Trevor-Roper, p.546

84 *Hitler's Table Talk*, ed. Hugh Trevor-Roper, p.265

85 *Road to Victory, Winston S Churchill 1941-45*, Martin S Gilbert, p.137

86 *The Goebbels Diaries, 1942-43*, p.36

87 Quoted in *Road to Victory, Winston S Churchill 1941-45*, Martin S Gilbert, p.216

88 *Road to Victory, Winston S Churchill 1941-45*, Martin S Gilbert, p.23

89 *Churchill: Taken from the diaries of Lord Moran*, Lord Moran, p.41

90 *The Reckoning*, Anthony Eden, p.331

91 *Hitler's Table Talk*, ed. Hugh Trevor-Roper, p.527

92 *Hitler's Table Talk*, ed. Hugh Trevor-Roper, p.574

93 *Hitler's Table Talk*, ed. Hugh Trevor-Roper, p.171

94 *Hitler's Table Talk*, ed. Hugh Trevor-Roper, p.538

95 *Hitler's Table Talk*, ed. Hugh Trevor-Roper, p.550

96 *Hitler's War*, David Irving, p.400

97 *Road to Victory, Winston S Churchill 1941-45*, Martin S Gilbert, p.217

98 *War Diaries*, Oliver Harvey, p.165

99 Churchill speech, 10 November 1942

100 *Road to Victory, Winston S Churchill 1941-45*, Martin S Gilbert, p.180

[101] *Road to Victory, Winston S Churchill 1941-45*, Martin S Gilbert, p.197
[102] Churchill broadcast, 29 November 1942
[103] *Hansard*, 11 November 1942
[104] *Road to Victory, Winston S Churchill 1941-45*, Martin S Gilbert, p.179
[105] *Goebbels, Mastermind of the Third Reich*, David Irving, p.357
[106] *Bomber Offensive*, Arthur Harris, p.105
[107] *Hitler's War*, David Irving, p.378
[108] *Hitler's War*, David Irving, p.390
[109] Hitler speech, 26 April 1942
[110] *Hitler's War*, David Irving, p.416-7
[111] Hitler speech, 30 September 1942
[112] *Road to Victory, Winston S Churchill 1941-45*, Martin S Gilbert, p.69
[113] *The Goebbels Diaries*, 1942-43, p.228
[114] *Road to Victory, Winston S Churchill 1941-45*, Martin S Gilbert, p.146
[115] Hitler speech, 9 November 1942
[116] *Road to Victory, Winston S Churchill 1941-45*, Martin S Gilbert, p.245
[117] War Cabinet papers, 14 December 1942
[118] War Cabinet papers, 23 December 1942
[119] *Road to Victory, Winston S Churchill 1941-45*, Martin S Gilbert, p.287
[120] *Hitler's Table Talk*, ed. Hugh Trevor-Roper, p.179
[121] *Hitler's Table Talk*, ed. Hugh Trevor-Roper, p.678
[122] *Hitler's Table Talk*, ed. Hugh Trevor-Roper, p.202
[123] *Road to Victory, Winston S Churchill 1941-45*, Martin S Gilbert, p.181
[124] *Road to Victory, Winston S Churchill 1941-45*, Martin S Gilbert, p.205
[125] Churchill Papers 20/82, quoted in *Road to Victory, Winston S Churchill 1941-45*, Martin S Gilbert, p.253
[126] Churchill speech, 12 October 1942
[127] Churchill papers 23/10, quoted in *Road to Victory, Winston S Churchill 1941-45*, Martin S Gilbert, p.271
[128] *Road to Victory, Winston S Churchill 1941-45*, Martin S Gilbert, p.281-2
[129] *Hitler's War*, David Irving, p.403

8

The Turn of the Tide (1943)

Throughout 1943, the Allies slowly gained the upper hand against the Axis on all fronts. For Churchill especially, this was clearly a huge relief, given the disasters which had overtaken Britain in the first three years of the war. This change in fortunes was fully reflected in Churchill's conversations about Hitler, and Hitler's discussion of Churchill. In February, Churchill spoke optimistically to Parliament about the war situation, celebrating British victories in Africa and in the campaign against the U-boats. Such an opportunity to taunt Hitler could not, of course, be lost:

> "Provided that the present intense efforts are kept up here and in the United States, and that anti-U-boat warfare continues to hold first place in our thoughts and energies ... we shall be definitely better off, so far as shipping is concerned, at the end of 1943 than we are now, and ... we shall be still better off at the end of 1944, assuming that the war continues until then. It may be disappointing to Hitler to learn that we are upon a rising tide of tonnage and not upon an ebb or shrinkage, but it is the governing fact of the situation"[1].

Nor was this an empty boast. That same month, the War Cabinet heard an analysis of the war situation which included the following paragraph:

> "Apart from the military situation described above, the following factors affect Germany's situation to-day. Economic shortages are making themselves increasingly felt in Germany, and economic difficulties, particularly as regards man-power, oil and transport, are having a growing effect on the armed forces. The subservience of the remaining European neutrals grows less. Germany must now reckon with the

possibility of the defection of Italy, Hungary, Roumania and Finland, or any of them. Japan can and will do little to relieve the immediate military pressure on Germany. Meanwhile the Allied bombing offensive continues with increasing weight. Evidence is accumulating of disagreement between the German High Command and Hitler".

The same meeting did, however, sound a note of caution about the situation at sea, in contrast to Churchill's speech earlier that month: "The only ray of light in the sombre picture confronting Germany is provided by the increasing scale of submarine attack on the shipping of the United Nations"[2]. Churchill's perpetual anxiety about the U-boat war was clearly justified.

The end of the War and after

More and more, Churchill looked forward to the end of the European war. The British had in fact received peace feelers from the German government, though these approaches were almost certainly unknown to Hitler. According to the War Cabinet minutes of 1943:

> THE SECRETARY OF STATE FOR FOREIGN AFFAIRS informed the War Cabinet that a telegram had been received from, our Minister in Sweden stating that a Swedish personality had made the following report to our Naval Attaché. The person in question bad been approached by a Swedish pro-Nazi businessman (Mr "X") who said that he had met at the German Foreign Office with Von Ritgracht and Grundler, who had expressed the general desire to contact British officials in Stockholm. This had led to a meeting between "X" and Himmler. According to Mr. "X", Himmler had said that he had had consultations with Göring and with Generals Milch and Rommel and had been authorised by Hitler to seek personal contact clandestine- between representatives of Germany and Britain. Himmler had proposed that Germany should nominate two representatives to confer with two British representatives in order to clarify what was meant by the term "unconditional surrender".

> THE SECRETARY OF STATE FOR FOREIGN AFFAIRS, who read to the War Cabinet the text of the telegram in question, said that this move might be connected with the German threat of forthcoming employment of their secret weapon. In any case, he thought that it was intended to make trouble for us. He thought that the right course was that we should

inform the United States and Soviet Governments of this approach and should ask whether they agreed that our reply should be to the effect that we had nothing to say to Hitler, Himmler and those associated with him, except that our terms were unconditional surrender.

The War Cabinet agreed that the Foreign Secretary should deal with the matter on the lines proposed"[3].

That summer, the fall of Mussolini clearly led to reflections on the fate of Hitler when the Allies were to capture him. In a Cabinet paper of 26 July, Churchill described his plans for the disposal of Hitler and his regime:

"At this moment above all others, our thoughts must be concentrated upon the supreme aim, namely, the destruction of Hitler, Hitlerism and Nazi Germany. Every military advantage arising out of the surrender of Italy (should that occur) must be sought for this purpose...

The surrender of, to quote the President, 'the head devil together with his partners in crime' must be considered an eminent object and one for which we should strive by all means in our power short of wrecking the immense prospects which have been outlined in earlier paragraphs. It may be, however, that these criminals will flee into Germany or escape into Switzerland. On the other hand, they may surrender themselves or be surrendered by the Italian Government. Should they fall into our hands, we ought now to decide in consultation with the United States and after agreement with them and the U.S.S.R. what treatment should be meted out to them. Some may prefer prompt execution without trial except for identification purposes. Others may prefer that they be kept in confinement till the end of the war in Europe, and their fate decided together with that of other war criminals. Personally I am fairly indifferent on this matter, provided always that no solid military advantages are sacrificed for the sake of immediate vengeance"[4].

On 5 October 1943, the War Cabinet discussed a paper by the Foreign Secretary, Anthony Eden, on Germany's political future, and agreed to encourage separatist movements within Germany where these were available, for example in Bavaria or Saxony. One view advanced at that meeting, however, possibly by Churchill, was that the growing power of Russia could make a united Germany more "expedient" for Britain. According to the minutes, "Another view put forward was that, even though it proved impracticable to secure that the whole of Germany was divided into separate States, there was in any event much to be said for isolating and possibly even dismembering Prussia, whose evil influence had twice been responsible for a European war, and at the same time encouraging the formation of a Danubian Federation based on Vienna"[5].

In a broadcast over the radio on March 21, Churchill looked forward to the end of the war, and, beyond that, the post-war world. "Speaking under every reserve and not attempting to prophesy, I can imagine that some time next year – but it may well be the year after – we might beat Hitler. By which I mean beat him and his powers of evil into death, dust and ashes … The day of Hitler's downfall will be a bright one for our country and for all mankind. Bells will clash the peal of victory and hope, and we will march forward together, encouraged and invigorated and still, I trust, generally united upon our further journey." The broadcast ranged over many subjects besides Churchill's views on the end of the war. It also discussed his plans for the post-war welfare state, a Council of Europe, a National Health Service and the revival of British industry[6].

Almost immediately after the Teheran conference, Churchill came down with pneumonia, in those days still a life-threatening complaint. "If I die, don't worry", he told his daughter, Sarah, "the war is won"[7]. He was, however, starting to be concerned about the next challenge: how to cooperate with the Americans to deter Russia: "we mustn't weaken Germany too much – we may need her against Russia", he apparently told the War Cabinet on 5 October 1943[8]. He evidently expressed this concern to many of his closest advisers around this time: "Now he sees he cannot rely on the President's support", his doctor wrote in his diary on November 29 1943. "It would be useless to try to take a firm line with Stalin… Will he become a menace to the free world, another Hitler? The PM is appalled by his own impotence"[9].

Even at the end of, what was, on balance, a successful year, Churchill knew that a hard road lay ahead. He had not shared the view of many "higher-ups" in Turkey, who apparently told Lord Moran in January that Germany would collapse by mid-1943[10]. At the Mansion House in the City of London, on 9 November, he reminded his listeners that Hitler still had 400 divisions under his control. There would clearly be heavy fighting ahead in Europe before Hitler was finally defeated[11].

In Parliament on 21 September 1943, Churchill referred for the first time in public to the rocket bombs which Hitler was shortly to unleash on Britain: "We must not in any circumstances allow these favourable tendencies to weaken our efforts or lead us to suppose that our dangers are past or that the war is coming to an end. On the contrary, we must expect that the terrible foe we are smiting so heavily will make frenzied efforts to retaliate. The speeches of the German leaders, from Hitler downwards, contain mysterious allusions to new methods and new weapons which will presently be tried against us. It would, of course, be natural for the enemy to spread such rumours in order to encourage his own people, but there is probably more in it than that. For example we now have experience of a new type of aerial bomb which the enemy has begun to use in attacks on our shipping, when at close quarters with the coast"[12].

Churchill's taunts in Parliament and the press reflected the change in fortunes that year, though he took every opportunity to remind the British that the war was far from won. In Parliament on 9 November 1943, an MP asked Churchill "Is not Hitler's only ally the hangman, and will my right hon. Friend reproduce as a Government paper his last speech proving it?" Churchill answered that "Hitler still has some other allies besides the one mentioned by my hon. and gallant Friend, on which no doubt he relies a great deal"[13]. As Germany's fortunes waned, even fanatical Nazis like Goebbels realised that the game was almost up, and that they should attempt to save what they could from the war. Hitler's estimations of the relative advantages of approaching Stalin and Churchill seem to have been influential in his rejection of Goebbels's ideas. Goebbels noted in his diary in September 1943:

> "Meeting the Führer at Rastenburg in East Prussia. I asked the Führer whether anything might be done with Stalin sooner or later. He said not for the moment. That is right, of course, considering the critical situation in the East. And anyway, the Führer believes it would be easier to make a deal with the English than with the Soviets. At a given moment, the Führer believes, the English will come to their senses. But I can't see that for the present".

The reason for Hitler's optimism about the English seems to have been a fundamental misunderstanding of Churchill's motivations. He seems to have thought that Churchill and the British wanted extra territory in Europe, which they never sought:

> "It is true of course, that Churchill is absolutely anti-Bolshevik. Churchill is naturally pursuing imperialistic British aims in this war. The seizure of Sicily gives him a great advantage. Sicily will never be restored to the Italians, for Sicily … will absolutely guarantee English domination in the Mediterranean and render it secure for all time. Undoubtedly the English will also snatch Sardinia and Corsica. If they can make their exit from this war with all this as booty, they will of course have made somewhat of a gain. The Führer believes they will then possibly be amenable to some sort of arrangement"[14].

Goebbels himself favoured approaching Stalin, regarding him as a "practical politician", while Churchill was a "romantic adventurer with whom one cannot talk seriously".

A few days after that discussion, Goebbels asked Hitler specifically whether he would be willing to negotiate with Churchill to end the war, or whether he refused to talk to his Nemesis on principle. If we can trust Goebbels's diary, Hitler gave an unclear and ambiguous answer that at any rate ruled out negotiations with Britain in the near future. "The Führer replied that in politics principles simply do not exist when it comes to questions of personality. He does not believe that negotiations with Churchill would lead to any result as he is too deeply wedded to his hostile views and, besides, is guided by hatred and not by reason. The Führer would prefer negotiations with Stalin, but he does not believe that they would be successful inasmuch as Stalin cannot cede what Hitler demands in the East"[15].

The War in the Mediterranean

In early 1943, the British and Commonwealth forces advancing from Libya and the Americans moving east from Algeria cornered the remnants of Rommel's army in Tunisia. In one of his increasingly numerous mistakes, Hitler began pouring reinforcements into North Africa. A small fraction of those reinforcements could have enabled Rommel to capture Egypt had they been available eighteen months earlier. Though they delayed the British and American assault on Italy, they would almost certainly have been more useful to Germany anywhere else in her shrinking empire.

Churchill was delighted by Hitler's miscalculation in reinforcing Rommel just in time for him to be defeated. On 6 April 1943, he telegraphed to Stalin, "Hitler, with his usual obstinacy, is sending the Hermann Göring and the 9th German Divisions into Tunisia … Our forces have a good superiority both in numbers and equipment. We are taking a very heavy toll of all the ships that go across with fuel, ammunition, vehicles &c [sic]… we are making every preparation to prevent a Dunkirk escape"[16]. Churchill argued to Stalin that the campaign in North Africa led to a delay in Hitler's summer offensive on the Eastern Front, "for which it seems great preparations were in existence six weeks ago"[17].

Even Stalin seems to have acknowledged the importance of the North African campaign, writing to Churchill that "with simultaneous pressure on Hitler from our front and from your side we could achieve great results. Such a situation would cause serious difficulties for Hitler and Mussolini. In this way the extended operations in Sicily and the Eastern Mediterranean could be expedited"[18]. Throughout the battle for Tunisia, which occupied the first four months of 1943, Churchill continued to read the German Army's innermost thoughts in the Enigma decrypts. These had a crucial impact on the conduct of the war in North Africa on several occasions, for example at the Battle of Medenine, in March. Because the British knew the exact strength, timing and location of the German attack, they were able completely to rout it, destroying 52 out of 140 German tanks without loss. This made the Germans suspicious of the Allies' secret, but they never tumbled to it[19]. Both Churchill and Hitler clearly followed the battle for Tunisia extremely closely, but Churchill never doubted the outcome. In April, Churchill wrote to his son Randolph that "the rascals [the Germans] … probably have a big disaster facing them in Africa, and I think they are now convinced they cannot win. What a change this is from the days when Hitler danced his jig of joy at Compiegne [accepting France's surrender in 1940]"[20].

The delayed but decisive Allied victory in Tunisia in May 1943, followed a few months after the equally decisive defeat of the Germans at Stalingrad which yielded almost 150,000 German and Italian prisoners. It allowed Churchill to gloat. In June, he told the House of Commons. "We cannot doubt that both Stalingrad and Tunisia are the greatest military disasters that have ever befallen Germany in all the wars she has made, and they are many. There is no doubt from the statements of captured Generals that Hitler expected his Tunisian army to hold out at least until August and that this was the view and intention of the German High Command"[21].

After the Allied successes of 1942 and early 1943 in North Africa, Churchill had wanted to invade Italy, in part to help the Russians. "Is it really to be supposed that the Russians will be content with our lying down … during the whole of 1943, while Hitler had a third crack at them?" he asked (rhetorically, one assumes) the Chiefs of Staff after they had proposed limiting the invasion to Sicily and Sardinia[22]. The Allies planned to invade Sicily as soon as it could be organised, following the clearance of the North African shore. To disguise their intention, Churchill approved one of the most remarkable deceptions of the war. The "Man Who Never Was" (also known as Operation Mincemeat) saw a dead body dressed up and given the identity of Major William Martin and placed in the sea close to Huelva in Spain. Faked documents were placed about the cadaver showing that the Allies intended to invade Sardinia and Greece, and any moves on Sicily were only a diversion, whereas the reverse was the case. The plan succeeded brilliantly, and Hitler told Dönitz on May 14 that:

"he believes that the discovered Anglo-Saxon order confirms the assumption that the planned attack will be directed mainly against Sardinia and the Peloponnese". Churchill knew almost immediately from Enigma decrypts that the Germans, from Hitler down, were swallowing this disinformation, despite understandable initial scepticism.

The British and Americans discussed the invasion of Italy after Sicily in Algeria on 31 May 1943. Churchill argued that it would be necessary to invade Italy to force the Germans to withdraw to the Alps, knock Italy out of the war and have a favourable effect on Turkey. In the event, only the second of those reasons turned out to be valid. Unfortunately, the Germans did not withdraw to the Alps, and the effect on Turkey, if any, was small. The invasion did, however, depose Mussolini and knock the Italians out of the war in fairly short order. It was the occasion for an uprising by the Fascist high command against Mussolini, who was dismissed by the King in July, and then imprisoned by the new Italian government. Churchill spoke to Parliament soon after. After welcoming the news, Churchill drew some lessons for the possible fate of the Nazi regime. He was optimistic, but clearly did not think that Hitler was about to go the same way as the Italian dictator:

> "The whole outlook of the Nazi Party and regime, their whole ideological outlook, as it is called, will be disturbed and darkened by the events which have happened and are going to happen in Italy, and the overthrow and casting down in shame and ruin of the first of the dictators and aggressor war lords strikes a knell of impending doom in the ears of those that remain.

> Nevertheless, let us not allow this favourable inclination of our fortunes to blind us to the immensity of the task before us, nor of the exertions still to be made and privations and tribulations still to be endured and overcome. The German national strength is still massive. The German armies, though seriously mauled by the three Russian campaigns, are still intact and quite unbroken. Hitler has under his orders over 300 German divisions, excluding the satellites"[23].

Arranging for Italy to surrender and switch sides to fighting the Germans occupied Churchill while he was in Quebec for another conference with Roosevelt. He had to decide whether to treat the new government in Rome as hostile or not. He argued to Eden that Marshal Badoglio, the new Prime Minister should be granted more generous terms if Italy switched sides. "Badoglio admits he is going to double-cross someone but his interests and the mood of the Italian people make it likely that Hitler will be the one to be tricked"[24].

Simultaneously, Hitler had to make the same decision. Badoglio had professed his loyalty to Germany, but Hitler saw through him fairly quickly. What seems to have helped him decide to treat the new regime as an enemy was an intercepted conversation between Churchill and Roosevelt. Churchill told his American counterpart about an "imminent armistice" with Italy, but it appeared that this armistice would not be immediate, because the terms had not yet been worked out, and it was necessary to prevent British prisoners being shipped to Germany[25]. To the Germans, this intercepted conversation was crucial. It was the trigger for several days of furious activity as the Germans planned to seize control of the Italian government, and set up a puppet regime, using Mussolini if possible, but without him if necessary. In one of the most daring operations of the war, an elite SS squad snatched Mussolini from captivity, enabling Hitler to set him up as a puppet in northern Italy. Churchill noted that Hitler had attempted to console his fellow dictator during his period of captivity:

> "The measures which the Badoglio Government took were carefully conceived and were the best they could do to hold Mussolini, but they did not provide against so heavy a parachute descent as the Germans made at the particular point where he was confined. It may be noticed that Hitler sent him some books of Nietzsche to console or diversify his confinement. The Italians could hardly have refused this civility and the Germans no doubt were thus pretty well acquainted with where he was and the conditions under which he was confined"[26].

Mussolini met Hitler after his rescue. According to Goebbels, Mussolini said that:

> "Churchill evidently wanted to await the liquidation of the Italian question, the English and American advance to the Brenner, the extradition of the Duce and his public exhibition in New York. This was prevented only by our stroke of genius [i.e. Mussolini's rescue]. The Duce told the Führer very happily that he had always believed in his liberation by the Germans and had firmly counted on it"[27].

After the conquest of Sicily had been completed on 17 August, the Allies moved troops across into Italy itself. Before that could happen, on 1 September, Badoglio indicated his intention to surrender. Hitler, however, learned of Italy's probable actions, despite her protestations of loyalty, and just managed to move enough troops into Italy to ensure that they could take control of most of the Italian state. Churchill realised that Hitler would see Italy's surrender as an act of treachery. As he later remarked to Parliament, "Herr Hitler has left us in no doubt that he considers the conduct of Italy treacherous and base in the extreme — and he is a good judge in such matters"[28].

Thousands of miles away, Churchill could afford to be more relaxed. "Here at the gateway of Canada", he broadcast to his Canadian hosts on 31 August, "in mighty lands which have never known the totalitarian tyrannies of Hitler and Mussolini, the spirit of freedom has found a safe and abiding home"[29]. Churchill found out that one, albeit the weakest, of his three enemies would throw in the towel on arriving in Washington from Quebec. A week later, Italy surrendered formally and renounced its German alliance. Hitler and Churchill were both immersed in the detail of the Italian campaign, as Lord Moran noted in his diary at the end of 1943:

> "Hitler, I said to the PM, seems not only to direct the policy of war, he even plans the details. 'Yes', the PM answered with a smile, 'that's just what I do'"[30].

Hitler in fact felt that Churchill should have struck north earlier, perhaps attacking somewhere around Rome[31]. There were very few German troops in Italy, and the Italian army, though nominally allied to Germany, was extremely unreliable. When they heard news of the Italian surrender, however, the Germans, as was their habit, reacted swiftly and aggressively. They occupied Rome and Northern Italy with remarkable efficiency, in the process sparking a civil war which lasted until the German surrender almost two years later.

Besides defeating the German army in Italy, ensuring the loyalty of the new government there, and helping Italian partisans as much as possible, Churchill had to consider a number of other factors in the campaign. For example, as he told Parliament in September 1943:

> "There were nearly 70,000 British prisoners of war and upwards of 25,000 Greek and Jugoslav prisoners in Italian hands. From the very first moment of Mussolini's fall we made it brutally clear to the Italian Government and King that we regarded the liberation of these prisoners and their restoration to our care as the prime, indispensable condition of any relationship between us and any Italian Government, and this, of course, is fully provided for in the terms of surrender. However, many of these prisoners in the North of Italy, and others in the Central and Southern part may have fallen into the power of the Germans... Henceforward we shall see the Germans holding down or trying to hold down the whole of Hitler's Europe by systematic terror. Whenever

Hitler's legions can momentarily avert their eyes from the hostile battle fronts which are closing in upon them, they can take their choice either of looking upon ruined cities of the German homeland, or of looking upon what is not a less awful spectacle, the infuriated populations which are waiting to devour them. The first point then is our prisoners, many of whom we hope will be rescued; and the second is this great development in the Balkans, which I cannot pretend to measure exactly and which in any case is not suitable for public discussion"[32].

Hitler seemed to derive a bizarre form of consolation from the invasion of his Italian ally. In his annual speech to the Party faithful in Munich in November 1943, he told his listeners:

"Every new landing will force them [i.e. the British and Imperial forces and Americans] to provide more and more space in their ships. This will dissipate the forces of our enemies and open up new venues for the deployment of our arms. Wherever such a landing takes place, we will be prepared. Then, they will experience, as Churchill put it, that 'it is one thing to land against Italy on Sicily and another to land against the Germans on the Channel coast, in France, Denmark, or Norway'. It will then become apparent whether our restraint in some areas was due to weakness or cool reason"[33].

In private, with Goebbels, Hitler was more realistic. After a conference with Hitler following the Italian invasion, Goebbels noted that "The Führer … believes that they will shortly try an invasion in the West…. But the Führer is on the lookout. He doesn't, under any circumstances, want to be surprised by Churchill and Roosevelt"[34].

Bombing of Germany

During 1943, the Germans faced an exponential growth in the air assault on their cities. This was the year when they first documented the terrible phenomenon of the firestorm (*Feuersturm*)*. The British and Americans attacked crowded

---

* Briefly, a firestorm occurs when fires burn so intensely that they suck oxygen in from the surrounding areas, causing hurricane-force winds and making normal fire-fighting impossible.

industrial towns throughout the year, and the destruction culminated in the attack on Hamburg in July. Hitler attempted to prepare the German people against this new threat, while designing new "wonder weapons" in an attempt to "defeat terror through terror". His Secretary, Bormann, was worrying about a terror weapon that the Allies could have used on German cities. Worrying about the dropping of "gas bombs, whether by mistake or not" by the British and Americans, Bormann ordered the "speedy issue of gas masks, etc., to the population of Obersalzberg"[35], where Hitler's country retreat was located. In October 1944, he was writing to his wife that "if the British want, they are, of course, in a position to smash up every house in Obersalzberg". In fact, Obersalzberg, which is about as far from Britain as it is possible to get in Germany, was not destroyed by the Allied Air Forces until February 1945.

In January 1943, Hitler was still trying to present the Second World War as having been forced on the Germans. He told his people:

> "Our soldiers fought heroically after England and France declared war on us but this hatred was still not there in the German race. The ruins of our old cathedrals, numerous dead and wounded women and children, the well-planned attacks on our military hospitals, and so on, only they brought about this change of heart in the German *Volk*. Mr. Roosevelt and Mr. Churchill taught Germany how to hate. Thus, the German *Volk* today works with grim wrath in the countryside and in the cities in the single determination that, this time, the war will end in such a manner that Germany's enemies will no longer feel like attacking us again for the next hundred years".

To stiffen morale, Hitler still attempted to pour scorn on his British adversary, though he must have realised by now that his speeches were sounding increasingly hollow. In November 1942, he addressed his Nazi Party faithful:

> "... today, when I compare our position with his - our bastions, our fronts advanced everywhere far beyond the borders - then I must say they are completely stupid if they imagine that they can ever crush Germany. And especially if they imagine that they could possibly impress me in any way or could make me afraid. I know perfectly well that the battle is a very hard one, for that is probably just the difference between me and, let us say, a man like Churchill. Churchill said that we - the Reichsmarschal [Göring] and I - had made whining speeches recently. I don't know if I hit someone right and left and then he says that is absolute defeatism, then one can have a good laugh".

He also mocked Churchill's organisational activity, with heavy irony:

> "If one compares the organization of such geniuses as – uh - Churchill
> and Duff Cooper and Chamberlain and all those people, or even
> Roosevelt, this organizer of . . . If one compares these people, then, from
> the point of view of organization, we, of course, were nothing but
> blunderers. That is true. But so far we have achieved one success after
> another".

Another tactic which Hitler tried to use to stiffen German morale was to stress to
his audience how awful the peace which the British and Americans were
planning to impose on Europe would be for them. From this point of view, the
Allied declaration that they would only accept unconditional surrender[†] was a
gift to him, even if it was not quite the godsend that Goebbels believed it to be.
Hitler's speech on 21 March 1943 (the Nazi Heroes Memorial Day) alleged that
Churchill was taking a leading role in crippling Germany:

> "Just as in the English parliamentary democracy the warmonger
> Churchill pointed the way for later developments with his claim in 1936,
> when he was not yet the responsible leader of Great Britain, that
> Germany had to be destroyed again, so the elements behind the present
> demands for peace in the same democracies today are already planning
> the state to which they seek to reduce Europe after the war".

He did not, however, take the one measure which could possibly have raised
morale significantly amongst the German people, even that late in the war.
Goebbels repeatedly urged him to appear in public to inspect air-raid damage.
Hitler did not, however, appear in person at the scene of any of the raids. A
British War Cabinet paper of 1943 records the effect of this failure on morale in
Germany:

> "In the Mosquito attack on the 12th August the Warsaw Bridge
> underground station was severely damaged by direct hits and the army
> clothing office for southeast Berlin, situated in Mariennen Strasse,
> Eichwalde, was burnt out with considerable loss of stores. An informant
> who left Berlin prior to the recent attack gave the following account of
> conditions when he left:

[†] The term was in fact originated in the American Civil War. General Ulysses S Grant's
demand for the "unconditional and immediate surrender" of Fort Donelson is the first
recorded use.

'The stories of the Hamburg attacks spread throughout Germany by the evacuees have played a greater part in undermining morale than any event that has yet taken place. In Berlin morale changed from a limited confidence to almost complete panic. Everyone who can takes steps to leave the city each night ... The general uneasiness has been increased by the fact that Hitler has neither appeared nor spoken'[36].

As Hitler never inspected the damage caused by an air-raid, and because there was no reliable way of measuring public opinion in Nazi Germany, we will never know if Hitler was right, or if the approach advocated by Goebbels and others could have borne fruit in better morale and increased war production. Churchill's visits to air raid damage certainly helped British morale in 1940 and long after, but Churchill had never claimed to be invincible, and had never boasted, as the Nazis had, that no bomb would ever fall on the capital city of his country.

Russia

Throughout 1943, the intense fighting between the Germans and the Russians dominated Hitler's waking hours, while it was rarely at the forefront of Churchill's mind. The British and American war efforts were focused on Africa and the Mediterranean, the bombing offensive against German cities and the war at sea. The year began badly for the Germans in the East. Stalin's 15 January telegram to Churchill, that "we are finishing the liquidation of the group of the German troops surrounded near Stalingrad" was highly welcome, but still left the Germans hundreds of miles inside Russia[37]. It was also rather premature: it was not until 2 February that Churchill was able to telegraph to Stalin his congratulations on Russia's "wonderful achievement"[38].

Churchill's relations with Stalin were never easy. Throughout 1943, the Russian dictator reproached Churchill for failing to invade France. Churchill clearly regarded these criticisms as rank hypocrisy from a regime which had been ready, indeed eager, to see the British Empire completely destroyed until it was, itself, attacked. Sometimes, Churchill's patience with Stalin's verbal assaults seemed to snap. One of his telegrams to the Russians reads as follows:

"Although until 22nd June 1941, we British were left alone to face the worst the worst that Nazi Germany could do to us, I instantly began to aid Soviet Russia to the best of our limited means from the moment that she was herself attacked by Hitler. Therefore the reproaches which you now cast upon your Western Allies leave me unmoved"[39].

Most importantly, and decisively for the Allies, Churchill refused to let Stalin bully him into a premature invasion of France. In October 1943, he told the Chiefs of Staff Committee that: "… by landing in Northwest Europe we might be giving the enemy the opportunity to … inflict on us a military disaster greater than that of Dunkirk. Such a disaster would result in the resuscitation of Hitler and the Nazi regime"[40]. Throughout 1942 and 1943, Churchill had to deal with similar arguments from the other side of the Atlantic. One example of Churchill's memos on the subject may suffice, as it deals with Hitler. A week after his statement to the Chiefs of Staff Committee, he made a similar point in a cable to Roosevelt: "Unless there is a German collapse, Hitler, lying at the centre of the best communications in the world, can concentrate at least 40 to 50 divisions against [an invasion of France or Allied forces in Italy] … I feel that if we make serious mistakes in the campaign of 1944, we might give Hitler the chance of a standing come-back"[41]. The implied comparison of the Nazi dictator with a spider at the centre of a web is unmistakable. It is an image which Churchill used in his history of the Second World War years later.

The major event on the Russian front in 1943 was undoubtedly the Battle of Kursk, the largest tank battle in history, in July. The German attack began on 5 July, but by 19 July, the War Cabinet was already aware that the Russians had retaken all the ground that Hitler's forces had won in the first week of the offensive[42]. "The entire British Empire sends [Stalin] our salutes on this brilliant summer campaign, and on the victories of Orel, Kharkov and Taganrog, by which so much Russian soil has been relieved and so many hundreds of thousands of its invaders wiped out", he said in his broadcast to the Canadian people in August 1943[43].

Churchill's detestation of the Communist government in Russia received powerful reinforcement in 1943. Details emerged of the Katyn massacre of Poles by the Red Army. The Germans blamed the Russians, and the Russians blamed the Germans, but the evidence seemed for once to lie clearly on Hitler's side. Churchill thought that the Russians were probably responsible: "alas, the Bolsheviks can be very cruel", he remarked to members of the Polish government-in-exile in London. Goebbels made all the propaganda capital he could out of the massacre. He was apparently untroubled by the hypocrisy which a senior Nazi had to show in complaining about others' atrocities. The Russians broke off relations with the London Polish government over its reaction to the incident. However, Churchill urged them to reconsider "after whatever interval is thought convenient", since "no-one will hate this more than

Hitler and what he hates most is wise for us to do"[44].

Churchill never played down the Red Army's achievements. In March 1944, he was to declare that the Red Army's advance "constitutes the greatest cause of Hitler's undoing"[45]. Despite these friendly statements, Polish affairs kept intruding in Anglo-Soviet relations during the last three years of the war. Britain had gone to war for Poland's integrity in 1939, but it became increasingly evident during 1943 that the Red Army would have the dominant voice in Poland's future. Stalin had no intention at all of relinquishing the half of Poland that the Red Army had occupied in 1939, and he wanted to set up a Communist government in the remainder of that country after the war. Churchill advised against this course of action in vain.

Casablanca and Teheran

In January 1943, Churchill had nine days of discussions with the Americans, led by Roosevelt at Casablanca in Morocco. The meeting at Casablanca had established the priority of "Hitler's extinction" over the defeat of the Japanese. Roosevelt demanded that Germany should surrender unconditionally. Germany would not be allowed to make conditions before being granted an armistice, as had happened at the end of the First World War. Instead, it would have to capitulate in such a way that future resistance was impossible. Even Churchill seems to have been open to some conditions on any peace with Germany as late as November 1941[46]. However, once the Americans and Russians entered the war, he had to consider their viewpoints as well. In addition, Churchill could now see, however distantly, the possibility of a final, decisive victory over Hitler. He did not, therefore, have the same degree of motivation to plan for a compromise peace as he had when Britain was fighting alone, and a total victory over Nazi Germany looked extremely unlikely.

It was clear that the Nazi regime would be dismantled by the Allies as soon as Germany surrendered. This demand for full capitulation has been controversial ever since. Many have argued that it stiffened the Germans' will to resist. It certainly made Hitler calculate that he had no alternative but to hold on until the end, though he was temperamentally predisposed to fight until the last man, so he may have done so in any case. According to his *Luftwaffe* adjutant, von Below, Hitler "mentioned the agreement repeatedly and stressed that any idea of 'coming round' would now be completely senseless"[47].

Some have argued that the Allies' demand for unconditional surrender discouraged the German resistance from killing Hitler and lifted German morale. Churchill always disagreed with this view. He did not feel that negotiations with Hitler would have been productive. "Negotiation with Hitler was impossible", he wrote to Harry Hopkins, "he was a maniac with supreme power to play his hand out to the end, which he did; and so did we"[48]. That playing the Allies' hand out to the very end may have cost thousands of lives does not seem to have occurred to Churchill, or if it did, it was clearly a price he felt worth paying for the unambiguous defeat of the Nazis and the destruction of the Hitler regime. Given that negotiations with Hitler were likely to be futile, by default, any compromise peace had to be arranged with someone else in charge. Irrespective of the difficulties of achieving Hitler's overthrow (for he would never have given up power voluntarily), such an outcome could have led to endless arguments in a post-war Germany about whether whoever overthrew Hitler had been committing treason or not. German politics after 1945 certainly avoided the claims which had beset the Weimar Republic after 1918, that the German armies in the field were sabotaged by treacherous and cowardly civilian politicians who had arranged an armistice.

The conference at Teheran in November 1943 saw an important discussion between Roosevelt, Stalin and Churchill on the best way to defeat Germany. There were lighter moments too, with Stalin and Roosevelt teasing Churchill about the fate of German officers and technicians. Stalin proposed shooting 50,000 of them after the war, as they were the people upon whom "the whole force of Hitler's mighty armies depended" to which Churchill reacted with horror. Roosevelt then offered a compromise: only 49,000 should be executed! Churchill walked out at this point, though Stalin and Molotov later assured him that they had only been joking[49]. Even more bizarrely, at a dinner hosted by Churchill the next evening, the Conservative Prime Minister and former scourge of the Bolsheviks and General Strikers proposed a toast to the "Proletarian Masses", while Stalin drank to the Conservative Party; more proof, if any were needed, that Hitler's aggression (when combined with large amounts of vodka) had made strange bedfellows[50].

Chapter 8

Japan

The war in the Pacific took much less of Churchill's and Hitler's attention in 1943 than it had immediately after Pearl Harbor. As argued previously, Churchill always saw Japan as a much lesser danger than Nazi Germany. The Casablanca conference had, to Churchill's satisfaction, affirmed the priority of "Hitler's extinction" over Japan's defeat[51]. He told the House of Commons that: "We have made no secret of the fact that British and American strategists and leaders are unanimous in adhering to their decision of a year ago, namely, that the defeat of Hitler and the breaking of the German power must have priority over the decisive phase of the war against Japan"[52]. Thinking about what would happen after that happy event, he told Roosevelt at Casablanca on 18 January, "that he wished it made clear that if and when Hitler breaks down, all of the British resources and effort will be turned towards the defeat of Japan"[53]. He repeated this point in the House of Commons the following month, telling MPs that, after the German defeat, "Great Britain will continue the war by the side of the United States with the utmost vigour until unconditional surrender has been enforced upon Japan"[54].

By July, Churchill felt able to plan the war against Japan "on the basis that Hitler and Mussolini are disposed of during 1944"[55]. In fact, this turned out to be over-optimistic, since both dictators lived until May 1945. Though the European war dominated his thoughts in 1943, Churchill nevertheless gave some thought to the war against Japan. He even thought about involving the Russians after their own army was free from its epic struggle against the Nazis. He told Eden that it might be possible to have Russian sailors manning a portion of the captured Italian fleet against the Japanese after the German defeat: "… on the defeat of Hitler … [we could establish] under the Soviet flag and [manned with] Russian sailors … a substantial naval force at some Pacific base … and the participation of this force of surface ships in the final phase of the war might come into view"[56]. The dropping of the atom bombs on Japan meant that this, and other plans, were never necessary.

---

[1] *Hansard*, 11 February 1943
[2] Cabinet papers, CAB/66/34/26 February 22 1943,
[3] Cabinet papers, CAB 65/40/17
[4] Cabinet papers, CAB 66/39/39
[5] War Cabinet minutes, Confidential Annex, 5 October 1943
[6] Churchill broadcast, 21 March 1943

[7] Lady Audley to Martin Gilbert, quoted in *Road to Victory, Winston S Churchill 1941-45*, Martin S Gilbert, p.606

[8] John Harvey diary, quoted in *Road to Victory, Winston S Churchill 1941-45*, Martin S Gilbert, p.518. According to Gilbert, the War Cabinet minutes of that day do not record this comment.

[9] *Winston Churchill, Struggle for Survival*, Lord Moran, p.141

[10] *Churchill at War, 1940-45*, Lord Moran, p.103

[11] Churchill broadcast, 9 November 1943, quoted in *Road to Victory, Winston S Churchill 1941-45*, Martin S Gilbert, p.437

[12] *Hansard*, 21 September 1943

[13] *Hansard*, 9 November 1943

[14] *The Goebbels diaries, 1942-43*, p.435

[15] *The Goebbels diaries, 1942-43*, p.477

[16] Prime Minster's Telegram, Churchill Papers, 20/109, quoted in *Road to Victory, Winston S Churchill 1941-45*, Martin S Gilbert, p.377

[17] Prime Minister's Personal Telegram, Churchill Papers 20/114, quoted in *Road to Victory, Winston S Churchill 1941-45*, Martin S Gilbert, p.438

[18] Churchill papers 20/106, quoted in *Road to Victory, Winston S Churchill 1941-45*, Martin S Gilbert, p.340

[19] *Road to Victory, Winston S Churchill 1941-45*, Martin S Gilbert, p.361

[20] Letter of 16 April 1943, Churchill papers 1/375, quoted in *Road to Victory, Winston S Churchill 1941-45*, Martin S Gilbert, p.386

[21] *Hansard*, 8 June 1943

[22] Prime Minster's Minute, Churchill Papers, 20/67, quoted in *Road to Victory, Winston S Churchill 1941-45*, Martin S Gilbert, p.253

[23] *Hansard*, 27 July 1943

[24] Cabinet papers, 120/94, quoted in *Road to Victory, Winston S Churchill 1941-45*, Martin S Gilbert, p.464

[25] *Hitler's War*, David Irving, p.550

[26] *Hansard*, 21 September 1943

[27] *The Goebbels diaries, 1942-43*, 23 September 1943

[28] *Hansard*, 21 September 1943

[29] Churchill broadcast, 9/195, quoted in *Road to Victory, Winston S Churchill 1941-45*, Martin S Gilbert, p.485

[30] *Winston Churchill, Struggle for Survival*, Lord Moran, p.158

[31] *Hitler's War*, David Irving, p.546

[32] *Hansard*, 21 September 1943

[33] Hitler speech, November 1943

[34] *The Goebbels diaries, 1942-43*, p.425

[35] *The Bormann Letters*, edited by HR Trevor-Roper, p.28-9

[36] War Cabinet Situation Summary, 2 September 1943

[37] Churchill Papers 20/105, quoted in *Road to Victory, Winston S Churchill 1941-45*, Martin S Gilbert, p.294

[38] Cabinet papers 120/714, quoted in *Road to Victory, Winston S Churchill 1941-45*, Martin S Gilbert, p.328

[39] Prime Minister's Personal Telegram, Churchill Papers 20/114, quoted in *Road to Victory, Winston S Churchill 1941-45*, Martin S Gilbert, p.437

[40] Cabinet papers 79/66, quoted in *Road to Victory, Winston S Churchill 1941-45*, Martin S Gilbert, p.534

[41] Prime Minister's Personal Telegram, Cabinet Papers 120/113, quoted in *Road to Victory, Winston S Churchill 1941-45*, Martin S Gilbert, p.538

---

[42] War Cabinet minutes, 19 July 1943

[43] Churchill broadcast, 9/195, quoted in *Road to Victory, Winston S Churchill 1941-45*, Martin S Gilbert, p.486

[44] Churchill papers 20/111, quoted in *Road to Victory, Winston S Churchill 1941-45*, Martin S Gilbert, p.390

[45] Broadcast of 26 March 1944, quoted in *Road to Victory, Winston S Churchill 1941-45*, Martin S Gilbert, p.720

[46] *In Command of History*, David Reynolds, p.323

[47] *At Hitler's Side*, Nicolaus von Below, p.164

[48] Robert E Sherwood, *The White House Papers of Harry L Hopkins*, Robert E Sherwood, p. 692-3, quoted in *Road to Victory, Winston S Churchill 1941-45*, Martin S Gilbert, p.310

[49] *The Second World War*, Winston Churchill, volume 5, p.330

[50] *Struggle for Survival*, Lord Moran, p.143

[51] Cabinet papers, 99/24, quoted in *Road to Victory, Winston S Churchill 1941-45*, Martin S Gilbert, p.307

[52] Hansard, 11 February 1943

[53] Cabinet Papers 99/24, quoted in *Road to Victory, Winston S Churchill 1941-45*, Martin S Gilbert, p.299

[54] Hansard, 11 February 1943

[55] Prime Minister's Minute, 19 July 1943, quoted in *Road to Victory, Winston S Churchill 1941-45*, Martin S Gilbert, p.446

[56] Prime Minister's Personal Telegram, Churchill Papers 20/122, quoted in *Road to Victory, Winston S Churchill 1941-45*, Martin S Gilbert, p.544

9

Churchill Triumphant
(1944 – August 1945)

Between the start of 1944 and May 1945, the Allies comprehensively defeated Nazi Germany. By early 1944, the strategic initiative had passed entirely to the British and Americans in the West and South, and the Russians in the East. Hitler could only react to their offensives as Germany's cities were systematically smashed from the sky, its war industries ruined and its armies irretrievably defeated. The long-promised Allied invasion of France happened on 6 June 1944. Together with the Russian summer offensive (code-named *Bagration*) and the Allied bombing offensive on Germany, it obviously meant doom for Hitler's empire. Churchill became more and more worried about the Russian menace throughout the latter stages of the war. "Winston never talks of Hitler these days; he is always harping on the dangers of Communism", Lord Moran noted in his diary on 21 August 1944. "He dreams of the Red Army spreading like a cancer from one country to another. It has become an obsession, and he seems to think of little else"[1].

Hitler refused to go to bed until the last Allied bomber had left Germany's skies, keeping his inner circle up too, since he frowned on those who left his evening gatherings. Sometimes, according to one of his secretaries, his staff would tell him that all bombers had left German airspace when there were still some there, "otherwise the day would never have come to an end"[2]. However, this show of solidarity seems to have been play-acting for his staff and perhaps posterity. An officer who was close to Hitler in the last year of the war never heard him "utter a word of compassion for …the bomb victims or the refugees. Human suffering was of no consequence to him …and… he had no wish to see it"[3]. As mentioned in previous chapters, Hitler never paid a visit to bombed areas in the way that

Churchill routinely had when London was being Blitzed, doubtless because he did not like being confronted with what even he had to recognise were the disastrous consequences of the war which he had unleashed on Europe. Indeed, when he had to drive through devastated areas, he asked that the curtains on the windows of his Mercedes be pulled shut[4]. He spoke less and less to the German people. Goebbels, his propaganda minister, frequently expressed his despair that Hitler would not appear in public to boost morale more, as Churchill had done throughout the war. To his mounting frustration, his pleas fell on deaf ears.

Churchill, Hitler and the liberation of Western Europe

Until the end of the Second World War, British, Commonwealth and American forces were engaging the Germans and their allies in Italy. This chapter of the war was also an Italian civil war of considerable savagery as partisans fought behind the lines. The Germans fought extremely skilfully, and were not finally defeated in Italy until the very end of the Third Reich. Churchill had described Italy as the "soft underbelly" of the Axis, but it had turned out to be extremely hard.

Churchill, however, turned even Germany's fierce resistance in Italy to his rhetorical purposes, telling the House of Commons in February 1944 that: "On broad grounds of strategy, Hitler's decision to send into the south of Italy as many as ... half a million Germans ... is not unwelcome to the Allies [because] we must fight the Germans somewhere"[5]. He repeated this point in a letter to the American General Douglas MacArthur, then fighting the Japanese in the Pacific theatre. "If Hitler likes to play on a front of 20 Divisions in Italy, we are quite agreeable and we could not have a better preliminary to 'Overlord' than this heavy fighting ... which keeps his troops away from the decisive theatre [in France]"[6]. Churchill also apparently knew from the Ultra decrypts of German communications that Hitler had been attributing his defeats in southern Russia to the collapse of the Italian resistance and the need to move large armies to Italy[7]. In fact, the Russians were far from grateful for this assistance. Stalin argued, probably correctly, that Italy was not of great importance for defeating Hitler, because "the Alps stood between"[8].

Churchill recognised, however, that Germany had to be defeated in France for the war to be won by the Western Allies. It would, though, be an extremely hazardous undertaking. "Unless there is a German collapse", Churchill telegraphed to Roosevelt on 17 October 1943, "the campaign of 1944", which would include the invasion of France, "will be far the most dangerous we have undertaken, and personally I am more anxious about its success than I was about 1941, 1942 or 1943"[9]. A week later, his anxiety had not lessened. "Personally", he told Roosevelt, I feel that if we make serious mistakes in the campaign of 1944, we might give Hitler the chance of a startling comeback"[10]. The story of the complex negotiations between the British and Americans about when they should liberate France from the Germans has been told many times. Briefly, the Americans pressed the British to invade in 1942, before the British considered that the Germans had been weakened sufficiently. Originally, the British thought that an invasion in 1943 might be possible. Responding to his Chiefs of Staff, who argued that a major land invasion of Continental Europe should be postponed until 1943, Churchill wrote: "When we consider the immense length of coastline which Hitler has to defend and the choice we have where to hit him, and that he will have to maintain a major Russian front ... I think there is a good chance of our being able to make five simultaneous Anglo-American landings on the Continent in the summer of 1943"[11]. Even Churchill was to be wildly overoptimistic, and mid-1944 was to arrive before the invasion was launched.

Churchill himself, however, did not like hearing Overlord referred to as an invasion or an assault, as he feared giving Hitler a propaganda weapon. "I hope that all expressions such as 'Invasion of Europe' or 'Assault upon the Fortress of Europe' may be eliminated henceforward", he telegraphed to the Chiefs of Staff Committee on New Year's Day 1944. He suggested that "liberation" and "entering" countries should be the words used instead. "... the word 'invasion' must be reserved for the time when we cross the German frontier. There is no need for us to make a present to Hitler of the idea that he is the defender of a Europe we are seeking to invade"[12].

Churchill also realised the need to provide against the failure of Overlord, and for alternative operations to land on the continent of Europe. The planning for the operation concerned him, on and off, for two years. In May 1942, for example, he put forward the idea of building artificial harbours to be put in place once the invasion had been successful. The idea was tested on the way to the Quebec conference in August 1943 in the Prime Minister's bathtub. General Ismay left a memorable picture of Churchill as "a stocky figure in a gown of many colours, sitting on a stool and surrounded by a number of ... 'Top Brass', while an Admiral flapped his hand in the water at one end of the bath in order to simulate a choppy sea, and a Brigadier stretched a lilo across the middle to show how it broke up the waves"[13].

Somewhat surprisingly, the artificial harbours, codenamed Mulberry, worked, at least until one was wrecked in the Channel by an unusually severe storm. Churchill was so proud of them that he gave them an entire chapter in his history of the Second World War, much more than he devoted to the battle of Stalingrad[14]. He was aware that the success of "Overlord" was far from guaranteed, however, and that Hitler could do more than anyone else to frustrate it. He realised that he had to develop contingency plans to tackle Germany and take more pressure off the Russians. He wrote that: "In the event of 'Overlord' not being successful or Hitler accumulating forces [in France] beyond our power to tackle, it would perhaps be necessary to adopt the flanking movements both in 'Jupiter' [the invasion of Northern Norway] and from Turkey and the Aegean in the winter of 1944/45"[15].

The best, and most unlikely, intelligence coup the Germans scored against the Allies during the Second World War was probably their recruitment of Cicero, the valet of the British Ambassador to Turkey. Working only for money, Cicero would copy the ambassador's paperwork while he took his morning swim. His reports gave Hitler important insights into both Churchill's mind, and his plans for the future direction of the war. In this way, Hitler heard what Churchill, Roosevelt and Stalin had discussed at their meeting at Teheran in November 1943. Hitler had already strongly suspected that an invasion of France would be attempted from Britain. Cicero reported that "Roosevelt had got his way over Churchill for northern France; Churchill wanted to go for northern Greece. Hitler decided from this that Churchill wanted to drive a wedge between the Germans and Russians. The Russians would not agree to this as it would tend to rob them of the influence they wanted in the Balkans"[16]. Citing any small, or even imaginary, difference between the Allies was to be a recurring feature of Hitler's conversation in the last two years of the Second World War.

Churchill tries to kill Hitler

What is surprising about British attempts to kill Hitler at this time, is not that one full scale attempt was approved, but that only one was, and that it was approved so late in the war. This can be explained by a combination of attitudes in British intelligence circles at the time. Higher-ups tended to see assassination as ungentlemanly. It could have made him a martyr to the underhanded tactics of his enemies, thereby perhaps making possible a revival of Nazism after the war. In any case it was not clear, particularly in the later stages of the war, whether Hitler's death would shorten the conflict at all. A replacement might have continued the war, but with greater military competence.

In 1939, Lord Halifax, then Foreign Secretary, had argued that Britain had "not reached that stage ... when we have to use assassination as a substitute for diplomacy"[17]. Once the war broke out, however, Britain slowly shed those inhibitions. Throughout the war, attempts were mounted on some leading Nazis, including Reinhard Heydrich, Himmler's deputy (which succeeded in killing him in Prague, but at the cost of Nazi reprisals which left 5,000 Czechs dead). The British also targeted Rommel with an attempted kidnapping, though they aborted this operation because Rommel was badly injured by a British fighter plane. In June 1941, when British intelligence heard (from a Bulgarian defector) that Hans Baur, Hitler's pilot, might fly the Führer to England without his knowledge, preparations were made to let his plane land at an airfield in Kent, take him to London and execute him. Sadly, however, no plane appeared. The Bulgarian agent turned out to have been wrong. A couple of other attempts were at least considered in 1941, but Hitler's increasing reclusiveness seems to have limited severely the possibilities of killing him[18].

In 1944, Churchill approved the only full-scale British attempt to assassinate Hitler which almost managed to get off the drawing board. Known as "Operation Foxley", it was developed by the Special Operations Executive (SOE), which he had set up in July 1940 with a mission to "set [Nazi-occupied] Europe ablaze" through sabotage. A number of options were considered, but the SOE finally recommended the use a two-man team, including a sniper, to shoot Hitler. A captured German soldier had told the Allies that when Hitler was present at a residence, a Nazi flag was raised there. In such circumstances, the sniper could shoot Hitler as he took his morning stroll in his Alpine retreat of Berchtesgaden. Churchill approved the plan, though, in fact, by the time it was submitted by SOE, in November 1944, Hitler had already paid his last visit there. The British never tried to put the plan into action, in part for fear that replacing Hitler with a more competent military leader might lead to a stiffening of the German war effort. In fact, however, the SOE continued to develop assassination plans, known as "little Foxleys" until Hitler's death[19].

While the British were considering how to kill Hitler, a group of courageous, though incompetent and ultimately doomed, German officers took action by themselves on July 20 1944. They had developed the July Bomb Plot without British knowledge or assistance. Though they managed to injure him slightly, the conspirators failed in their goal of killing Hitler. Reading the British government documents and the personal papers of those involved today, Sir Ian Kershaw's verdict that the British and Americans regarded the German resistance to Hitler as "little more than a hindrance"[20] seems spot on. Churchill himself described them as the "bravest of the best", but this was a long time afterwards, and his lack of support for German opposition groups during the war has been heavily criticised[21]. He referred to the July Bomb Plot infrequently after news of it had reached London. In an address to British airmen, three days after the assassination attempt, he expressed the hope that, as the Germans "are shooting each other ... the fighting might come to an end earlier than we have the right to say"[22]. In an 11,000 word speech to the Commons on the war situation just before it rose for the summer recess in August 1944, he devoted only half of one sentence directly to the Plot: "The highest personalities in the German Reich are murdering one another, or trying to..."[23] The passage of time did not change his opinion of the plot's lack of significance either. In his 1.9 million word history of the war, it barely rates a paragraph. There is some indication, however, that he might have taken a different line with perfect hindsight. He told one of the survivors of the German opposition that he now thought that "during the war he had been misled by his assistants about the considerable strength and size of the German anti-Hitler resistance"[24]. In Parliament in July 1949, he remarked that he was not sure that a "new situation" might have arisen had the plot succeeded (equally, presumably, he was not sure that it would not have)[25].

Two months later, Churchill was to use the failure of the plot to pour scorn on Hitler's military abilities. In this, he was possibly influenced by a Foreign Office note, which made the argument that Hitler's death could have opened the way for peace feelers from the German government[26]. In September 1944, following the liberation of most of France, Belgium and a part of Holland, Churchill made a famous speech in the Commons. After listing the recent Allied victories, and refusing to compare Hitler to Napoleon, he referred to Hitler using the semi-insulting and (to English ears) slightly ridiculous name "Schickelgruber*" (the use of which also cast doubts on Hitler's parentage):

> "I always hate to compare Napoleon with Hitler, as it seems an insult to the great Emperor and warrior to connect him in any way with a squalid caucus boss and butcher. But there is one respect in which I must draw a parallel. Both these men were temperamentally unable to give up the tiniest scrap of any territory to which the high watermark of their hectic fortunes had carried them ... Hitler has successfully scattered the German armies all over Europe, and by obstinating at every point from Stalingrad and Tunis down to the present moment, he has stripped

---

* In fact, the first "e" is superfluous: the name is spelt without it. It is not clear whether Hansard or Churchill made the mistake.

himself of the power to concentrate in main strength for the final struggle.

He has lost, or will lose when the tally is complete, nearly 1,000,000 men in France and the Low Countries...

When Herr Hitler escaped his bomb on 20th July he described his survival as providential; I think that from a purely military point of view we can all agree with him, for certainly it would be most unfortunate if the Allies were to be deprived, in the closing phases of the struggle, of that form of warlike genius by which Corporal Schickelgruber has so notably contributed to our victory"[27].

According to one of his aides, Hitler had "abandoned the vital area of politics so as to devote himself to matters of military commend"[28] and considered himself the "sole judge ... as to whether an artillery unit or engineer battalion should be sent east or west"[29]. In so doing, he had set himself up for such gibes once Germany's position began to fall apart.

Hitler apparently authorised various attempts on Churchill's life. These never came as close to success as the attempts on Hitler's life mounted by his enemies. Nevertheless, Churchill's staff, including his long-time bodyguard, Walter "Tommy" Thompson, had to take them seriously. At Algiers in 1942 and Teheran in 1943, the Germans tried to kill Churchill. According to one Secret Service agent years after the war, "I have it on the authority of General Erwin Lahousen, Deputy Chief of German Intelligence, that Hitler gave orders for an attempt to be made on your life"[30]. None of the assassins apparently came anywhere near their target. It is possible that the actor Leslie Howerd was mistaken for Churchill in Lisbon. German fighters shot down the scheduled BOAC flight, on which he was travelling back to London, over the Bay of Biscay. In fact, this seems unlikely - the Germans would probably have known that Churchill was in England at the time, and that he would be unlikely to travel by scheduled flight, rather than by Royal Air Force plane.

Thunderbolts from the sky

The British and American bombing offensive against Germany reached its terrible climax in 1944 and the start of 1945. The German counter measures caused horrifying losses amongst the Allied crews, of whom 71% were killed or went missing overall; 80% failed to complete their tours of duty unscathed at some times of the war[31]. The offensive failed to cripple German armaments production until mid-1944[32]. Nevertheless, it is undoubtedly true that Germany would have produced far more weapons, and German civilian morale would have been far higher during the last two years of the war, had its large cities not been systematically reduced to rubble from the air. Understandably, the German people were thoroughly aroused against the bomber crews. *Luftwaffe* fighter pilots who attacked them never had any of the problems with morale which the German armed forces faced in other theatres of war. Allied pilots who survived their planes being shot down over Germany were often lynched by an enraged populace.

Hitler's main hope in 1944 was that vengeance weapons, such as the V-1 and V-2 rockets, would destroy London, in the way that German cities were being wrecked. His secretary had him forecasting that, when they were fired, "Panic will break out in England. The effect of these weapons will wear their nerves down so badly that they won't be able to hold out for long. I'll pay the barbarians back for shooting women and children and destroying German culture"[33].

As the military situation turned against him, Hitler's speeches more and more relied on these and other wonder weapons in development, to keep up German morale and disconcert the Allies. There were indeed various new weapons under development in Germany, aside from the rocket bombs. There were also new types of U-boat which could recharge their batteries without surfacing and jet fighters as well, but without exception they failed to live up to expectations. Answering Hitler's speeches which promised these miracle weapons presented something of a problem for Churchill, however, since he could not definitely say that the weapons would not be successful. As early as September 1943, months before the first V-1s began to rain down on London, Churchill was clearly preparing public opinion for unpleasant news, while at the same time attempting to reassure it. He said in the Commons:

> "The speeches of the German leaders, from Hitler downwards, contain mysterious allusions to new methods and new weapons which will presently be tried against us. It would, of course, be natural for the enemy to spread such rumours in order to encourage his own people, but there is probably more in it than that. For example we now have experience of a new type of aerial bomb which the enemy has begun to use in attacks on our shipping, when at close quarters with the coast. This bomb, which may be described as a sort of rocket-assisted glider, is released from a considerable height, and is then apparently guided towards its target by the parent aircraft ... I can only assure the House

that unceasing vigilance and the most intense study of which we are capable are given to these possibilities. We have always hitherto found the answer to any of the problems which have been presented to us..."[34]

Eventually, the rocket bombs were launched. "Hitler has started [using] his secret weapon upon London", Churchill cabled to Stalin on 16 June 1944, "we had a noisy night"[35]. Hitler thought that the V-1s would undermine British morale, and so force Churchill out of office, and Britain to withdraw from the war. It turned out that this hope was completely misplaced. The V-2, which was first launched against London three months later, was an even greater and more expensive failure. Hitler referred again and again to the power of his vengeance weapons, often as a way to deflect awkward questions about the increasingly disastrous military situation, but there were simply nothing like enough of them to make any difference at all by this stage in the war. The 9,181 tons of explosives which fell on Britain in 1944 were a poor reply to the 1,188,577 tons which the Allies dropped on Germany in that year[36]. Even if there had been far more of them, the evidence of Britain's morale during the Blitz earlier in the war and Germany's later in the war surely suggests that the effect would have been much less than Hitler supposed. Even the latter, much heavier, total, did not cause German civilian morale to collapse completely in the way that Hitler hoped that the V-weapons would undermine British morale.

Ramblings in the bunker

Hitler's opinions about Churchill inevitably became even more bitter during his final year, as he saw his life's work destroyed, in large part by a man he despised leading a country he still, to some extent, admired. Throughout the last four years of the war, Hitler inhabited a series of bunkers which were Spartan, joyless and uncomfortable. One civil servant said of Rastenburg, Hitler's East Prussian headquarters for the first part of the Russian war, that it was made up of:

> "Cold and clammy bunkers, in which we freeze to death at night, can't sleep for the constant rattle of the electric ventilation system and its frightful draft, and wake up every morning with a headache"[37].

It was situated in a marshy area, and so plagued by mosquitoes. His Ukrainian headquarters at Vinnitsa, to which he later moved, was even worse, icy cold at night and extreme heat by day. It also had swarms of malarial mosquitoes during the summer months. Hitler suffered splitting headaches there and detested the camp[38]. He managed many fewer breaks in his mountain retreat at

Berchtesgaden, and none at all after July 1944. The Berlin bunker to which he moved in November 1944[†] was just as Spartan and depressing. The almost unrelentingly gloomy war news which the Führer had to hear clearly did not help, nor did the collapse in his health. Positive thoughts about anything would have been difficult at this time, and Hitler's views on Churchill became, if possible, even more embittered. He referred to Churchill as a "henchman of the Jews" on 4 February 1945, and clearly hoped for his death. "A Churchill may disappear and then everything may change"[39], he wrote.

As noted in Chapter 7, Martin Bormann's record of Hitler's lunch and dinner conversations restarts briefly in February 1945, though the seventeen conversations which he arranged to be noted in that month are not included in the book *Hitler's Table Talk*, as they were lost at the end of the war and then rediscovered. Published as *The Testament of Adolf Hitler* in 1961 (and not to be confused with his Political Testament – see below), they are different from the monologues recorded in 1941-4, as they concern only the war. Churchill features fairly frequently. On 4 February, Hitler apparently delivered himself of a long rant comparing his British adversary to the great eighteenth-century Prime Minister, William Pitt the Younger. Pitt had attempted to preserve the balance of power in Europe by fighting Napoleon:

> "Churchill seems to regard himself as a second Pitt, What a hope! In 1793, Pitt was thirty-four years old. Churchill unfortunately is an old man, capable, and only just capable at that, of carrying out the orders of that madman, Roosevelt".

But, Hitler argued, what Britain now had to realise was that it was not the balance of power in Europe, but over the whole world that mattered. Competition between European powers was less important now: Europe had to hold its own against the United States and the Soviet Union. Of course, the argument was couched in much cruder terms than this summary implies, and much of the abuse was directed at Hitler's most persistent foe. The Nazi dictator referred to him as: "a senile clown", "this Jew-ridden, half-American drunkard", "bound hand and foot to the Jewish chariot", who had "condemned his country to a policy of suicide". He was also, with Roosevelt, a lackey of the Jews, and a "punishment chosen [for Britain] by Providence".

[†] He moved to a bunker in the west to direct the Ardennes offensive at the end of 1944, but was there for only about five weeks.

Getting carried away in the course of his rant, Hitler reversed his Anglophilia of previous years. He clearly relished the thought that the British Empire was doomed and that "the future of the British people is to die of hunger and tuberculosis on their cursed island" [40]. Two days later, however, he was willing to be slightly more generous to the British, if only Churchill would die:

> "If Churchill were suddenly to disappear, everything could change in a flash. The British aristocracy might perhaps become conscious of the abyss opening before them— and might well experience a serious shock! These British, for whom, indirectly, we have been fighting and who would enjoy the fruits of our victory…" [41]

On 15 February, Hitler again criticised the "stupid leaders" of the British people, who refused to recognise the German dominance of Europe while Russia remained undefeated[42]. Eleven days later, he announced what he regarded as the final proof of Churchill's stupidity. Churchill should have taken the German mistake, in halting before Dunkirk in 1940, as a hint that Hitler felt no hostility towards the British: "Churchill was quite unable to appreciate the sporting spirit of which I had given proof by refraining from creating an irreparable breach between the British and ourselves. We did, indeed, refrain from annihilating them at Dunkirk"[43].

During the final years of the war, Hitler broadcast less and less to the German people, doubtless because he had less and less good news to impart, and he did not want his citizens to associate him with failure or defeat. Goebbels suggested to Hitler that he broadcast to the nation. "I cite the examples of Churchill during the British crisis and Stalin during the Russian. They then found the right words to inspire their people… Basically the Führer is in agreement with my proposals", but Hitler then changed the subject to military matters, without Goebbels realising what he was doing. Goebbels left with the impression that Hitler was fully determined to make his speech as soon as possible, but nothing happened[44]. Churchill also travelled to see the war for himself, though Goebbels also held this against him: "Churchill is of course once again visiting troops on German soil. He is lazing in the sunshine of his fame … undoubtedly told him of certain jealousies which have arisen between him and Eisenhower"[45].

Goebbels, perhaps echoing Hitler, even managed to blame Churchill for the economic devastation caused by the war which his master had started: "Food riots are reported from all over Europe. Churchill and Roosevelt have in fact succeeded in plunging this part of the world into frightful chaos"[46]. The Nazi propaganda minister may have had slightly more reason to blame Churchill for the horrific damage to German cities, given Churchill's championing of the doctrine of strategic bombing. "For the first time Churchill has actually seen the results of his air war. He was in Jülich and, according to Reuters, surveyed the expanse of ruins … with an air of satisfaction. …. A better symbol of the chaos and ruin into which Anglo-American policy has plunged Europe is hardly conceivable"[47]. Later, Goebbels noted in his diary that "Churchill took malicious pleasure in what he saw during a visit to Aachen. He expressed himself extraordinarily satisfied with the extent of the damage wrought by the air terror. This is completely in character. He is a top class gangster …"[48]

Peace feelers

As the Third Reich crashed into ruin about its founder's head, it was inevitable that the question of whether and how to try to negotiate a peace treaty should be raised. Churchill's doctor noted that, in September 1944, "Hitler was rumoured to be suing for peace", though nothing ultimately came of this approach[49]. The obvious manoeuvre for Germany was to approach either the Western Allies or the Russians, to try to split the formidable coalition which was smashing the Third Reich to pieces. Since Churchill and Roosevelt were almost as firmly in charge of their respective countries' diplomacies as Hitler was of Germany's, there was no aspect of the Second World War in which the leaders' personalities were more important.

Hitler mostly took the realistic view that Churchill was irreconcilably hostile towards Nazism. Roosevelt had called for Germany's unconditional surrender and therefore was unlikely to negotiate a peace treaty, and Churchill and his Cabinet subsequently endorsed Roosevelt's policy. By default, this left Hitler with only one allied leader to approach: Stalin. The Russian dictator had a big advantage over his Western counterparts, Hitler felt, since he could ignore public opinion, whereas Roosevelt and Churchill would have to pay attention to it[50]. As early as the autumn of 1943, Ribbentrop and Goebbels had tried to persuade Hitler to attempt a negotiated peace with Stalin. Ribbentrop had hated the British since the failure of his ambassadorship in London, and Goebbels was always amongst those Nazis who hated capitalist democracy even more than Marxism. According to von Below, his *Luftwaffe* adjutant, Hitler repeated his view that a negotiated peace with Churchill (or Stalin) would be impossible:

> "Ribbentrop and Goebbels … attempted to win Hitler over [to a separate peace in autumn 1943]. What they had in mind was an agreement with Stalin. Hitler said that basically he was so inclined, but it would only be possible from a position of strength … Any agreement with the Western

powers was out of the question, however. Churchill was his enemy from innermost conviction and would not rest until Germany was destroyed, even if he lost the British Empire in doing so. [Hitler] could not go for a compromise with the Soviets, for the Communists were the enemy of the Reich"[51].

Throughout the final years of the war, Hitler believed that the coalition between his enemies was bound to break up. Warlimont records him as saying, in August 1944, as the Western Allies were liberating Paris and the German army was in headlong flight towards the Rhine:

> "The time's not ripe for a political decision ... Moments like that arrive when you've had victory. I've proved that I've done everything to come to terms with England. In 1940 after the French campaign I offered an olive branch and was ready to give things up. I wanted nothing from them. On 1 September 1939 ... I proposed an alliance in which Germany would guarantee the British Empire. It was primarily Churchill and the anti-German crowd around Vansittart who were against the proposal; they wanted war and today they can't go back on it. They are reeling to their ruin"[52].

In fact, it was Hitler who was reeling towards his ruin, though, in mid-1944, Churchill still believed that his final defeat could be some way off. In September 1944, the Chiefs of Staff told him that the war could end in 1944. Churchill replied "it is at least as likely that Hitler will be fighting on the 1st January as that he will collapse before then. If he does collapse before then, the reasons will be political rather than purely military"[53]. At the same time, von Below noted the following conversation:

> "Hitler ... was himself waiting for the moment when the Anglo-American coalition broke up. He could not imagine that the British would accept a permanent American presence in Europe. I replied that I differed. Churchill's politics proved that he stood shoulder to shoulder with the Americans. Anyway, the Americans were so strong in Europe now that they would suit themselves as to how things were done. Hitler did not respond to this".

As usual in the later part of the war, Hitler totally misread his opponents' opinions and fatally underestimated their hatred of him and his government. When he heard that Roosevelt, Churchill and Stalin had met at Yalta to seal the fate of Germany and Europe, "Hitler was ... curiously disinterested, rather as if it had nothing to do with him any more"[54]. At the conference, Stalin had asked whether the Allies should negotiate with a German government after Hitler's overthrow. Churchill's reply, set out in Cabinet papers, was that:

> "If Hitler or Himmler were to come forward and offer unconditional surrender, it was clear that our answer should be that we would not negotiate with any of the war criminals ... It was more probable that Hitler and his associates would have been killed and that another set of people would offer unconditional surrender. In that case the three great Powers must immediately consult and decide whether such people were worth dealing with or not..."[55]

In contrast to some of his colleagues, Hitler's view of Churchill meant that he thought it better to approach Stalin first. Several times in these weeks, he talked to Goebbels about the prospects for peace, and whether to approach the British or the Russians. After one such discussion, Goebbels wrote in his diary that:

> "The Führer is convinced that, if any country on the other side is willing to take the initiative in opening talks with us, it will be the Soviet Union. Stalin is having the greatest difficulties with the Anglo-Americans ... The Führer is right when he says that Stalin is in the best position to do an about turn in war policy, since he need take no account of his public opinion. It is rather different with England. It is quite immaterial whether Churchill wants to pursue a different war policy; even if he did, he couldn't; he is too dependent on internal political forces".

Later that day, however, Goebbels learned from Ambassador Hewel that, though Ribbentrop had been making peace overtures, "Churchill's and Roosevelt's attitude is completely negative"[56]. Three days later, Goebbels spoke to Himmler. "[Himmler] thinks that England will come to her senses, which I rather doubt ... Stalin seems to me more realistic than the trigger-happy Anglo-American"[57].

> "As far as our enemies' situation is concerned, the Führer is convinced that the hostile coalition will break up. He no longer thinks, however, that England will be the instigator of this... Churchill is a gangster who has now got into his head the crazy notion of destroying Germany no matter whether England goes down in the process. So we have no alternative but to look around for other possibilities. Perhaps this is just as well since, if we could come to some arrangement with the East, we should then have an opportunity of giving England the coup de grace and this war would then really have achieved its true purpose"[58].

Goebbels even managed to air a bizarre conspiracy in his diary around this time. Chamberlain had died of cancer in November 1940, six months after resigning the Prime Ministership. However, Goebbels used innuendo to besmirch Churchill's name: "People on the British side even suspect that Churchill commissioned the Secret Service to administer poison to Chamberlain. I do not believe this but ... Churchill was not particularly downcast at Chamberlain's death"[59]. How Goebbels could have known what Churchill's reaction was is unclear. He did not speculate on what Churchill's motive for killing Chamberlain, when he had already obtained the Premiership, might have been.

Later in the month, Hitler and Goebbels were still clutching at straws, hoping that one of the Allies might approach Germany for a separate peace. In fact, neither of the three main Allied powers had the slightest motivation to come to terms with the Germans when they were about to achieve total victory over the regime which they had been fighting for so long. This did not stop Goebbels and Hitler discussing the subject endlessly, however. Barely a month before the end of the war, Goebbels noted Hitler's view in his diary: "As far as the hoped-for collapse of the enemy coalition is concerned, the Führer thinks that this is more likely to come from Stalin than from Churchill and Roosevelt. Stalin is a marked realist and so from our point of view there is more to be done with him than the others. The Führer is inclined to think that the San Francisco conference will never take place. The conflict in the enemy camp will have become so intense by that time that they will not dare parade their differences."[60] To Goebbels, Hitler described Churchill, who had sabotaged his policy of peace with Britain as the "true father of this war"[61]. Goebbels's diary records a further conversation, just before the end of the war:

> "... A reversal of war policy is very difficult if not impossible to achieve both in Britain and the United States since Roosevelt and even more Churchill have to take too much account of their public opinion. With the Kremlin it is totally different ... A separate peace in the East would naturally alter the war situation fundamentally...
>
> ... The programme divulged to me by the Führer is grandiose and persuasive. The only objection is that there is no means of achieving it."

Himmler's view, by contrast, was that Britain and America were more likely to preserve the Nazi regime. On the morning of April 25, Churchill heard that Himmler had offered to surrender on the Western front, but not in the East. Himmler had said that Hitler was so desperately ill that he might be dead already and would be so in two days' time. The British and Americans were not fooled, however, and demanded unconditional surrender on all fronts simultaneously[62]. On the 27 April 1945, three days before his suicide, after the Russians had surrounded Berlin and broken through into the city centre, Hitler was still pinning his hopes on the illusion that the coalition would break up. After Hitler had given him a cyanide capsule, von Below, recorded their conversation:

> "I asked Hitler whether, in view of the circumstances in Berlin, … break-out stood any chance of success. He replied, 'I believe that the situation has now changed. The Western Allies will no longer insist on the unconditional surrender demanded at Casablanca. It appears quite clear from the foreign Press reports of recent weeks that the Yalta conference was a disappointment for the United States and Britain. … I have the impression that the three big men at Yalta did not leave as friends. Now Roosevelt is dead, and Churchill has never loved the Russians. He will be interested in not allowing the Russians to advance too far through Germany'"[63].

In fact, no salvation came. The V-weapons, the divisions between the Allies, and the German armies were all insufficient to save Hitler.

Hitler on trial?

As Germany's defeat approached, the Allies had to decide what to do with Hitler and his senior henchmen. As will be remembered, Churchill had topped the Gestapo's list of people to be arrested, and presumably executed, had Germany conquered Britain in 1940. With the Allies now all-conquering, Churchill, who had opposed bringing Kaiser Wilhelm II to trial and executing him at the end of the First World War, nonetheless thought that no such mercy should be extended to Hitler. In July 1941, he had been relatively lenient, proposing to strangle Mussolini "like Vercingetorix in old Roman fashion", while segregating Hitler and the Nazis "on some island, though he [Churchill] would not so desecrate St Helena [where Napoleon had been exiled after his defeat at Waterloo]"[64]. Churchill's attitude evidently hardened as the war progressed. He would treat the question of Hitler's punishment flippantly on occasion. At the end of the war, he wrote to his wife about the son of the King of Norway's laugh, "Certainly it is the silliest laugh I have ever heard. One of Hitler's punishments ought to be being tied up and made to listen to it for twelve hours a day"[65].

Churchill's opinion that Hitler should be executed was formed before the most dreadful evidence of the worst Nazi crimes was uncovered as Auschwitz, Bergen-Belsen and the other extermination camps were not liberated until 1945. However, news of the magnitude and awfulness of the Holocaust began to reach the British and Americans in 1942. Already in November 1943, therefore, Churchill had written that, once captured, the leading men in the Axis powers should be "shot to death ... without reference to a higher authority" after their identities had been established. Allied awareness of Nazi atrocities increased steadily during the last three years of the war. In July 1944, Churchill wrote to Anthony Eden that the Nazi regime had committed "probably the greatest and most horrible crime ... in the history of the world ... It is quite clear that all concerned ... who may fall into our hands ... should be put to death after their association with the murders has been proved"[66]. "Proof" in this context is ambiguous: it might or might not have included some form of trial. In August 1944, he wrote that a short list of the war criminals to be executed should be published. "It is very important to show the German people that they are not on the same footing as Hitler, Göring, Himmler and other monsters, who will infallibly be destroyed"[67]. There was no mention of a trial or legal process in this minute. In October 1944, Churchill's doctor wrote in his diary on the way to Moscow about a conversation he overheard between his patient and Eden, in which Churchill said: "I'd like sixty or seventy of the people round Hitler shot without any trial, but I am against shooting all the German General Staff"[68]. At that time, Churchill had not seen the extensive evidence which later came to light concerning German army atrocities, especially in the East.

The Lord Chancellor and the Attorney General set out the British government's reasons for opposing a judicial trial of the top Nazis (sometimes the note mentions Hitler, sometimes "Hitler, Himmler, etc.") in some detail in a paper dated 16 April 1945. It argued that a trial would face considerable practical difficulties. Firstly, it would be exceedingly long and elaborate, given that Hitler would be afforded the opportunity to present his case, and that "according to British ideas ... his defence could not be forcibly shut down or limited because it involves a great expenditure of time". Secondly, the trial might be seen as a "put-up job" and public opinion in the Allied countries might soften during the course of a lengthy procedure. Thirdly, it was not clear that one of the proposed charges, that of starting an aggressive war, could be sustained under international law. The paper proposed, instead, a procedure whereby an indictment would be handed to the accused, who might be able to answer it, with the decision being left to the Allied government in whose charge he was[69].

The summary execution of leading Nazis had its supporters in Washington, and doubtless in Moscow too, though there it was only Stalin's view that counted. Churchill had wanted to discuss the whole issue with Roosevelt and Stalin at the

Yalta Conference in 1945, but neither man was willing to express his opinion at that stage. Stalin had staged hundreds of show trials in the 1930s, and knew the value of the appearance of justice. According to Richard Overy, arguments and pressure from the Russians and the Americans changed the British position on summary execution. Only after Hitler's death, on 5 May 1945, did the British agree to a trial of war criminals. Churchill "penned a brief minute for Eden that the British Government was at last willing to accept American and Soviet views 'in principle'..."[70].

Such was the genesis of the Nuremberg trials of Nazi war criminals. Hitler's suicide made the judicial process fought over by the Allies irrelevant as far as he was concerned, though it doomed many of his henchmen. The trials also contributed greatly to the historical record of the Third Reich. Witness testimony and the presentation of documents as evidence were both hugely illuminating about the history of Nazi Germany.

Hitler's death

As the end of the war approached, Churchill would worry occasionally that Hitler might slip through his fingers. At Yalta in February 1945, he asked Stalin what Stalin would do if Hitler moved south "say to Dresden". Stalin answered, "the Red Army would follow him [Hitler], and the intention was to give the Germans no rest"[71]. Churchill occasionally speculated on how Hitler would act when his defeat loomed. On 8 April 1945, with the end of the war in sight, he remarked at dinner that he thought that Hitler should admit personal responsibility to the Allies, but then invite them to spare his people. One of his guests, the Duchess of Marlborough, argued that in that case, the only course of action would be "to take him back and drop him by parachute over Germany", presumably in the hope that the Germans would lynch him[72]. Churchill thought that this would present the Allies with a dilemma about how to assign guilt amongst the Nazis and the German people generally.

On 28 April 1945, news arrived in Britain that Mussolini had met his end, strung up in a town square in Italy alongside his mistress. "Ah, the beast is dead", Churchill told his guests at Chequers when he heard the news[73]. The worse beast outlived his Italian ally by two days. Hitler shot and poisoned himself on 30 April 1945, deserting the German people for whom he had always expressed his boundless love. His excuses for doing so were that he was not able to fight the Russians as he could not hold a pistol because of his shaking hands, possibly caused by Parkinson's disease, and that he was not willing to be captured by them[74].

Hamburg radio broadcast to the German people that Hitler had died a heroic death "fighting to his last breath against Bolshevism". Churchill cabled to his wife, who was in Russia, that "both our great enemies are dead"[75]. He evidently believed the German radio's broadcast that Hitler had died fighting the Russians. He remarked to some friends on hearing the news, "Well I must say, I think that he was perfectly right to die like that". His long-time friend, Lord Beaverbrook, was closer to the mark, however, in saying that Hitler had obviously not died in this way[76]. In fact, Hitler had been discussing the best way to die with his entourage for a week. "'The best way is to shoot yourself in the mouth. Your skull is shattered and you don't notice anything' ... But the women were shocked. 'I want to be a beautiful corpse', said Eva Braun"[77].

Just before his death, Hitler dictated an uncharacteristically brief political testament. It is a strange document, a self-justifying tirade, which is unintentionally revealing about the state of his mind as the end approached. For instance, he claimed that he "had never wished that, after the appalling First World War, there would be a second against ... America", evidently forgetting that he had enjoyed the First World War, and that he had declared war on America in December 1941. He had clearly learned nothing from the twelve years of the Third Reich. The only Briton directly mentioned in Hitler's testament is, unexpectedly, Sir Neville Henderson, the pro-appeasement ambassador to Berlin in 1939. Though Hitler blamed the war on "international statesmen either of Jewish origin or working for Jewish interests", he did not mention Churchill by name. The document also repeated Hitler's view that the First World War was "forced upon the Reich", and as Churchill was the most anti-German member of the British Cabinet in the key week before Britain declared war on Germany, this might be a subtle dig at his most persistent enemy.

Hitler's private will expressed his wish that his body should be burnt. Some soldiers attempted to undertake this unpleasant task using gasoline outside the bunker, but they were not able to burn his body completely. According to Russian documents obtained after the fall of the Soviet Union, Red Army soldiers found his remains. Bizarrely, the Russians repeatedly exhumed and reburied his body in secret until 1970, when they threw his remains into an East German river.

Chapter 9

Hitler and the problems of reconstruction

Churchill never had any doubts about the decisiveness of the victory over Nazi Germany. In 1953, he was working with an assistant on his war memoirs at Chequers. The assistant had written that, after the war, "Nazi Germany was occupied and partitioned". Churchill told him, "the word you want is *crushed*"[78]. Despite Hitler's death, Churchill, in common with almost everybody at that time and since, continued to lay the blame for the disastrous state of Germany and the rest of Europe in 1945, and for years afterwards, squarely on his shoulders. As the new leader of the Opposition, just after the end of the war with Japan, Churchill said in Parliament:

> "The character of Hitler's Nazi party was such as to destroy almost all independent elements in the German people. The struggle was fought to the bitter end. The mass of the people were forced to drain the cup of defeat to the dregs. A headless Germany has fallen into the hands of the conquerors. It may be many years before any structure of German national life will be possible, and there will be plenty of time for the victors to consider how the interests of world peace are affected thereby"[79].

Churchill, though determined to punish the Nazis, had always been determined to protect the German people from what he saw as unreasonable vengeance. He once remarked that he did not believe in creating "pariah nations", and would welcome Germany back to the councils of Europe after the war. It might be a shrunken Germany: in 1941, he had mused briefly about separating Bavaria from Prussia, though "to raise such issues publicly now would only be to rally all Germans round Hitler"[80]. He had also responded to a proposal to kill all German babies after the war with a flippant comment "Need we wait as long as that?"[81] To Stalin in Moscow in October 1944, Churchill proposed separating Bavaria, Wuerttemberg, Baden and Austria from Prussia, and subjecting the industrial area on the River Rhine to international control. Prussia should receive "hard treatment", and the other parts of Germany "soft treatment". That Austria and Bavaria, rather than Prussia, had produced and schooled Hitler, however, does not seem to have troubled either Churchill or Stalin. Later in the same meeting, Churchill argued that the Nazis had rearmed using factories built under the democratic Weimar Republic. "… no-one dared go into production until Hitler appeared … Hitler only pulled the lever. It should not happen again. Industrial armament was the important thing. To begin with, the machine tools must be taken away"[82]. Stalin wholeheartedly agreed.

Churchill wrote to his wife that he was "saddened" by reports of the long refugee columns of German women and children, though he was "clearly convinced that they deserve it"[83]. What exactly German children had done to deserve being expelled from their homes in the February snows, he did not say. He could be magnanimous, however. When the American Treasury Secretary Morgenthau came up with his notorious plan, in 1944, to partition Germany and dismantle her heavy industry, Churchill at first opposed it. When he changed his mind, it was not because of any vengeful feelings towards Germany, but because Britain needed American goodwill and aid, and because he had been convinced by his old friend Lindemann (now Lord Cherwell) that a deindustrialised Germany would benefit British trade. (His agreement to

Morgenthau's proposal allowed Goebbels to use the monstrously hypocritical headline "Roosevelt and Churchill agree to Jewish murder plan"[84]). Four years after the end of the war, he expressed in public his regret for initialling the Plan, which he later said had "dropped to one side". He said that he felt differently when fighting for life in a fierce struggle than when that enemy was defeated, though in fact, as his initial reluctance to approve the Plan shows, he had not been particularly vengeful even during the war[85].

By far the biggest long-term problem faced by Europe liberated from the Nazis was Russian aggression. In fact, as much as half of Europe had simply exchanged one tyranny for another. Churchill was aware, long before he made his famous "Iron Curtain" speech in Missouri in 1946, that the Russians were intending to occupy Eastern Europe. He foresaw that they would administer any countries they controlled using techniques remarkably similar to those that Hitler had used. They had no intention of keeping the promise they had made to himself and Roosevelt at Yalta in February 1945, to allow free elections in Eastern Europe. The example of Hitler clearly informed Churchill's thinking and that of the Americans towards the Stalinist menace. Already, in May 1945, Truman had written to Churchill about Russian and Yugoslav tactics "which are all too reminiscent of those of Hitler and Japan"[86]. Knowing that he had Truman's support, Churchill warned the world in a broadcast the next day, that:

> "On the Continent of Europe, we have yet to make sure that the ... honourable purposes for which we entered the war are not brushed aside or overlooked ... There would be little use in punishing the Hitlerites for their crimes if law and justice did not rule"[87].

Churchill visits Berlin, July 1945

Churchill and the new American President, Truman, met Stalin in July 1945 at Potsdam to attempt to agree on how to rebuild a shattered Europe. Potsdam is just outside Berlin. Churchill's doctor, Lord Moran, accompanied him, and they used the opportunity to visit Hitler's Chancellery, which had been wrecked by allied bombing. A Russian officer conducted the tour, speaking through a British interpreter. According to Lord Moran, Churchill went down one flight of stairs into Hitler's bunker, but, being over 70 years old, gave up the idea of going down the remaining two flights of stairs. According to Churchill, however, he went down "to the bottom" of the bunker "and saw the room in which [Hitler] and his mistress had committed suicide and ... the place where his body had been burned"[88]. The electric lighting system may have been out of order, and the bunker would have been very gloomy by torchlight[89]. According to Moran, "At the top [of the stairs, Churchill] sat down on a gilt chair, mopping his brow. 'Hitler', he said, 'must have come out here to get some air, and heard the guns getting nearer and nearer'".

The *Manchester Guardian* reported that, "as [Churchill] came out of the shelter, a shallow trench near the entrance was pointed out to him, and he was told that it was in this trench that the bodies of Hitler and of Eva Braun ... are said to have been burned"[90]. Martin Gilbert quotes a witness as recalling "how, as Churchill looked over the ruins of the bunker, he remarked: 'This is what would have happened to us if they had won the war. We would have been the bunker'"[91]. Churchill did not, apparently, make much comment on Hitler's study, which he had built for himself, and where, in fact, he never worked[92, ‡]. Churchill clearly saw the megalomania which such rooms implied. "It was from here that Hitler planned to govern the world", Churchill mused. "A good many have tried that, and failed"[93]. Afterwards, Churchill walked around Berlin without any security precautions in "an astonishingly informal tour"[94]. Few Berliners recognised Churchill. One who did apparently muttered, "So that is supposed to be a tyrant, is it?"

The Russians were not the only foe which Churchill had to face now that the Nazis had collapsed, though they may have been the most malignant. While Germany had been completely defeated, Japan fought on for more than three months. Most in Britain thought that defeating Japan might take two more

---

‡ Hitler would receive official visitors whom he wanted to impress in his absurdly large office, while working elsewhere.

years, and cost hundreds of thousands or millions of Allied lives. Fortunately, there now was at hand the means to finish it much more quickly, though at a horrific cost in the lives of Japanese civilians. Justifying the use of the atom bombs on Hiroshima and Nagasaki, Churchill made the obvious, if hypothetical and doubtfully relevant, point that, had Hitler developed nuclear weapons, he would undoubtedly have used them on Britain:

> "Six years of total war have convinced most people that had the Germans or Japanese discovered this new weapon, they would have used it upon us to our complete destruction with the utmost alacrity"[95].

In Britain, Churchill faced a different opponent in the Labour Party, whose leader, Clement Attlee, had been his deputy for five years. Soon after Germany surrendered, the wartime coalition was dissolved, and Britain held a general election. The result was a Labour landslide, and Churchill spent the summer of 1945, in deep depression. "A very formidable event has occurred in Britain", he wrote to Sir Alexander Cadogan a few days later, "and I fear it will diminish our national stature at a time when we most need unity and strength"[96]. Hitler had cast his long shadow even over internal British politics: some have attributed the result in small measure to a remark Churchill made, that the Labour Party's policies of economic control would require "some form of a Gestapo, no doubt very humanely directed in the first instance" to implement them. This remark was felt by many to be grossly unfair to politicians who, whatever their faults, had spent five years fighting Nazism. Without detailed opinion polls, however, we cannot be sure what, if any, effect that remark had on people's voting intentions, and some Conservatives thought that the speech actually put Labour on the back foot[97].

---

[1] *Winston Churchill, Struggle for Survival*, Lord Moran, p.173

[2] *Until the Final Hour, Hitler's Last Secretary*, Traudl Junge, p.82

[3] *In the Bunker with Hitler*, Bernd Freytag von Loringhoven, p.88

[4] *Hitler's War*, David Irving, p.608

[5] *Hansard*, 20 February 1944

[6] Churchill Papers 20/137, quoted in *Road to Victory, Winston S Churchill 1941-45*, Martin S Gilbert, p.437

[7] *Road to Victory, Winston S Churchill 1941-45*, Martin S Gilbert, p.737

[8] *Road to Victory, Winston S Churchill 1941-45*, Martin S Gilbert, p.570

[9] Churchill telegram to Roosevelt, 20/121, quoted in *Road to Victory, Winston S Churchill 1941-45*, Martin S Gilbert, p.531-2

[10] Churchill telegram to Roosevelt, 20/122, quoted in *Road to Victory, Winston S Churchill 1941-45*, Martin S Gilbert, p.538

[11] Premier Papers 3/499/2, quoted in *Road to Victory, Winston S Churchill 1941-45*, Martin S Gilbert, p.21

[12] Churchill Papers 20/179, quoted in *Road to Victory, Winston S Churchill 1941-45*, Martin S Gilbert, p.633

[13] *The Memoirs of General Lord Ismay*, General Ismay, p.308

[14] *The Second World War, Volume 5, Closing the Ring*, Winston Churchill, Chapter IV

[15] Prime Minister's Personal Minute, Churchill Papers 20/152, quoted in *Road to Victory, Winston S Churchill 1941-45*, Martin S Gilbert, p.437

[16] *At Hitler's Side*, Nicolaus von Below, p.187

[17] *Killing Hitler*, Roger Moorhouse, p.147

[18] For this paragraph, see, in particular, *Killing Hitler*, Roger Moorhouse, p.163-7

[19] See the National Archives, HS 6/623-5

[20] *Hitler, 1936-45, Nemesis*, Ian Kershaw, p.663

[21] See, for instance, *The Unnecessary War*, by Patricia Meehan, or *Plotting Hitler's Death* by Joachim Fest

[22] *Road to Victory, Winston S Churchill 1941-45*, Martin S Gilbert, p.861

[23] *Hansard*, 2 August 1944

[24] *The Unnecessary War*, Patricia Meehan, p.7

[25] *Hansard*, 21 July 1949

[26] See *Road to Victory, Winston S Churchill 1941-45*, Martin S Gilbert, p.868

[27] *Hansard*, 28 September 1944

[28] *In the Bunker with Hitler*, Bernd Freytag von Loringhoven, p.79

[29] *In the Bunker with Hitler*, Bernd Freytag von Loringhoven, p.81

[30] *Beside the Bulldog*, Walter Thompson, p.23-4

[31] *The Fringes of Power*, John Colville, p.437

[32] *The Storm of War*, Andrew Roberts, p.443

[33] *Until the Final Hour, Hitler's Last Secretary*, Traudl Junge, p.121

[34] *Hansard*, 21 September 1943

[35] Prime Minister's Personal Telegram, Churchill Papers 120/858, quoted in *Road to Victory, Winston S Churchill 1941-45*, Martin S Gilbert, p.809

[36] *Air Superiority in War*, Marshal of the RAF Lord Tedder, quoted in *The Storm of War*, Andrew Roberts, p.452

[37] Quoted in *Hitler's War*, David Irving, p.278

[38] Quoted in *Hitler's War*, David Irving, p.404

[39] *Hitler's Letters*, Werner Maser, p.363

[40] *The Testament of Adolf Hitler*, 4 February 1945

[41] *The Testament of Adolf Hitler*, 4 February 1945

[42] *The Testament of Adolf Hitler*, 15 February 1945

[43] *The Testament of Adolf Hitler*, 26 February 1945

[44] *The Goebbels Diaries, 1944-45*, 27 March 1945

[45] *The Goebbels Diaries, 1944-45*, 6 March 1945

[46] *The Goebbels Diaries, 1944-45*, 6 March 1945

[47] *The Goebbels Diaries, 1944-45*, 6 March 1945

[48] *The Goebbels Diaries, 1944-45*, 6 March 1945

[49] *Winston Churchill, Struggle for Survival*, Lord Moran, p.175

[50] *The Goebbels Diaries, 1944-45*, 6 March 1945

[51] *At Hitler's Side*, Nicolaus von Below, p.179

[52] *Inside Hitler's headquarters*, W Warlimont, p.452

[53] Prime Minster's Personal Minute, 8 September 1944, quoted in *Road to Victory, Winston S Churchill 1941-45*, Martin S Gilbert, p.943

[54] *At Hitler's Side*, Nicolaus von Below, p.227

[55] Cabinet Papers, 120/170, quoted in *Road to Victory, Winston S Churchill 1941-45*, Martin S Gilbert, p.1179

[56] *The Goebbels Diaries, 1944-45*, 4 March 1945

[57] *The Goebbels Diaries, 1944-45*, 7 March 1945

[58] *The Goebbels Diaries, 1944-45*, 11 March 1945

[59] *The Goebbels Diaries, 1944-45*, 12 March 1945

[60] *The Goebbels Diaries, 1944-45*, 21 March 1945

[61] *The Goebbels Diaries, 1944-45*, 28 January 1945

[62] On this episode, see War Cabinet papers, 25 April 1945, and *Road to Victory, Winston S Churchill 1941-45*, Martin S Gilbert, p.1310

[63] *At Hitler's Side*, Nicolaus von Below, p.239

[64] *The Fringes of Power*, John Colville, p.358

[65] Letter to Clementine Churchill, 6 April 1945, quoted in *Road to Victory, Winston S Churchill 1941-45*, Martin S Gilbert, p.1284

[66] Churchill to Eden, 11 July 1941, quoted in *Triumph and Tragedy*, Winston Churchill

[67] Prime Minster's Personal Minute, 23 August 1944, quoted in *Road to Victory, Winston S Churchill 1941-45*, Martin S Gilbert, p.921

[68] *Winston Churchill, Struggle for Survival*, Lord Moran, p.194

[69] See Annex B of CAB 65/66/31

[70] *Interrogations,* Richard Overy, p.15

[71] Cabinet Papers, 120/170, quoted in *Road to Victory, Winston S Churchill 1941-45*, Martin S Gilbert, p.1173

[72] *The Fringes of Power*, John Colville, p.553-4

[73] *Beside the Bulldog*, Walter Thompson, p.133

[74] *Until the Final Hour, Hitler's Last Secretary*, Traudl Junge, p.178

[75] *Speaking for Themselves*, Mary Soames, p.529

[76] *The Fringes of Power*, John Colville, p.562-3

[77] *Until the Final Hour, Hitler's Last Secretary*, Traudl Junge, p.177

[78] *Never Despair*, Martin Gilbert, p.892

[79] *Hansard*, 16 August 1945

[80] *Churchill War Papers, Vol. III, The Ever-Widening War*, Martin Gilbert, p.1659

[81] *Churchill War Papers, Vol. III, The Ever-Widening War*, Martin Gilbert, p.974

[82] Prime Minster's Personal Minute, 23 August 1944, quoted in *Road to Victory, Winston S Churchill 1941-45*, Martin S Gilbert, p.1024-5

[83] *Speaking for Themselves: the personal letters of Winston and Clementine Churchill*, ed. Mary Soames, p.512

[84] *Volkischer Beobachter*, 22 September 1944

[85] *Hansard*, 21 July 1949

[86] Churchill Papers 20/218, quoted in *Never Despair*, Martin Gilbert, p.8

[87] *Never Despair*, Martin Gilbert, p.13

[88] *The Second World War, Volume 6, Triumph and Tragedy*, Winston Churchill, p.546

[89] *The Diaries of Sir Alexander Cadogan*, p.763

[90] *Manchester Guardian*, 17 July 1945

[91] *Never Despair*, Martin Gilbert, p.61

[92] *The Diaries of Sir Alexander Cadogan*, p.763

[93] *Churchill at War*, Lord Moran, p.334

[94] *Manchester Guardian*, 17 July 1945

[95] *Hansard*, 16 August 1945

[96] *The Diaries of Sir Alexander Cadogan*, p.774

97 *Never Despair*, Martin Gilbert, p.32-5

10

Churchill Alone
(July 1945 - 1965)

Following his resounding defeat in the British general election of July 1945, Churchill had significant leisure time for the first time in six years. He remained Leader of the Opposition, though that post was far less demanding than it is now. He combined his part time role as Leader of the Opposition with frequent overseas travel around Europe and the United States in particular. He delegated much of the more mundane work to Anthony Eden and other colleagues, to their considerable annoyance. He often would refer to Hitler occasionally in public and, even more frequently, in private.

Despite increasingly blunt hints from colleagues, Churchill did not retire from front line politics in the late 1940's, and his persistence was rewarded in 1950 and again in 1951, when his party first almost eliminated Labour's large majority, and then gained a small overall majority of its own. Foreign and defence matters remained important in British politics in the late 1940's and 1950's, and Churchill's policies in those areas were heavily influenced by his views on Hitler. In his speeches, conversation and writings, Churchill would use the German dictator in three main ways: in his historical writings; to make political points; and to reminisce with friends and colleagues. This chapter therefore deals with each of these in turn.

Chapter 10

Hitler in Churchill's war memoirs

Churchill devoted much of his time between 1945 and 1951 to composing his history of the Second World War, which blends autobiography and history. Churchill had long been aware that he would write a history of his involvement in the Second World War, similar to that which he had written about the First World War. He saw the two books as making up a history of the twentieth century's own Thirty Years War, and therefore his history of the Second World War actually begins in 1919, at the end of the First.

Churchill argued for, and received, access to many government documents which would not otherwise have been made public for decades, though he could not mention many of the more sensitive aspects of the war, such as the Ultra decrypts. It is certainly not a definitive history of the War, nor did its author think that it could be: that belonged, he said, to a subsequent generation. Nevertheless, it is an extremely important statement of Churchill's thoughts about the War, and about the main actors in it.

Needless to say, the six-volume, 1.6 million* word[1] book is full of illustrations of Churchill's attitude towards Hitler. When he was working on his history of the First World War twenty years before, he had remarked to Lord Beaverbrook about the "great difficulties in writing this kind of contemporary history when one has friendly relations with the actors"[2]. This was clearly not a problem in talking about Hitler, who was dead, and in any case Churchill had never had friendly relations with him. However, as many writers have subsequently shown, Churchill needed to spare the feelings of many of the actors still on the world stage, especially the Americans and his fellow British politicians. Accordingly, his account must be treated with considerable scepticism in many areas.

Though the glow of victory enabled Churchill to make favourable references to former opponents or antagonists such as Neville Chamberlain or the anti-British French Admiral Darlan, there is no sign of a similar mellowing in his attitude towards the Nazi dictator. It would obviously be unrealistic to expect Churchill suddenly to take a different attitude to the man he had spent fifteen years condemning. Understandably, the war which Hitler had unleashed on Europe and the atrocities of the Nazi regime meant that Churchill's views on Hitler in his history of the Second World War are far harsher than they had been before

---

* 1.9 million including appendices.

the Second World War, for example in his 1935 essay on Hitler in the *Strand* magazine.

The writing of the book is a fascinating story in itself, ably told by David Reynolds in his stimulating *In Command of History*. Churchill assembled an able group of assistants, and they wrote much of the book, but Churchill was both chairman of the Syndicate, as it was known, and editor of the work. As Reynolds remarks, Churchill operated "less as an author, more as what scientists today would recognise as head of a research group"[3]. The book is, as its author admitted, a personal statement: "this is not history; this is my case".

There are many errors and inaccuracies in the book's 1.6 million words, some of which involve Churchill's views on Hitler. In the space of five pages describing the first thirty-five years of Hitler's life[4], he makes several mistakes, though none are of great significance. He refers to Hitler as a "house painter" in Munich and Vienna, which implies that Hitler would decorate people's houses for a living, when in fact he painted watercolours and postcards (albeit often *of* houses). Churchill dates Hitler's anti-Semitism to his life in Vienna, following his account in *Mein Kampf*. However, there is no conclusive evidence that Hitler was an anti-Semite at this time, and some evidence that he got on reasonably well with the Jewish soldiers in his regiment during the war[5], after he had left Vienna. Churchill's book states that Hitler's sentence for his attempted *coup* in Munich in 1923 was four years, whereas in fact the sentence was five years[6], though Hitler was allowed credit for the four months and two weeks which he had already served in jail while waiting for his trial. Churchill also refers to Hitler as a Corporal, whereas, as argued in Chapter 2 above, this arguably overstates his rank (interestingly, early drafts seem to have referred to Hitler as a Private – this was later changed, for reasons which are not apparent). Finally, early drafts refer to Hitler as having been poisoned by chlorine gas in 1918, though this was subsequently corrected to mustard gas.

Churchill chronicles Hitler's rise to power in some detail. He focuses more on the backstairs intrigues of von Schleicher and von Papen than on Hitler's electoral successes or mass appeal. In particular, he notes that, at the elections just before Hitler became Chancellor, the "Nazis lost ground, ... the Communists gaining the balance" and that Hindenburg only consented to Hitler's appointment as Chancellor "at last reluctantly"[7]. Churchill does not dwell on the gangster-like methods of the Nazi Party and its paramilitary wing, the SA, or on the backing which Hitler received from German industry, though he mentions both. In chronicling Hitler's rise to power, Churchill also notes that Hitler made a poor impression on both President Hindenburg and Mussolini. He quotes Hindenburg as saying about Hitler, "That man for Chancellor? I'll make him a postmaster and he can lick stamps with my head on them"[8]. He says that Mussolini remarked to an aide when he first saw Hitler in June 1934, "I don't like the look of him", and then dismissed his fellow dictator in three words: "a garrulous monk"[9]. He does not, however, quote any of the dozens of people whom Hitler met during these years upon whom he exerted a hypnotic fascination.

On Hitler's purge of the SA in 1934, Churchill says that "it will long be disputed in Germany whether Hitler was forced to strike by the imminence of the Röhm plot or whether he and the generals, fearing what might be coming, resolved on a clean-cut liquidation … It is certain that … [the SA] were forestalled … [Hitler's] promptitude and purpose had saved … no doubt his life"[10]. In fact, it is extremely unlikely that there was any threat of a coup: with a dictator's enthusiasm for pre-emptive action, Hitler was simply eliminating rivals for power.

Churchill chronicles Hitler's early foreign policy triumphs, interspersing his history with his own contemporary speeches and writings. He also goes into some detail about German rearmament in the mid-1930s. He spends an entire chapter on Britain's loss of air parity with Germany, against which he campaigned strenuously (see Chapter 3 above). Any unbiased observer must come away with an impression of Churchill's prescience about the German menace. Interestingly, Churchill also blames Hitler indirectly for his exclusion from office in 1936, when the post of Minister of the Coordination of Defence was created: "Apparently … the German entry into the Rhineland on March 7 was decisive against my appointment. It was certainly obvious that Hitler would not like it". He describes this exclusion as a "heavy blow", but then devotes the next page of his book to saying how lucky it turned out to be, as he was not officially associated with the foreign policy disasters of the next three years[11]. He records Hitler's fury at the chaos in the German army during its invasion of Austria, when "In spite of perfect weather and road conditions, the majority of tanks broke down … [and] the road from Linz to Vienna was blocked with heavy vehicles at a standstill"[12]. He is in no doubt that Hitler outmanoeuvred Britain and France at Munich, noting that Hitler could have been overthrown by Halder and other generals, and that the year's respite gained was not worth the sacrifice of the Czechs[13]. He notes, however, that Hitler's gratitude for Britain's betrayal of the Czechs at Munich "found only frigid expression"[14]. On the change in British foreign policy following the German seizure of Prague the following year, he argues that "Hitler completely underrated the nature of the British Prime Minister. He mistook his civilian aspect and passionate desire for peace for a complete explanation of his personality ... He did not realise that Neville Chamberlain had a very hard core, and that he did not like being cheated"[15].

As war loomed, Churchill recognised that the German "fifth column" in Britain could have been a danger to him personally, because of his anti-Hitler stance. "There were known to be twenty thousand organised German Nazis in England at this time ... I had at that time no official protection and I did not wish to ask for any; but ... I had enough information to convey to me that Hitler recognised me as a foe. My former ... detective, Inspector Thompson, was in retirement. I told him to come along [to Chartwell] and bring his pistol with him. While one slept the other watched"[16].

Once the war began, Churchill's memoirs pay somewhat less attention to Hitler. He focuses more on his departmental responsibilities at the Admiralty. His memoirs devote the same amount of space to his "War Cabinet Problems" as to Hitler's conquest of Poland. He gives Hitler credit for the "ruin of Poland", attributing it to "Hitler's method" and "Hitler's plan"[17]. According to Andrew Roberts, he was wrong to do so: the plan for the invasion of Poland "was drawn up by OKH† planners, with Hitler merely putting his imprimatur on the final document"[18]. He also gives credit to Hitler for understanding the low level of French morale. However, "He did not understand the profound change which takes place in Great Britain once the signal for war has been given ... He could not comprehend the mental and spiritual force of our Island people"[19]. According to Churchill - Britain's blood was on the boil. "It never occurred to him for a moment that Mr Chamberlain and the rest of the British Empire ... now meant to have his blood or perish in the attempt"[20].

Churchill gave "Hitler and his Generals" full credit for the devastating German attack through the Ardennes in May 1940[21], though also blaming the Belgians for refusing to coordinate their military plans with the French[22], and the French for failing to guard their frontier with Belgium better[23]. On the key question of who halted the German tanks before Dunkirk, allowing most of the British Army to escape, Churchill gives the blame to the German General in charge on the scene, von Rundstedt, not Hitler. He also gives credit to the British resistance at Calais for holding the waterline of Gravelines[24]. Churchill also argued that "Hitler's belief that the German Air Force would render escape impossible, and that therefore he should keep his armoured formations for the final stroke of the

---

† *Oberkommando des Heeres*, the German General Staff.

campaign, was a mistaken but not unreasonable view"[25]. He speculated that Hitler would have been better to defeat the French armies in northern France, then allow a month for the French army in southern France to recover, so that Britain could have felt obliged to help it, thereby weakening its defence of its own island. "The more we urged the French to fight on, the greater was our obligation to aid them, and the more difficult it would become to make any preparations for defence in England …"[26]

Churchill devotes two entire chapters to discussing the possibility of the invasion of Britain from the British and the German points of view. "Our excellent Intelligence [i.e. the Enigma decrypts, though Churchill could not mention these by name] confirmed that the operation "Sea Lion" had been definitely ordered by Hitler and was in active preparation. It seemed certain that the man was going to try"[27]. The possibility that he might, and the outcome if he had, clearly intrigued Churchill for the rest of his life. "In 1940", his doctor quotes him as saying in 1952, "three-quarters of a million Germans would have been needed to give invasion any chance of success; in 1941 the number had risen to a million and a half. If Hitler had turned on all his factories to making landing craft … [Churchill apparently trailed off at this point, leaving the thought incomplete]"[28]. Churchill chronicles Hitler's vacillations and ambiguous views on the invasion, both on its desirability and its chances of success[29].

The German dictator is largely absent from Churchill's accounts of the Battle of Britain, the Blitz, and the North African campaign of the winter of 1940, but reappears briefly in his account of Hitler's failed wooing of Vichy France and Spain. Churchill's account of Hitler's turn towards Russia, however, sees him reappear and he gives a full account of Molotov's disastrous visit to Berlin in November 1940[30], though he argues that the visit "made no difference to Hitler's deep resolve [to attack Russia]". Hitler, he claims, tried to deceive Russia in two ways: by discussing with her the dismemberment of the British Empire, and by occupying Eastern Europe militarily[31].

Churchill describes in detail Hitler's spasm of rage at the Yugoslav coup of March 1941. "'The Yugoslav *coup* came suddenly out of the blue. When the news was brought to me on the morning of the 27th I thought it was a joke'", he has Hitler remarking a month later. He quotes Hitler as wanting to "destroy Yugoslavia militarily and as a national unit"[32]. He also discusses at some length Hitler's clumsy intervention in Iraq in May 1941, which, if conducted earlier, could have caused the British serious embarrassment, but which, in the end, was a damp squib. "Hitler certainly cast away the opportunity of taking a great prize for little cost in the Middle East" [33], was Churchill's verdict.

Churchill writes, uncontroversially, that the Russians were far stronger than Hitler imagined[34]. He regarded Hitler's decision not to concentrate on taking Moscow in the early summer as wrong[35]. Yet again comparing Hitler to Napoleon, he gloated that, later in 1941, "like the supreme military genius who had trod this road [to Moscow] a century before him, Hitler now discovered what Russian winter meant. He bowed to inexorable facts ... Henceforth, Hitler took personal command in the East"[36]. He gives Hitler credit for "at last" transferring a German Air Fleet to Sicily in December 1941, which materially worsened British prospects in North Africa[37]. But three days later, the Japanese attacked Pearl Harbor. Churchill claims that Hitler was "astonished"[38]. Writing about his thoughts just after Pearl Harbor, he made his famous comment that "Hitler's fate was sealed", even though the Americans and Germans were not yet at war[39]. Churchill argues that Hitler could have inflicted far greater damage on Allied shipping during 1942 had German heavy warships been sent into the Atlantic, though the fate of the battleship *Bismarck* the previous year was not encouraging. "Hitler was however obsessed with the idea that we intended to invade Northern Norway at an early date. With his powerful one-track mind he sacrificed the glittering chances in the Atlantic... In vain, the admirals argued for a naval offensive"[40]. He gave Hitler full credit for the Channel Dash of the two pocket battleships. However, he thought that that operation was a strategic mistake, however brilliant it had been tactically[41]. Churchill criticised Hitler for his decision to order Dönitz to move U-boats to guard against an attack on the Azores or Madeira[42].

Churchill blamed Hitler's nerves for the lack of a German invasion of Malta. The German dictator apparently hoped that he could force the island to surrender by air attack alone[43]. "Hitler himself had not been confident of success against Malta as he mistrusted the ability of the Italian troops who would have formed the major part of the expedition". However, Churchill argued that the loss of Tobruk spared Malta from invasion[44]. Because Hitler was still confident of taking Egypt, he "postponed the attack on Malta until the conquest of Egypt was complete"[45].

Churchill only gives a paragraph and then, later, a few pages to the Battle of Stalingrad, while giving a whole chapter to the insignificant affair of Admiral Darlan, and several chapters to manoeuvres in the House of Commons. He blames Hitler for ordering the German general on the spot, Paulus, to hold his ground: "but Hitler would not countenance any suggestion of withdrawal ... Thereafter, [the German Sixth Army's] doom was certain"[46]. Churchill has Hitler lecturing Laval in an attempt to align Vichy France closer with Germany, and comments on Hitler's "theatrical sense of history"[47]. Finally, he notes that at the end of May 1943, "Hitler still had to pay the full penalty of his fatal error in trying to conquer Russia by invasion. He had still to squander the immense remaining strength of Germany in many theatres not vital to the main result"[48].

Churchill says that Hitler made "a crowning error" in trying to hold all the ground he had occupied, without accumulating a central reserve. With his usual gift for arresting animal metaphors, he writes that Hitler had "made a spider's web and [had] forgotten the spider"[49]. He does not give Hitler credit for the ruthless German takeover of Italy after the Allied invasion, but mentions his role in the recapture of Mussolini[50]. He states that Hitler's decision to fight for Italy helped the Allies with their invasion of France, by diverting troops to what would become a secondary theatre of war[51], though he credits Hitler with occasional tactical strokes, such as the ruthless, and almost successful, German counterattack on Anzio: "Hitler, for his was the will-power at work ..." he begins[52].

Churchill repeatedly, and on the whole justifiably, criticises Hitler's repeated orders to German troops to fight until the last man. "Hitler's method of fighting to the death on all fronts lacked the important charm of selection"[53], he comments about German manoeuvring after D-Day. It is a major theme in the last book of his memoirs in particular. He refers to it when outlining the Allied invasion of Southern France (Operation Anvil)[54], when relating his strategy discussions with Marshal Tito of Yugoslavia[55], and again when chronicling the Allied victory in Italy in 1945[56]. Occasionally, however, as in Hitler's decision to hold on to Rhodes, he admits that it was the right choice[57]. In this case, though, Churchill could have wanted to deflect blame onto the Americans, who thwarted his desire to invade those islands after the Italian collapse.

As noted in the previous chapter, Churchill devotes only a paragraph to Stauffenberg's assassination attempt. "All the fury of [Hitler's] nature was aroused by this plot, and the vengeance which he inflicted on all suspected of being in it makes a terrible tale"[58], he writes, though he did not seem to feel obliged to tell the tale himself. He is clearly aware of Hitler's involvement in the detail of the rocket bomb attacks on London in 1944 and 1945, and referred to his order to construct 30,000 of the very expensive V-2s, which "shows the absurd ideas on which he lived"[59]. Churchill also refers to the "stubborn hopes" which Hitler places on the V-weapons for many months[60]. Churchill assigns Hitler responsibility for the Ardennes offensive[61]. He also notes intense speculation about Hitler's plans as Germany crumbled, in particular whether he planned to retreat to the Alps and hold out there[62]. He chronicles Hitler's last week factually and does not reflect on his record at all[63].

At various points of writing his book, Churchill attempted to see into Hitler's mind. He speculates on whether Hitler or Stalin loathed their non-aggression pact most. "Both", he claims, "were aware that it could only be a temporary expedient[64]. He often combined this with an analysis of counterfactuals, those "what ifs?" of history that always fascinated him. For example, he correctly assumed that Hitler must have been very annoyed by the hostile Yugoslav *coup d'etat* in the spring of 1941. He wrote to an assistant of his, Bill Deakin, on the *coup d'etat* in Belgrade passage "Can we also have a paragraph on Hitler's *fury* at the Yugoslav volte-face? He must have been vy [sic] much vexed"[65]. He even attempted some empathy with the Nazi tyrant: "Here we are at the end of March 1941, with Hitler massing his forces to destroy Russia and these foolish commissars, the Kremlin gang, let the whole Balkans go to pieces. Our feeble intervention, such as it was, gained them five weeks in which Hitler lost the necessary time to take Moscow before the winter"[66]. In fact, Churchill was probably wrong to attribute the delay in Barbarossa to the British intervention in Greece. The unusually wet spring of 1941 was likely to have meant that Blitzkrieg warfare of the type that the German army of the 1940s had used to such devastating effect on Poland, Belgium and France was not possible until mid-June, whether or not Britain had intervened in Greece. Churchill's unwise extension of the war to south-eastern Europe therefore did not buy the Soviets any time at all.

The critical reception of the six-volume book was generally favourable as it was published over several years, though one British review was distinctly unpleasant. Michael Foot, extreme left-wing journalist, MP and future leader of the Labour Party, wrote a review in the Tribune which actually compared the first volume of Churchill's book to *Mein Kampf*. In "personal conceit and arrogance there is some likeness between the two [books]", he wrote. Churchill was not entitled "to write bad history for the benefit of the Churchill legend"[67]. Foot made one demonstrable mistake in his review of volume 3. "The suggestion that Mr Churchill was anything other than convinced of the Russian inability to withstand the German attack amounts to a downright falsehood … the main strategy of the war as directed from Downing Street was not altered for several months by Hitler's huge plunge eastwards". Colville wrote to Churchill on 3 August 1950, reminding Churchill that he had said on 22 June 1941, "I will bet anybody here a monkey to a mousetrap that the Russians are still fighting, and fighting victoriously, two years from now"[68].

Churchill's war memoir was only one of the means he used to argue his "case" in the decade after the Second World War. He also occasionally made speeches, in Parliament and elsewhere, which talked about Hitler, particularly when he felt that his wartime record was being unjustifiably attacked. One subject on which he clearly felt strongly was the British government's attitude towards the German resistance. Though the British government approved an attempt on Hitler's life, it was rather more distant when dealing with the occasional contacts from members of the German government or Army who were aiming at the same goal. To a German opponent of Hitler, Fabian von Schlabrendroff whom he met at Chartwell in 1949, however, Churchill questioned the British government's attitude to the German resistance during the war. He said that he had realised that "during the war he had been misled by his assistants about the considerable strength and size of the German anti-Hitler resistance"[69]. Blaming unnamed "assistants" was a handy alibi, though in this case it could have been true. Whether Churchill would have acted differently, and what he would have done had he known its true size and strength, must remain speculation. He was clearly sceptical about whether any help from Britain would have been effective. In 1949, the Labour politician, Richard Crossman, told the Commons that if Churchill had called the conspirators in the Stauffenberg plot "patriotic Germans" in 1944, Hitler might have been overthrown. Churchill replied:

> "I am not at all sure that that is true. I am not going to plunge into a lengthy argument, but I am not at all sure that, if Hitler had been murdered by some of the plots which were levelled against him by men whom I do not hesitate to call patriotic Germans, a new situation would have arisen. I believe there was the force and vigour to carry on the fight, as it was carried on, to the very last gasp. He and the band of guilty men around him were in the position that they could not look for any pardon or any safety for their lives and they would certainly have fought to the death"[70].

The Cold War

Three questions above all dominated British foreign and defence policy during the last two decades of Churchill's life: the Cold War; the retreat from Empire; and the recovery of Europe in general, and Germany in particular. Of those, the Cold War was the most immediate threat to western civilisation in general, and Britain in particular. Even in Opposition, Churchill routinely drew on his experience confronting Hitler in the 1930's to suggest how the Soviets might be contained. As early as November 1945, he was warning the Belgian Senate publicly against appeasement of the Soviets based on Britain's experience before the Second World War:

> "Do not forget that twice the German people ... voted against Hitler, but the Allies and the League of Nations acted with such feebleness ... that each of Hitler's encroachments became a triumph for him over all moderate and restraining forces until, finally, we resigned ourselves without further protest to the vast process of German rearmament and war preparation which ended in a renewed outbreak of destructive war ... If the allies had resisted Hitler strongly in his early stages ... the chance would have been given to the sane elements in German life, which were very powerful – especially in the High Command – to free Germany from the maniacal system into the grip of which she was falling" [71].

Churchill's most famous speech on Russian expansionism, at Fulton, Missouri, in March 1946, accused the Soviets of drawing an "Iron Curtain" across Eastern Europe[‡]. A significant part of that speech was dedicated to showing how lessons learned in opposing Hitler in the 1930's should have taught the British and Americans to stand up to Stalin in the late 1940's:

> "From what I have seen of our Russian friends and Allies during the war, I am convinced that there is nothing they admire so much as strength, and there is nothing for which they have less respect than for weakness, especially military weakness ...
>
> Last time I saw it all coming and I cried aloud to my own fellow-countrymen and to the world, but no one paid any attention. Up till the year 1933 or even 1935, Germany might have been saved from the awful fate which has overtaken her and we might all have been spared the miseries Hitler let loose upon mankind. There never was a war in history easier to prevent by timely action than the one which has just desolated such great areas of the globe. It could have been prevented in my belief without the firing of a single shot, and Germany might be powerful, prosperous and honoured today; but no one would listen and one by one we were all sucked into the awful whirlpool. We surely must not let that happen again. This can only be achieved by reaching now, in 1946, a good understanding on all points with Russia under the general

---

[‡] A large literature has grown up around the origins of that famous phrase. It seems that Goebbels was the first to use it ("*ein eisener Vorhang*") in this context in early 1945 – Martin Gilbert, *Never Despair*, p.7

authority of the United Nations Organization and by the maintenance of that good understanding through many peaceful years, by the world instrument, supported by the whole strength of the English-speaking world and all its connections".

Many American papers criticised Churchill heavily. The *Wall Street Journal*, for example, wrote that "The United States wants no alliance ... with any other nation", and the internationalist *Chicago Sun* referred to the "poisonous doctrines" of the speech[72]. Though Churchill had no official position, the reaction to his speech from Moscow was explosive. Just as the Nazis had seen him as a menace when he was a backbencher in the 1930s, so Stalin clearly did after the Second World War. Stalin wrote in the Communist newspaper, *Pravda*:

"Mr Churchill is now in the position of a warmonger ... Mr Churchill and his friends are strikingly reminiscent of Hitler and his friends. Hitler began the process of unleashing war by pronouncing his racial theories, declaring that only those people whose mother tongue was German could be considered a full–blooded nation. Now Mr Churchill is starting his process of unleashing war also with a racial theory, declaring that only those people who speak English are full-blooded nations, whose vocation it is to control the fate of the whole world. The German racial theories brought Hitler and his friends to the conclusion that the Germans ... were destined to rule over other nations. The English racial theories have brought Mr Churchill and his friends to the conclusion that those nations who speak English ... must rule over the other nations of the world ... But the nations spilled their blood during five years of cruel war for the freedom and independence of their countries, and not in order to change the rule of the Hitlers for the rule of the Churchills. It is most probable therefore that the nations who do not speak English ... do not agree to walk into a new slavery"[73].

That night, Churchill was at a dinner in New York, hosted by Henry Luce, the owner of *Time* magazine. A journalist present at that dinner wrote to Martin Gilbert in 1987:

"In the main reception hall outside the dining room stood an American eagle carved in ice. It was hot in the room and water was already dripping from the eagle's wings. Commented Churchill, 'The American eagle seems to have a cold'. Stalin's reaction to his speech seems to have cheered Churchill. 'You know', he suggested half-seriously, 'if I had been turned loose on Winston Churchill, I could have done a much better job' ... The thought gave him pleasure".

Churchill then recalled the 1930's.

> "Brightening perceptibly, he went on to tell how Hitler had attacked him in almost identical terms: 'warmonger, inciter of wars, imperialist, reactionary, has been – why, it is beginning to sound almost like old times'".

He also referred to his admiration for the Russian people and their war record. "We all remember what frightful losses Russia suffered in the Hitlerite invasion"[74].

Churchill ended his American tour in 1946 by granting an interview to his son, Randolph, "I enjoyed [the tour] very much. I came here for a rest cure and now I am going home to have a rest after the rest cure". Randolph asked his father about his views on the Soviets: "I suppose we may take it that you are still an opponent of International Communism?" Churchill replied with a response that showed that he was far from forgiving the Nazi-Soviet pact of 1939: "I have never been able to get to like it very much. We must not forget that all the Communists in the world would have seen England sunk beneath the waves by Hitler's Germany, and that it was only when Soviet Russia was attacked that they put themselves in line with the modern world". He made a distinction between Communists and the Russian Army, however: "I always admire the bravery and patriotism of the Russian Armies in defending their own soil, when it was invaded by Hitler's legions. But I made it clear in my broadcast of 22 June 1941, that my support of Russia in no way weakened my opposition to Communism"[75].

His concern about a possible Soviet attack on Western Europe in the late 1940s is palpable, however. This worry, together with the memory of Hitler's aggression, are the two key threads running through his second great speech of 1946 given in Zurich. Churchill proposed a Franco-German alliance as a first step towards a united Europe. Though not mentioning Hitler by name, he dwelt extensively on Nazi atrocities and the devastation which they had inflicted on Europe:

> "Among the victors there is a babel of jarring voices; among the vanquished the sullen silence of despair.
>
> That is all that Europeans, grouped in so many ancient States and nations, that is all that the Germanic Powers have got by tearing each

other to pieces and spreading havoc far and wide.

…

We must build a kind of United States of Europe.

…

We all know that the two world wars through which we have passed arose out of the vain passion of a newly united Germany to play the dominating part in the world.

In this last struggle crimes and massacres have been committed for which there is no parallel since the invasions of the Mongols in the fourteenth century and no equal at any time in human history.

The guilty must be punished. Germany must be deprived of the power to rearm and make another aggressive war.

But when all this has been done, as it will be done, as it is being done, there must be an end to retribution"[76].

Hitler had occasionally referred to the possibility of a united Europe during the war, though he meant a Germanic slave empire rather than a voluntary association of free peoples. But European unification was far ahead, and in 1946, Soviet penetration of Europe was the most urgent foreign policy problem on the minds of most European statesmen. On 26 November 1946, Churchill wrote to his wartime ally (and sparring partner) General de Gaulle about Soviet intentions, "Soviet advance westward to the sea … It is evident that they have the power to do it at any time. On the other hand, the end might not be so agreeable as the beginning. This was certainly Hitler's experience and it might be a deterrent"[77]. Churchill's turbulent relationship with the head of the Free French, General de Gaulle, has been well documented. At one point, he accused the General of displaying "symptoms [of becoming] a budding Führer"[78]. Soviet advances in Eastern Europe clearly made strange bedfellows.

Semi-serious nostalgia for the Nazis is also evident in Churchill's October 1946 remarks that:

"It was easier in Hitler's day to feel and forecast the general movement of events. But now we have not to deal with Hitler and his crude Nazi-gang. We are in the presence of something very much more difficult to measure. We are in the presence of a collective mind whose springs of action we cannot judge"[79].

Having confronted Hitler in the 1930's, Churchill felt that he had some knowledge of the tactics which dictators would use in peacetime to fool other nations and their politicians. He used the Nazi practice of soothing declarations after an act of aggression to warn against taking soft Soviet statements seriously. In a broadcast of 14 October 1947, he talked about Soviet foreign policy: "If their minds are set on war I cannot believe that they would not lull the easy-going democracies into a false sense of security". Hitler had been a master of this, and "before or during some act of aggression, he uttered soothing words or made non-Aggression Pacts"[80].

It is clear that Churchill was not the only politician thinking along these lines. President Truman also thought of the Nazi menace as a precedent for the dealing with the Soviet Union. In September 1947, he wrote to Churchill: "The world is facing many serious problems ... Our Russian 'friends' seem most ungrateful for the contribution which your great country and mine made to save them. I sometimes think perhaps we made a mistake – and then I remember Hitler. He had no heart at all. I believe that Joe Stalin has one but the Polit Bureau won't let him use it"[81]. History has not borne out the final part of his argument. It is clear that the Politburo in the 1930's and 1940's did whatever Stalin told it to.

Two years after Churchill's Iron Curtain speech, the Russian menace had not abated. Indeed, one of the most dangerous phases in the Cold War, the Berlin Blockade, began in June 1948. The Russians began blockading the British, French and American zones of occupation in that city, which were well inside Soviet East Germany. Food, fuel and other provisions immediately begun running short in the Western zones, and the British and Americans undertook a massive airlift to maintain a minimum level of supply. In August of that year, Churchill wrote to a former American Secretary of State after talking about Soviet advances in Germany and Czechoslovakia: "We are now confronted with the designs and ambitions of despots as wicked as Hitler and even more absolute. How right you were to stand up firmly to them about Persia in 1945"[82].

Churchill thought that there was nothing new in the Soviet threat. On October 9, in North Wales, he remarked in a speech that "the gulf which was opening between Asiatic Communist Russia and the Western Democracies, large and small, was already brutally obvious to the victorious War Cabinet of the

National Coalition even before Hitler destroyed himself and the Germans laid down their arms"[83]. During this crisis, Churchill ratcheted up his anti-Soviet rhetoric, often invoking Hitler's memory to do so. In New York in March 1949, he told an audience that:

> "we are now confronted with something which is quite as wicked but much more formidable than Hitler, because Hitler had only the *Herrenvolk* [master race] stuff and anti-Semitism. Well, somebody said about that – a good starter but a bad stayer. That's all he had. He had no theme. But these fourteen men in the Kremlin have their hierarchy and a ... fifth column ... everywhere"[84].

Even the end of the blockade did not find Churchill jumping for joy, in part because of his memories of Hitler's aggression. On 12 May 1949, he told Parliament that:

> "the lifting by the Soviet government of the blockade of Berlin has not been taken by Stalin as an occasion for proclaiming that an important peace gesture has been made ... Before the last war, I do remember how, every time Herr Hitler made some reassuring statement, such as 'This is my last territorial demand', people came to me and said 'There, now, you see ... he says this is his last territorial demand'; but the bitter experience we all have gone through ... has made us more wary of these premature rejoicings upon mere words and gestures"[85].

The problems which Hitler's aggression had caused Britain and the world continued to be felt well into the 1950's, though the Nazi dictator and the war itself were slowly receding from memory. The greatest issue for Britain and the West in these years was clearly the Russian presence in Eastern Europe. As Churchill argued in Parliament, "That [Soviet aggression] should have eclipsed in a few years, and largely effaced, the fearful antagonism and memories that Hitlerism created for the German people is an event without parallel"[86]. He saw nuclear deterrence as a crucial means for protecting Western Europe against Russia, although: "[t]he deterrent does not cover the case of lunatics or dictators in the mood of Hitler when he found himself in his final dug-out"[87].

Churchill also realised that without American support, the Western European democracies could not cope with the Russian menace. He made this point forcefully when he addressed the Guildhall on 9 November 1951. It was the first occasion that he had done so as Prime Minister. "The explanation is convincing. When I should have come here as Prime Minister, the Guildhall was blown up and before it was repaired I was blown out! [i.e. defeated in the 1945 general election]" He could not resist teasing the Americans slightly, by referring to their supine isolationism in the 1930's:

> "The sacrifices and exertions which the United States are making to deter ... Communist aggression from making further inroads upon the free world are the main foundation of peace. A tithe of the efforts now being made by America would have prevented the Second World War and would have probably led to the downfall of Hitler with scarcely any blood being shed except perhaps his own"[88].

Churchill realised that the Russian threat to Western Europe, and the Red Army's presence in Eastern Europe was partly caused by Russian fear (or paranoia) of yet another invasion from Germany through Poland:

> "Russia has a right to feel assured that as far as human arrangements can run the terrible events of the Hitler invasion will never be repeated, and that Poland will remain a friendly Power and a buffer, though not, I trust, a puppet State"[89].

In an attempt to dissuade the Americans from what he regarded as an excessively aggressive posture towards the Russians, he emphasised the Soviet need for security from another invasion like Hitler's at the Bermuda summit with President Eisenhower in 1953: "they had a right to ... reassurance that they would not have another dose of Hitler", though their possession of most of Eastern Europe could not be either "permanent or tolerable"[90]. This did not mean he was going soft on the Russians, however. In 1953, he described his policy as "peace through strength"[91].

In November 1954, Churchill's opposition to Russian expansionism in 1945 came back to haunt him, when he made something of a gaffe. He noted peaceful overtures he had made to the Russians, but then said: "Even before the war ended, I telegraphed to Lord Montgomery directing him to be careful in collecting the German arms, to stack them so that they could easily be issued again to the German soldiers whom we should have to work with if the Soviet advance continued"[92]. He had clearly thought that this was a sensible precaution, and proof of his far-sightedness. However, for some in the press it showed that he was a tactless, indiscreet warmonger. "What on earth made him say it?" *The Times* asked the following day. Other papers were calmer. "Extremists in both camps are using this reference as a means of trying to lessen Sir Winston's standing", according to the *Manchester Guardian*'s political correspondent[93]. The storm quickly blew itself out.

Five years later, the Soviet Premier Nikita Krushchev attacked Churchill, calling him the author of the Cold War. Churchill had been out of office for four years, but this had done little to reduce his appetite for controversy. He answered the Soviet dictator: "I am certainly responsible for pointing out to the free world in 1946 ... the perils inherent in complacently accepting the advance of Communist imperialism. But apart from this, my conscience is clear. It was not Britain who in 1939 so cynically compounded with Hitler and later so greedily devoured the half of helpless and hapless Poland while the Nazis took what was left... On the contrary, I suppose we are the only nation who fought throughout the war against Germany, and who, far from receiving any reward, have greatly diminished in our tenure on the surface of the globe... But we are willing to forget old scores"[94].

Using Hitler to attack the Labour government

As Leader of the Opposition, Churchill frequently used Hitler to attack the Labour Government. He used any example he could, however trivial. For example, he criticised it for raising £500 by "selling Hitler's bust to a parcel of malignant crackpots"[95]. In agreeing with the Labour government's conscription bill, Churchill taunted them with having opposed compulsory military service before the war:

> "Why, these were the very politicians who, four months before the outbreak of the war, led their followers into the Lobby against the principle of compulsory military service, and then had the face to accuse the Conservative Party of being "guilty men." I and a handful of others have a right to criticise and censor the lack of preparation for the late war, but the Prime Minister and his friends have no right to do so; the whole effort of their party was designed to make every preparation for defence of the country and resistance to Hitler so unpopular, that it was politically impossible. Now, in the long swing of events, the Prime Minister and the Minister of Defence, who refused in May, 1939, to vote for conscription against Hitler and Nazism, when that was proposed by Mr. Hore-Belisha in Mr. Chamberlain's Government, come forward in a time of peace and victory, to ask us to support conscription against some other danger, some other dictatorship [i.e. Russia]"[96].

Churchill, however, clearly saw that the relevance of Hitler to post-war debates had its limits. He refused to talk about Hitler's relevance to a scuffle in the House of Commons cafeteria in 1946[97]. Churchill also exonerated the Labour government from being as bad as the Nazis but when it demanded yet more powers for itself from Parliament, he took it to task, using his devastating wit:

> "The blameless and reputable Home Secretary, the other night, used language very similar to that which was in the mouths of Hitler and his associates. I do not think he is a second Hitler; I do not think Right Hon. Gentlemen opposite are likely to be second Hitlers. They may use his words, but they have not got his guts, nor, I am glad to say, his criminality"[98].

When the Government wanted to emasculate the House of Lords, with its inbuilt Conservative majority, Churchill did not hesitate to compare its actions to those of the Nazis. As part of a long and rather hysterical speech, he said:

> "As a free-born Englishman, what I hate is the sense of being at anybody's mercy or in anybody's power, be he Hitler or Attlee. We are approaching very near to dictatorship in this country, dictatorship that is to say — I will be quite candid with the House — without either its criminality or its efficiency"[99].

His attacks on the post-war Labour government were clearly exaggerated, as is common with Opposition attacks on any British government. However, this particular sally did his reputation little good.

Churchill, Hitler and Germany's place in Europe

Throughout the war, Churchill had advocated the partition of Germany, though he recognised that "to raise such issues publicly" before the war was won "would only be to rally all Germans around Hitler"[100]. Churchill's advocacy of the Morgenthau Plan (see the previous chapter) was an uncharacteristic hiccough in his generally humane and realistic attitude towards the German people. They certainly needed help immediately after the Second World War, as the country was devastated and starving. In New York in March 1946, as a guest of the Mayor of New York at the Waldorf Astoria Hotel, he encouraged the United States to help in the "noble work … of averting famine, of healing the awful wounds of Hitler's war and rebuilding the scarred and shattered structure of human civilisation"[101]. "I always felt in the war", he remarked in America in 1952, "that we must strike down the tyrant, but be ready to help Germany up again as a friend"[102].

Before the Second World War, Churchill had had a powerful ally in Sir Robert Vansittart, Permanent Secretary of the Foreign Office. According to Churchill in his war memoirs, Vansittart "never removed his eyes for one moment from the Hitler peril"[103]. In 1938, just as his warnings were being justified by events, Vansittart was "kicked upstairs", given an honorary post and deprived of an effective chance to influence British foreign policy. Churchill and Vansittart differed strongly, however. Vansittart criticised Churchill for making a "fallacious" distinction between German and Nazi. Churchill told him that Germany should not be kept in permanent subjection: "I definitely disagree with your line on this. I contemplate a reunited European family in which Germany will have a great place. We must not let our vision be darkened by hatred"[104].

Six years later, again Prime Minster, Churchill was once more generous to the Germans, this time in London. "There can be no effective defence of European culture and freedom unless a new Germany, resolved to set itself free from the ghastly crimes of Hitlerism, plays a strong and effective part in our system", he said in the Guildhall in London in 1952[105]. Though he occasionally succumbed to the anti-German feelings common to many in Britain during and after the Second World War, Churchill inclined to those who wanted to place the blame for the catastrophe on Hitler and the Nazis, rather than the German people as a whole. As Lord Moran noted in his diary in July 1953:

> "[Churchill's] generous heart seems, as the days pass, to be flushed with kindly thoughts ... even about the Germans. He has always admired them, they are a great people. He admired their Army, and would have liked, he once said, to go to Germany to appeal to young Germans to wipe out the disgrace of Hitler and of the cruel murder of the Jews"[106].

He still believed that "safeguards against another Hitler"[107] were required, but he viewed allowing Germany to rehabilitate itself as both morally right and as expedient, given the need to confront the Soviet Union. What one of these safeguards might have been is evident from a comment he made to Stalin at the Potsdam conference in July 1945: "... the Germans had always believed in a symbol. If a Hohenzollern had been allowed to reign after the last war, there would have been no Hitler. They certainly were like sheep"[108]. In 1951, according to his doctor's diary, he told Eden that "if a grandson of the Kaiser had been left on the throne after 1918, Hitler would never have seized power. But it's no use saying this to the Americans. The only kind they think of is George III"[109]. The Russians, like the Americans, agreed with Hitler, who had remarked in 1941 that "monarchy is an out-of-date form ... the age of princes is over", at least in Europe. The Allies did not restore the German monarchy in

1945 or subsequently[110].

In December 1948, Churchill spoke to Parliament during a debate on foreign affairs. He looked forward to the revival of Germany and the "resurrection of the German spirit", "I look forward to the day when all this hateful process of denazification trials and even the trials of leaders or prominent servants of the Hitler regime may be brought to an end … surely enough blood has been shed … I would not take another life because of the quarrels, horrors and atrocities of the past"[111]. The provisional West German government ended denazification and amnestied many lesser offenders in 1951. The results were to be controversial in Germany and abroad for decades, especially as former Nazis could now serve in the West German government. The Soviet puppet East German regime even used the presence of Nazis in the West Berlin government as an excuse for building the Berlin Wall.

Churchill's support for denazification extended only to those who had not been participants in "the crimes of the regime". When Prime Minister again, he argued in Parliament:

> "there are many people in Germany who were Nazis to support their country, but who did not associate themselves with the crimes of the Nazi regime. I believe it is a great factor in the peace of the world to separate those who were the active and vigorous servants and supporters of Hitler and his crimes and tyrannies from those who tried to keep the honour of the German name clear from those charges"[112].

In advocating admitting Germany to the Council of Europe in the House of Commons, Churchill argued that Germany had only sabotaged the League of Nations because "the Hitler Revolution had taken place", rather than because of something inherent in the German character. The former Labour Foreign Secretary, Bevin, argued that "the Hitler revolution did not change the German character very much. It expressed it", to which Churchill replied with a flat "No". Churchill even argued for German soldiers to serve alongside the British, French and Americans in defending Western Europe from the Red Army, at a time when this was still unthinkable to many[113].

Churchill also agreed to allow General Speidel, former chief of staff to Field Marshal Rommel, who was now German representative on the European Defence Council, to visit Britain. At the Guildhall banquet in November 1952, Churchill discussed NATO and German rearmament, "There can be no effective defence of European culture and freedom unless a new Germany, resolved to set itself free from the ghastly crimes of Hitlerism, plays a strong and effective part in our system." Anybody who tried to prevent "that healing process is guilty of undermining the foundations upon which the salvation of all mankind from tyranny and war depends"[114]. He viewed Rommel's opposition to "the Hitler tyranny, which cost him his life, as an additional distinction to his memory"[115].

Churchill's generosity towards Germany had its limits, and he did not forget Mussolini's tyranny either. In response to a paper by Truman advocating a friendly treatment of Italy, Churchill listed some of the Mussolini regime's crimes:

> "Special detachments of Italian aircraft had been sent to bomb London, and ... Italy had made a most dastardly and utterly unprovoked attack upon Greece ... she had seized Albania by a most lawless act. All these things had happened while we had been alone. It could not therefore be denied that we had suffered grievously at the hands of the Italian state. Nor could we acquit the Italian people entirely of their responsibility for these acts, any more than we could acquit the German people for the actions taken by them under the yoke of Hitler"[116].

British decline

Churchill had recognised, during the war, that British influence was declining thanks, at least in part, to its role in the defeat of Hitler. He believed, however, that the decline in its military power should be arrested, or at least slowed, as much as possible. Concerned at a proposal to send British jet fighters to friendly and neutral foreign governments, he wrote to the Prime Minster, Clement Attlee, on 22 September 1949:

> "A defenceless Britain can play no part in the defence of Europe... In 1940 we ... ran great risks to help France, sending almost our last divisions abroad, but the other thing we did not ever give way upon was sending the twenty-five fighter air squadrons. This is always considered to have been a cause of our salvation. Distributing 'jets' to Allied European countries or to our Dominions or still more selling them to strangers, while they are so scarce and precious, is ... exactly on a footing with distributing the 25 last fighter squadrons in 1940 ..."

Nor was there any doubt as to who was to take Hitler's role in the possible war that Churchill was attempting to provide against:

"Nothing is more likely to bring upon a Soviet air attack on Western Europe than the knowledge that they could … overwhelm, by mass attacks, the air defence of Britain, which would others, in the long run, be fatal to them as it was to Hitler"[117].

Churchill recognised that Labour's pre-war record in opposing military spending to combat Hitler was a strong weapon which he could use against its politicians after the war. On 12 October 1951, during the election campaign of that year, he criticised Attlee directly on his voting record before the war. On 10 November 1935, Attlee had claimed that the National Government was preparing a great programme of rearmament which will endanger the peace of the world. "Such was the language of the Socialist leaders in the years while Hitler's Germany was rearming night and day". For good measure, Churchill also mentioned Attlee's vote against conscription in April 1939[118].

Despite Churchill's hostility to Russian expansionism, his main goal for his second term as Prime Minister was to open a détente with Moscow. Perhaps over-sensitive to the "warmonger" taunts which had dogged him for decades in one form or another, he seems to have wanted to be seen as a peacemaker instead. One revealing anecdote concerns his Nobel Prize for Literature, awarded in 1953. A disputed story has it that he wanted to win the Nobel Prize for Peace, and, on hearing that he had won the Literature Prize instead, seemed to lose interest. Whether or not this is true, Churchill apparently felt that the death of Stalin in March 1953 opened up the possibility of a breach in the Iron Curtain. This sits somewhat oddly with his view during the Second World War (and President Truman's after it), that Stalin had been reasonable while shadowy forces in the Politburo forced him to take a harder line. However, in May 1953, he made an appeal for a new approach to the Soviet Union after the death of Stalin. He recalled the Locarno Treaty with which "I was closely acquainted" as Chancellor of the Exchequer in the government which negotiated it. He then repeated his view that "Russia has a right to feel assured that as far as human arrangements can run the terrible events of the Hitler invasion will never be repeated, and that Poland will remain a friendly Power and a buffer, though not, I trust, a puppet State"[119].

Later that year, in Bermuda, Churchill met the American President, Eisenhower, and the Canadian Prime Minister, Laniel. Again, he argued about the need to open relations with Russia, "contacts, infiltration, trade leading to greater prosperity, reassurance that they would not have another dose of Hitler – and they had a right to this – and at the same time make it clear that we do not regard the position of the satellites [as] … permanent"[120]. His arguments had no noticeable effect on American policy, however, which was entering its most anti-

Soviet phase. Given the pressures of American politics at the time, it seems unrealistic for him to have expected that he could have had such an effect.

Three days later, Churchill again attributed Russian insecurity to their memory of Hitler, "When the second world war was in its late phases he had been profoundly impressed with the deep grievance and passionate desire of the Soviets for effective protection against another Hitler ... and he had felt the deepest sympathy with that anxiety. If they had not been carried away by victory, something much better for all would have been feasible"[121]. Churchill failed to carry his point, however – the Russians as well as the Americans were unreceptive. Eisenhower responded to Churchill at Bermuda "in the coarsest terms", comparing Russia to a "woman of the streets" and proposing to "drive her off her present 'beat' and into the back streets". On détente with the Soviets, Churchill was at least a decade ahead of his time.

The Cold War with the Russians was not the only area of foreign policy on which Churchill brought his experience of dealing with Hitler to bear. One of the major problems caused by the collapse of the British Empire was the Israel/Palestine conflict, which has scarred the Middle East ever since. Britain reluctantly allowed the creation of Israel in 1948. Churchill had always admired the Jews, and the Israeli government quoted him as saying, in 1954, at a time of tension between Israel and Egypt, "I am a Zionist. Let me make that clear ... I think it a most wonderful thing that this community should have established itself so effectively, turning the desert into fertile gardens and ... should have afforded a refuge to millions of their co-religionists who had suffered so fearfully under Hitler, and not only Hitler, persecution"[122]. Why advanced irrigation practices gave the Jews a right to land occupied by Palestinian Arabs, he did not say.

Throughout his second term as Prime Minister, Churchill's attitude to the growing power of Nasser's Egypt was informed, not only by his Zionism, but also by his experience of the appeasement of Hitler during the 1930s. He had reservations about Eden's 1953 agreement to withdraw British troops from the Suez Canal because of this. The agreement was nevertheless concluded, and British troops left. Had Churchill's reservations prevailed, the Suez crisis which overwhelmed Eden, who had trusted Nasser, would never have occurred, at least not in the form in which it did. Churchill was appalled at Eden's indecisiveness over Suez, remarking to Colville in one of his most famous asides, "I would never have dared; and if I had dared, I certainly would never have dared stop"[123]. During the Suez crisis Randolph Churchill made another comparison to Hitler, for which Eden never forgave him. Eden had taken a winter holiday in the West Indies, in the days when such vacations were an unimaginable luxury for most people. He wrote to the *Manchester Guardian* that Britain's disastrous position at Suez was like that of the Germans at Stalingrad. "But even Hitler did not winter in Jamaica"[124].

Private conversation and anecdotes

After his shattering defeat in the 1945 General Election, Churchill took a holiday to Lake Como in Italy. He stayed in a villa put at his disposal by Field Marshal Alexander. A Brigadier Edwards recorded his remarks about Hitler's military record: "He cannot understand Hitler's prodigal dispersal of troops and his extravagant usage of them. 1200 were sunk (or at least had to swim) in the first attack on Leros[§]. The second 1200 Germans did the trick"[125].

During that same holiday, Churchill's love of painting nearly landed him in trouble with an Italian mob. A Colonel Walthen, who had been there with Churchill, recorded that:

> "Apparently he came across a bombed railway viaduct and hoses at Recco and started to paint... a ... crowd gathered and started to boo and shake their fists. The crowd probably didn't recognise him, but didn't take kindly to a foreigner painting their bombed homes. Without any more ado, Mr Churchill packed up and came home [to his villa]. The incident upset him somewhat, but he readily admitted that it was a tactless thing to do and said that he would have been damned annoyed if Hitler had started to paint the bomb damage in London"[126].

In the process of writing his history of the Second World War, Churchill clearly thought much about Hitler's place in history. He would occasionally speak of it to his close associates. According to Colville's diary, after tea in 1952, Churchill went for a walk with Montgomery:

> "Monty in the role of grand inquisitor ... Was Hitler great? (PM said No – he made too many mistakes)"

[§] In November 1943, the Germans dislodged a British and Italian garrison in the Greek island of Leros in the Dodecanese. The successful 1957 book and subsequent film, *The Guns of Navarone* was based on this battle.

Chapter 10

His answer to a further question of why Hitler was not great if Napoleon was, is unrecorded[127]. Churchill apparently never tired of comparing the two. In 1958, when Churchill was 83, his doctor recorded Jock Colville as saying, "when he gets very bored with me I have a special technique. I say to him: 'Don't you think Napoleon was the Hitler of the nineteenth century?' Then he wakes up with a start. 'How dare you say such a thing?' Winston exclaims, and it is some time before he relapses into a state of apathy"[128]. According to an anecdote which Churchill's grandson, Nicholas Soames, told Roy Jenkins, Churchill had no doubts about his own claim to greatness. One day in 1955, the six-year-old Soames broke into his grandfather's study at Chartwell. "Grandpapa, is it true that you are the greatest man in the world?" the boy asked. "Yes," the greatest man apparently replied, "and now bugger off"[129].

The greatest man in the world died peacefully in his bed on 24 January 1965 at the age of ninety. His body lay in state for three days and a state funeral was held at St Paul's Cathedral, which, unusually, attended. In all, 112 countries were represented officially at the ceremony. In accordance with his wishes, he was then buried in the family plot at St Martin's Church, Bladon, near Blenheim Palace, where he had been born nine decades before. The contrast between Churchill's natural death and magnificent funeral, and the bizarre circumstances of Hitler's suicide and the odd journey which his body seems to have taken after 1945 may mean that there is, after all, a small measure of justice in this world.

---

[1] *In Command of History*, David Reynolds, p.532

[2] *The Churchill Documents, Volume 11, The Exchequer Years*, Martin Gilbert, p.885

[3] *In Command of History*, David Reynolds, p.74

[4] *The Second World War, Volume 1, The Gathering Storm*, Winston Churchill, p.47-51

[5] *Hitler, Hubris, 1889-1936*, Ian Kershaw, p.95

[6] *Hitler, Hubris, 1889-1936*, Ian Kershaw, p.216

[7] *The Second World War, Volume 1, The Gathering Storm*, Winston Churchill, p.62-63

[8] *The Second World War, Volume 1, The Gathering Storm*, Winston Churchill, p.62

[9] *The Second World War, Volume 1, The Gathering Storm*, Winston Churchill, p.86

[10] *The Second World War, Volume 1, The Gathering Storm*, Winston Churchill, p.88-90

[11] *The Second World War, Volume 1, The Gathering Storm*, Winston Churchill, p.180-1

[12] *The Second World War, Volume 1, The Gathering Storm*, Winston Churchill, p.242-3

[13] *The Second World War, Volume 1, The Gathering Storm*, Winston Churchill, see Chapters 16, 17 and 18, especially p.301-3

[14] *The Second World War, Volume 1, The Gathering Storm*, Winston Churchill, p.294

[15] *The Second World War, Volume 1, The Gathering Storm*, Winston Churchill, p.309

[16] *The Second World War, Volume 1, The Gathering Storm*, Winston Churchill, p.358

[17] *The Second World War, Volume 1, The Gathering Storm*, Winston Churchill, p.395-396

[18] The Storm of War, Andrew Roberts, p.20

[19] *The Second World War, Volume 1, The Gathering Storm*, Winston Churchill, p.430

[20] *The Second World War, Volume 1, The Gathering Storm*, Winston Churchill, p.436

[21] *The Second World War, Volume 2, Their Finest Hour*, Winston Churchill, p.34

[22] *The Second World War, Volume 2, Their Finest Hour*, Winston Churchill, p.32

[23] *The Second World War, Volume 2, Their Finest Hour*, Winston Churchill, p.33-34 and 42-3

[24] *The Second World War, Volume 2, Their Finest Hour*, Winston Churchill, p.69-73

[25] *The Second World War, Volume 2, Their Finest Hour*, Winston Churchill, p.95

[26] *The Second World War, Volume 2, Their Finest Hour*, Winston Churchill, p.227

[27] *The Second World War, Volume 2, Their Finest Hour*, Winston Churchill, p.261

[28] *Winston Churchill, The Struggle for Survival*, Lord Moran, p.365

[29] *The Second World War, Volume 2, Their Finest Hour*, Winston Churchill, p.266-278

[30] *The Second World War, Volume 2, Their Finest Hour*, Winston Churchill, p.512-518

[31] *The Second World War, Volume 2, Their Finest Hour*, Winston Churchill, p.518

[32] *The Second World War, Volume 3, The Grand Alliance*, Winston Churchill, p.144

[33] *The Second World War, Volume 3, The Grand Alliance*, Winston Churchill, p.234

[34] *The Second World War, Volume 3, The Grand Alliance*, Winston Churchill, p.337

[35] *The Second World War, Volume 3, The Grand Alliance*, Winston Churchill, p.347

[36] *The Second World War, Volume 3, The Grand Alliance*, Winston Churchill, p.476-7

[37] *The Second World War, Volume 3, The Grand Alliance*, Winston Churchill, p.513

[38] *The Second World War, Volume 3, The Grand Alliance*, Winston Churchill, p.547

[39] *The Second World War, Volume 3, The Grand Alliance*, Winston Churchill, p.539

[40] *The Second World War, Volume 4, The Hinge of Fate*, Winston Churchill, p.97

[41] *The Second World War, Volume 4, The Hinge of Fate*, Winston Churchill, p.99-101

[42] *The Second World War, Volume 4, The Hinge of Fate*, Winston Churchill, p.108

[43] *The Second World War, Volume 4, The Hinge of Fate*, Winston Churchill, p.266

[44] *The Second World War, Volume 4, The Hinge of Fate*, Winston Churchill, p.378

[45] *The Second World War, Volume 4, The Hinge of Fate*, Winston Churchill, p.389

[46] *The Second World War, Volume 4, The Hinge of Fate*, Winston Churchill, p.525, and p.637-639

[47] *The Second World War, Volume 4, The Hinge of Fate*, Winston Churchill, p.560

[48] *The Second World War, Volume 4, The Hinge of Fate*, Winston Churchill, p.743

[49] *The Second World War, Volume 5, Closing the Ring*, Winston Churchill, p.48-49

[50] *The Second World War, Volume 5, Closing the Ring*, Winston Churchill, p.103-104

[51] *The Second World War, Volume 5, Closing the Ring*, Winston Churchill, p.215

[52] *The Second World War, Volume 5, Closing the Ring*, Winston Churchill, p.433

[53] *The Second World War, Volume 6, Triumph and Tragedy*, Winston Churchill, p.17

[54] *The Second World War, Volume 6, Triumph and Tragedy*, Winston Churchill, p.51

[55] *The Second World War, Volume 6, Triumph and Tragedy*, Winston Churchill, p.80

[56] *The Second World War, Volume 6, Triumph and Tragedy*, Winston Churchill, p.455

[57] *The Second World War, Volume 5, Closing the Ring*, Winston Churchill, p.185

[58] *The Second World War, Volume 6, Triumph and Tragedy*, Winston Churchill, p.25

[59] *The Second World War, Volume 5, Closing the Ring*, Winston Churchill, p.205

[60] *The Second World War, Volume 6, Triumph and Tragedy*, Winston Churchill, p.49

[61] *The Second World War, Volume 6, Triumph and Tragedy*, Winston Churchill, p.238

[62] *The Second World War, Volume 6, Triumph and Tragedy*, Winston Churchill, p.401

[63] *The Second World War, Volume 6, Triumph and Tragedy*, Winston Churchill, p.463-465

[64] *The Second World War, Volume 1, The Gathering Storm*, Winston Churchill, p.351

[65] Churchill papers, 4/19, quoted in *Never Despair*, Martin Gilbert, p.416

[66] Churchill papers, 4/19, quoted in *Never Despair*, Martin Gilbert, p.417

[67] *Tribune*, 8 October 1948, quoted in *In Command of History*, David Reynolds, p.143

[68] *Never Despair*, Martin Gilbert, p.549-550

[69] *The Unnecessary War*, Patricia Meehan, p.7

[70] *Hansard*, 21 July 1949

[71] *Never Despair*, Martin Gilbert, p.171

[72] *Churchill*, Roy Jenkins, p.811

[73] Article in *Pravda*, Joseph Stalin, 14 March 1946

[74] *Never Despair*, Martin Gilbert, p.212-5

[75] *Never Despair*, Martin Gilbert, p.219

[76] Churchill speech in Zurich, 19 September 1946

[77] *Never Despair*, Martin Gilbert, p.285

[78] In Command of History, David Reynolds, p.411

[79] *Hansard*, 23 October 1946

[80] *Europe Unite*, Randolph Churchill

[81] *Never Despair*, Martin Gilbert, p.351

[82] Churchill papers, 2/146, quoted in *Never Despair*, Martin Gilbert, p.428

[83] *Never Despair*, Martin Gilbert, p.437

[84] *In the Balance*, Randolph Churchill, speech 25 March 1949, New York, quoted in *Never Despair*, Martin Gilbert, p. 464

[85] *Hansard*, 12 May 1949

[86] *Hansard*, 1 March 1955

[87] *Hansard*, 1 March 1955

[88] *Stemming the Tide*, Randolph Churchill, p.187-90

[89] *Hansard*, 11 May 1953

[90] *Never Despair*, Martin Gilbert, p.922

[91] *Never Despair*, Martin Gilbert, p.1070

[92] *Never Despair*, Martin Gilbert, p.1070

[93] *Manchester Guardian*, 26 November 1954

[94] *The Unwritten Alliance*, Randolph Churchill, p.311-5

[95] *Hansard*, 6 December 1945

[96] *Hansard*, 31 March 1947

[97] *Hansard*, 10 February 1947

[98] *Hansard*, 11 August 1947

[99] *Hansard*, 11 November 1947

[100] Churchill papers 20/47, quoted in *Road to Victory, Winston S Churchill 1941-45*, Martin S Gilbert, p.16

[101] *Never Despair*, Martin Gilbert, p.215

[102] *Winston Churchill, The Struggle for Survival*, Lord Moran, p.362

[103] *The Second World War, Volume 1, The Gathering Storm*, Winston Churchill, p.163

[104] *Never Despair*, Martin Gilbert

[105] *Never Despair*, Martin Gilbert, p.774

[106] *Winston Churchill, The Struggle for Survival*, Lord Moran, p.446

[107] *Never Despair*, Martin Gilbert, p.1003

[108] *Never Despair*, Martin Gilbert, p.64

[109] *Winston Churchill, The Struggle for Survival*, Lord Moran, p.352

[110] *Hitler's Table Talk*, p.121

[111] *Hansard*, 10 December 1948

[112] *Hansard*, 29 April 1953

[113] *Hansard*, 17 December 1953

[114] *Never Despair*, Martin Gilbert, p.774

[115] *Hansard*, 29 April 1953

[116] *Never Despair*, Martin Gilbert, p.80

[117] Churchill papers, 2/229, quoted in *Never Despair*, Martin Gilbert, p.490

[118] *Stemming the Tide*, Randolph Churchill, p.142-5

[119] *Hansard*, 11 May 1953

[120] *Never Despair*, Martin Gilbert, p.922

[121] *Never Despair*, Martin Gilbert, p.935

[122] Government of Israel press statement, 24 February 1955

[123] *The Fringes of Power*, John Colville, p.721

[124] *Never Despair*, Martin Gilbert, p.1224 n6

[125] *Never Despair*, Martin Gilbert, p.141

[126] *Never Despair*, Martin Gilbert, p.151-2

[127] *The Fringes of Power*, John Colville, p.608

[128] *Winston Churchill, The Struggle for Survival*, Lord Moran, p.738

[129] *Churchill*, Roy Jenkins, p.849n

Conclusion

Mid-June 1940 was one of the most critical points of the Second World War. France was about to surrender and Britain was evacuating her troops from the Continent as quickly as possible. Late on the evening of the 15th, Churchill was pacing around the Rose Garden at Chequers, spasmodically murmuring, "Bang, bang, bang goes the farmer's gun, run rabbit, run rabbit, run, run, run". He declared to Colville that the French should be told "that if they let us have their fleet we shall never forget, but that if they surrender without consulting us we shall never forgive. We will blacken their name for a thousand years". He then made one of the few direct comparisons he ever made between himself and the figure who dominated his thoughts for a decade: "he and Hitler only had one thing in common – a hatred of whistling"[1]. Churchill frequently dictated messages which he never intended to send, in order, apparently, to order his thoughts. This message was apparently one of those. At any rate, his office never sent it.

As a cursory examination of their respective biographies reveals however, Hitler and Churchill had far more in common than Churchill - doubtless facetiously – claimed at Chequers that night. The obvious similarity is that both men were heads of government of their respective countries during the Second World War. However, they had far more in common besides that. Neither man was entirely from the country which he later led during the most critical phase in its history – Hitler was an Austrian, and Churchill was half-American. Both men had unsatisfactory upbringings, in Churchill's case caused by absentee parents, and in Hitler's by a domineering father and an over-protective mother. Both men were under fire for the first time in their 20's – in Churchill's case, in Cuba on his twenty-first birthday[2], and in Hitler's case at the age of 25 in Flanders. Both men saw active service on the Western Front during the First World War, in

Conclusion

Churchill's case relatively briefly, and in Hitler's for four years, until he was gassed by the British. Neither man excelled during their school years, and both left school more or less as soon as they could. Neither went to university, though both men had strong views on their respective countries' education systems. Both men were voracious readers at various points in their lives, when time permitted. Both men were published authors, in Hitler's case of one book (as discussed in the Introduction, his second, much shorter, work was not published until 1961), in Churchill's case of 43. Both men wrote extensively for newspapers, in Hitler's case solely for the Nazi Party's, and in Churchill's, during his time in Opposition, for almost any newspaper that would pay him.

Both men were great orators, inspiring their countrymen through difficult times with their rhetoric. Both were capable of humour – Hitler was apparently a competent mimic, and many of Churchill's witticisms seem likely to be immortal. Both men had physical courage, in Hitler's case demonstrated by his Iron Crosses, First and Second Class, awarded during the First World War, and in Churchill's by his record in the Boer War and on the North-West Frontier of India. Both men declared themselves ready to die for their countries should the Second World War end in defeat, though neither man ever put this into practice – Churchill because he never had to, and Hitler because he took an easier way out by committing suicide. Both men aspired to be the saviours of their countries, in Churchill's case preserving Britain from Hitler and the Nazi regime, and in Hitler's, saving Germany from the imagined Jewish peril and the frighteningly real Communist danger. Both men imprisoned political opponents for years, though Churchill always considered this practice "in the highest degree odious" and released the very few such prisoners which he took as soon as he safely could. Hitler on the other hand relished it, and murdered thousands of his political opponents. One example may suffice to demonstrate that last difference. At one point during the war, a Miss Elsie Orrin was sentenced to five years' imprisonment for saying that Hitler was "a good ruler, a better man than Mr Churchill". Churchill heard about her case in some way, and told his Home Secretary that the sentence was "far too heavy for expressions of opinion, however pernicious, which are not accompanied by conspiracy"[3]. Had she been overheard comparing Churchill to Hitler favourably in Germany, especially in the last year of the war, her life expectancy could have been measured in hours.

Both men were deeply interested in their respective countries' histories, though Churchill's knowledge of Britain's was far deeper and broader than Hitler's of Germany's. Both men were fascinated by warfare, and immersed themselves in the details of military operations throughout the Second World War. Both men considered that terror bombing could shorten the Second World War, by undermining morale in the other's country. Both men seriously underestimated one or more of their country's enemies – in Churchill's case Japan, in Hitler's case Russia and the United States. Both men seem to have overestimated Italy's military might, and to have been shocked at the speed of the French collapse in May and June 1940. Both men, however, had serious limitations as wartime commanders and often displayed poor judgement in military matters. Both men believed that their respective countries were destined to control vast empires. Indeed both men respected the role which they considered the British Empire played in promoting Western civilisation. Both men had key roles in their countries' turbulent histories during the 1920's. Churchill was Chancellor of the Exchequer in the Baldwin government for five years, and helped defeat the General Strike in 1926. Hitler led an attempted coup in 1923. Both men advocated substantial rearmament for their countries during the 1930's. Both men had attitudes towards non-European races which would place them on the lunatic fringe today. Both men believed that the Versailles Treaty, which ended the First World War, had been to some extent harsh on Germany. Both men had a horror and a loathing of the Communism which had taken root in Russia at the end of the First World War, and admired Mussolini's success in crushing that danger in Italy. This did not stop each man praising Stalin at different stages of the Second World War.

Neither man had a conventional religious faith, though both occasionally invoked "Providence" or some deistic "God" in their speeches, and both sometimes used religious quotes or imagery to suit their rhetorical purposes. Both men were more interested in foreign affairs and defence than in domestic or economic policy. Indeed, neither man really understood economics, though some argue that Churchill showed sounder instincts than many professional economists in the 1920's, by feeling deeply uneasy about Britain's return to the gold standard in 1925.

Both men were involved in car accidents in the early 1930's, though Churchill's injuries were much more serious than Hitler's. Both men had strong views on diet, albeit diametrically opposed to the other's. Hitler became a vegetarian and was a teetotaller, while Churchill drank large amounts of alcohol and loved rich food. Both men enjoyed the company of people with "flaws in the weave". Both men were reasonable, though not outstanding, painters. Both men possessed a country house, whose atmosphere was important to them for relaxation. Both men were night owls, routinely keeping their subordinates and guests awake past 2 am.

Despite these similarities, the two great European tribal leaders of the 1940's ended up both hating and despising each other. According to Speer, Hitler thought that it would be a mistake to encourage nationalism in other European

Conclusion

countries, since it would weaken Germany's position[4]. It is interesting to speculate what might have happened had they met in the 1930's. It could have happened if Hitler had taken Hanfstäengl's advice in Munich in 1932, or if Churchill had accepted one of Ribbentrop's invitations to visit Nazi Germany. It is unlikely that Churchill's future politics or his opinions of Nazi Germany would have changed greatly, given how firmly entrenched they were, and how they were supported by Hitler's acts of aggression throughout that disastrous decade.

This account has argued that, despite the tumultuous times through which they lived the two men's views of each other changed little during the course of the Second World War, and can help explain some of the decisions each man made during that epic conflict. Churchill's rhetoric, writing and private conversation about the "danger" posed by Hitler to Britain in particular and Europe in general changed relatively little from his first recorded mention of the German in his conversation with Prince Bismarck in 1930 to the end of the Second World War and beyond. What did change, however, was that Churchill started to highlight Nazi atrocities once their human rights record became known in Britain. Even after Hitler was dead, he still used the lessons which he had derived from his experiences in confronting the German dictator in the 1930's and early 1940's in a number of contexts, including the Cold War and the Arab-Israeli conflict.

Hitler's views of Churchill were also fairly consistent from the mid-1930's, when he first took note of his future nemesis, to the end of his life. They were a mixture of contempt and incomprehension, based on false or misleading information, warped by his Nazi ideology. From his first recorded mention of Churchill, to Hanfstängl in 1932, to that recorded by his *Luftwaffe* adjutant three days before his death, when he hoped that the coalition facing him would break up, there is very little evidence of a significant change. Hitler rarely changed his views on any matter, and his attitude to the British Prime Minister who did so much to undermine his work was no exception.

---

[1] *The Fringes of Power*, John Colville, p.158
[2] *Road to Victory, Winston S Churchill 1941-45*, Martin S Gilbert, p.506
[3] *Churchill War Papers, Vol. III, The Ever-Widening War*, Martin Gilbert, p.959
[4] *Inside the Third Reich*, Albert Speer, p.182

Bibliography

Books

Ansel, Walter

> *Hitler confronts England*

Ashley, Dr Maurice

> *As I Knew Him, Churchill in the Wilderness, talk to the International Churchill Society*

Asquith, Margot

> *Autobiography*

von Below, Nicolaus

> *At Hitler's Side*

Bloch, Michael

> *Ribbentrop*

Bullock, Lord Alan

> *Hitler: A Study in Tyranny*

Cadogan, Sir Alexander

> *The Diaries of Sir Alexander Cadogan*

Bibliography

Chamberlain, Neville

The Neville Chamberlain Diary Letters, Vols. 1-4

Channon, Sir Henry, MP

Chips – The Diaries of Sir Henry Channon

Churchill, Randolph

In the Balance

Stemming the Tide

Europe Unite

The Unwritten Alliance

Winston S Churchill, Young Statesman, 1901-1914

Churchill, Winston L.S.

Ahistory of the English-Speaking Peoples (4 vols.)

Arms and the Covenant or While England Slept

Great Contemporaries

Into Battle

My Early Life

Step by Step

Savrola

The Gathering Storm

The Second World War (6 vols)

The World Crisis (5 vols)

Thoughts and Adventures

Churchill, Winston S.

His Father's Son

Colville, Sir John

The Fringes of Power

Conradi, Peter

Hitler's Piano Player

Cowling, Dr. Maurice

The Impact of Hitler: British Politics and British Policy 1933-1940

Dahlerus, Birger

The Last Attempt

Eden, Sir Anthony, Earl of Avon

The Eden Memoirs, The Reckoning

von Engel, Gerhard

At the Heart of the Reich

Fest, Joachim C.

Hitler

Plotting Hitler's Death

Gilbert, Sir Martin

Winston S Churchill (8 vols.)

Winston S Churchill Companion documents (17 vols.)

Bibliography

In Search of Churchill

The Wilderness Years

Goebbels, Dr Paul Josef

The Goebbels Diaries, 1939-41

The Goebbels Diaries, 1942-43

The Goebbels Diaries, 1944-45

Halder, Colonel General Franz

The Private War Journal of Colonel General Franz Halder

Hanfstaengl, Dr Ernst

Hitler; The Missing Years

Hanson, Neil

First Blitz

Harris, Arthur

Bomber Offensive

Harvey, Oliver

War Diaries

Henderson, Sir Neville

Failure of a Mission

Hewel, Walther

Diary of Ambassador Hewel

Hitler, Adolf

>   *Mein Kampf*

>   *Secret Book, a.k.a. Second Book*

Hoffman, Heinrich

>   *Hitler was my Friend*

Holmes, Richard

>   *In the footsteps of Churchill*

Hoare, Sir Samuel, Viscount Templewood

>   *Nine Troubled Years*

Irving, David

>   *Goebbels, , Mastermind of the Third Reich*

>   *Göring, A Biography*

>   *Hitler's War*

>   *The Secret Diaries of Hitler's Doctor*

Ismay, General Lord

>   *The Memoirs of General Lord Ismay*

Jaeckel, Eberhard and Kuhn, Axel

>   *Hitler, Saemtliche Aufzeichnungen 1905-1924*

Jenkins, Roy

>   *Churchill, A Life*

Bibliography

Junge, Traudl

    Until the Final Hour, Hitler's Last Secretary

Kershaw, Sir Ian

    Hitler, 1936-1945, Nemesis

    Hitler, 1936-1945, Hubris

Kirkpatrick, Yvonne

    The Inner Circle

Kubizek, August

    The Young Hitler I Knew

von Loringhoven, Bernd Freytag

    In the Bunker with Hitler

Lukacs, John

    Churchill, Visionary, Statesman, Historian

Macmillan, Margaret

    Peacemakers

Mack Smith, Denis

    Mussolini

von Manstein, Field Marshal Eric

    Lost Victories

Maser, Werner

    Hitler's Letters

Massie, Robert

    Castles of Steel

Meehan, Patricia

    The Unnecessary War

Moir, Phyllis

    I was Winston Churchill's Private Secretary

Moorhouse, Roger

    Killing Hitler

Moss, Norman

    Nineteen Weeks

Nel, Elizabeth

    Mr Churchill's Secretary

Neitzel, Soenke

    Tapping Hitler's Generals

Nicolson, Nigel (ed.)

    The Harold Nicolson Diaries, 1907-1963

Overy, Richard

    The Morbid Age: Britain Between the Wars

    Interrogations: The Nazi Elite in Allied Hands

Read, Anthony

    The Devil's Disciples, Hitler's Inner Circle

Bibliography

Reynolds, David

In Command of History

Roberts, Andrew

Eminent Churchillians

Hitler and Churchill, Secrets of Leadership

Masters and Commanders

Napoleon and Wellington

The Holy Fox: A Biography of Lord Halifax

The Storm of War

Ryback, Timothy

Hitler's Private Library

Schmidt, Dr Paul

Hitler's Interpreter

Schroeder, Christa

Er war mein Chef

Sereny, Gitta

Albert Speer: His Battle with the Truth

Sheean, Vincent

Between the Thunder and the Sun

Sherwood, Robert E

The White House Papers of Harry L Hopkins

Shirer, William L

　　Berlin Diary

　　The Nightmare Years

　　The Rise and Fall of the Third Reich

Soames, Mary

　　Speaking for Themselves: The Personal Letters of Winston and Clementine Churchill

Speer, Albert

　　Inside the Third Reich

Stapleton, Julia

　　Sir Arthur Bryant

Tedder, Marshal of the RAF Lord

　　Air Superiority in War

Thompson, Walter

　　Beside the Bulldog

Thorpe, D.R.

　　Eden

Toye, Richard

　　Lloyd George and Churchill, Rivals for Greatness

Trevor-Roper, Hugh, Lord Dacre

　　The Bormann Letters

Bibliography

The Last Days of Hitler

(ed.) *The Testament of Adolf Hitler*

(ed.) *Hitler's Table Talk*

Warlimont, General Walter

Inside Hitler's Headquarters

Weber, Thomas

Hitler's First War

Welles, Sumner

Report on Mission to Europe

Wilson, Sir Charles, Lord Moran

Churchill at War

Winston Churchill – Struggle for Survival

Winterbotham, F.W.

The Ultra Secret

Wheeler-Bennett, John

King George VI

Zoller, Albert

Hitler Privat

Newspapers and magazines

British: The Times, The Manchester Guardian, the Daily Mail, the Daily Express, the Daily Herald, the Tribune, Daily Dispatch, Strand magazine, Finest Hour

German and Austrian: Neue Freie Presse, Berliner Zeitung, Der Stürmer, Deutsche Algemeine Zeitung

Other: Time, Pravda, New Republic

Official records

Hansard

War Cabinet Papers

Cabinet Papers

Nuremberg Trial Proceedings

Index

CPSIA information can be obtained
at www.ICGtesting.com
Printed in the USA
LVHW100759240420
653803LV00006B/96